MW01119833

2009 01 06

EDGAR ALLAN POE

Edgar Allan Poe
Rhetoric and Style

BRETT ZIMMERMAN

McGill-Queen's University Press
Montreal & Kingston · London · Ithaca

© McGill-Queen's University Press 2005
ISBN 0–7735–2899–7

Legal deposit second quarter 2005
Bibliothèque nationale du Québec

Printed in Canada on acid-free paper that is 100% ancient forest free
(100% post-consumer recycled), processed chlorine free.

This book has been published with the help of a grant from the Canadian Federation
for the Humanities and Social Sciences, through the Aid to Scholarly Publications
Programme, using funds provided by the Social Sciences and Humanities Research
Council of Canada.

McGill-Queen's University Press acknowledges the support of the Canada Council
for the Arts for our publishing program. We also acknowledge the financial support of the
Government of Canada through the Book Publishing Industry Development Program
(BPIDP) for our publishing activities.

Library and Archives Canada Cataloguing in Publication

Zimmerman, Brett, 1958–
    Edgar Allan Poe: rhetoric and style / Brett Zimmerman.

    Includes bibliographical references and index.
    ISBN 0–7735–2899–7

    1. Poe, Edgar Allan, 1809–1849 – Literary style. 2. Poe, Edgar Allan, 1809–1849 –
Technique. I. Title.

PS2644.Z54 2005   813'.3   C2005–900574–2

This book was typeset by Dynagram Inc. in 11/14 Garamond.

For introducing me to
the adventure of stylistics,
this book is gratefully and affectionately
dedicated to
ROBERT ADOLPH
– mentor, colleague, friend.

Contents

Tables and Figures

Acknowledgments

I would like to thank several editors and managers of refereed journals for their very kind permission to reprint portions of this book. The first published essay here was "'Moral Insanity' or Paranoid Schizophrenia: Poe's 'The Tell-Tale Heart'." A version of this article originally appeared in *Mosaic, a Journal for the Interdisciplinary Study of Literature*, volume 25, no. 2 (spring 1992), 39–48. My thanks to former editor Evelyn J. Hinz for accepting the piece and to Jackie Pantel for granting permission to reprint it here. As well, thanks to Karl Simms for providing permission to reprint "'I could read his prose on salary, but not Jane's': Poe's Stylistic Versatility." An early version appeared in volume 5 of *Language and Discourse*, 97–117, in 1997. I would also like to extend my gratitude to David E.E. Sloane, who published "*Allegoria* and Clock Architecture in Poe's 'The Masque of the Red Death'" in volume 29 of *Essays in Arts and Sciences*, 1–16, in October 2000, and to Robert Greenberg, who gave me permission to reprint. Many thanks as well to Linda Watson for allowing me to reprint several articles, or excerpts from articles, that appeared in *Style*: "Frantic Forensic Oratory: Poe's 'The Tell-Tale Heart'," in volume 35 (spring 2001), 3–49; "A Catalogue of Selected Rhetorical Devices Used in the Works of Edgar Allan Poe," in volume 33 (winter 1999), 637–57; and "A Catalogue of Rhetorical and Other Literary Terms from American Literature and Oratory," in volume 31 (winter 1997), 730–59. Thanks also to James Mellard, who was editor when those essays were accepted for publication in *Style*.

I would also like to acknowledge Karen L. Kilcup, who accepted "Poe's Linguistic Comedy" for publication in *Studies in American Humor*. After her readers had already helped me polish the essay, I – rather embarrassingly – decided to withdraw it to improve the ratio of new material to old in this manuscript, which I then chose to send away to McGill-Queen's University Press. Ms Kilcup was sympathetic to my dilemma and very good-natured about my poor timing, and I am deeply appreciative. Finally, I cannot sufficiently express my gratitude to the editors of McGill-Queen's University Press – Coordinating Editor Joan McGilvray, Editor Roger Martin, and Senior Editor Don H. Akenson – for their wisdom, patience, support, and guidance. I so enjoyed working with them on *Herman Melville: Stargazer* that I wanted to repeat that experience with the present project. Thanks also to my copy editor for *Edgar Allan Poe: Rhetoric and Style*, Lesley Andrassy.

Introduction

To me his prose is unreadable. [Mark Twain]

His style is highly finished, graceful, and truly classical. [James Russell Lowell]

Poe's serious style at its typical worse makes the reading of more than one story at a sitting an almost insuperable task. [Allen Tate]

[Poe's tales] are masterpieces of style. [George Bernard Shaw]

This brief sampling of pronouncements – for an amplification, see chapter 1 – shows vividly how wide apart Poe readers can be on the volatile issue of his style; but insufficient critical attention has been paid to that style to swing the judgment to one side or the other once and for all. Pronouncements, when they come at all, often tend to be negative, as if a brief dismissal in the spirit of Mark Twain or Allen Tate (or Henry James or Yvor Winters or T.S. Eliot or Harry Levin) is sufficient: "Poe was an awful stylist; now let's move on to the more serious concerns of his themes and symbolism or to the sordid details of his gin-soaked, opium-saturated, pathological life." A colleague once e-mailed me the following query: "How come so many astute readers have so much trouble with Poe (and not with Melville, Hawthorne, etc.)? That is, What is it exactly about Poe's style that excites such reactions?" My colleague begs the question at least twice: *are* the readers who despise Poe's style indeed all that astute? and do readers indeed have no trouble with the styles of Melville and Hawthorne? I have not explored stylistic criticism of Hawthorne's prose, so I am not in a position to comment; as for Melville, some readers, in his own day as well as our own, certainly have shown reservations about his style(s). One example will suffice. Of *Moby-Dick*, Melville's contemporary, British editor and novelist William Harrison Ainsworth, wrote, "The style is maniacal – mad as a March hare – mowing, gibbering, screaming, like an incurable Bedlamite, reckless of keeper or strait-waistcoat" (620). And when was the last time someone actually enjoyed reading *Pierre* – that is, enjoyed it on the *sentence level*? Yet Melville's sometimes nearly unreadable prose still, apparently, has not elicited the same hostility as Poe's writing.

This is not to say that Poe's prose has been completely ignored or commented on solely by unfriendly readers. As I make my way down this particular critical path, I find the footprints of other Poe enthusiasts before me: William Mentzel Forrest, James W. Gargano, Joseph R. McElrath, Richard M. Fletcher, Sandra Whipple Spanier, Michael J.S. Williams, Donald Barlow Stauffer – and most of these are actually quite sympathetic to Poe as a stylist. The combined efforts of those scholars, however, have not dispelled the smog of critical hostility that hangs over the Poe canon. More remains to be done to convince the world that Poe's prose deserves more critical attention and that the hostility it has engendered is largely misguided. Proceeding from a position of sympathy, then, I thought it high time that someone devoted a book-length study, a stylistical approach, to Poe's prose. As far as I can tell, no one has done this before; Fletcher's *The Stylistic Development of Edgar Allan Poe* comes close but he deals considerably with Poe's poetry and does not concentrate to the same extent that I do on the tropes and schemes of classical rhetoric where the prose is concerned (this, by the way, is by no means a criticism of Fletcher). I have found several insightful essays by Stauffer, and certainly his impressive knowledge of language and rhetoric – stylistics – may become manifest in book form. As yet, however, I have not seen it (see appendix 1).

By stylistics I mean, of course, linguistics, grammar, lexis, syntax, phonology, typology, punctuation, but especially classical rhetoric – figures of thought and figures of speech, the schemes and tropes. The study of these rhetorical devices was, after all, the first stylistics. Unfortunately, a distrust of "mere rhetoric" goes back at least as far as Plato, and we certainly encounter it again and again through the ages (see the conclusion of chapter 2); even now my own colleagues attempt to discourage me from teaching it to undergraduates: "They're only first-year students,

Brett; you can't teach them that stuff." Why, even a colleague who professed to be an expert on Shakespearean language would have nothing to do with rhetoric (even though we cannot fully understand Shakespeare's language without appreciating his use of the rhetorical tradition, with which he was thoroughly conversant). But I believe what the ancient Greek, Roman, and Renaissance rhetors did: by employing the various figures, writers and speakers are able to express the full range of human emotions and subtleties of thought – and most naturally. I also maintain that Poe (like Melville) had rhetorical training, and in chapter 2 I take up the question of where and when he picked up this training.

That Poe was profoundly sensitive to style, that he was aware of the traditional typologies, and that he even knew the names of classical figures of rhetoric (some of them, anyway) – all this is easily demonstrated. Well, I should not say *easily*, since it took several years and several hundred pages for me to make the demonstration. However, had those critics and professional authors who are hostile to Poe's prose taken the time to read through his literary criticism, they would have found ample evidence to disprove what they insist on believing: that Poe was a sloppy prose writer who really knew nothing, or very little, about style. Nothing can be farther from the truth, as the chapters in this study are designed to illustrate. Allow me to begin the process of substantiation here (briefly).

One of the earliest references to issues of style in the Poe canon appears in an epistle to Thomas White (30 April 1835). Poe is discussing "Berenice" and Gothic tales generally, promising the editor more of this type of fiction because it sells and can help magazines gain a sure hold in the market: "To be appreciated you must be *read*, and these things are invariably sought after with avidity" (Ostrom, 58). One must be careful with horror stories, however: "*great attention must be paid to style, and much labor spent in their composition*, or they will degenerate into the turgid or the absurd" (my italics). Ironically, Poe's prose often *has* been called turgid, but his comments make it clear that he was a very careful, deliberate, and conscientious prose stylist – and if his style now and then *is* turgid, I would be prepared to guess that he wrote it that way for a reason (typically to reveal certain aspects of his narrator's mind – see chapter 1).

Very few of the numerous critical reviews Poe wrote are without comments about the author's style; this alone shows his sensitivity to the *how* of the writing not just the *what*. Sometimes his comments are as vague as those I quoted earlier from Ainsworth – they constitute what Louis T. Milic termed *metaphysical stylistics* (see the catalogue); on the other hand, quite often they are much more precise. Witness these remarks about Ann S. Stephens:

Her style is what the critics usually term "powerful," but lacks real power through its verboseness and floridity. It is, in fact, generally turgid – even bombastic – involved, needlessly parenthetical, and superabundant in epithets, although these latter are frequently well chosen. Her sentences are, also, for the most part too long; we forget their commencements ere we get at their terminations. (*The Literati of New York City*, 15: 57)

Poe's critical vocabulary is fairly clear, explicit – contrast it with the rather vague and meaningless nonsense from William Harrison Ainsworth. For *verboseness* rhetors might use *macrologia*; for *florid* they might try *poicilogic*; for *bombastic* and *turgid* they might substitute *bomphiologic*; for *parenthetical* they might say *hypotactic*. The phrase *superabundant in epithets* works sufficiently, but a modern stylistician might say, instead, that Stephens has an *adjectival style*. My point is this: we can understand Poe's critical terminology quite well; the words he employs give us a fairly accurate idea of Ann S. Stephens' stylistic signature. At the same time, we *can* find accurate substitutions for Poe's precise terminology from the rhetorical handbooks – further evidence of how carefully he thought about style. Try the same exercise with the terms from Ainsworth. What rhetorical labels can we exchange for *maniacal, mad, mowing, gibbering, screaming*? No terms exist, because the ancient Greeks, those superb cataloguers and analysts, were far more precise than that.

As additional evidence of Poe's stylistical expertise, consider the several statements about style that we find in his Marginalia, letters, and critical reviews. That he was sensitive to stylistic concision is shown by his comments on Gibbon's prose: "The mere terseness of this historian is, however, grossly over-rated ... The most truly concise style is that which most rapidly transmits the sense" (16: 15–16; see also 9: 137). In another place Poe demonstrates his ability to recognize concision, and the lack of it, in identifying in a passage from Henry Cary some unnecessary verbosity: "Now the conjunctions which I have italicized ['*and* then,' '*and* yet'] are pleonastic" (95). Poe's knowledge of traditional typologies, stylistic paradigms, is evident elsewhere. Again, of Cary, he says, "His style is pure, correct, and vigorous," and although this is clearly "metaphysical" (see "metaphysical stylistics" in the catalogue), Poe is more precise when he goes on to call it "a judicious mixture of the Swift and Addison manners" (94). Poe recognized, then, aspects of what is (or *was*) rather sweepingly called the "Restoration" style. In a letter (12 July 1841) to his friend Dr Snodgrass, Poe praises a satire by L.A. Wilmer as being "really good – good in the old-fashioned Dryden style" (Ostrom, 175). Later he mentions another Restoration writer and makes clear his understanding of Ciceronianism as well:

The only noticeable demerit of Professor Anthon is diffuseness, sometimes running into Johnsonism, of style [see also 9: 159; 15: 35]. The best specimen of his manner is to be found in an analysis of the Life and Writings of Cicero, prefacing an edition of the orator's Select Orations. This analysis ... is so peculiarly Ciceronian, in point of fullness, and in other points, that I have sometimes thought it an intended imitation of the Brutus, sive de Claris Oratoribus. (103)

Poe's knowledge of the Ciceronian style appears again in his review of *The Works of Lord Bolingbroke*: "The euphony of his sentences is like the liquid flow of a river. No writer in the English tongue so much resembles Cicero – to our mind – as Bolingbroke" (10: 173). Indeed, one characteristic of Ciceronian prose is its *euphoniousness*. Finally, a reference to yet another traditional typology is found in Poe's condemnation of Thomas Carlyle's "linguistic Euphuisms": "I would blame no man of sense for leaving the works of Carlyle unread, merely on account of these Euphuisms" (99). Euphuism is characterized by antithesis, parallelism (*isocolon*), alliteration, rhyming, and every other possible device of sound (Cluett/Kampeas, 30); it became fashionable for a brief time during the Renaissance largely because of John Lyly's *Euphues* (1572). Apparently Poe thought these euphuistic features great for poetry (witness his own) but felt them to be obnoxious when overused in prose. Elsewhere, he expands on this theme in discussing the works of other Transcendentalists than Carlyle: "The quips, quirks, and curt oracularities of the Emersons, Alcotts and Fullers, are simply Lyly's Euphuisms revived" ("About Critics and Criticism," 13: 195). Given Poe's impressive knowledge of style and stylistic models – his sensitivity to various kinds of prose – it is hard to imagine Poe the sloppy writer that some would make him out to be (see also the discussion of "the tone laconic, or curt," in "How to Write a Blackwood Article" [2: 275]).

We see, then, that Poe had some formal or informal education in prose styles and typically would have been a highly conscientious craftsman in these matters. His criticism even proves that he knew the classical names for some rhetorical figures. In his review of Bulwer's *Night and Morning*, he demonstrates his awareness of the rhetorical name for personification: "Nor does the commonplace character of anything which he wishes to personify exclude it from the prosopopœia" (10: 131; see also 10: 75; 13: 19). In "The Rationale of Verse," he illustrates his knowledge of another fancy Greek term: "*Blending* is the plain English for *synæresis* – but there should be *no* blending" (14: 231). Poe uses the adjective *synæretical* in *Eureka* (16: 187). In his review of *The Dream, and Other Poems*, he displays his familiarity with the device *solecismus*: "Mrs. Norton will now and then be betrayed into a carelessness of diction; Mrs. Hemans was rarely, if ever, guilty of such solecisms" (10: 100; see also 12: 133).[1] That Poe knew the esoteric name for personification, and that he knew the little known *synæresis* and *solecism*, shows that he was indeed familiar with some of the classical terms for literary devices – again, more evidence of his understanding of *style*.

In chapter 1 – really the core chapter of the book – I continue this examination and defence of Poe as a stylist. I expand the survey, begun here in the introduction, of the notable critical remarks (condemnatory and laudatory) made about his writing; dispel the erroneous assumption that Poe wrote in a single style, and a bad one at that; demonstrate Poe's appreciation of writers who were stylistically versatile and show this versatility in his own prose masterpieces; destroy the silly assertion that the overwrought and turgid utterances of his narrators are essentially those of their creator – that, in other words, Poe could not distance himself from his own story-tellers; abolish the equally silly assumption on the part of some scholars that these narrators all have the same style; explain Poe's reasons for the more "obnoxious" features of his writing that have been condemned by patronizing critics; and use "The Tell-Tale Heart" as a case study to show that the stylistic features in Poe's best tales are brilliantly appropriate – that style advances, complements, such things as theme, technique, and especially characterization. In other words, the linguistic is related successfully to the extralinguistic – surely one sign of a literary master.

In chapter 2 I further our examination of Poe as a linguistic craftsman but this time less as a stylist and more as a rhetorician. That is, while this text examines the classical schemes and tropes as a way of exploring Poe's prose works at the microscopic level of the sentence (for the most part), in "Frantic Forensic Oratory and the Rhetoric of Self-Deceit" we look at the figures for their *suasive* force in "The Tell-Tale Heart" and "The Black Cat"; we consider two of his murderous narrators as self-conscious but deluded rhetoricians. Additionally, we put *Poe* the rhetorician against the larger backdrop of his time and place, suggesting possible sources (both ancient and modern) for his knowledge of the classical devices and traditional argumentative appeals.

In chapters 1 and 2 I present, among other things, detailed examinations of "The Tell-Tale Heart," and both chapters to some extent depend on my argument that the homicidal narrator in that tale is a paranoid schizophrenic. I relate some devices of speech and thought uncovered there directly to certain manifestations of that illness (for instance, *ecphonesis* to the narrator's mood swings and *paradiastole* to his lack of insight). These chapters in themselves, however, do not fully make the case that the narrator is schizophrenic, yet they depend on that thesis. So that I do not simply ask readers to take my word for it, I include my article "Paranoid Schizophrenia in 'The Tell-Tale Heart'" as an appendix. It is an appendix rather than a main chapter because it is not primarily a stylistical examination – but it is necessary for a fuller appreciation and understanding of my remarks in chapters 1 and 2. While improving that essay in several small ways, I have also updated it: when it appeared originally in *Mosaic*, in 1992 (as "'Moral Insanity' or Paranoid Schizophrenia: Poe's 'The Tell-Tale Heart'"), the latest edition of the *Diagnostic and Statistical Manual of Mental Disorders* had not appeared; I therefore have revised it to reflect the most recent edition of this manual.

Four of the five chapters in this book may somewhat overwhelm readers – those unfamiliar with the hundreds of rhetorical figures of speech and thought and even those well acquainted with them – with the sheer *number* of devices mentioned, defined, and exemplified. Such readers may prefer chapter 3, where I narrow the focus to examine in "The Masque of the Red Death" Poe's use of only two figures, *allegoria* and *chronographia* – among the most frequent devices in the Poe canon. While considering his use of time images and symbols, *chronographia*, we home in on another component of Poe as stylist: his complex use of allegory. Simultaneously, I provide a new reading of "Masque" and clear up some critical confusion on the part of other scholars.

In the final two chapters, we return to the repertory of Greek and Roman rhetorical terms. Chapter 4, "Poe's Linguistic Comedy," begins with a survey of many of the most important statements about Poe's humour: it shows his alienation; it paradoxically also shows how he was part of his *Zeitgeist*; it fits into these and those comedic categories; it can also be found in his Gothic tales; it compares with Swift and Rabelais; it features numerous puns. After the survey, I begin my stylistic analysis and discuss – in addition to the device *cacemphaton* and why it is rarely seen in Poe – the devices one does find there, particularly in those tales in which the comedy is foregrounded. I demonstrate that his use of rhetorical figures is related largely to characterization: the devices present are determined by whether the characters are, say, pompous, urbane, or "linguistic bumpkins." Simultaneously, we see how Poe's verbal playfulness anticipates the prose of Mark Twain (especially) and even some more contemporary American comic writers. In short, in certain ways – and this may surprise readers – Poe's comedy, particularly his *dialectal* humour, is very much in the tradition of American humour. In other ways, it transcends its time and place.

In the sense that Poe's literary reviews were occasionally quite funny in his delicious use of linguistic weaponry for satire, chapter 5 might be seen as an offshoot of chapter 4. Least impressive are such devices as *bdelygma* through name-calling, *tapinosis*, parody, and *hyperbole*. Next on the list of linguistic or rhetorical inventiveness we find his many figures of vehemence (such as *sarcasmus* and *antiphrasis*); somewhat more sophisticated are the several devices of argument (including certain types of rhetorical questions); perhaps most impressive is the way Poe employs particular devices of repetition, not satirical *per se*, but certainly given a derisive application in his hands. Poe broadens the usefulness of some rhetorical figures by giving them applications not typically associated with them, all in the name of critical tomahawkism. Thus, in chapter 5, as in the others, I easily demonstrate Poe's stylistic versatility, inventiveness, innovation – and his love of language, his linguistic sportiveness.

These five chapters alone (with the supplemental appendix on schizophrenia) would suffice to make my multi-faceted case. But there is more. The *backbone* of this study is the catalogue comprising 300 (mostly rhetorical) devices taken solely from the Poe *oeuvre*. This dictionary fulfills several functions. For sophisticated Poe specialists or students relatively new to Poe, it demonstrates one way of *getting into* his works in the hope of inspiring further stylistical analyses. It shows that classical rhetoric provides a critical vocabulary to enable us to describe with precision the stylistic features of a writer's prose. It involves more than mere labelling, however: it sensitizes us to an author's language; increases our appreciation of that writer's craftsmanship; helps us to distinguish between great, good, mediocre, and poor stylists; and opens up exegetical possibilities closed to readers who look for themes but neglect style.

The rhetorical catalogue represents no mere pedantic listing of devices; it is not simply an alphabetical compilation of figures with definitions and exemplifications from the Poe canon. True, some of the entries are little more than definitions and brief illustrations, for many of the figures listed seem merely incidental and appear to add nothing significant, stylistically or thematically, to the works from which they were excerpted. Quite often, on the other hand, I provide mini-essays on the devices that function significantly in illuminating aspects of Poe's writing – his themes, styles, techniques, characters, and aesthetic credo. Readers may want to pay particular attention to the mini-essays provided under the following terms, especially if they are not discussed at length in the chapters: *adynata, allegoria, amphibologia, anadiplosis,* analogy, *anoiconometon, antonomasia, aphelia, astrothesia, auxesis* (#2), *barbarismus, bathos, brachylogia, chiasmos, chronographia,* climax, *dicaeologia, ellipsis, enargia, epanalepsis, epicrisis, erotesis,* the various fallacies, *hyperbaton, hyperbole, hypotaxis,* imagery, *inclusio,* left-branching sentence, *leitmotif, meiosis, metanoia, metaphora,* metaphysical stylistics, morphological set, *non sequitur,* notional set, parenthesis, *polysyndeton, praemunitio, praeparatio, prosopopoeia,* pun, seriation, *soraismus,* and *topothesia.* Also interesting are (for instance) the mini-essays for *diacope,*

enthymeme, palindrome, parallelism, *parataxis, ploce, reductio ad absurdum,* simile, *syllepsis, syncope,* triplet, and *zeugma.* Here, then, are dozens
of the 300 figures in the catalogue that function significantly somewhere
or other in the Poe canon. I am content to let other critics pore over the
catalogue to see whether they might detect patterns of significance that I
have missed. That approach is pretty much the way the chapters in this
book started: I recorded all the stylistic features I found in the tales then
sat back to see whether I could detect patterns of meaning. The result:
five large essays and dozens of mini-essays illuminating Poe's talents and
techniques as stylist and rhetorician.

EDGAR ALLAN POE

Look at *me!* – how I labored – how I toiled – how I wrote! Ye Gods, did I *not* write? I knew not the word "ease." By day I adhered to my desk, and at night, a pale student, I consumed the midnight oil. You should have seen me – you *should.* I leaned to the right. I leaned to the left. I sat forward. I sat backward. I sat upon end. I sat *tête baissée,* (as they have it in the Kickapoo,) bowing my head close to the alabaster page. And, through it all, I – *wrote.* Through joy and through sorrow, I – *wrote.* Through hunger and through thirst, I – *wrote.* Through good report and through ill report, I – *wrote.* Through sunshine and through moon-shine, I – *wrote. What* I wrote it is unnecessary to say. The *style!* – that was the thing. I caught it from Fatquack – whizz! – fizz! – and I am giving you a specimen of it now.

"The Literary Life of Thingum Bob, Esq."

"I could read his prose on salary, but not Jane's": Poe's Stylistic Versatility

Allow me to begin with an anecdote (*paradiegesis*). In 1979, while attending a prestigious Canadian university, I participated in an undergraduate survey course on nineteenth-century American literature. We did most of the classic writers: Thoreau, Melville, Dickinson, Mark Twain, Hawthorne, Whitman – they hardly need to be enumerated. When we came to the section on Poe, however – and we had only reserved a single one-hour lecture for him – the professor announced that next week's class on Poe was optional. Consequently, only four students in a course of over 100 showed up. A lover of Poe's Gothic tales, science fiction, and sweet-sounding poetry since high school, I was among the four. Our professor took the opportunity to confess his keen dislike for Poe – more precisely, for "his style." When I was a graduate student years later at another prestigious Canadian university, this experience was duplicated when a second expert in American literature, and in stylistics, admitted a distaste for Poe due to "his style." Sadly, these specialists in u.s. fiction had little knowledge to impart when it came to Poe because they could never overcome their hatred of his prose.

One wonders how much of this critical contempt for Poe is the result of his literary style and how much pertains more to his personal weaknesses (his alcoholism, his alleged drug addiction and womanizing) or opinions (his endorsement of slavery, hatred of democracy, belief in autography, phrenology, physiognomy). How much of it is really due to his subject matter and themes? It may be, rather, that those academics who express disdain for America's foremost gothicist have been influenced by magisterial pronouncements from other scholars and literary giants. Henry James believed that to take Poe "with more than a certain degree of seriousness is to lack seriousness one's self. An enthusiasm for Poe is the mark of a decidedly primitive stage of reflection" (*Recognition of Edgar Allan Poe*, 66). This remark does not seem to be directly pertinent to the issue of Poe's style, although James W. Gargano quotes it in that context ("The Question of Poe's Narrators"). He also cites Yvor Winters, who ridiculed "the traditional reverence for Poe as a stylist, a reverence which I believe to be at once unjustified" (*Recognition*, 177). Winters complains about numerous grammatical errors in Poe, quotes several passages of prose, condemning without going to the trouble of analysing them, and concludes that Poe's poetry (not prose, mind you) "is an art to delight the soul of a servant girl; it is a matter for astonishment that mature men can be found to take this kind of thing seriously" (200). Gargano also cites T.S. Eliot, who claims to find in Poe "slipshod writing" (*Recognition*, 205), noting, for instance, like Margaret Fuller over 100 years earlier (*Recognition*, 18), an "irresponsibility towards the meaning of words" in Poe's writings (210). He announces that "the work of Poe is such as I should expect of a man of very exceptional mind and sensibility, whose emotional development has been in some respect arrested at an early age" (231) – "the intellect of a highly gifted young person before puberty" (212). Observe that these remarks refer not to Poe's prose style but to his themes and subjects; Gargano seems oblivious to this. At any rate, perhaps my professors did not want it said of them that they were stuck at a primitive stage of reflection or possessed the minds of servant girls.

Maybe other critical judgments have influenced my teachers in their critical disdain for Poe. They likely had read or heard about Mark Twain's letter to William Dean Howells, written on the centenary of Poe's birth: "To me his prose is unreadable – like Jane Austin's [sic]. No, there is a difference. I could read his prose on salary, but not Jane's" (*Letters*, 830). Harold Bloom sounds a similarly infuriating note: "how does 'William Wilson' survive its bad writing? Poe's awful diction, whether here or in 'The Fall of the House of Usher' or 'The Purloined Letter,' seems to demand the decent masking of a competent French translation" (4); "Uncritical admirers of Poe should be asked to read his stories aloud (but only to themselves!)" (3). Another notable critic, Allen Tate, although recognizing that Poe could write lucidly and well on occasion, confesses that "Poe's serious style at its typical worst makes the reading of more than one story at a sitting an almost insuperable task" ("Our Cousin, Mr. Poe," 48). Like so many others who condemn Poe's style, however, Tate never actually does a stylistic analysis of that prose; he merely refers to it as "glutinous." I am not aware of "glutinous" among the traditional typologies of styles. Tate's pronouncement is an instance of what Louis T. Milic calls "metaphysical stylistics": vague, imprecise statements about style that tell us more about the reader than the writing (see the entry for "metaphysical stylistics" in the catalogue of rhetorical terms). Another example of such irresponsible impressionism comes from Julian Symons, who records that Poe's "style is only too often rusty or rhetorical Gothic" (210). We have among recognized typologies the "biblical," the "baroque," the Ciceronian ("high," "grand," "ornate"), the Attic, the Rhodian, the Asiatic, the Euphuistic, the Gorgianic, the Senecan ("pointed"), the Elizabethan, the Restoration, the "middle" style, the "low" ("plain," "humble"), the "modifying," "nominal," "passive," and "verbal" styles. Nowhere do I find "rusty" or "Gothic" on the list of typologies. Eager to have his say, Harry Levin writes that "Poe's style is comparable to the patter of a stage magician, adept at undermining our incredulity with a display of sham erudition, scientific pretensions, quotations from occult authorities, and misquotations from foreign languages" (135). Levin fails to realize that he is commenting on technique rather than style. The same flaw permeates the case made by James M. Cox in "Edgar Poe: Style as Pose." Cox condemns most meanmindedly Poe's alleged "style" – "so ridden with clichés that it seems always something half borrowed, half patched. And not in the worst stories only is this evident, but in the best" (69) – but his argument has almost nothing to do with style as I understand it (as something that can be evaluated through stylistics – linguistics, grammar, classical rhetoric, lexis, syntax, phonology, typography, punctuation), and more to do with characterization, technique, theme.

So far, then, we have seen scathing condemnations of Poe's prose from writers and scholars who cannot be bothered to analyse in detail that prose in order to make their case, and equally scathing dismissals from scholars who do not understand enough about stylistics to avoid making purely "metaphysical" statements. Arthur H. Quinn, on the other hand, admires Poe's writing, calling him "one of the greatest creators of phrases the world has known" (114), but even some readers who like Poe's prose do not write of it with precision. Here is an early admirer, James Russell Lowell: "His style is highly finished, graceful, and truly classical" (*Recognition*, 14). These adjectives mean nothing to me. While Lowell calls Poe "the master of a classic style" (15), George Bernard Shaw simply says that Poe's tales "are masterpieces of style" (*Recognition*, 99). James A. Harrison insists that Poe "always contrived to invest his compilations with the singular charm of his style, so cameo-clear in its distinction and so absolutely free from the verbal ambiguities for which he did not hesitate to rate even Macaulay" (14: vi). Placing Poe within the Southern tradition of the "Ciceronian ideal" – "the ideal of rational man reaching his noblest attainment in the expression of an eloquent wisdom" (25) – Herbert Marshall McLuhan calls Poe "the master of a prose whose lucidity and resilience are unmistakably owing to a society in which good talk is common" (30). Donald B. Stauffer, who seems to have done more good work on the issue of Poe's prose than anyone else, calls him "One of the great stylists of the nineteenth century" ("The Language and Style of the Prose," 465–6). R.D. Gooder has noted that Poe's "tales are held together with a tight logic of development, and with a careful and calculated attention to style," which Gooder calls "brilliant and deliberate" (121). I agree wholeheartedly, but when Gooder concludes by referring to the "*hard brilliance* of Poe's style [my italics]," we know we have read a "metaphysical" statement and not one resulting from a close stylistic analysis.

All these statements raise the question: what *is* Poe's "style"? Readers have called it everything from elegant, lucid, and classic to glutinous, rusty, and Gothic. Certainly "quantitative" critics of the "individualist" school, like Milic and Robert Cluett, might like to consider the question and improve on earlier critical impressions by using the "stylostatistical" approach of the computer. I have no access to such a piece of high-tech machinery and, somehow, merely counting grammatical parts of speech in Poe's work would take the life out of him. I do not care much whether Poe's prose is nominal, verbal, passive, or modifying – whether there is a high or low count of determiners, prepositions, or pattern markers. I also hesitate to place Poe within any traditional but misleading typology such as Ciceronianism, Senecanism, Euphuism. Instead, part of my thesis here is that Poe uses different styles, which depend, for instance, on the nature of the particular mental illness and obsessions of his individual narrators. At least Allen Tate recognized Poe's stylistic diversity nearly half a century ago, in both "Our Cousin, Mr. Poe" and "The Angelic Imagination". In the latter, he writes of

the variations of his prose style, which range from the sobriety and formal elegance of much of his critical writing, to the bathos of stories like *Ligeia* and *Berenice*. When Poe is not involved directly in his own feeling he can be a master of the ordonnance of eighteenth century prose; there are passages in *The Narrative of Arthur Gordon Pym* that have the lucidity and intensity of Swift. (*Recognition*, 241)

These remarks are a little vague, but at least Tate has come to the right conclusion – a conclusion at which more and more scholars have finally arrived: Stauffer quotes Richard Wilbur as saying, "Poe chose numerous styles for his several modes and purposes, distinguishing between the means appropriate to criticism, fiction, and verse, and attuning the language of his tales to the genres ... and the nature of his narrators." Stauffer comments that this is "the single most important fact about Poe's prose style" ("The Language and Style of the Prose," 448). *Because* Poe employs different styles, it is difficult to place him within any particular paradigm, typology, owing to his linguistic (rhetorical, syntactical, lexical) versatility. That Poe approved of writers who were able to employ various prose styles is shown by a criticism he makes in his Marginalia about "The author of 'Cromwell'," who, "to render matters worse ... is as thorough an unistylist as Cardinal Chigi, who boasted that he wrote with the same pen for half a century" (16: 66). He praises W.E. Channing for the "purity, polish and *modulation of* [his] *style*" (*Autography*, 15: 227; my italics). In writing of Kennedy's novel *Horse-Shoe Robinson*, Poe says approvingly that the style "varies gracefully and readily with the nature of his subject" (8: 9). He commends James Paulding for the same thing: "In regard to the style of Mr. Paulding's Washington, it would scarcely be doing it justice to speak of it merely as well adapted to its subject, and to its immediate design" (9: 15–16). Of another writer, Poe says, "The *style* of Mr. Wilmer is not only good in itself, but exceedingly well adapted to his subjects" (8: 236). A similar point appears in his review of *The Prose Works of John Milton*: "it is only by *the degree of its adjustment* to the result intended, that any style can be justly commended as good or condemned as bad" (12: 245; Poe's italics). In other words, *it was part of Poe's authorial credo that style should vary according to subject – should be adapted to the subject.* Consider, finally, a statement in Poe's review of *The Doctor*, which sums up nicely all those I have just quoted: "That man is a desperate mannerist who cannot vary his style *ad infinitum*" (9: 68).[1]

In the following pages I show a variety of stylistic features in Poe's prose. Because some of these belong to entirely antithetical typologies, I hope to discourage once and for all any further sloppy talk of "Poe's style" on the part of students, scholars, and literary giants. As well, I hope to defend Poe as a stylist, offering explanations for some of the more "obnoxious" features of his prose that have been condemned by patronizing critics. Finally, I also intend to use "The Tell-Tale Heart" as a case study to suggest that the stylistic features used by Poe in his best tales are brilliantly appropriate. By showing that in his best works style advances and complements such things as theme, technique, and characterization – that Poe relates successfully the linguistic to the nonlinguistic – I want to prevent once and for all any further condescension and wrong-headedness in critical judgments of Poe as a prose writer.[2]

If we could consider a writer's "style" as something unvarying, as so many oversimplifying critics, scholars, and literary giants have done for so long, presumably we could place the writer within one of the traditional typologies, classifications, defined by some group of characteristic stylistic features. The so-called "plain" style, for example, supposedly refers to prose that is unadorned (lacking in poetic and oratorical devices), to relatively short sentences without or with very little expansion, pleonasm, or amplification. We might expect to find a lot of *parataxis*, for instance – phrases or independent clauses set one after the other without subordination and often without coordinating conjunctions (such as *and, but, or*); as well, we might find a lot of *asyndeton* – a scheme of omission involving unlinked independent clauses side by side without subordination or interlinking conjunctions. If we could say that Poe has a plain style we should expect to find such prose features throughout his writings. Certainly we can find some *asyndeton* and *parataxis* in "The

Tell-Tale Heart": "A shriek had been heard by a neighbour during the night; suspicion of foul play had been aroused; information had been lodged at the police office" (5: 93). Edward P.J. Corbett says, quite rightly, that "The principal effect of asyndeton [and parataxis] is to produce a hurried rhythm in the sentence" (435). Consider how the addition of conjunctions and other connectors would have slowed the passage. Here is another paratactic piece from "The Premature Burial": "She presented all the ordinary appearances of death. The face assumed the usual pinched and sunken outline. The lips were of the usual marble pallor. The eyes were lustreless. There was no warmth. Pulsation had ceased" (5: 257). Note that paratactic sentences are also linear (they depend on the normal word order of subject-verb-object). Certainly the above excerpts can hardly be called "glutinous," "rusty," or "Gothic." I have hitherto neglected the term "right-branching." Linguists call a right-branching sentence one that begins with a main (independent) clause followed by at least one dependent clause. This type of sentence, also referred to as "loose" or "unsuspended," is complete grammatically well before the end; the material that follows in the dependent clause(s) seems incidental. The following quote from "The Tell-Tale Heart" exemplifies this type of syntax: "I knew what the old man felt, and pitied him, although I chuckled at heart" (5: 90). If the paratactic, asyndetonic, unadorned, linear, right-branching, brief sentences I have just quoted were found throughout the Poe canon (and surely "The Cask of Amontillado" is a classic Poe tale in which aspects of the plain style are foregrounded), we could indeed speak of his "style" and label it "plain."

But things are not so simple, for we also find stylistic features antithetical to those I have just demonstrated. Case in point: *hypotaxis* – a complicated syntax employing phrases or clauses arranged in dependent or subordinate relationships. Here is an instance in "The Fall of the House of Usher":

From the paintings over which his elaborate fancy brooded, and which grew, touch by touch, into vagueness at which I shuddered the more thrillingly, because I shuddered knowing not why; – from these paintings (vivid as their images now are before me) I would in vain endeavour to educe more than a small portion which should lie within the compass of merely written words. (3: 283)

The main idea in this long-winded and complicated passage is, "From the paintings I would in vain endeavour to educe"; however, note all the intervening phrases and clauses between the beginning and end of the excerpt. Obviously, a hypotactic sentence structure can be very difficult to read, and we can look to Henry James and some of Melville's later prose for this feature. Another relevant term that applies in discussions of *hypotaxis* is "nested syntax," which Cluett and Kampeas define as "Multiple inclusion, or the placing of subordinate and relative clauses inside other subordinate and/or relative clauses" (42). Interestingly, in his Marginalia, Poe himself uses this nest metaphor in a condemnation of Sir Edward Bulwer-Lytton's style, which he calls "atrociously involute": "He wraps one sentence [clause?] in another ad infinitum – very much in the fashion of those 'nests' of boxes sold in our wooden-ware shops, or like the islands within lakes, within islands within lakes, within islands within lakes" (16: 66). That Poe could even make such an observation shows his sensitivity to issues of style; for a parody of the hypotactic style turn to the first paragraph of "A Predicament: The Scythe of Time." We also see that he condemns in another writer a stylistic feature of which he himself was capable. *Hypotaxis* is clearly the opposite of *parataxis*, which we have likewise seen, and while *parataxis* can speed up a passage, *hypotaxis* tends to slow the pace because of the syntactic interruption.

Hypotactic sentences are sometimes left-branching, too (like the one above), which adds to their difficulty. Called a "periodic" or "suspended" sentence by most English teachers and *hirmus* by rhetors, a left-branching sentence is one in which full grammatical completeness is left until the end. It begins with a phrase or at least one dependent rather than independent clause (contrast with the "right-branching sentence" we saw earlier). Here is an extremely long left-branching sentence describing quite vividly the horrors of premature burial:

The unendurable oppression of the lungs – the stifling fumes from the damp earth – the clinging of the death garments – the rigid embrace of the narrow house – the blackness of the absolute Night – the silence like a sea that overwhelms – the unseen but palpable presence of the Conqueror Worm – these things, with thoughts of the air and grass above, with memory of dear friends who would fly to save us if but informed of our fate, and with consciousness that of this fate they can never be informed – that our hopeless portion is that of the really dead – these considerations, I say, carry into the heart, which still palpitates, a degree of appalling and intolerable horror from which the most daring imagination must recoil. (5: 263)

The main thought in this long structure is at the very end, but we must wade through twelve dependent clauses before we get there. Afraid that we would lose the sense of his meaning long before he concludes the sentence, Poe must employ not one but two summarizing phrases (*epanalepsis*) to help carry the sentence along: "these things" and "these considerations." Clearly, long left-branching sentences can retard the pace of a passage; Poe does so deliberately and thus forces us to consider at torturous length the horrors of being buried alive (premature burials of various kinds occur several times in Poe's fiction and, as is well known, he himself may have suffered from taphephobia – fear of premature interment). Furthermore, a lengthy left-branching sentence like this is the linguistic equivalent to the physical action of holding our breath – an "unendurable oppression of the lungs." Here, style advances theme. From the same tale is another considerably periodic passage that also resorts to *epanalepsis*:

Apart, however, from the inevitable conclusion, à priori, that such causes must produce such effects – that the well known occurrence of such cases of suspended animation must naturally give rise, now and then, to premature interments – apart from this consideration, we have the direct testimony of medical and ordinary experience, to prove that a vast number of such interments have actually taken place. (5: 256)

The combination of *hypotaxis* and periodicity is one characteristic of the grand, the high style, but other features of Ciceronianism are missing from the above examples of Poe's prose. The best we can say so far is that sometimes Poe exhibits qualities of the grand style, other times the plain.

Let us return briefly to one aspect of the "plain" style, *asyndeton*, to contrast it with its opposite, *polysyndeton*, another feature found occasionally in Poe's prose. It involves the use of conjunctions to join a series of words, phrases, or clauses. *Polysyndeton* can be used not only to indicate a series of things but also to emphasize an abundance either of objects or of events passing. The device is frequent in the Bible and some writers use *polysyndeton* to give passages a biblical "flavour" – to suggest that what they are writing has the weight of biblical pronouncement and truth. Here, for instance, is the ending of "The Masque of the Red Death":

And now was acknowledged the presence of the Red Death. He had come like a thief in the night. And one by one dropped the revellers in the blood-bedewed halls of their revel, and died each in the despairing posture of his fall. And the life of the ebony clock went out with that of the last of the gay. And the flames of the tripods expired. And Darkness and Decay and the Red Death held illimitable dominion over all. (4: 258)

Pym similarly ends with foregrounded *polysyndeton*, complementing the biblical themes in that work. Arthur Quinn suggests that "the indefiniteness of 'and' envelops biblical narratives ... in mystery. Occasionally, in the Bible and elsewhere, repeated polysyndetons have an almost hypnotic power" (12). He also notes that *polysyndeton* can slow a passage, "thereby adding dignity to what we say, much like the slow motion of a ceremony" (13). Can we now conclude that Poe has a "biblical" style? Although William Mentzel Forrest has demonstrated several stylistic features that Poe's prose and the Bible have in common (syntactical simplicity, repetitions, parallelisms, refrains, inversions, obsolete words), these, along with *polysyndeton*, are not foregrounded, prominent, in his entire canon; thus, we cannot conclude that Poe's style is exclusively biblical.

Polysyndeton as a scheme of addition involves long-windedness and repetition (of conjunctions), but verbosity and redundancy cannot be said to characterize Poe's style exclusively either. As well as schemes of addition, Poe now and then uses schemes of omission. Sometimes referred to as "minus additioning," schemes of omission can impart terseness, brevity, to a writer's prose. We have already seen one, *asyndeton*, but we can cite instances of *ellipsis* – the exclusion of a word or words that would be necessary for full grammatical completeness but not for understanding. In the following quote from "The Premature Burial" I place in brackets the words that Poe omits: "In all that I endured there was no physical suffering, but of moral distress [there was] an infinitude ... The ghastly Danger to which I was subjected, haunted me day and night. In the former, the torture of meditation was excessive – in the latter, [the torture of meditation was] supreme" (5: 266). Schemes of omission often indicate heightened, even increasing, emotional agitation because of the economy of expression involved: who employs them feels an urgency to say what needs to be said as quickly as possible. Also employing *ellipsis* is another device of omission, *diazeugma* – the use of many verbs with their subject expressed only once. Here are two instances from "The Black Cat":

Upon my touching him, he [subject-pronoun] immediately arose [verb], purred [verb] loudly, rubbed [verb] against my hand, and appeared [verb] delighted with my notice. This, then, was the very creature of which I was in search. I at once offered to purchase it of the landlord; but this person [subject-noun] made [verb] no claim to it – knew [verb] nothing of it – had never seen [verb phrase] it before. (5: 149)

Clearly, *diazeugma* is an effective way to emphasize action and to help ensure a swift pace to the narrative – a sense of many things happening, and quickly. The device figures several times in the tale of detection, "Thou Art the Man"; I indicate the missing subject-pronoun *he* with a caret: "He followed his victim to the vicinity of the pool; there [/\] shot his horse with a pistol; [/\] despatched the rider with its butt end; [/\] possessed himself of the pocket-book; and, supposing the horse dead, [/\] dragged it with great labour to the brambles by the pond" (5: 307). Finally, Poe employs a third scheme of omission, *prozeugma* – the expression of a verb in the first clause that is left out (yet understood) in subsequent clauses. In the following description of Ligeia I insert a caret to mark the missing verb *became*: "Those eyes! those large, those shining, those divine orbs! they became to me twin stars of Leda, and I [/\] to them devoutest of astrologers" (2: 252). *Prozeugma* means "to join in front," and we see how the initial verb joins (governs) words in subsequent clauses. This device is one of several that can speed up the pace of a passage and make for expressive concision.

According to the traditional typologies of style, schemes of omission are found typically in Senecan prose, as is a loose sentence structure, all of which can be found in the above passages. We cannot conclude, however, that Poe's "style" is exclusively Senecan because not all of the so-called Senecan features are found together, or at all times, in Poe's prose; and because, as we have seen, frequently he employs stylistic features that belong to other alleged typologies. Even in this short survey, then, I have compiled considerable evidence to argue against the tendency of reductionist readers to refer to "Poe's style." We have seen that Poe uses a variety of stylistic devices belonging to several of the conventional typologies, but none of these appears to dominate. At best we might be safest to suggest that Poe exhibits a middle style insofar as his prose displays a moderate blend of characteristics belonging to both the grand and the plain – for instance, a mixture of *parataxis* and *hypotaxis,* of right- and left-branching sentences, of schemes of addition but also of omission.

When students, critics, and literary figures complain about Poe's prose, however, they do not rant about his "middle style." No one ever gripes about the moderate style, one typically associated with the lucidity of eighteenth-century prose-writers such as Addison and Dryden (or Swift, as Tate suggests in "The Angelic Imagination"). Those inclined to condemn normally draw attention to those features of Poe's prose typically found in his Gothic tales, stylistic qualities considered excessive, obnoxious. After recording his impression that Poe's "writing smells of the thesaurus" and that "his vocabulary tends to be abstract," Levin regrets that "Typography lends its questionable aid, with an excess of capitals, italics, dashes, and exclamation points. There are too many superlatives and intensitives and ineffables" (133). Perhaps this sweeping pronouncement influenced one of my aforementioned professors, who had been one of Levin's students. Where Levin can be faulted is in making no detailed stylistic analysis or exegetical leap in an attempt to understand why Poe may use these features. Frequently, scholars who comment on Poe's writing can also be faulted for assuming that his style is homogeneous – uniformly bad (or good) throughout his canon. A second erroneous assumption is that the "style" of any given Poe narrator is essentially Poe's – an assumption made by Cox: "all of Poe's narrators are remarkably similar – are in effect a single narrator who tells, under various names, practically all of Poe's stories. *There is really no fallacy in equating this narrator's style with Poe's style*" (70; my italics). Sandra Whipple Spanier also accepts this conclusion (312).

Apparently, neither Spanier nor Cox was persuaded by one of the most intelligent defences ever written of Poe as a stylist: Gargano's "The Question of Poe's Narrators." I cannot express my approval of, my enthusiasm for, Gargano's point of view in that essay sufficiently – but I shall quote him at length:

the contention that he is fundamentally a bad or tawdry stylist appears to me to be rather facile and sophistical. It is based, ultimately, on the untenable and often unanalyzed assumption that Poe and his narrators are identical literary twins and that he must be held responsible for all their wild or perfervid utterances; their shrieks and groans are too often conceived as emanating from Poe himself. I believe, on the contrary, that Poe's narrators possess a character and consciousness distinct from those of their creator. These protagonists, I am convinced, speak their own thoughts and are the dupes of their own passions. In short, Poe understands them far better than they can possibly understand themselves. Indeed, he often so designs his tales as to show his narrators' limited comprehension of their own problems and states of mind; the structure of many of Poe's stories clearly reveals an ironical and comprehensive intelligence critically and artistically ordering events. (165)

To summarize, then: the style in which each narrator relates his story is not Poe's – he and his narrators are entirely distinct; Poe as a deliberate, conscious, and careful craftsman maintains an aesthetic detachment from his protagonists. Victor Vitanza supports Gargano's insight: "only a naive reader would continue to confuse Poe with his characters, would insist that the babblings of his characters are the result of what some early critics alleged to be Poe's own mental state and poor craftsmanship" (137). Another essential point Gargano insists on, although he does not engage in a stylistic analysis to substantiate it, is that "there is often an aesthetic compatibility between his narrators' hypertrophic language and their psychic derangement" (166) – a compatibility between the linguistic and the extralinguistic. In the context of "Ligeia," Stauffer agrees: "The predominantly emotional quality of its style may be defended by its appropriateness to both the agitated mental state of the narrator and to the supernatural events he relates" ("Style and Meaning," 323). Poe believed what ancient rhetoricians, and surely such Renaissance giants as Shakespeare and Ben Jonson, believed – that (to quote Jonson) *oratio imago animi*: "speech is the image of the mind." The stylistic features of any given narrator – rhetorical tropes and schemes, punctuation, notional sets, italics, diction, syntax – reflect the personalities, the emotions, concerns, obsessions, even

madness, of Poe's story-tellers. "Language most shewes a man," wrote
Jonson; "speake that I may see thee" (*Timber or Discoveries* [1640]).

We discover several passages in Poe's literary criticism substantiating
his belief that the character of a persona and his/her narrative or speaking style should be compatible. Reviewing Catherine Sedgwick's novel
The Linwoods, Poe, after praising the author for her "generally excellent
style," complains that, "Now and then, we meet with a discrepancy between the words and the character of a speaker" (8: 98; see also 15: 111).
Style should also be used to *differentiate* characters. In his review of
Orion, Poe says, "We might urge, as another minor objection, that all
the giants are made to speak in the same manner – with the same
phraseology. Their characters are broadly distinctive, while their words
are identical in spirit. There is sufficient individuality of sentiment, but
little or none, of language" (11: 266). Finally, any Poe scholar who has
bothered to read his *Autography* knows about his belief that style reflects
character. His examination of the chirography of over a hundred authors
and editors is laced with deductions showing his belief that a signature
can indicate much about a signatory's writing style, and that it also tells
us about his or her mental qualities. If my logic is correct, then, a connection between style and personality can be made through the interme-
diary of the written name. One quote should suffice to demonstrate the
link between chirography, literary style, and mental characteristics: writing of Judge Story, Poe says, "His chirography is a noble one – bold,
clear, massive, and deliberate, betokening in the most unequivocal manner all the characteristics of his intellect. The plain, unornamented style
of his compositions is impressed with accuracy upon his hand-writing,
the whole air of which is well conveyed in the signature" (15: 242). Each
person has a distinctive signature that indicates each person's distinctive
mental characteristics, which are conveyed in each person's distinctive
literary/narrative style.

The final section will justify the use of certain stylistic features so disliked by some commentators and will demonstrate that Poe can be considered separate from his protagonists as a stylistic craftsman (as
Gargano, Vitanza, and Stauffer maintain) and that these narrators are
also distinguishable from one another.

As a starting point, let us return to Levin's criticism that Poe uses too
many superlatives; I call him the "king of superlatives." Those of us who

have read Poe's review of *Twice-Told Tales* are familiar with Poe's praise of Hawthorne in the following parallelistic passage (which would fit into the typology of Euphuism, this time): "He has the purest style [whatever that means], the finest taste, the most available scholarship, the most delicate humor, the most touching pathos, the most radiant imagination, the most consummate ingenuity" (13: 155). The generous use of superlatives – which might compel some critics to label Poe's a "modifying" style – is only one aspect of Poe's occasionally hyperbolic writing. Think of the trope *hyperbole* itself – exaggeration, overstatement, often used for emphasis or comical effect. The use of *hyperbole* is appropriate for a uniquely American type of humour, the tall tale, which often depends on gross exaggeration. We see it sometimes in Irving and Melville, for instance, and frequently in Mark Twain, but consider these (noncomedic) exemplifications from *Pym*: "suddenly, a loud and long scream or yell, as if from the throats of a thousand demons, seemed to pervade the whole atmosphere around and above the boat" (3: 10); "he found himself beneath the surface, whirling round and round with inconceivable rapidity" (15); "I felt, I am sure, more than ten thousand times the agonies of death itself" (3). I would argue that Poe, retaining an objective, even amused, detachment from his narrators, is well aware of Pym's use of *hyperbole* here, and that, by this absurd level of exaggeration, Poe wants us to question Pym's reliability as a narrator. Or we may consider this *hyperbole* a deliberate clue to the attentive reader that *Pym* is in fact a hoax (it is well known that Poe loved hoaxing the American public) – that *Pym* itself can be seen within the tall-tale tradition. That the novel may indeed be a deception on Poe's part is suggested by the centrality of deceit as a theme (see Ketterer's *The Rationale of Deception in Poe*). Largely a story about oceanic mishaps, *Pym* introduces one of three main characters, Augustus Barnard, who loved to relate his own stories of the ocean, "more than one half of which I [Pym] now suspect to have been sheer fabrications" (17). Thus, Augustus himself appears to be a teller of tall tales marked by *hyperbole*. The novel not only is full of hoaxes perpetrated by the characters but also is itself a hoax perpetrated by the author. Poe weaves a few anomalies, inconsistencies, into Pym's narrative to join with the absurd *hyperbole* in tipping off the wide-awake reader to the tall-tale quality of his only novel.

Another rhetorical name for, or another type of, *hyperbole* is *adynata* – exaggeration that involves the magnification of an event by reference to the impossible (Dupriez, 18), a confession that words fail us (Lanham, 3). This is what Levin refers to when he complains of all the "ineffables" in Poe's prose, and *adynata* figures often enough in Poe's tales of the fantastic. Occasionally a Poe narrator is unable to express some aspects of his incredible experiences; they are ineffable. We find the device four times in "Ligeia," for instance (see Stauffer, "Style and Meaning," 323–4), and five times in "The Fall of the House of Usher." Here are several instances from that tall tale, *Pym*: "The night was as dark as it could possibly be, and the horrible shrieking din and confusion which surrounded us it is useless to attempt describing" (3: 99); "Of a sudden, and all at once, there came wafted over the ocean from the strange vessel (which was now close upon us) a smell, a stench, such as the whole world has no name for – no conception of – hellish – utterly suffocating – insufferable, inconceivable" (111); "I am at a loss to give a distinct idea of the nature of this liquid" (186). While a few of Poe's narrators lack the lexical versatility to describe certain phenomena, in his Marginalia Poe himself claimed greater expressive competence: "How very commonly we hear it remarked, that such and such thoughts are beyond the compass of words! I do not believe that any thought, properly so called, is out of the reach of language ... For my own part, I have never had a thought which I could not set down in words, with even more distinctness than that with which I conceived it" (16: 88). If we can take him at his word, then, Poe himself claimed to be able to express any mere thought through words, but some of his own narrators confess an inability to convey verbally certain thoughts related to their own extraordinary experiences. This discrepancy between Poe's linguistic facility and that of his narrators suggests the aesthetic distance that Poe keeps in relation to them. That is to say, the issue of *adynata* helps support Gargano's assertion that the stylistic "excesses" sometimes found in Poe's works must not be blamed on Poe but are the responsibility of his narrators, who therefore speak their own thoughts (or cannot, as the case may be): "Poe's narrators possess a character and consciousness distinct from those of their creator."[3]

I have offered some hermeneutical suggestions about the appearance of superlatives and "ineffables" in Poe's prose; but Levin also complains about "italics, dashes, and exclamation points." Surely the work in which these particular devices are most prominent is "The Tell-Tale

Heart," and it remains for me to briefly analyse that piece to defend those and other foregrounded stylistic features – features that must be considered insufferably obnoxious to readers hostile to Poe's prose. In "Paranoid Schizophrenia in 'The Tell-Tale Heart'" (see appendix 2), I demonstrate that the narrator suffers from several symptoms of that disease: the superstitiousness of the prodromal phase and, of the active phase, hallucinations, a lack of insight, delusions of grandeur and of persecution, shifts of mood, wrong and/or inappropriate emotions, violence, anxiety, anger, argumentativeness – all being manifested within the expected time-span according to current psychoanalytical findings. Many of these symptoms can be related to the "style" in which the work is written – in which the narration is given by the emotionally overwrought narrator.

Let us begin with those seemingly ubiquitous exclamation marks (Poe called them "admiration marks"). The rhetorical term for a vehement exclamation expressing emotion is *ecphonesis*. Even a rather unsophisticated quantitative analysis of this device in the tale yields some interesting insights. I am referring to a mere counting of exclamation marks, paragraph by paragraph. In Table 1, the eighteen columns represent the eighteen paragraphs in "The Tell-Tale Heart"; the rows represent the number of exclamations in each paragraph. For instance, we see that in column 1 two rows are shaded, meaning that two instances of *ecphonesis* occur in the first paragraph. Although the narrator begins by bragging of how "calmly" he can relate his story, the number of exclamation marks he employs suggests that he is not consistently calm at all – quite the reverse. Eight exclamation marks can be found in his first three paragraphs; he then relaxes a little until the seventh. The next three paragraphs show no *ecphonesis*, but once the narrator recounts how he leapt into the room to murder the old man, and then concealed the dismembered limbs, his vehemence, as suggested by the increased number of exclamations, undermines his earlier claim to tranquility. He settles down again for three more paragraphs but by the tale's climax the number of exclamation marks nearly shoots off my chart (nineteen in the penultimate paragraph). The pattern of *ecphonesis* in "The Tell-Tale Heart" reveals at least two insights. The first is that the narrator suffers from one typical symptom of schizophrenia, a lack of insight – not only into the nature of his psychological illness ("why *will* you say that I am mad?"), but also into

Table 1
Instances of *Ecphonesis* in "The Tell-Tale Heart"

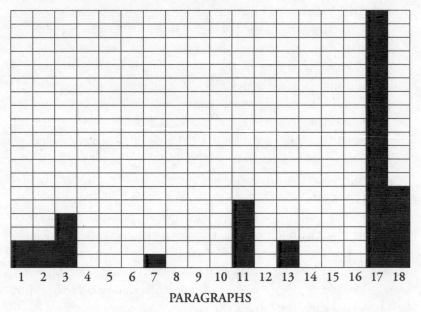

PARAGRAPHS

his own character: he claims to be serene but is in fact emotionally volatile. The second is that he exhibits yet another expected symptom of
schizophrenia: shifts of mood. The pattern of exclamations is one of
peaks and valleys: his mood shifts from expressive violence to relative
tranquility and back again to vehemence – time and again. Thus Poe's use
of *ecphonesis* as a foregrounded stylistic device in "The Tell-Tale Heart" is
deliberate: it enables him to illustrate at least two features of his protagonist's mental sickness: mood shifts and a lack of insight (and this latter
supports Gargano's assertion that "Poe understands them [his narrators]
far better than they can possibly understand themselves").

While the heavy-handed use of *ecphonesis* is one of the more obvious
signs of the madman's frenzy, he is never entirely unruffled even when he
avoids exclamations. Other stylistic features in "The Tell-Tale Heart"
show that, even in those emotional valleys between the peaks of his loud
and frantic outbursts, the narrator's rage and anxieties are simmering.
His patterns of expression prove that his vehemence is always present,
like the background radiation astronomers have detected behind the

more distinctly observable wavelengths in the electromagnetic spectrum. One stylistic feature of this background vehemence is the rhetorical question (*erotesis*) accompanied by a device frequent in Poe, italics (about which Levin complains, as we have seen): "why *will* you say that I am mad?" (5: 88). As Corbett reminds us, "The rhetorical question is a common device in impassioned speeches" (454). The above example of *erotesis* might even be interpreted by some as *epiplexis* instead – a question asked not to elicit information but to reproach, upbraid, rebuke. *Epiplexis* is clearly a device of vehemence. We also find some imperative statements, various exhortations (*adhortatio*) to the narrator's auditors: "Hearken! and observe how healthily – how calmly I can tell you the whole story" (88). The first paragraph also involves some instances of *hyperbaton* – the inversion of normal word order for emphasis: "Object there was none. Passion there was none" (88). This word order allows the narrator to emphasize the usual motives for crime (object, passion) and to stress that they were completely absent through the repetition of the word *none* at the end of two successive sentences (*epistrophe*). Moreover, his syntax is more emphatic and attention-grabbing than "I had no motive, such as passion, for committing the crime" (the important words *motive* and *passion* get lost in the middle of this version and so are deemphasized rather than emphasized). Then follows another instance of *hyperbaton*, "For his gold I had no desire" (88), instead of "I had no desire for his gold." It is true that a word order departing from the normal can be a sign of heightened emotions: we often do not speak in a calm, linear syntax when emotionally aroused. Dupriez says "Most theorists ... have been content to return to the definition of hyperbaton as an inversion which expresses 'a violent movement of the soul' (Littré)" (214).[4] Like *ecphonesis*, these devices – *hyperbaton*, rhetorical questions, italics, and imperative statements – undermine the narrator's vaunted ability to discuss his deeds calmly.

What is particularly foregrounded in this narrator's style are devices of repetition. Take simple *ploce*, for instance, such as the frequency of the word *eye* in the second paragraph: "I think it was his eye! yes, it was this! He had the eye of a vulture – a pale blue eye, with a film over it" (88). We see how the reappearance of a word can suggest a speaker's obsession, and certainly this narrator is a monomaniac where the old man's eye – an eye perhaps merely covered with cataracts – is concerned. Two other devices of repetition are prominent: Lanham says that *diacope* (repetition of a word with one or few words between) is used "to express strong emotion," and calls a similar device, *epizeuxis* (repetition with no inter-ruption), "another vehement emphasizer" (49–50). Schemes of redun-dancy always indicate emphasis, often emotional in nature. Both figures appear in the very first sentence of the confession: "True! – nervous – very, very dreadfully nervous I had been and am" (88). Often, as in that case, when Poe uses both schemes simultaneously, the words constitut-ing the *epizeuxis* are found to come between those comprising the *dia-cope*: "I moved it [the lantern] slowly – very, very slowly" (89); "I resolved to open a little – a very, very little crevice in the lantern" (91); "It [the eye] was open – wide, wide open" (91). Thus, we have a kind of double emphasis and thus a doubled sense of vehemence. We find a great deal of *epizeuxis* and *diacope* throughout the tale: "I put in a dark lantern, all closed, closed" (89); "I undid the lantern cautiously – oh, so cautiously – cautiously" (89); "there I was, opening the door, little by lit-tle" (89); "I kept pushing it on steadily, steadily" (90); "just as I have done, night after night" (90); "He shrieked once – once only" (92); "he was stone, stone dead" (92); "I bade them search – search well" (93). A final device of redundancy I should point out is *anadiplosis*, the repeti-tion of the last word or words of one clause at the beginning of the next: "he had been trying to comfort himself with these suppositions: but he had found all in vain. *All in vain*" (91). Again, the repetitiousness, inten-sified by the italics, emphasizes the narrator's mounting frenzy, quite at odds with the calmness with which he had promised to tell the story.

Another stylistic feature regretted by Levin is the overabundance of the dash in Poe's prose, and certainly it appears often in "The Tell-Tale Heart." As with every other feature of Poe's best writing, the overuse of the dash is not accidental. In his Marginalia Poe discourses at surprising length on punctuation and on the usefulness of this particular feature. Unlike Melville, who seems to know nothing about the proper use of punctuation, certainly the semicolon, Poe was very reflective: "That punctuation is important all agree; but how few comprehend the extent of its importance! The writer who neglects punctuation, or mis-punctuates, is liable to be misunderstood" (16: 130). After suggesting the necessity of a treatise on the topic, Poe continues: "let me say a word or two of the dash," the nearly total disuse of which "has been brought about by the revulsion consequent upon its excessive employment about twenty years ago. The Byronic poets were all dash [what would Poe have thought of Emily Dickinson's verses!]. John Neal, in his earlier novels, exaggerated its use into the grossest abuse" (131). Poe, then, is sensitive to the overuse of the dash, so we must deduce an intelligent artistic rationale for its obvious overuse in "The Tell-Tale Heart." Normally the dash, Poe believes, is exploited to represent *a second thought – an emendation"* (and Poe in these words illustrates its very use); "The dash gives the reader a choice between two, or among three or more expressions, one of which may be more forcible than another, but all of which help out the idea. It stands, in general, for these words – *'or, to make my meaning more distinct"* (see *metanoia* and *epanorthosis* in the catalogue). The dashes in "The Tell-Tale Heart" do indeed function this way *sometimes* but not always. Often the words coming after the dash are merely the same that came before, so they are not emendations but emphatic repetitions (see *epizeuxis* and *diacope*, above). Thus, in "The Tell-Tale Heart" Poe departs from a use of the dash that would presumably figure in the prose of calm and thoughtful writers. In this mad narrator's usage the dash helps out, highlights, the frenzied repetition, and certainly its frequency also detracts from the smoothness of the narrator's sentences – adds a jerky, staccato rhythm quite in contrast to the Ciceronian smooth-flowingness in much of Milton's prose, for instance. That quality might have helped convince us of the calmness of the narrator; instead, the syntactic abruptness of his monologue, brought on by the dashes, suggests the opposite: emphatic vehemence.[5]

Having offered exegetical explanations for Poe's use of punctuation, italics, and a variety of rhetorical figures in "The Tell-Tale Heart," I shall examine briefly the primary notional set in the work as a final way to show how style complements theme and characterization. A notional set, linguists remind us, is a group of words linked on the basis of meaning. The words in such a set do not necessarily overlap semantically but they are related in theme, idea ("notion"). When we isolate notional sets in dialogues, monologues, or first-person narratives, we can truly unlock the mind of a character, giving us a real sense of his or her concerns and values, even obsessions.

Scholars have noticed how often images and words relating to time appear in Poe's writings – clocks, watches, pendulums, hour and minute

hands, ticking sounds, midnight (see chapter 3 and, in the catalogue,
chronographia). Gargano has explored the imagery and significance of
this motif in his essay "The Theme of Time in 'The Tell-Tale Heart',"
reinforcing my belief that no first-person or omniscient narrator in any
Poe story is so wildly obsessed with time and time passing as the schizophrenic here. While Gargano does not give us a list, we can provide a
notional set relating to temporality:

day and night	by degrees – very gradually
the whole week before	every night, about midnight
It took me an hour	every morning
every night, just at twelve	Upon the eighth night
A watch's minute hand	Never before that night
For a whole hour	in the meantime
Many a night, just at midnight	I had waited a long time
such as a watch makes	Meantime the hellish tattoo
louder every moment	the dead hour of the night
for some minutes longer	The old man's hour had come!
In an instant	But, for many minutes
held it there many minutes	The night waned
during the night	much such a sound as a watch makes

it was four o'clock – still dark as midnight
night after night, hearkening to the death watches
for seven long nights – every night just at midnight

Here are twenty-nine references to time in a five-page short story. Time
must play some significant thematic role, then. Gargano suggests that the
narrator's real enemy is not so much the Evil Eye as what it represents. It is
a vulture eye, and the vulture reminds one of death – and death is brought
about by the passing of time: "His quarrel, then, is not with a ravaged individual but with Time, which on one level is symbolized by the omnipresent
'watches' and on another by the 'tell-tale heart'" (379). Gargano proposes
that the madman has a "compulsive obsession with images and sounds that
evoke the rhythm of time" (379), and our notional set clearly supports that
suggestion. The narrator hates the eye of an old man who has become re-
volting because of the passing of time, and he hears the symbols of time ev-
erywhere, even within the centre of our being – at the heart (our "ticker").

He deludes himself, however, in thinking he can escape time and death by simply destroying the individual who reminds him of those abstractions. Like it or not, he is "caught in the temporal net," bound "to the earth and time" (381). He cannot transcend his human limitations, says Gargano. This works as a symbolic reading and accounts well for our notional set of time images and words. It is not necessarily at odds with my interpretation of the narrator as a paranoid schizophrenic, for I have explained his symptoms but have not attempted to suggest the source of his obsession and anxieties. Gargano can be seen to have done that much.

A sensitivity to notional sets in Poe's first-person tales not only can lead to interpretative insights but also can support the contention that Poe's narrators are distinct from one another and from their creator. In relation to "The Black Cat" specifically, McElroy has concluded that the tale "has two simultaneous perspectives: the narrative and the authorial" (103), but surely this is true of all of Poe's most famous stories of murder. While the schizophrenic in "The Tell-Tale Heart" is obsessed with time and time passing, the narrator in "The Black Cat" is profoundly superstitious (despite his claim to rationality). He is terrified not of time and death but of "demonic" black cats, damnation, the Devil, and an angry, punishing God. What makes this tale so much like those of Hawthorne is the language of religion and folkloristic superstition. Like Hawthorne's Puritans, he has a Manichean view of the world as divided into forces of pure good and pure evil, and of the human soul as a battleground of those forces. Consider the following notional set pertaining to ideas of the supernatural in "The Black Cat":

soul	Fiend	demon
fiendish	damnable	remorse
deadly sin	my immortal soul	High God
demoniacal	guilt	Arch-Fiend
hell	damned	damnation
witches		demons

mercy of the Most Merciful and Most Terrible God

This is vocabulary we would expect to find in Hawthorne or in the novels of that fallen Calvinist, Mark Twain, but the tormented murderer in "The Black Cat" really believes he is one of Jonathan Edwards' sinners in

the hands of an angry God (see chapter 2). This notional set is unique to
"The Black Cat"; it is not found in "The Tell-Tale Heart" or "The Cask
of Amontillado," for instance.

Finally, let us consider one of Poe's more obscure tales, "The Business
Man," to see yet another notional set – this one reminiscent of Ben
Franklin's *Autobiography* and "The Way to Wealth," for instance:

account(s)	Advertisement	advertiser
Amount	attorney	bankrupt corporation
banks	bargaining	bill
bonus of five	business	hundred per cent
business habits	business purposes	calling
charge	cheap	competition
copper	corporation(s)	Costs
counting-house	customer	damages
Day-Book	dry-goods dealer	economy
employers	employment	Exchange
fifty cents	fifty per cent	firm
flourishing trade	fortune	fourpence
good income	interest	invested
labored	Ledger	livelihood
lucrative	lucrative business	made man
making money	manufacturer	merchant(s)
merge	moderate charge	money
Net profit	occupation(s)	outlay of capital
overcharged	partner	pay
pennies	penny	premium
price	prime cost	profession
profit	profitable	punctuality
purchase	purchasing	quality
retail business	running account	sale
shilling	sixpence	sold
speculation	sum	swindling
trade	unprofitable	

This "business" notional set very much reflects the American *Zeitgeist*:
nineteenth-century America. It reminds us of the old saying that the

business of America is business and suggests as well that, contrary to the legend of Poe as an artist isolated from his time and place, he was very much in tune with his environment. At any rate, had Cox and Spanier paid a little more attention to the notional sets in Poe's tales, they would not have concluded that Poe's narrators are stylistically indistinguishable from one another or from him or that he was, to use one of his own terms for another writer, a "unistylist."

A close look at Poe's prose reinforces my contentions. First, to do justice to Poe as a writer we must be willing to engage in patient stylistical analyses; in this way we can avoid sloppy "metaphysical" pronouncements about his prose. Second, because such things as lexis, syntax, punctuation, typography, and rhetorical figures really do vary from work to work, we cannot easily place Poe within any conventional or impressionistic typology (although "individualist" scholars would say this is true of any writer). Ciceronian is no more helpful than Senecan, Euphuistic, "biblical," "classic," "elegant," "finished," "rusty," "Gothic," or "glutinous." Third, although he is surely guilty of the occasional semantic or grammatical lapse (and who is not?), Poe as a stylist is much more conscientious and deliberate than many readers realize or are willing to acknowledge: the stylistic features in any given tale, displayed by any given narrator, are suited to theme, technique, and characterization ("there is often an aesthetic compatibility between his narrators' hypertrophic language and their psychic derangement"). Fourth, although we have seen some stylistic overlapping from tale to tale (we found *diazeugma* in "The Black Cat" and "Thou Art the Man," for instance), the styles of the narrators are as various as their particular mental illnesses or world views, balanced or obsessive. The fifth point follows from the fourth: Poe is therefore distinct from his protagonists; he maintains a psychological, an artistic, a stylistic, distance from them. It is hoped that this study, and others to come, will rescue Poe once and for all from the dungeon of critical condescension – from the hands of such censorious inquisitors as Henry James, Yvor Winters, T.S. Eliot, Mark Twain, Harold Bloom, Julian Symons, Harry Levin, and my two unforgiving and uncomprehending professors of olden days.

Frantic Forensic Oratory and the Rhetoric of Self-Deceit: "The Tell-Tale Heart" and "The Black Cat"

In chapter 1 I defend Poe as a stylist, and in part that involves examining his dexterous use of rhetorical tropes and schemes; yet rhetoric involves not only figures of speech and eloquence but also persuasive force. I have no idea what Ezra Pound meant when he complained that Poe is "A dam'd bad rhetorician half the time" (quoted in Hubbell, 20). Perhaps he was referring to Poe's literary criticism, but what concerns me here is the rhetoric of some of Poe's murderous narrators, for John P. Hussey is certainly correct when he notes that "Poe created a series of rhetorical characters who try to persuade and guide their readers to particular ends" (37). The protagonists of "The Tell-Tale Heart" and "The Black Cat," especially, have a considerable grasp of the techniques of argument but, like damned bad rhetoricians, they fail in their rhetorical performances even while striving desperately to convince. That does not mean that Poe himself is a damned bad rhetorician, for what John McElroy says of "The Black Cat" is equally true of "The Tell-Tale Heart": both stories have "two simultaneous perspectives: the narrative and the authorial" (103). The author, Poe, puts various rhetorical figures of speech and thought, and argumentative appeals, into his narrators' explanations of the horrible events they have witnessed, then sits back with his perceptive readers to watch the narrators *fall short* in their attempts at persuasion. The result is an irony that alert readers detect and a conviction – on my part, anyway – that Poe is a far better literary craftsman than even some of his critical champions have realized.

POE AND THE TRADITION OF RHETORIC
AND ORATORY: HIS TIME AND PLACE

We cannot say for sure which rhetorical handbooks Poe was familiar with, but that he *was* familiar with some is shown by a remark he makes in "The Rationale of Verse": "In our ordinary grammars and in our works on rhetoric or prosody in general, may be found occasional chapters, it is true, which have the heading, 'Versification,' but these are, in all instances, exceedingly meagre" (14: 211). To be more particular, scholars attempting to demonstrate a nineteenth-century writer's familiarity with the rhetorical tradition often begin with the eighteenth-century Scottish divine and professor of rhetoric, Hugh Blair, whose *Lectures on Rhetoric and Belles Lettres* "went through 130 British and American editions between 1783 and 1911" (Short, 177n). Hussey shows no diffidence at all in insisting that Poe's art is grounded "in the specific injunctions of the [rhetorical] handbooks," Blair's in particular. For *Eureka*, specifically, Poe needed appropriate personae for his narrator and a rigidly structured pattern or mould, for which he turned to the "classical address, again as Blair describes it, with six major sections: the Introduction (Exordium), Proposition and Division, Narration, Reasoning or Arguments, the Pathetic, and the Conclusion (Peroration)" (41). These divisions are centuries old and as such did not originate in *Lectures on Rhetoric and Belles Lettres*; however, Hussey makes a case for Poe's indebtedness to Blair by showing how the poet-cosmologist follows certain *dicta* expounded in the *Lectures*. Although he makes no attempt to prove his case, Donald B. Stauffer *takes for granted* that Poe took some of his ideas about style from Blair ("The Language and Style of the Prose," 454). Finally, Robert D. Jacobs insists that Poe adopted his rules for metaphors from Blair – see Jacobs' long footnote on these dicta in *Poe: Journalist and Critic*, 198–9.

While Blair's rhetoric was most prevalent in Eastern colleges until 1828 – "Until the middle of the nineteenth century it was one of the most widely used textbooks of rhetoric" (Thomas, 204; see also Corbett, 568) – other extant works were George Campbell's important *Philosophy of Rhetoric* (1776), which achieved a circulation comparable to Blair's after 1830 (Thomas, 204), Richard Whately's *Elements of Rhetoric* (1823), and Professor Samuel P. Newman's *Practical System of Rhetoric* (1827), which would go through more than sixty editions, according to Matthiessen (203n).

Short also cites Alexander Jamieson's *Grammar of Rhetoric and Polite Literature*, first published in 1818 and "in its twenty-fourth American edition by 1844" (178n). Other works known in American colleges include Charles Rollin's *Belles Lettres*, John Stirling's *System of Rhetoric* (1733), John Holmes's popular *Art of Rhetoric Made Easy* (1739), John Mason's *Essay on Elocution and Pronunciation* (1748), John Lawson's *Lectures Concerning Oratory* (1758), John Ward's influential *System of Oratory* (1759), James Burgh's *Art of Speaking* (1761), Thomas Sheridan's *Lectures on Elocution* (1762), Joseph Priestley's *Course of Lectures on Oratory and Criticism* (1777), John Walker's *Elements of Elocution* (1781), John Quincy Adams's two-volume *Lectures on Rhetoric and Oratory* (1810), and William Enfield's *The Speaker* (1826). Less widely circulated were contributions to the teaching of oratory and rhetoric by certain American college professors, including President John Witherspoon of Princeton, "whose lectures on rhetoric, delivered at the New Jersey college from 1758 to 1794, were posthumously collected and printed"; then there is *Lectures on Eloquence and Style*, by Ebenezer Porter, holder of the Bartlett Professorship of Sacred Rhetoric at Andover Academy from 1813 to 1831 (Thomas, 205). He also produced *Analysis of the Principles of Rhetorical Delivery as Applied in Reading and Speaking* (1827), "one of the most widely used college elocutionary texts before 1850" (Thomas, 207 n2). While John Quincy Adams and Joseph Priestley do appear in Pollin's *Word Index to Poe's Fiction*, we find no reference to any of the above texts (Blair is mentioned in *Exordium*). Still, it seems almost inconceivable that Poe would not have read at least some of these at one time or another, especially when we consider that, as Kenneth Cmiel puts it, "From the seventeenth to the end of the nineteenth century, rhetoric saturated American culture" and was "critical to the school curriculum, pulpit, political forum, and court of law." Poe's career as a schoolboy and professional author fits, after all, between the years 1820 and 1860, "the golden age of American oratory" (592). Jacobs calls oratory "the most admired form of Southern rhetorical expression in Poe's time" ("Rhetoric in Southern Writing," 76). "It was," says biographer Allen, "the age of the spoken word" (176).[1]

It certainly seems that speechmaking went on at Poe's childhood home, for his domestic environment and education were responsible for initiating Poe's knowledge of rhetoric as both eloquence and persuasion. An early biographer, George Woodberry, tells us that, at the home of his foster parents, the Allans, Poe even as a young boy was encouraged to give speeches to visitors: "his talent was to declaim" – an aptitude he had "perhaps by inheritance," both dead parents having been actors (15). A later biographer, James A. Harrison, confirms and elaborates by quoting a former acquaintance of Poe, Col. Thomas H. Ellis, who paid tribute to Poe in the *Richmond Standard* on 7 May 1881: "Talent for declamation was one of his gifts. I well remember a public exhibition at the close of a course of instruction in elocution which he had attended ... and my delight when, in the presence of a large and distinguished company, he bore off the prize in competition with ... the most promising of the Richmond boys" (1: 24).[2] It is hard to imagine a precocious Virginia boy being unaware of rhetoric, given his environment: "Little Edgar's childhood and youth were passed in an atmosphere of sociability, open-air sports, oratory, and elocution. Patrick Henry, the great orator of the Revolution, lay in the neighboring churchyard of Old St. John's; Chief-Justice Marshall, the greatest of the justices of the Supreme Court, and John Randoph of Roanoke, celebrated for silver voice and stinging sarcasm, were familiar figures in Richmond streets; retired presidents like Jefferson, Madison, and Monroe" were also to be seen occasionally (1: 13). A recent biographer, Jeffrey Meyers, goes further, speculating – probably following Arthur Hobson Quinn (102) – that Poe had met the author of "The Declaration of Independence," one of the most brilliant pieces of rhetoric ever penned by an American: "Every Sunday Mr. Jefferson regularly invited some of the students to dine with him at Monticello [but see Bittner, 45], and Poe must have met him on several social and academic occasions" (22).

Not only did the young Poe have the example of contemporary orators such as Jefferson ("Old Man Eloquent") constantly in front of him but his formal education acquainted him as well with the great rhetoricians of the past. When a young scholar in England, Poe attended John Bransby's school at Stoke Newington, where he learned Latin, so important for a knowledge of ancient rhetoric. Back in America, in the English and Classical School of Richmond, Virginia, a barely adolescent Edgar "read the ordinary classical authors of the old preparatory curriculum" (Woodberry, 19). A.H. Quinn is more specific, quoting the schoolmaster Joseph H. Clarke, who wrote in an 1876 letter, "When I left Richmond ... Edgar's class was reading Horace and Cicero's Orations in

Latin" (83). At Jefferson's newly opened University of Virginia, Poe enrolled in the Schools of Ancient and Modern Languages, later to excel in French and, again, Latin (Norman, 72).[3] Harrison records that Poe impressed his associates with "his remarkable attainments as a classical scholar" (1: 48). As another biographer, Kenneth Silverman, notes, Poe also joined "the Jefferson Society, a debating club, [where] it was said, [he] 'grew noted as a debater'" (30). What better forum for the practice of rhetoric?[4]

These scholarly achievements are occasionally reflected in Poe's writings, where we certainly find some references to rhetoric and oratory. In "Some Words with a Mummy," for instance, Poe provides a rather comical picture of modern oratorical gestures: "Mr. Gliddon ... could not make the Egyptian comprehend the term 'politics,' until he sketched upon the wall, with a bit of charcoal, a little carbuncle-nosed gentleman, out at elbows, standing upon a stump, with his left leg drawn back, his right arm thrown forward, with the fist shut, the eyes rolled up toward Heaven, and the mouth open at an angle of ninety degress" (6: 125). Poe would have known this cartoon orator to be partaking of the "mechanistic" concept of elocution, which was overwhelmingly popular in the 1800s.[5] (In other words, here Poe shows his awareness of the last of the traditional five parts of rhetoric: delivery.) Furthermore, in "The Purloined Letter," Dupin suggests to the narrator that "some color of truth has been given to the rhetorical dogma, that metaphor, or simile, may be made to strengthen an argument, as well as to embellish a description" (6: 47; see also 10: 143–4). His knowledge of both ancient and modern rhetoric is shown by some remarks Poe makes in his Marginalia:

We may safely grant that the *effects* of the oratory of Demosthenes were vaster than those wrought by the eloquence of any modern, and yet not controvert the idea that the modern eloquence, itself, is superior to that of the Greek ... The suggestions, the arguments, the incitements of the ancient rhetorician were, when compared with those of the modern, absolutely novel; possessing thus an immense adventitious force – a force which has been, oddly enough, left out of sight in all estimates of the eloquence of the two eras.

The finest Philippic of the Greek would have been hooted at in the British House of Peers, while an impromptu of Sheridan, or of Brougham, would have carried by storm all the hearts and all the intellects of Athens. (16: 62; see the nearly identical remarks in a Poe review [10: 58–9])

Elsewhere in the Marginalia we find a reference to Cicero's speeches: "The best specimen of his manner [Professor Charles Anthon's] is to be found in an analysis of the Life and Writings of Cicero, prefacing an edition of the orator's Select Orations. This analysis … is so peculiarly Ciceronian, in point of fullness, and in other points, that I have sometimes thought it an intended imitation of the *Brutus, sive de Claris Oratoribus*" (16: 103). In fact, Poe reviewed Anthon's *Select Orations of Cicero* for the *Southern Literary Messenger* in January 1837 (9: 266–8). In "The Man of the Crowd" the narrator refers to "the mad and flimsy rhetoric of Gorgias" (4: 134), the fourth-century Sicilian rhetorician and chief adversary of Socrates in Plato's *Gorgias*. The forensic oratory of Gorgias employed "highly musical forms of antithesis, involving isocolon, homoioteleuton, parison, paramoion and – above all – abundant paranomasia" (Cluett/Kampeas, 33) – figures Poe himself uses on occasion in his own prose. Poe shows his familiarity with another ancient rhetor in his discussion of the mystical Ralph Waldo Emerson: "Quintilian mentions a pedant who taught obscurity, and who once said to a pupil 'this is excellent, for I do not understand it myself'" (15: 260). At any rate, Allen Tate, after acknowledging Poe's "early classical education" (and Christian upbringing), is certainly wrong when he goes on to say that Poe "wrote as if the experiences of these traditions had been lost" ("Our Cousin, Mr. Poe," 49).

We do not have to be denouncing bitterly the King of Macedon or carrying on in the British House of Peers to engage in the art of persuasion, however, for we employ rhetoric every day of our lives, usually for the most ordinary of needs; nor do we need to have all our mental faculties in good working order to exploit rhetoric – as Poe demonstrates through the desperate narrators in his tales of homicide. For instance, in "The Tell-Tale Heart" and "The Imp of the Perverse," the mentally disturbed murderers want to convince their auditors of the reasonableness of their crimes and/or their subsequent manoeuvrings – to make their audience understand that these things are comprehensible according to ordinary motives of human behaviour and psychology. The profound irony, of course, is that these protagonists employ the traditional, the classical, language of reason (and primarily the Aristotelian appeal to *logos*) to justify and defend the actions of unreason. Readers should adopt the same stance of ironic detachment as Poe himself enjoys; that is, we should be aware of the discrepancy between his narrators' irrational actions, motives, and their techniques of rational argument, their forensic oratory. Like another American literary psychologist, Herman Melville, Poe recognized that victims of mental diseases do not appear to be psychologically ill all the time – that hysterical ravings and incomprehensible babblings do not always identify the insane (also the lesson in "The System of Dr. Tarr and Professor Fether" [see especially 6: 72]). Poe would have appreciated Melville's psychoanalysis of John Claggart:

Though the man's even temper and discreet bearing would seem to intimate a mind peculiarly subject to the law of reason, not the less in heart he would seem to riot in complete exemption from that law, having apparently little to do with reason further than to employ it as an ambidexter implement for effecting the irrational. That is to say: Toward the accomplishment of an aim which in wantonness of atrocity would seem to partake of the insane, he will direct a cool judgment sagacious and sound. These men are madmen, and of the most dangerous sort. (*Billy Budd*, 76)

Like Melville's Ahab, Poe's madman in "The Tell-Tale Heart" particularly employs reason not only to carry out irrational acts but also to justify them. He behaves like an orator striving to convince an audience to take up a cause or like a defence attorney advocating a point of view.[6] We have to acknowledge that Poe's depraved rhetoricians – like Ahab, many of Shakespeare's evil characters, and the Satan of Milton's *Paradise Lost* – have fairly impressive powers of argument even while we recognize the absurdity of their attempts to justify themselves, or recognize at least the *pathos* of their attempts to explain the events in which they have played a role.

FRANTIC FORENSIC ORATORY: "THE TELL-TALE HEART"

In appendix 2 I demonstrate that the homicidal narrator in "The Tell-Tale Heart" is a paranoid schizophrenic, noting that symptoms of the disease include anxiety and argumentativeness. These symptoms, especially his disposition to dispute, are manifested not only when he "arose and argued about trifles" (5: 95) but also throughout the account. "The Tell-Tale Heart" is an extended example of what classical Greek and Latin rhetors called *antirrhesis* (the rejection of an argument or opinion because of its error, wickedness, or insignificance). Obviously, the prisoner's captors have named his crime for what it is, the act of an anxiety-ridden madman; *this* is the argument that the narrator – illustrating another symptom of schizophrenia, lack of insight – rejects as erroneous, impertinent, absurdly false; this is the thesis to which he attempts to provide the antithesis. Acting as his own defence lawyer, he is not concerned with the issue of his responsibility in the crime, or with the quality of the evidence against him, or with the nature of the law broken, or with determining the extent of harm done to the victim – all important issues in forensic oratory (see Corbett, 137–8). That is, he is not concerned with *whether* something happened but with the *quality* of what happened: his motives – the causes of his murderous actions and his subsequent manoeuvrings. He wants to demonstrate, rhetorically, that they were the actions of a sane rather than an insane man – wants, therefore, to refute not the charge that he committed the crime but the charge that he is mad. In doing so he bases his argument on the topos of comparison, specifically the sub-topic of *difference* ("I differ from homicidal madmen in several important respects").

As a specimen of courtroom oratory, "The Tell-Tale Heart" displays several parts of the classical speech: it begins, as it should, with an *exordium* or *prooemium* (introduction), which we might consider the first two paragraphs. Part of the introductory material is the *narratio,* a brief, clear statement of the case; the narrator knows that this is a principal component of forensic oratory. Speeches, however, do not always use or need every part of the classical division, and Poe's narrator omits a *partitio* (*divisio* – division of the issue into its constituent parts). He then combines the standard fourth and fifth sections – the *confirmatio* (one's strongest positive arguments) and *confutatio* (refutation of contrary viewpoints); these make up the bulk of the tale and are anticipated in the opening two paragraphs. It is telling that this speech lacks the final part of a classical oration, the *peroratio* (conclusion). Had the narrator been able to retain his initial tranquility, he might have been able to produce some closing remarks (a summary of his case and a terminal flourish), but by the end of the speech his forensic powers have degenerated into complete and utter frenzy: he succumbs to his schizophrenic symptoms again, specifically a violent mood swing comprising anger and anxiety.

At the start, he knows that his audience has already determined what they think of him, knows that they are hostile and have labelled him a nervous "madman." He is aware that his case is what Cicero would have called a *difficult* one (as opposed to being "honorable," "mean," "ambiguous," or "obscure"), involving as it does an audience whose sympathies are alienated by the horrendous nature of his crime. Thus, the narrator uses his *exordium* as it is meant to be used: he attempts to win the goodwill of his auditors, at least to the extent that they are willing to hear him out patiently. While the rest of the speech is an appeal to *logos*, reason, at the beginning he must resort to an appeal to *ethos* to lessen the audience's hostility and make them more receptive. He begins, therefore, with *restrictio* in accepting part of their judgment: "True! – nervous – very, very dreadfully nervous I had been and am" (88). He makes a concession (*paromologia*), and what better way to capture the audience's sympathies than by agreeing with their pronouncement – in effect congratulating them on their astuteness, their medical acumen. It is true that he qualifies their diagnosis with his rhetorical questions ("why *will* you say that I am mad?"; "How then am I mad?") – in this sense he is using what Richard Whately called the *introduction corrective* (see Corbett, 284–5) – but he has already shown his goodwill (*eunoia*) towards his listeners by agreeing with at least part of their judgment. Corbett discusses the strategic usefulness of the concession as part of the ethical appeal: "The audience gets the impression that the person capable of making frank confessions and generous concessions is not only a good person but a person so confident of the strength of his or her position that he or she can afford to concede points to the opposition" (316).

Poe's clever forensic rhetorician uses other devices to "soften up," to *condition*, his audience. The first and second paragraphs of "The Tell-Tale Heart" also involve a device used often by Poe's narrators: *praeparatio* (preparing an audience before telling them about something done). Several of Poe's tales begin with short essays on various themes or concepts that will be illustrated by the following narrative accounts; thus, the narrators prepare the audience to understand the specific cases to follow by illuminating the theories first. "The Murders in the Rue

Morgue" commences with an essay on certain mental skills before we hear about their display by the amateur detective C. Auguste Dupin. "The Premature Burial" starts with several illustrations of untimely interment before we hear about how the narrator himself was apparently buried alive. "The Imp of the Perverse" begins with a short dissertation on that destructive and irresistible human impulse before the narrator provides three examples of it and finally his own case. I agree with Sandra Whipple Spanier (311), who quotes Eugene R. Kanjo with approval: "This essay-like introduction is not a failure of craft, as one critic contends, but a measure of Poe's craftiness" (41). This craftiness lies in Poe's use of the rhetorical tradition – here, in his employment of *praeparatio*. When used to preface a criminal defence, this device can make what would otherwise seem to be merely cold, hard, ugly, incriminating facts more understandable, even more acceptable – or, at least, less *un*acceptable. At the same time, most significantly, the forensic narrator combines the ethical appeal with the appeal to *pathos* (emotions): he attempts to enlist the sympathies of his hostile auditors by portraying *himself* as the real victim. He tries to weaken the charges against him by discoursing on his misfortunes, his difficulties: I *loved* the old man, but I was persecuted, hounded, harassed, and haunted day and night by his wretched Evil Eye (Crowley says "a rhetor's ethos may be a source of good will if she … elaborates on her misfortunes or difficulties" [176]).

In his use of *praeparatio*, the narrator in "The Tell-Tale Heart" differs from the Watson-like biographer of Dupin and the protagonists of "The Imp of the Perverse" and "The Premature Burial" in that he does not provide any general theories or other cases of his particular illness, but he does prepare us to understand it nevertheless. He wants us to recognize, first, that he suffers from overacute senses and, second, that the vulture eye of the old man, not hatred or greed (rather trite, uninteresting, normal motives), is what compelled him to commit his atrocity (here is also *expeditio*, if we can accept the term as meaning not just the rejection of all but one of various reasons why something should be done but also of why something was done). Also embedded within the larger trope, *praeparatio*, is *aetiologia* – giving a cause or reason for a result (Lanham, 3): "He had the eye of a vulture – a pale blue eye, with a film over it. Whenever it fell upon me, my blood ran cold; and so by degrees – very gradually – I made up my mind to take the life of the old man, and thus rid

myself of the eye forever" (88). Here the narrator employs another topos
frequent in forensic oratory: the topos of relationship and its sub-topic,
cause and effect. The pathetic irony in all this, of course, is that the narrator really believes his *aetiologia* to be reasonable, comprehensible, easily
justifiable.

Poe maintains an objective distance with us and watches the ironic *aetiologia*. What characterizes most of the rhetorical devices in Poe's tales of
homicide is the conscious, the deliberate, irony with which he uses these
techniques of argumentation. Overlapping with the ironic *aetiologia* is *dicaeologia*: defending one's words or acts with reasonable excuses; defending
briefly the justice of one's cause. As with the *aetiologia*, what gives an interesting twist to the use of *dicaeologia* in some of Poe's tales is the extent to
which the narrators' auditors and we, the readers, might find the defence,
the excuse, outrageously unconvincing and bizarre. The same is true of the
use on the part of the "Tell-Tale Heart" narrator of what Cicero called
praemunitio – defending yourself in anticipation of an attack; strengthening your position beforehand: "If still you think me mad, you will think so
no longer when I describe the wise precautions I took for the concealment
of the body" (92). Here the *praemunitio*, which is a normal component of
the confirmation/refutation part of a classical oration, is pathetic, ironic,
because clearly inadequate, ludicrously implausible to anyone except the
narrator – more generally, to anyone who is outside society's codes of
moral behaviour and lacking the conscience of the *superego*.

The bragging narrator, however, believes that he, as a man of superior
powers (note his delusions of grandeur, another sign of schizophrenia), not
only can plan and carry out the perfect crime and conceal the evidence but
also can convince his prosecutors that his actions were entirely reasonable.
"The Tell-Tale Heart" is an extended exemplification of *antirrhesis* but it
is, as well, extended *diallage* – a bringing together of several arguments to
establish a single point: his sanity. Argument 1: I am not mad but suffer
from overacute senses, especially of the auditory capacity ("And have I not
told you that what you mistake for madness is but over acuteness of the
senses?" [91]). Argument 2: "Madmen know nothing. But you should
have seen *me*. You should have seen how wisely I proceeded – with what
caution – with what foresight – with what dissimulation I went to work"
(88). A lunatic, he believes, would be incapable of sagacity, caution,
foresight, and deception in planning and executing a murder ("would a

madman have been so wise as this?" [89]). Argument 3: "If still you think me mad, you will think so no longer when I describe the wise precautions I took for the concealment of the body."[7] Not only sagacity in execution but sagacity in concealment is a sign of sanity, he believes.

His auditors, however, likely do not share the positive *slant* that he puts on his actions. After all, this shrewd forensic rhetorician seems to make use of what is sometimes considered a rather disreputable device: *paradiastole* (making the best of a bad thing; the euphemistic substitution of a negative word with something more positive). In his introduction to Machiavelli's *The Prince*, David Wootton calls chapters 16 to 18 of that work "a virtuoso exercise in *paradiastole*, the redescription of behavior in order to transform its moral significance" (xxxiv). For example, what we call hypocrisy in a ruler, Machiavelli would call *craftiness* or *expediency*; in other words, what most people consider a negative trait, Machiavelli considers positive. We see, then, how the device, a technique of argument, can involve essentially a Nietzschean revaluation of values. As part of his forensic oratory, the Machiavellian narrator in "The Tell-Tale Heart" seems to employ *paradiastole*, especially in the third paragraph. Consider his use of nouns and adverbs: "You should have seen how *wisely* I proceeded – with what *caution* – with what *foresight* – with what *dissimulation* I went to work! ... Oh, you would have laughed to see how *cunningly* I thrust it in!" (88–9; my italics). What we might call *perfidiously,* he calls "wisely"; what we might call *sneakiness,* he calls "caution"; what we might call *scheming,* he calls "foresight"; what we might call *treacherously,* he calls "cunningly." Even the one word in that catalogue that has negative connotations, "dissimulation," he would translate as *ingenuity.* Certainly his accusers, those whom he is addressing, have evaluated his conduct and might have expressed it thus: "We should have seen how perfidiously you proceeded – with what sneakiness – with what scheming – with what hypocrisy you went to work! Oh, we would have been appalled to see how treacherously you thrust in your head!" But the narrator, using *paradiastole*, has redescribed his behaviour, putting it in a positive light according to *his* twisted values and assuming that his audience would be persuaded to adopt those values also.

Let us summarize the rhetorical appeals, topoi, and devices that Poe's paranoid schizophrenic employs, within a classical arrangement, to win the skeptical audience to his point of view. We have seen that he employs four of the six parts of a classical oration. His *exordium* attempts to make the hostile audience more receptive to his point of view through *restrictio* and an initial, friendly concession (*paromologia*), part of his brief appeal to *ethos* (simultaneously, his introduction is of an inoffensively corrective nature in that he insists that his judges have misunderstood the nature of his illness and, hence, his case). Next, he continues his strategy of softening the auditors with *praeparatio*. His statement of the case (*narratio*), told in the plain style as it should be (according to Quintilian), also features *expeditio*, *aetiologia*, and *dicaeologia*. The fourth and fifth parts of this forensic speech, the *confirmatio* and *confutatio*, begin with the third paragraph and employ *paradiastole*, *praemunitio*, *progressio*, *antirrhesis*, and *diallage*. Additionally, the narrator's forensic oratory involves the topos of comparison (with its sub-topos of difference) and the topos of relationship (with its sub-topos of cause and effect); all these comprise a five-page appeal primarily to *logos*, reason – with a useful bit of *ethos* and *pathos* thrown in at the beginning.

What is so tragic about the narrator's frantic forensic rhetoric, however, is his psychopathic inability to appreciate the *moral gravity* of his deeds, despite his – shall we say it? – otherwise brilliant capacity to construct a powerful piece of persuasion, of reasoning. Paige Matthey Bynum puts it this way: "Poe's narrator is maintaining a causal sequence – I can reason; therefore I am not insane – which Poe's audience had just discovered was false" (148). It is evident immediately to the reader, and increasingly as the narrative progresses, that the narrator is clearly ill and, as John Cleman says, "The irony of ostensible sanity signalling insanity could not have been lost on Poe" (632). Let us narrow the focus from the broad and vague term "insanity" to the particular illness from which Poe's forensic orator suffers. His revaluation of values, his *paradiastole*, is really a manifestation of his schizophrenia, which, remember, refers to a split between thought and feeling: his thoughts of the grisly murder he committed are not accompanied by the feelings of disgust that mentally healthy people would feel. His feelings are of delight rather than disgust. That is why he is able to turn *perfidiously* into *wisely*, *sneakiness* into *caution*, *scheming* into *foresight*, *treacherously* into *cunningly*, and to define *dissimulation* as *ingenuity* rather than *hypocrisy*. We recognize this rhetorical revaluation of values as a sign of schizophrenia; the narrator does not.

THE RHETORIC OF SELF-DECEIT: "THE BLACK CAT"

Several ingenious interpretations of "The Black Cat" have been put forward over the last three or four decades, all of them, of course, at odds with one another to a greater or lesser extent – although there have been some points of agreement, too. For instance, earlier readers seemed inclined to take the narrator's explanation of the "imp of the perverse" at face value, while later readers – more perceptive ones, I think – largely agree that this psychological theory is not to be credited within the context of "The Black Cat" (although I believe Poe offers it more seriously as a psychological description of human behaviour in "The Imp of the Perverse").[8] Another exegetical tendency has been for critics to lean toward naturalistic rather than supernaturalistic interpretations of the fantastic events as recorded by the condemned narrator – and here is where I part company.[9] Although some clever naturalistic explanations of the tale have been put forward (see, for instance, Susan Amper, McElroy, William Crisman, T.J. Matheson), I am still inclined, like Gayle Anderson and Mabbott (who calls "The Black Cat" a "story of 'orthodox' witchcraft" [*Works*, 848]), to favour a reading that considers the horrendous events as genuinely supernatural. Certainly the narrator believes them to be, and a key to understanding "The Black Cat" in this light is the influence that Hawthorne's tales of New England witchcraft must have had on Poe in 1843, the imagery and structure of the tale, the language (especially what I call the "supernatural notional set"), and the narrator's own inner-directed rhetoric (especially his use of *meiosis* and *litotes*). All the hermeneutical performances published so far have ignored the combination of these key factors, an attention to which has enabled me to produce a new reading of the tale.

From a stylistic and rhetorical point of view, the language in "The Black Cat" is interesting right from the opening paragraph. *This* narrator, like that of "The Tell-Tale Heart," employs *praeparatio* in explaining his motives for confessing his crime:

For the most wild, yet most homely narrative which I am about to pen, I neither expect nor solicit belief. Mad indeed would I be to expect it, in a case where my very senses reject their own evidence. Yet, mad am I not – and very

surely do I not dream. But to-morrow I die, and to-day I would unburthen my
soul. My immediate purpose is to place before the world, plainly, succinctly,
and without comment, a series of mere household events. (5: 143)

One wonders what he means by "without comment," for – as other
scholars have noted (James W. Gargano, McElroy, Richard Badenhausen, Matheson) – he does more than simply relate the events: he explains throughout the effect they have had on him; as well, he theorizes
about such things as the "imp of the perverse." Thus, we seem to have
here an extended instance of the figure of thought *paraleipsis*, pretending
not to mention something while mentioning it. The narrator promises
that he will not comment – but he cannot help commenting; he wants
to come off as nonchalant but it quickly becomes evident that he cannot
keep up the appearance, so emotionally overwrought is he.

While, rhetorically, "The Tell-Tale Heart" is an extended example of
antirrhesis – rejecting an argument as erroneous (the argument of his
captors that the narrator is mad), in "The Black Cat" the rhetoric is
more inner-directed. Badenhausen claims that this murderous storyteller seeks both understanding and approval from his audience (489),
and Matheson insists that the narrator, who borrows "the language and
rhetoric from the temperance tale" (80), attempts to elicit our sympathy
through appeals to *ethos* (his good character) and *pathos* (our emotions).
However, I think it is possible to overstate the extent to which the narrator wants us to pity him as a previously sensitive and "passive victim"
(Matheson's phrase) of alcoholic excesses. The rhetorical appeals to *ethos*
and *pathos* (my terms, not Matheson's) seem rather incidental; except for
the narrator's briefly explained theory of perversity (an appeal to *logos* –
reason), he does not expect to persuade his audience of *anything* regarding his narrative: "I neither expect nor solicit belief. Mad indeed would I
be to expect it." This narrator seems more concerned with convincing
not so much his readers but *himself* of something.[10] What is that something?: that he has *not* been duped by a witch-cat into murder or exposed by a vengeful witch-cat; that he is *not* doomed by an angry
Jehovah to eternal punishment. He wants desperately to believe that the
narrative he is about to relate is *not* one of supernatural retribution;
rather, he insists on calling it a *homely* (ordinary, unremarkable) narrative
(see Fred Madden's discussion of the German term *heimlich*). Essential

to this man's inner-directed rhetoric is *meiosis*, a lessening, sometimes belittling a thing or person with a degrading epithet (Lanham, 98) – under-emphasis. A few lines later the confessor uses *meiosis* again in referring to the "series of *mere* household events [my italics]." Anyone who has read "The Black Cat" knows that the mutilation and hanging of a cat, the murder of a wife (uxoricide) with an axe, and the attempt to hide the corpse behind a brick wall in a basement are anything but mere household events. The narrator's ridiculous use of *meiosis* is a fore-grounded stylistic feature that differentiates him from other Poe narrators (who tend to use *hyperbole* and *adynata* – figures of exaggeration), and through *meiosis* he attempts to de-emphasize the events and their possible implications for his soul. When he mentions the apparent shape of the white fur on the second cat as resembling a gallows, he again tries to downplay the significance of the phenomenon by referring to it as "one of the *merest* chimaeras it would be possible to conceive" (my italics; 150). He frantically wants to believe that the gallows on the cat's fur is a mere trick of the imagination and not a portent of his doom. As Pamela J. Shelden puts it, "his terror of the supernatural is a very urgent concern" (78). Indeed, and he uses all his suasive powers to battle his own superstitious nature. *That* is the rhetorical crux of the tale.

Supernatural are typically balanced by natural explanations of the events in a Poe tale of terror, but the narrator in "The Black Cat" seems unable – despite his best rhetorical efforts – to convince himself of the validity of rational interpretations. No wonder he has such difficulties, for *this* time Poe seems to have weighted the story on the side of the genuinely supernatural.[11] For instance, as in one of Hawthorne's New England Gothic tales, here Poe uses the folkloristic belief about black cats being disguised witches. During the New England witchcraft trials of 1692, one of the accused, Martha Carrier, was charged with appearing before her daughter in the shape of a black cat. Martha was hanged on 19 August, along with the alleged "wizards" John Willard, George Burroughs, George Jacobs, Sr, and John Proctor. Hawthorne refers to Martha in "Young Goodman Brown" and "Main Street." That Poe would use the idea of black cats as witches shows that, like Hawthorne, he could use folklore as a literary tool. But note the *litotes* – denying the contrary; like *meiosis*, another form of understatement – that the narrator employs: "In speaking of [the cat's] intelligence, my wife, who at heart was *not a little* tinctured with superstition, made frequent allusion to the ancient popular notion, which regarded all black cats as witches in disguise [my italics]." He then tries to downplay the idea, and we may wonder whether he is being honest: "Not that she was ever *serious* upon this point – and I mention the matter at all for no better reason than that it happens, just now, to be remembered" (144). He pretends that the belief in the demonic nature of black cats is a mere afterthought.

That it is much more, however, is suggested by the narrator's language and imagery, which reveal that *he* is the superstitious party, whether his wife really is or not (again, Shelden: "he is more fearful of superstition than he will concede" [78]). What makes this tale so much like those of Hawthorne, in addition to the use of folklore, is the language of religion. Like Hawthorne's Puritans, this religionist also has a Manichean view of the world. Stephen Peithman would agree: "the narrator sees everything in terms of black or white. There is no middle ground" (143). The narrator expresses his Manichean view and emphasizes the dark side of his soul with *epanalepsis* – beginning and ending a clause with the same words: "the feeble remnant of the good within me succumbed. Evil thoughts became my sole intimates – the darkest and most evil of thoughts" (151). A nice bit of reinforcement: the syntactical arrangement of the sentence suggests that evil became the very *alpha* and *omega* of the narrator's world view – that he would always begin and come around again inevitably to malevolence. Contributing to his religious view of the world is the *notional set* pertaining to ideas of the supernatural – a set of words and corresponding images that has been almost completely ignored by other critics, especially those attempting naturalistic explanations of the text. As the notional set of time reveals the obsession of the protagonist in "The Tell-Tale Heart" (see chapter 1), so the notional set of the supernatural tells us about the obsessions, the view of the world, held by the protagonist in "The Black Cat": (again, see chapter 1). This narrator's religious view of life contributes to his superstitious dread of divine portents and punishment. Had he been an agnostic or atheist, he would not have attached any supernatural significance to the events and images he witnessed, but his fervent belief in the world of the supernatural is his source of terror and the target of his self-directed rhetorical efforts.[12]

Other literary aspects of "The Black Cat" lean heavily towards a supernatural interpretation and would seem, therefore, to buttress the narrator's worst fears. Interestingly, the first cat's name is *Pluto*, the name of the god of Hades in Roman mythology. Here is a connection with witches, who, as servants of the Devil, are also associated with the underworld. The imagery in the story also suggests the underworld, Hell, notably the fire imagery – the second cat has a "red extended mouth and solitary eye of fire" (155) – and the "fireplace." Another allusion, a rather abstruse one, suggests that the narrator's black cat may indeed be demonic in nature. He confesses that, during each night, "I started, hourly, from dreams of unutterable fear, to find the hot breath of *the thing* upon my face, and its vast weight – an incarnate Night-Mare that I had no power to shake off – incumbent eternally upon *my heart!*" (151). As only Anderson has noticed, but almost incidentally (43), Poe is alluding to the famous Gothic painting *The Nightmare*, by John Henry Fuseli. That Poe was familiar with Fuseli's work is proved by a reference in "The Fall of the House of Usher" where the narrator writes of the paintings of Roderick Usher: "For me ... there arose out of the pure abstractions which the hypochondriac contrived to throw upon his canvas, an intensity of intolerable awe, no shadow of which felt I ever yet in the contemplation of the certainly glowing yet too concrete reveries of Fuseli" (3: 283). In the second version of Fuseli's painting (1790–91), a creature with cat-like ears sits heavily upon the chest of a sleeping woman who, judging from her unnatural, contorted, position, seems to be having a bad dream. Nicolas Powell, the author of an entire book on this work, calls the creature on the woman's chest a "nightmare" (34) and says that it is understood to be an "evil spirit" (43), a *demon*. Thus, Poe's esoteric allusion to the cat-like demon in *The Nightmare* suggests that the narrator's black cat, *his* "Night-Mare," may be demonic, too.[13]

In addition to the imagery and the allusions to the underworld adding a sense of the supernatural, the very structure of the tale – the parallelism of the terrible events – reinforces the supernatural interpretation he entertains so reluctantly (see also Gargano's "Perverseness Reconsidered," 176–7). First, consider the appearance of the second black cat, so much like the first (each has only one eye): it would appear that Pluto has been reincarnated. A theme that Poe also deals with in "Ligeia" and "Metzengerstein" is metempsychosis, the passage of a soul from one body to another. Furthermore, as other scholars have observed, the appearances of each cat split the tale into two halves – and note that the

roles of the narrator and the cat are *reversed* in the second half. In the
first half, the narrator is fond of the black cat ("Pluto ... was my favorite
pet and playmate" [144]); in the second half, the black cat is fond of the
narrator ("It followed my footsteps with a pertinacity which it would be
difficult to make the reader comprehend" [150]). In the first, after the
narrator has butchered Pluto by cutting out one of its eyes, the cat comes
to be terrified of the narrator ("He ... fled in extreme terror at my approach" [146]); in the second, the narrator becomes terrified of the cat
("I came to look upon it with unutterable loathing, and to flee silently
from its odious presence, as from the breath of a pestilence" [150]). In
the first, the narrator causes the black cat to be hanged ("I slipped a
noose about its neck and hung it to the limb of a tree" [146]); by the end
of the second, we know that the black cat has caused the narrator to be
condemned to be hanged ("the hideous beast ... whose informing voice
had consigned me to the hangman" [155]). In short, for the most part,
what the narrator does to the first black cat (Pluto), the second black cat
causes to be done to the narrator, who seems to realize that he may be
the victim of Old Testament justice. We have already seen evidence of
his intense religiosity in the notional set that characterizes his vocabulary, and surely *this* fideist would be aware of the Book of Exodus (21:
23–5): "And if any mischief follow, then thou shalt give life for life,/ Eye
for eye, tooth for tooth, hand for hand, foot for foot,/ Burning for burning, wound for wound, stripe for stripe" – and terror for terror, hanging
for hanging. The bipartite structure of the tale mirrors what we often
call the "eye-for-an-eye" structure of the ancient Hebrew justice system,
and surely Poe has the narrator cut out one of Pluto's *eyes* (as opposed to
some other form of mutilation) to remind the attentive reader of the
"eye-for-an-eye" code in the Old Testament: the punishment must be
equal to the crime, must mirror the crime. The narrator, then, has reason
to fear the revenge of a reincarnated witch-cat and recognizes the irony
of a *demonic* creature working out for him the Jehovic code of justice: "a
brute beast to work out for *me* ... so much of insufferable wo!" (151).

Considering the imagery, the allusions, and the very structure of the
tale, then, we see that the narrator indeed would seem to have reason to
dread the supernatural, and a main concern in the story is how he copes
with the apparent manifestations of those forces. A primary feature of

his mind is a struggle between rationality and superstitious fear – what I call the "Gothic psychomachy" (a terror-inspired war within the psyche). At the beginning of the tale, through his use of *meiosis* and *litotes*, we see the narrator's rhetorical attempts to downplay but comprehend the events that "have terrified – have tortured – have destroyed me" (143). He says, "Hereafter, perhaps, some intellect may be found which will reduce my phantasm to the common-place – some intellect more calm, more logical, and far less excitable than my own, which will perceive, in the circumstances I detail with awe, nothing more than an ordinary succession of very natural causes and effects." The type of person he longs for is, like Poe's detective Dupin, the very model of rationality. Such a person could explain apparently supernatural manifestations rationally. This is exactly what Dupin does in "The Murders in the Rue Morgue": he "imposes upon a world of irrational horror the semblance of order, proves over and over that the most grotesque nightmare … can be understood, given acumen and a talent for analysis" (Fiedler, 497).

The narrator's inner-directed rhetoric, his attempt to persuade himself that he has witnessed only natural events, is also manifested when he refers to the fiery destruction of his house after the brutal hanging of Pluto: "I am above the weakness of seeking to establish a sequence of cause and effect, between the disaster and the atrocity" (147). That is, attempting to employ a Dupinesque rationality, he does not want to believe that there is any supernatural connection between the crime and the destroyed house, as if an undead witch-cat were seeking to punish him. The narrator is trying to avoid superstition. Then he attempts rather *desperately* to account for the mysterious apparition of the gigantic cat on the remaining wall of his destroyed house:

When I first beheld this apparition – for I could scarcely regard it as less – my wonder and my terror were extreme. But at length reflection came to my aid. The cat, I remembered, had been hung in a garden adjacent to the house. Upon the alarm of fire, this garden had been immediately filled by the crowd – by some one of whom the animal must have been cut from the tree and thrown, through an open window, into my chamber. This had probably been done with the view of arousing me from sleep. (148)

Yet, notice the hedging terms ("must have," "probably"), his use of which suggests the weakness of his reckless attempt to explain the phenomenon rationally, naturalistically. He violates Occam's Razor, the principle that assumptions used to explain something must not be multiplied beyond necessity: we should always accept the simplest explanation for a phenomenon. *He* might argue that he is actually trying to uphold Occam's Razor; however, the terms "must have" and "probably" both show the assumptions, the guesses, he is willing to resort to in his search for a rational theory. But his is hardly rational, simple, or sensible. It is downright silly: Aubrey Maurice Weaver calls it an "outlandish," extravagant construct (320); Matheson labels it "far-fetched and unconvincing" (78) and Amper a spurious explanation "so preposterous that it ranks among American literature's all-time whoppers" (480). McElroy also applies the term "preposterous" (108) to this "cock-and-bull explanation" (106) – "the funniest thing in 'The Black Cat'" (110): "The reader should be falling off his seat with laughter at this point" (111). Still, to our frantic narrator, even a ludicrous interpretation of the events is preferable to the alternative explanation – that the events signify exactly what he inwardly fears: supernatural portents. He continues to try to avoid superstition and the hint of the supernatural when he speaks of the gallows-shaped splash of white fur on the second black cat: he says his "Reason struggled to reject it as fanciful" (151). The story is something like an allegory, with Reason (like a good angel) battling Superstition (a bad angel) for control of the narrator's mind. (For more on *allegoria* in Poe, see chapter 3.)

In the end, however, just as the frantic forensic oratory of the "Tell-Tale Heart" narrator fails to convince his auditors (and readers), so the rhetoric of the tortured protagonist in "The Black Cat" apparently fails to convince *him* that he is not the victim of supernatural malice. In the final paragraph he says that the second cat's *craft* had seduced him into murdering his wife (155). He can only mean "craft" in the sense of witchcraft. His language again gives him away (recall the notional set): regardless of his wife's alleged superstitiousness, it is *he* who has (reluctantly) believed all along that black cats are indeed disguised witches. Supporting his supernatural interpretation of events is the narrator's treatment of Pluto. After all, what is the American punishment for a witch but *hanging*? Like that amateur historian of the New England Puritans,

Hawthorne, Poe would have known that five men and fourteen women accused of being witches in New England in 1692 died by the gallows: in addition to Martha Carrier and her four doomed companions who died on 19 August, the Puritans hanged Bridget Bishop on 10 June, Sarah Good, Elizabeth How, Susanna Martin, Rebecca Nurse, and Sarah Wilds on 19 July, and, on 22 September, Martha Corey, Mary Easty, Alice Parker, Mary Parker, Ann Pudeator, Wilmot Reed, Margaret Scott, and Samuel Wardwell. The Bible says, "Thou shalt not suffer a witch to live" (Exodus, 22:18), and the intensely religious narrator surely would hold by that book.[14] If this is the real reason why he killed Pluto, then his explanation of perversity is merely a rationalization or an outright lie (thus, I do not quite agree with Richard Frushell's assertion that, because this is a "near-death confession, his sincerity and motives are unimpeachable" [43]).[15] To confess to the *real* motive for hanging the cat would be to betray his reason and his rhetoric by admitting to a Puritanical fear of the supernatural. Better to employ the rhetoric of self-deceit, especially *meiosis* and *litotes*, and downplay the events and their significance. To do otherwise would be – unbearable.

PERORATIO

Despite the glorification of oratory and rhetoric in Poe's time and place, in "The Tell-Tale Heart" and "The Black Cat" we find Poe demonstrating that rhetoric can *fail*. Did Poe therefore *distrust* that ancient art of persuasion? As we know, contempt for and suspicion of rhetoric is a tradition at least as old as Plato, who, in his *Gorgias*, has Socrates liken that art to teaching a cook how to give poison a pleasing taste. This attitude certainly carried into the Renaissance: in Marguerite de Navarre's *Heptameron*, academics are rejected as good story-tellers because "Monseigneur the Dauphin didn't want their art brought in, and he was afraid that rhetorical ornament would in part falsify the truth of the account" (69). In his essay "On the Education of Children," Montaigne writes of the ideal student who "knows no rhetoric, nor how, by way of preface, to *capture the benevolence of the candid reader*; nor has he any wish to do so. In fact, all such fine tricks are easily eclipsed by the light of a simple, artless truth. These refinements serve only to divert the vulgar" (77). Even Machiavelli dissociates himself from the tradition in the second paragraph of

The Prince: "I have not ornamented this book with rhetorical turns of phrase, or stuffed it with pretentious and magnificent words, or made use of allurements and embellishments that are irrelevant to my purpose, as many authors do" (5). And Shakespeare, most obviously, shows through the many *linguistic Machiavellians* in his plays the necessity of qualifying Quintilian's definition of the rhetor as "a good man skilled at speaking" (*Institutes of Oratory*). Poe, like Milton and Melville also, recognizes that *bad* men could speak well.

But I do not believe that Poe – the contemporary of Thomas Jefferson, Chief-Justice Marshall, John Randoph, Daniel Webster – held the rhetorical tradition in contempt. Like the Renaissance humanists cited above who claimed to despise rhetoric, he was trained in it and put it to good use. Yet, like them, he was wise enough to recognize how powerful a tool it could be and to hold it in suspicion. As well, he was fascinated by the ironic spectacle of the actions of unreason being justified through the linguistic tradition of reason – the *jarring collocation* of insanity employing the Aristotelian appeal to *logos*. Poe may indeed have been trained in the classical tradition – the brilliant oratory, rhetoric, and logic of the wisest ancient Greeks and Romans – but he was also a student of the new science of abnormal psychology. Poe, the devotee of sweetness and light, gives in to the impulses of Dark Romanticism. A Poe narrator may strive to convince us that his mind is a Greek temple with its glorious friezes, fluted Doric columns, solid stylobates – but *we* know what kind of ruin it is. The classical man will give way: Cicero will succumb to the barbarian hordes of his psyche, Quintilian to the inner demons, Aristotle to the beast within.

Allegoria, Chronographia, and Clock Architecture in "The Masque of the Red Death"

Several scholars have drawn attention to the imagery of time, the fore-grounded *chronographia,* in Poe's tales: clocks, watches, pendulums, hour and minute hands, ticking sounds, and the frequency of that most Gothic of hours, midnight. For instance, in "The Theme of Time in 'The Tell-Tale Heart,'" Gargano, noting the "images and sounds that evoke the rhythm of time" in the story, concludes that the mad narrator has become obsessed with the passing of the hours and that "His quarrel, then, is not with a ravaged individual but with Time, which on one level is symbolized by the omnipresent 'watches' and on another by the 'tell-tale' heart" (379). Edward William Pitcher writes of "Horological and Chronological" time in "The Masque of the Red Death." Dennis W. Eddings has written a monograph, *Poe's Tell-Tale Clocks,* while in "Edgar Poe or The Theme of the Clock" Jean-Paul Weber also demonstrates "the omnipresence of clocks in Poe's writings" (79), including "The Fall of the House of Usher" ("the House of Usher clearly represents the clock"), "The Devil in the Belfry," "The Raven," "The Scythe of Time," "A Descent into the Maelström," "MS. Found in a Bottle," "The Tell-Tale Heart," "The Pit and the Pendulum," "The Black Cat," "The Cask of Amontillado," "Silence – A Fable," "Shadow – A Parable," "The Un-paralleled Adventure of One Hans Pfaall," "Hop-Frog," "The Gold Bug," and "The Business Man" (previously entitled "Peter Pendulum"). Weber finishes the essay by referring to Poe as "the maniac of time" (97).

Here I am concerned specifically with Weber's observations about "The Masque of the Red Death." I would like to build on and extend some of Weber's insights and thus strengthen his interpretation about the time and clock imagery and the allegorical nature of that tale. For it is indeed an extended instance of what rhetoricians call *allegoria*, as other scholars (such as Buranelli, May, Peithman, Watson, Wilbur, Zapf) have argued, against those (such as Ruddick and Symons) who caution against seeing "The Masque of the Red Death" this way. The allegorists, however, are not subtle enough in their interpretations of the tale, insisting as they each do on one allegorical meaning (though their interpretations differ) and on one type of allegory. M.H. Abrams reminds us (4–7) that in literature we can find more than one type of allegory: for instance, one of ideas, in which literal characters represent abstractions "such as virtues, vices, states of mind, modes of life, and types of character," and one of "things," in which one literal thing represents itself as well as another literal thing. In "The Masque of the Red Death" Poe employs both types – but the work is also a *parable*, yet another type of allegory, one that illustrates a moral lesson of universal applicability. The manifold layers of suggestive meaning in this complex work almost make the "fourfold method of exegesis" desirable when interpreting it. Thus, while building on Weber's insights (which have largely been ignored), this chapter improves on his exegesis and constitutes a new way of reading "The Masque of the Red Death" that clears up some critical confusion and illuminates Poe's technique as an allegorist.

The many references to time passing in "The Masque of the Red Death" – "after the lapse of sixty minutes, (which embrace three thousand and six hundred seconds of the Time that flies,) there came yet another chiming of the clock" (4: 253) – tell us that time must indeed figure significantly in the tale, and supporting this theme and one of the allegorical readings is the architecture of Prospero's edifice. Richard Wilbur senses that "The Masque" contains "an obvious example of architectural allegory" (118) but *Weber* was the first to realize that the abbey is shaped like "a clock or a dial plate" (85). However, Weber justifies this conclusion weakly by reference to external evidence (the clock-shaped borough in "The Devil in the Belfry") rather than to the preferable internal evidence of the tale itself – and so does not go further in his interpretation to explain the significance of the seven rooms of the abbey's suite. Here is part of the description of the rooms:

The apartments were so irregularly disposed that the vision embraced but little more than one at a time. There was a sharp turn at every twenty or thirty yards, and at each turn a novel effect. To the right and left, in the middle of each wall, a tall and narrow Gothic window looked out upon a closed corridor which pursued the windings of the suite. (251)

Some readers have assumed that the words "irregularly disposed" describe a suite of rooms that twists and turns haphazardly with no real discernible pattern; Jeffrey Meyers, for instance, writes of the "zigzag construction of the rooms" (134). Certainly the suite does not "form a long and straight vista," to use Poe's own words, but the architecture does have a recognizable pattern. Eddings guesses that "the progression of the colored rooms is circular rather than in a straight line" (12) – but he is only partly correct. Rather, the seven rooms taken together form a *half circle*, one half of a clock's face, with each room representing one of the seven hours between 6 p.m. and twelve inclusive (see Fig. 1). As for the dimensions, the turn "at every twenty or thirty yards" can be taken to mean that the walls of each room – certainly the middle five – are thirty yards in length while the walls of the two endmost rooms are twenty. Poe's minor disquisitions on mathematical reasoning in the tales of ratiocination; the complex estimates of astronomical distances in *Eureka*; the attention to precise measurement on the part of Legrand in "The Gold-Bug": these show that he was an amateur mathematician, so he likely would have been very precise about the mathematics of the layout in "The Masque of the Red Death." That is, I doubt that he chose the figures of thirty and twenty yards randomly. Note, also, that the suite is said to *wind*. In the diagram the rooms have easily been drawn to wind around the centre of the clock-abbey while maintaining dimensions of thirty or twenty yards (three units or two). Also, the vision of someone standing well within any given room would indeed embrace "but little more than one at a time," especially if the folding doors do not slide back entirely to the walls on either side.

Figure 1
Prospero's Clock-Abbey

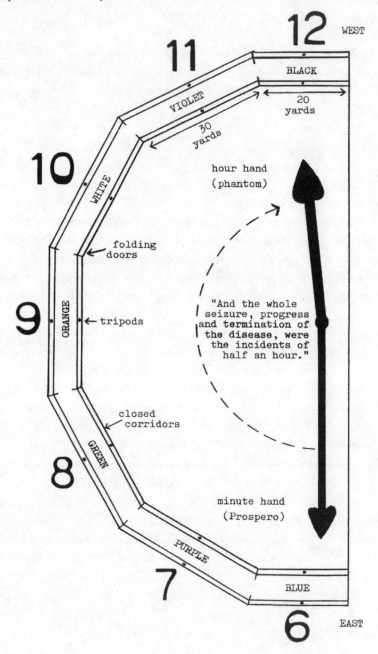

Some readers, going back to Walter Blair, maintain that these seven rooms stand for the "seven ages of man" (Roppolo, Ketterer, Vanderbilt).[1] Mabbott suggests "the seven days of the week, the seven deadly sins, and even seven parts of a day" (677), but makes no attempt to justify these interpretations with reference to the text. Pitcher (73) mentions the "seven decades of life's conventional span," probably alluding to the Bible: "The days of our years are threescore and ten" (Psalms, 90: 10). Ruddick notes (271) Angus Fletcher's observation that seven is also the traditional number of planets or the "windows" (orifices) of the head, but the text has nothing that substantiates these ideas. Patrick Cheney relates seven to its significance in the Bible and to Catholic liturgy (37), and Peithman summarizes the importance of seven in Christian thought and also relates it to Shakespeare's *As You Like It* (116 n12). We need not suggest any such symbolism, however, because seven is the inevitable number of rooms we must have if the abbey is shaped like half a clock. Still, my interpretation does not necessarily preclude those others, and I would be inclined to see the explanations relating to *time* as more relevant to my own exegesis: not only does the very structure of Prospero's Gothic edifice emphasize the theme of time's passage in terms of minutes and hours, but some readers may also see the seven rooms as symbolizing weekdays and decades.

Poe, however, seems more concerned with the passing of the final minutes and hours of Prospero and his guests, for a clock measures *these* temporal units, not weekdays or decades. Furthering the allegorical importance of the abbey's shape are Prospero and the phantom of the Red Death, the two central figures that move on the face of the abbey-clock. Weber suggests that they represent two hands of that clock:

the phantom advances "with a slow and solemn movement," moves with "deliberate and stately step," with "solemn and *measured*" step, makes his way *"uninterruptedly,"* as if impelled by some kind of inner necessity: one must agree that this uninterrupted, measured, solemn, and slow gait accords strikingly with the slow, regular tempo of the hour hand.

In this case Prospero must represent the *minute hand,* and a conjunction must take place between the two ... That Prospero is something of a blade, like a minute hand, the bare blade which he carries suggests at once. That he acts the part of the minute hand is apparent from the circuit he travels and from his

speed: he moves successively through the same chambers which the Masque of
the Red Death had traversed, but Prospero moves precipitously, not slowly. At
the end of the tale "the tall figure" stands "erect and motionless, within the
shadow of the ebony clock": the hour hand (the phantom) is indeed standing
erect ... at about twelve o'clock. As for Prospero, he falls "prostrate in death" a
few feet from the specter. (86)[2]

We must distinguish between literal and allegorical time, here, though.
When the phantom is first seen, the ebony clock is already striking the
midnight hour, literally, but at this point Poe's allegorical time becomes
important as Prospero moves quickly from the blue room to the black to
catch the slowly moving phantom. Yet, Prospero (the minute hand) does
not begin his pursuit until the phantom (the hour hand) is almost at midnight: indeed, the figure makes it all the way "to the violet [room], ere a
decided movement had been made to arrest him" (257). He and the
phantom begin to "take on" their respective hour- and minute-hand sig-
nifications just as the prince begins his pursuit from the blue room. On
the level of *literal* time, Prospero does not take a full half-hour to go from
the easternmost to the westernmost room, but he does on the level of *allegorical* time. At the end of this half-hour he falls dead. Thirty minutes is
exactly how long it takes for someone who has caught the Red Death to
die: "And the whole seizure, progress and termination of the disease, were
the incidents of half an hour" (250). The Prince and his guests catch the
disease at about 11:30 p.m. – literally and figuratively – and die at midnight after he enters the midnight room. The tale's apocalyptic climax
comes as the literal and allegorical time spans converge. Thus we solve the
confusion that has plagued Martin Roth, Burton R. Pollin, Patricia H.
Wheat, and Hubert Zapf. Zapf states, "The manner of the prince's death
– he dies on the instant ... is significantly not identical with the character
and the progress of the disease as it is described at the beginning of the
text" (217). On the contrary, the red-browed Prince has been dying for
half an hour; the disease finally kills him at the climactic moment when
he catches up to the allegorical representative of the plague.[3]

   On another stratum of meaning and action, however, Prospero can be
seen to stand for humanity in general: as the head and representative of
the "thousand hale and light-hearted friends from among the knights
and dames of his court" (250), he is an Everyman figure; and the

phantom represents exactly what its name implies – the Red Death – which disease contaminates all seven rooms, from blue to black. On this level the figure functions as part of the allegory of ideas, abstractions, representing as it does the abstraction (or personification) of the plague. One cannot see a disease, only its physical manifestations. That the figure of the Red Death *is* a mere abstraction is suggested by the emptiness, the lack of a "tangible form," that the revellers find when they rip off its corpse-like mask. As Wheat points out, "It is obviously fruitless to try to seize, unmask, and hang a personification of death" (55).

The revellers do not realize that the plague has entered, but one or two lines in the tale suggest that they, and Prospero, have caught the disease: "these other apartments were densely crowded, and in them beat feverishly the heart of life" (255). We can seize upon the word *feverishly* to suggest one manifestation of disease. And when he becomes infuriated by the figure of the Red Death, Prospero's "brow reddened with rage" (256). Never mind about his "rage" – a blood-red face is one of the symptoms of the plague: earlier we are told about the "scarlet stains upon the body and especially upon the face of the victim" (250). The Red Death has this appearance: "His vesture was dabbled in blood … and his broad brow, with all the features of the face, was besprinkled with the scarlet horror" (256).

So, the masquerade, Prospero's dance of life, has become a *danse macabre,* a medieval dance of death, and the parable ends in biblical tones accentuated by what William Mentzel Forrest (*Biblical Allusions in Poe,* 86) calls the "genitive of possession" (the frequently appearing preposition *of*) and the repetition of the conjunction *And* (the rhetorical scheme *polysyndeton*):

And now was acknowledged the presence of the Red Death. He had come like a thief in the night. And one by one dropped the revellers in the blood-bedewed halls of their revel, and died each in the despairing posture of his fall. And the life of the ebony clock went out with that of the last of the gay. And the flames of the tripods expired. And Darkness and Decay and the Red Death held illimitable dominion over all. (258)

Cheney also notes the *polysyndeton* without using the label (34); and, following in the wake of Forrest and Killis Campbell ("Poe's Knowledge of the Bible"), he revealingly explores Poe's use of biblical phrases, images, and allusions. We might note in this context that the image of the "thief in the night" can be found several times in the Bible: "the day of the Lord so cometh as a thief in the night" (1 Thess., 5: 2; see also 2 Peter, 3: 10, Job, 24: 14, and Matthew, 24: 43). We might guess that some weighty meaning is suggested by the biblical diction, imagery, and tone; although, as Ruddick points out, the end of the tale suggests no orthodox Christian lesson or eschatology – Darkness, Decay, and the Red Death constitute "a highly unorthodox trinity of deities presiding over an equally unorthodox apocalypse" (273). Nevertheless, the rhythms and images do suggest a parable (about the tragic human condition) that has the weight of biblical pronouncement.

That pronouncement, the "moral" of the story, is indeed what most scholars have said it is. Prince Prospero and a thousand guests lock themselves into one of his castellated abbeys to keep safe from the contagion outside the walls. Irresponsible, they are isolated in a kind of stationary ark, trying to enjoy a hedonistic forgetfulness of death, a *carpe diem* philosophy. The variety of their masks and professions – "There were buffoons, there were improvisatori, there were ballet-dancers, there were musicians" (251) – is so great that all manner of humans is suggested, from the beautiful to the grotesque; the revellers thus represent a microcosm of the human race (what Melville liked to call an "Anacharsis Clootz deputation"). But the black clock within the black room serves the symbolic purpose of reminding ephemeral humanity that *tempus fugit* – "time flies"; the ebony clock keeps chiming the passing hours as the revellers move closer and closer to the moment of their own deaths. Frail humanity can never escape the inevitable ravages of time – *here* is the "moral," the truth of universal applicability. Supporting this theme is the allegorical architecture of the abbey itself, the gigantic type of the smaller ebony clock. Contrary to Ketterer's insistence that the "reality of time is hidden by the arrangement of the rooms" (201), the arrangement of the chambers *reinforces* the awful reality of time as it leads inexorably to disease, death, darkness, and dissolution.

It is well known that Poe claimed to disapprove of *allegoria*. In an often-quoted review of Hawthorne's *Twice-Told Tales*, he states, "In defence of allegory, (however, or for whatever object, employed,) there is scarcely one respectable word to be said" (13: 148). The review in which this statement appears was first published in *Graham's Magazine* in May 1842, the same edition in which "The Masque of the Red Death" was first published. It is almost as if, while preparing the review for publication, Poe, thinking of Hawthorne's allegories, decided to submit one for publication himself – perhaps to show the world how allegory can be done well.[4] That Poe did not disdain to write this kind of literature is shown by scholars who insist that several of his other tales can also be read this way. Darrel Abel suggests that "The Fall of the House of Usher" "is a consummate psychological allegory" (185). Edward H. Davidson holds that "The Imp of the Perverse" is "more an allegory than a tale" (xvi) and that "'Hop-Frog' is almost straight allegory" (xx); he also refers to *Pym* as a "symbolic allegory" (xxiii) and, as the interpretations of several other prominent Poe scholars (Fiedler, Levin, Kaplan, Ketterer, Harold Beaver) demonstrate, the second half of the novel constitutes a kind of geographical allegory. Clark Griffith maintains that "Ligeia" is "an allegory of terror almost perfectly co-ordinated with the subtlest of allegorized jests" (quoted by Robert Regan, who agrees with this reading – "Hawthorne's 'Plagiary,'" 295). David Galloway reminds us of the "allegorical mannerisms" of "The Devil in the Belfry" (18). Walter Stepp sees the emblem in "The Cask of Amontillado" as having an allegorical significance (56) and is inclined to see Fortunato as representing "guileless, trusting innocence" (60). Victor Vitanza calls the heroes of several Poe tales "allegorical figures of impulse and reason: they act out a dramatic dialogue of 'body' and 'soul'" (147). "William Wilson" is universally recognized as *allegoria*. Let us remember, for instance, the case made in Ottavio Cassale's essay "The Dematerialization of William Wilson: Poe's Use of Cumulative Allegory"; and consider Liliane Weissberg's "In Search of Truth and Beauty: Allegory in 'Berenice' and 'The Domain of Arnheim'." The most recent study, and a book-length one, is Jeffrey DeShell's *The Peculiarity of Literature: An Allegorical Approach to Poe's Fiction*. Richard Wilbur summarizes more generally: "as for Edgar Allan Poe ... we can make no sense about him until we consider his work – and in particular his prose fiction – as deliberate and often brilliant allegory" (98–9); "All of Poe's major stories are allegorical presentations" of his characteristic themes (102). Lastly, Regan cites as an example of Poe's duplicity his "repeated denunciations of allegory when he was a confirmed and confessed allegorist" ("Hawthorne's 'Plagiary,'" 292).[5]

If we do not want to entertain the notion that Poe was deceitful, we still must somehow reconcile the scoffer at allegories and the author of them. Perhaps Poe was aware that in writing works such as "The Masque of the Red Death" he was apparently contradicting one aspect of his own theory of composition. He might have said with the Walt Whitman of "Song of Myself," "Do I contradict myself?/ Very well then I contradict myself,/ (I am large, I contain multitudes)"; or agreed for once with that other Romanticist, Ralph Waldo Emerson: "A foolish consistency is the hobgoblin of little minds" ("Self-Reliance"). I would propose, however, that the contradiction is not as real as it seems; and indeed, other scholars have remembered that in his review of *Twice-Told Tales* Poe says that allegory is acceptable if the literal and the suggested meanings are not connected too clearly: "Where the suggested meaning runs through the obvious one in a very profound under-current so as never to interfere with the upper one without our own volition, so as never to show itself unless called to the surface, there only, for the proper uses of fictitious narrative, is it [allegory] available at all" (13: 148). Then, after making some disparaging comments about the type of shallow (and didactic) allegory he despises, *Pilgrim's Progress*, Poe offers Baron de la Motte Fouqué's *Undine: A Miniature Romance* as a work in which the allegory is subdued because the hidden meanings are seen only "by suggestive glimpses." In other words, Poe the symbolist approves of allegory only when it approaches symbolism in offering suggested meanings rather than explicit equations.

As for "The Masque of the Red Death," then, the tale on the layer of the allegory of abstractions (the phantom = plague; Prospero = Everyman) functions less successfully according to Poe's definition of allegory "properly handled" because these meanings are relatively accessible to the reader. On this level "The Masque" is more like *Pilgrim's Progress* than Poe might want to admit. On the other hand, the work on the level of the allegory of things (the phantom suggests an hour hand, Prospero a minute hand, the abbey half a clock face) functions more successfully because these meanings are less accessible. The meaning of the "time motif" that Poe hints at runs "through the obvious one in a very profound under-current" indeed.

When we add the tale's parable to the mix, we see that "The Masque" seems sufficiently complex to warrant a "fourfold method of exegesis."

Regan, in his discussion of *allegoria*, recognizes the possibility of many layers of meaning in a typical Poe tale: "approaching the tales in the spirit of the 'fourfold method' will alert us to the special way in which they operate. We shall not grasp Poe's full accomplishment in fiction until we hear each of the several voices of a tale as at once discrete and part of a harmonious totality" (Introduction, 11–12). St Thomas Aquinas and others proposed that in interpreting the Bible we distinguish between (1) the literal meaning (what happened), (2) the allegorical meaning (New Testament truth), (3) the tropological meaning (the moral truth), and (4) the anagogic meaning (spiritual/eschatalogical truth). In "The Masque of the Red Death" Poe does give us a literal series of events (Aquinas' first meaning) and something like a tropological meaning – the parable, the "moral" of the story (the third). The tale on the level of the allegory of ideas comes closest to representing Aquinas' second meaning. As for an anagogic significance, it appears either to be missing altogether or profoundly subversive: the closing words offer no hopeful Christian eschatology.

Cheney is very good on this point and elaborates considerably: "Where the mythic pattern" of the Bible "depicts man's victory over sin, death, and time, Poe's mythic pattern depicts the triumph of these agents of destruction over man" (32); "In Poe's mythology, the Red Death replaces Christ as the reigning force in the universe. Hence, the Red Death is said to have 'dominion over all' – a reversal of Paul's statement in Romans 6: 9, in which 'death hath no more dominion' because of Christ's resurrection ... In Poe, the blood and dew of the Red Death replace the blood of Christ and the dew of heaven" (34); "In presenting an image of man helpless against the apparition of death, Poe suggests the inefficacy of Christ's triumph over death" (36). All in all, this subversive tale constitutes Poe's "grim reversal of the Christian drama," a production perhaps more characteristic of the skeptical Melville.

It also anticipates twentieth-century atheistic existentialism as well as the existential poetry of someone closer to Poe's own day who enjoyed reading him: Emily Dickinson. Both Poe and Dickinson present grim visions of the human condition while otherwise surrounded by the optimism of their Transcendental contemporaries and the sentimental Christianity of everyone else (but Melville). Neither Christians nor Transcendentalists would be receptive to the perverse eschatology of "The Masque of the Red Death," however, so Poe camouflages his meaning in layers of allegory: like Dickinson, he would "Tell all the Truth but tell it slant – / Success in Circuit lies" (#427). Poe was deeply familiar with the Bible, as were Dickinson and Melville (who "quarreled with God"), but at some profound level Poe, like them, seems to have intuited the possibility of a godless universe where the eschatological promises of the Christian Bible are empty, meaningless. Like the prisoner in "The Pit and the Pendulum" (another allegory), we grope blindly in the dark, attempting in vain to use our reason and senses to determine the nature of our environment. But, like his, our epistemology is flawed and, like him, we are tormented physically, emotionally, and psychologically, waiting for the inevitable descent of the destroying pendulum. Indeed (and this is also the perception of literary naturalism), we are left with nothing but our biological and mental selves at the mercy of indifferent and overwhelming forces over which we have no control, eternally victims of Time. *This* existential depiction of humanity's condition in "The Masque of the Red Death" is the most terrifying thing in all of Poe's fiction, beside which his Gothic accounts of vampires, black cats, witches, metempsychosis, and reanimated mummies are mere "bugaboo tales."

CHAPTER FOUR

Poe's Linguistic Comedy

Whatever tends to the amusement of man tends to his benefit.

Review of *Stanley Thorn*, 11: 12

The phrase "Poe's comedy" may seem to many a contradiction in terms, or a jarring collocation. J. Marshall Trieber offers a quip about "the old charge that a study of Poe's humor might consist of twenty blank pages" (32). Certainly those readers who know Poe only by his most famous tales and consider him primarily a gothicist are surprised to learn that he wrote comedic tales as well. We can imagine their surprise when they pull from their library shelves *Comic Tales of Edgar Allan Poe*, edited by Angus Wolfe Murray, or *The Other Poe: Comedies and Satires*, edited by David Galloway.[1] Poe specialists, on the other hand, are fully aware of the comic strain in his prose, although they differ as to the extent to which they are amused.[2] Jack Kaufhold and Donald Weeks are perhaps most sympathetic to Poe's attempts to induce laughter. Perhaps with a little *hyperbole*, the former considers some of Poe's stories "wildly funny" (143); the latter comments briefly on each of Poe's comedic tales, often comparing the humour in them to that of twentieth-century comic writers and performers. "Poe easily could have become a writer for humorous solo comedians," Weeks asserts (87).[3] Stauffer also believes "that Poe is funny, and that he is funnier than he is often given credit for" (*Merry Mood*, 5). Paul Lewis (532), on the other hand, quotes H.P. Lovecraft's complaints about Poe's "blundering ventures in stilted and labored pseudo-humor." Neither is Tom Quirk amused, as the title of his essay suggests: "What if Poe's Humorous Tales Were Funny?" In the context

of "Berenice" and the burlesque of "X-ing a Paragrab," Quirk argues
that Poe's humour "is not funny because it is fundamentally anti-
social ... he is laughing up his sleeve, immunized against the social contagion of general good humor and fellow feeling" (41). Trieber seems to
say something similar, arguing that to understand Poe's comedy we have
to consider not what we find funny or what his contemporaries found
funny but what *he* found funny. Poe's humour is very personal, Trieber
believes: it is the humour of the "grin" that "springs from a feeling of
pleasure in triumphing over an adversary" (33). Some of his characters
experience this feeling (diddlers, Montresor, Dupin), and he himself felt
it in his hoaxes – a "delight in overcoming others" (34). Robert Kierly
makes an astonishingly similar claim: "Poe's idea of a good 'joke' was often that of a trick by which he could 'get back' at someone" (37). Perhaps
this is the sort of explanation David Tomlinson has in mind in saying
that Poe's jocularity "is more laughing at people than leading them to
laugh along with him" ("Poe's Humor in Summary," 1). Hennig Cohen
agrees, comparing Poe with Melville: "They played with their readers,
toying with them and pushing them about, sometimes not so gently,
often making them the butt of their jokes" (86).

   That point of view would seem to apply to those Poe tales in which
humour is primary, particularly the satires, but scholars have also discovered that within another group of tales, specifically the Gothic ones, humour also exists but is secondary or covert (see especially the essays in
The Naiad Voice: Essays on Poe's Satiric Hoaxing). I find some of their arguments a bit forced – Procrustean. For instance, Lewis, in an otherwise
important and insightful essay, finds the narrator in "Ligeia" "briefly
amusing" and his "inflated, romance-seeking descriptions" of Ligeia ludicrous. Assuming that our response is the same as his, Lewis suggests
that we need to "[blink] back our laughter" (537). In "Ligeia," I would
propose, Poe the conscientious craftsman is not attempting to be
"funny"; he has selected deliberately the narrator's inflated diction as an
aspect of his style – to reveal character. Focusing on another Gothic tale,
John Clendenning suggests that a certain kind of humour can even be
found in "The Cask of Amontillado." After discussing the many ironies
in the tale and noting that "There is a comic absurdity in irony" (15), he
draws our attention to the claims made about wine by Montresor and
Fortunato:

The misspellings of Médoc and Graves, the inappropriate selection of these wines, the outrageous mishandling of them, and especially the ignorance of a well-known wine such as Amontillado – these details are a vital part of a grotesque level of the story. They expose Montresor and Fortunato as imposters, whose sincerity is generically that of Laurel and Hardy. They are, in fact, essentially and finally comic characters; they belong to the tradition of burlesque humor. (24; see also Bier, 372, and Galloway, 22)

B.F. Fisher considers "Usher" a parody of Gothicism ("Germanism") generally and some of Poe's own tendencies as a fictionist specifically: "Although he composed other tales that mingle tragic with comic substance, nowhere else was he so artistic" ("Playful 'Germanism' in 'The Fall of the House of Usher': The Storyteller's Art," 371). John Harmon McElroy finds something funny in another tale of terror, "The Black Cat." He refers to the narrator's wild explanation for the image of the cat that appears in his bedroom wall (see chapter 2):

He would have us believe that an onlooker in attendance the night his house went up in flames did the following: perceiving the deadly danger to the house's sleeping inhabitants and spotting the carcass of a cat hanging from the limb of a tree in the garden, this Unknown cut that down and dexterously whanged it through an open window to arouse the people of the house to the fire. But wait, dear reader, there is more: this charitable flinger of cats, according to the narrator's account, hurled the carcass in a nice trajectory so that it landed (thud) and lodged between the narrator's bed (the headboard) and the freshly plastered wall against which it stood, *without waking him.* (110)

McElroy considers the narrator's explanation hilarious: "The reader should be falling off his seat with laughter at this point" (111). Perhaps Constance Rourke is considering this mixture of the risible with the horrible when she notes that Poe's "laughter was of a single order: it was inhuman, and mixed with hysteria" – "a gross and often brutal comedy" (148). Bier relates Poe's work to black humour (see also Weeks, 76, 81; and Kierly, 34) and even finds amusement in "The Pit and the Pendulum," "The Tell-Tale Heart," and "The Murders in the Rue Morgue."[4] Bier reflects on the tales of ratiocination: "in these stories, particularly of Dupin, we ought to be on the lookout for comic traces in the ratiocinative logic itself. Many of the associations of ideas, masked as inevitable reason, that characterize Dupin's mental processes are disguised jokes" (372). Stauffer also sees much to laugh about in "The Purloined Letter" and "Thou Art the Man" (*Merry Mood*, 19–20).

We are seeing attempts, then, to label Poe's comedy, to categorize it. Some categories are regional. Rourke relates Poe's humour – "Hans Pfaall," for instance – to the Western tall tale, noting that Poe had a "sense of native comedy" (146); Cohen also suggests that Poe was not "far removed from the tradition of frontier humor" (99). Bier discusses Poe in a chapter on Southwestern humour, referring to the "senseless violence and cavorting evil" in Longstreet, Harris, Hooper, Baldwin, and Thorpe, whose works constitute "probably our first movement of sick humor"; "And when we link these figures legitimately with Poe, the whole group stands as an early indication of the deepest sources of American humor" (62).[5] Stephen L. Mooney considers Poe's "devil farces" – "The Duc de l'Omlette," "Bon-Bon," and "The Devil in the Belfry" – maintaining that in his farcical use of Satan "Poe is in the main stream of American humor, which is noted for presenting the native as an eiron who through superior astuteness in plotting is able to outwit the forces of supernatural evil [recall "The Devil and Daniel Webster"]" ("Comic Intent in Poe's Tales," 432). Cohen also relates some Poe tales to popular culture and folklore (87). Thus, on one hand we have scholars (Rourke, Bier, Cohen, Mooney) connecting Poe to what is *native* about his comedy, suggesting that he is very much part of his *Zeitgeist*; on the other hand, some (Trieber, Quirk, Kierly, Tomlinson) suggest that Poe's humour shows how he is *alienated* from his fellows. Both antithetical claims are true, paradoxically. Poe's famous hoaxes, for instance, partake of the tall-tale tradition in American humour (as does *Pym* to some extent); his satires, on the other hand, with their (sometimes esoteric) in-jokes and topicality – such as "Tales of the Folio Club" – show how he was at once aware of the literary scene of New England, New York, and Britain, and at the same time alienated from it (see also Kierly, 37). Poe's "humor of scorn" (Trieber, 34), whether he is ridiculing his fellow authors or certain other groups, is the derisive laughter of someone who considers himself superior to his fellows and who would expose their foibles. It is a humour of anger: "There are lapses and excesses in all the jokes indicative of an energy contrary to the very premises of conventional humor," says Kierly; "the comic rationality ... is strained and weakened by an anger ... of the artist himself" (37). Poe's is an *estranged* humour – but not always.

I have used the terms *estranged* and *alienated* to describe a certain facet of Poe's comedy, but the most commonly employed terms applied to his attempts to be funny are traditional: *hoax, satire, lampoon, farce, burlesque, spoof, parody, black* (as in *black humour*); Mooney even likes *vaudeville* ("The Comic in Poe's Fiction," 433). These aspects of Poe's humour have been amply documented, so I do not intend to go over well-covered ground.[6] One term that is rarely applied to Poe, *slapstick*, is appropriate in the context of a scene in "Some Words with a Mummy" (almost the only passage in all of Poe that actually made me – I admit it – laugh out loud). Here the scientists are attempting to revive the mummy using an electric charge from a battery:

Re-adjusting the battery, we now applied the fluid to the bisected nerves – when, with a movement of exceeding life-likeness, the Mummy first drew up its right knee so as to bring it nearly in contact with the abdomen, and then, straightening the limb with inconceivable force, bestowed a kick upon Doctor Ponnonner, which had the effect of discharging that gentleman, like an arrow from a catapult, through a window into the street below. (6: 122; see also Weeks, 85)

We also see acrobatic humour, something like vaudevillian clowning, in the otherwise grim "Hop Frog" (the king and his ministers monkeying around disguised as orangutans); consider also the tarred-and-feathered "orangutans" in "The System of Dr. Tarr and Professor Fether." The physical comedy of these tales may also remind us of certain Mark Twain works.

Some scholars, however, look before Poe rather than ahead of him in the chronology of literary comedy. For instance, Galloway suggests that Poe's comedic techniques "are sometimes reminiscent of Swift and Rabelais" (8) – but, we might guess, surely *without* the bawdy and scatological components. Consider Poe's censorious words in the review of *The Quacks of Helicon*:

We are also sure that the gross obscenity, the filth – we can use no gentler name – which disgraces the "Quacks of Helicon," cannot be the result of innate impurity in the mind of the writer. It is but a part of the slavish and indiscriminating imitation of the Swift and Rochester school. It has done the book an irreparable injury, both in a moral and pecuniary view, without effecting anything whatever on the score of sarcasm, vigour, or wit. "Let what is to be said, be said plainly." True; but let nothing vulgar be *ever* said, or conceived. (10: 184)

He strikes a similar note of disapproval when discussing Laughton Osborn's satirical poem "The Vision of Rubeta": "it was … very censurably indecent – *filthy* is, perhaps, the more appropriate word" (*The Literati of New York City,* 15: 47). Certainly, though, there are indeed Swiftian or Rabelaisian aspects to some of Poe's humour, and we know from some of his critical pieces that he was acquainted with both writers. In *The Literati of New York City* he calls the humour of John W. Francis "a compound of Swift, Rabelais, and the clown in the pantomime" (15: 27); in his review of *Hyperion: A Romance* he mentions "the heartier drolleries of Rabelais" (10: 39); in his article on *Wakondah* he refers to "the appetite of a Grandgousier," one of Rabelais' giants (11: 25). I am almost inclined to believe that *Gargantua* and *Pantagruel* were on the list, if ever there was one, of forbidden undergraduate readings, the sort of books that Poe's fellows might have passed around and read behind their professors' backs (and Poe read Rabelais in the original French – see 10: 194). Although he seems to approve of the hearty "drolleries" of Rabelais, it is hard to imagine the genteel and uptight Poe actually approving, being amused by, the raw sexuality of many passages in the French satirist. Thus, one device we might *not* expect to find in Poe's comedy (it appears occasionally in Melville and Mark Twain) is *cacemphaton* – a scurrilous jest, lewd allusion, or double entendre (Lanham, 30). In his review of *The Damsel of Darien,* he condemns the author for using this device: "amid a passage of great beauty, he pauses to quote from the 'Seige of Corinth' the well-known image about 'peeling the fig when the fruit is fresh' – an image whose disgusting application where it originally stands has been often made the subject of severe and very justifiable censure" (10: 54).

Poe specialists are aware, however, that he often practiced that for which he condemned others in his capacity as reviewer. Davidson seems to have been the first to find instances of *cacemphaton* in Poe. In *A Critical Study,* he refers to "Poe's early device of hiding some not very clever pornography behind the bland appearance of innocent double-talk" (279 n10). Davidson does not use the term *cacemphaton,* opting instead for "verbal violence" – "the employment of profane or forbidden words in contexts which would ostensibly belie any profanity or lewdness but which would nonetheless allow the writer ... to be explosive and irreverent" (145). He suggests, specifically, that "Lionizing" is probably not about the nose but about the penis. In "Poe's 'Lionizing': The Wound and the Bawdry," John Arnold later took up this suggestion and developed it, citing this passage (53), among others:

"He is coming!" said somebody on the staircase.
"He is coming!" said somebody farther up.
"He is coming!" said somebody farther still.
"He is come!" exclaimed the Duchess ...
A marked sensation immediately ensued.

G.R. Thompson gives credit to Arnold and Davidson for their insights, and concurs. Davidson also notices the scatological component of "A Tale of Jerusalem," particularly in the name "Abel-Shittim" (147). Again, Thompson agrees; then he returns us to "Lionizing" and the following passage: "As I felt within me the divine *afflatus* ... I determined to follow my nose" ("On the Nose – Further Speculation on the Sources and Meaning of Poe's 'Lionizing,'" 96). Finally, Davidson notes that Poe, who was "unaccustomed to profanity and obscenity" (148), revised these tales and never again in his later authorial career returned to these "verbal contrivances" (147).

The maturer Poe came to disapprove of Swiftian/Rabelaisian *cacemphaton*, then, opting instead for other comedic strategies. One term that is not inappropriately applied to some humorous passages in Poe is *bathos*. Perhaps the most obviously bathetic scene in all of his works appears in "The Premature Burial." Most of this tale is devoted to preparing the readers for the climactic finale in which the narrator himself is buried alive – but Poe deliberately surprises us with a rather comical anticlimactic ending:

And now, amid all my infinite miseries, came sweetly the cherub Hope – for I thought of my precautions. I writhed, and made spasmodic exertions to force open the lid: it would not move. I felt my wrists for the bell-rope: it was not to be found. And now the Comforter fled for ever, and a still sterner Despair reigned triumphant; for I could not help perceiving the absence of the paddings which I had so carefully prepared – and then, too, there came suddenly to my nostrils the strong peculiar odor of moist earth. The conclusion was irresistible. I was *not* within the vault. I had fallen into a [cataleptic] trance while absent from home – while among strangers – when, or how, I could not remember – and it was they who had buried me as a dog – nailed up in some common coffin – and thrust, deep, deep, and forever, into some ordinary and nameless *grave*.

As this awful conviction forced itself, thus, into the innermost chambers of my soul, I once again struggled to cry aloud. And in this second endeavor I succeeded. A long, wild, and continuous shriek, or yell, of agony, resounded through the realms of the subterrene Night.

"Hillo! hillo, there!" said a gruff voice in reply.

"What the devil's the matter now?" said a second.

"Get out o' that!" said a third.

"What do you mean by yowling in that ere kind of style, like a cattymount?" said a fourth; and hereupon I was seized and shaken without ceremony, for several minutes, by a junto of very rough-looking individuals. They did not arouse me from my slumber – for I was wide awake when I screamed – but they restored me to the full possession of my memory.

This adventure occurred near Richmond, in Virginia. Accompanied by a friend, I had proceeded, upon a gunning expedition, some miles down the banks of the James River. Night approached, and we were overtaken by a storm. The cabin of a small sloop lying at anchor in the stream, and laden with garden mould, afforded us the only available shelter. We made the best of it, and passed the night on board. I slept in one of the only two berths in the vessel – and the berths of a sloop of sixty or seventy tons, need scarcely be described. That which I occupied had no bedding of any kind. Its extreme width was eighteen inches. The distance of its bottom from the deck overhead, was precisely the same. I found it a matter of exceeding difficulty to squeeze myself in. Nevertheless, I slept soundly; and the whole of my vision – for it was no dream, and no nightmare – arose naturally from the circumstances of my position – from my ordinary bias of thought – and from the difficulty, to which I have alluded, of collecting my senses, and especially of regaining my memory, for a long time after awaking from slumber. The men who shook me were the crew of the sloop, and some laborers engaged to unload it. From the load itself came the earthy smell. The bandage about the jaws was a silk handkerchief in which I had bound up my head, in default of my customary nightcap. (5: 271–2)

In short, instead of having been interred prematurely, the narrator had been simply sleeping between wooden boards on a small boat filled with dirt. Poe takes us from the terrifying idea of untimely burial to a rather ridiculous anticlimax, and the reader who had been looking forward to the Gothic horror that we have come to expect from Poe might very well feel somehow cheated (see *Merry Mood*, 5–6). As for the narrator, he made a complete ass of himself – and this bathetic ordeal had a cathartic effect on him. The Gothic has turned into the comedic, even the satirical, when we consider that Poe is having some fun at the expense of his rather silly, paranoid, monomaniacal narrator.[7]

Hoax, satire, lampoon, farce, burlesque, spoof, parody, black humour, slapstick, bathos: all these terms work well to describe Poe's *techniques* or comedic *genres*. I would like to leave them behind, however, to discuss a component of Poe's lighter prose that has been largely ignored: the *linguistic*. While much – although not enough – has been written on Poe's prose styles, as far as I can tell little has been said about the stylistic features that contribute to his comedy. The one feature of Poe's linguistic playfulness that *has* attracted attention is the *pun*. Bier reminds us of the lightly "symbolic puns upon names" that abound in Poe's tales (371) – was Rabelais an influence here? – while Michael J.S. Williams discusses specifically the puns in "The Gold-Bug": "The puns are most obvious in the transcriptions of Jupiter's speech – where visual as well as aural puns are at work – but they also pervade the narrative" (176). He then recalls the scene in which the narrator, Legrand, and Jupiter are digging in a grave-like pit for treasure, and how Jupiter, to silence the yelping of their dog, exits the pit and with a "dogged" air of deliberation ties up its mouth, then returns to the pit with a "grave" chuckle (5: 115–16). In a review of the prose and poetry of Thomas Hood, however, Poe shows contempt for writers like Hood who use puns too often (12: 213–15; see the catalogue). Still, Poe often could not resist a good pun – or a bad one. Here are some further samples: "In Spain they are [use] *all* curtains – a nation of hangmen" ("The Philosophy of Furniture," 14: 101); "Some of our foreign lions [celebrities] resemble the human brain in one very striking particular. They are without any *sense* themselves, and yet are the centres of *sensation*" (my italics; "Fifty Suggestions," 14: 171). Stauffer discusses Poe's "verbal horseplay" – not only puns but also clichés, funny names, variations in diction – at length (*Merry Mood*, 13ff). Julian

Symons is not impressed with Poe's wordplay, however, insisting that "he uses an abundance of appalling puns" (208). Rourke also loses patience with Poe's linguistic dallying: his "command of verbal humor was uncertain; his puns often fall below tolerable levels" (148).

While agreeing with Rourke that Poe's punning often makes one wince, I must pause at her insistence that Poe's "command of verbal humor was uncertain," for that verbal humour is precisely the subject of my investigation. I would argue, rather, that (some bad puns notwithstanding) Poe's command of linguistic humour is precise, deliberate, and masterful – just as he was more generally a precise, deliberate, and masterful literary craftsman. Where his obvious comedies are concerned (I do not refer to the humour allegedly found in his Gothic tales), we can identify certain devices for which classical rhetoric (ancient stylistics) has provided names. Here, as usual, I employ the categories of tropes and schemes ("The Terms by Type") in Lanham's *Handlist*. With that aid, we can see that most of Poe's sentence-level comedic devices can be categorized under certain headings: metaphorical substitutions and puns (such as *asteismus*); addition, subtraction, and substitution of letters and syllables (*antistoecon, epenthesis, metathesis, prothesis*), or of words, phrases, and clauses (*parelcon, zeugma*); ungrammatical, illogical, or unusual uses of language (*barbarismus, acyrologia* [malapropism]); amplification (*bomphiologia*); and the repetition of words (*anadiplosis, polyptoton, epanalepsis*). I make no claim that these devices make up a comedy that is knee-slappingly, gut-wrenchingly funny – but what in Poe *is*? At any rate, this precise stylistical approach to Poe's comedy enables us to increase the magnification on our analytical microscope and take that study to a deeper level than scholars have hitherto achieved.

Since we have already seen some of Poe's punning, let us finish with that comedic feature. The device *asteismus* is defined thus: "Facetious or mocking answer that plays on a word" (Lanham, 25); "A contrived turning or twisting of the meaning of something said so that it implies something else" (Cuddon, 64). We find an instance of this device in "The Purloined Letter," when Dupin, with an anecdote, teases the Prefect of the Parisian police about his inability to solve the crime:

"a certain rich miser conceived the design of spunging upon this Abernethy for a medical opinion. Getting up, for this purpose, an ordinary conversation in a private company, he insinuated his case to the physician, as that of an imaginary individual.

"'We will suppose,' said the miser, 'that his symptoms are such and such; now, doctor, what would *you* have directed him to *take*?'

"'*Take*!' said Abernethy, 'why, take *advice*, to be sure.'" (4: 38)

Rhetors (see especially those quoted by Lee Sonnino [188]) stress that *asteismus* does not involve sarcasm or rudeness; it is an inoffensive "civil jest," a "merry scoff" the likes of which has come to be associated with the urbane wit of the sophisticated city-dweller. And who is a more sophisticated city-dweller than Dupin, whose wit is evident here?[8] Lanham offers an example of *asteismus* from *The Goon Show*: "Did you put the cat out?"; "No, it wasn't on fire" (25). My personal favourite instance is the answer I give to those roaming evangelists who proselytize from door to door: "Have you heard the Word, brother?"; "The word *brother*? Yes, it means 'a male sibling'.." At any rate, that Poe could use this clever linguistic device shows that we do not have to agree completely with Mooney, who insists that "Poe's wit ran, not to sophistication and controlled urbanity, but rather to the extravagant and outrageous" ("The Comic in Poe's Fiction," 434). Poe's comedy often *is* extravagant and outrageous, but at other times his humour displays a linguistic sophistication and sportiveness. Stauffer is right when he notes that Poe's emphasis in comedy is often "intellectual rather than emotional: for his humor is more closely allied to wit than to goodnaturedness" (*Merry Mood*, 6).

Take *zeugma* as another example of Poe's playfulness with language, his verbal wit. A scheme of omission, *zeugma* describes a situation in which one verb – or another kind of word – is used for two or more objects to each of which it stands in a different relation. Some of the most famous examples of the device are, of course, the bathetic instances in Pope's *The Rape of the Lock*: "Here, Thou, Great *Anna*! whom three Realms obey,/ Dost sometimes Counsel take – and sometimes *Tea*" (3.7–8); "When Husbands or when Lap-dogs breathe their last" (3.158). Lanham provides a more contemporary example from *The Goon Show*: "take this pencil and draw the blinds!" (161). Here is an exemplification from Poe's review of *Peter Snook*, suggesting indeed that he appreciated *zeugma*: "The consequence is, that Mr. Snook falls, thirdly, asleep, and fourthly, overboard" (14: 77). Here is another: "[An abused writer,] having starved through the month (he and his family) completes at length the month of

starvation and the article" ("The Magazine Prison-House," 14: 163). Poe
gives us another instance of *zeugma* and combines it literally with gallows humour and a pun: "I forbear to depict my sensations upon the
gallows ... I may just mention, however, that die I did not. My body
was, but I had no breath *to be* suspended" ("Loss of Breath," 2: 160). In
"King Pest," we get a description of the intoxicated Hugh Tarpaulin and
Legs being "brimful of courage and of 'humming-stuff!'" (2: 173). That
example confirms Dupriez's remark that, "In English, zeugma frequently
unites an abstract with a concrete term": the abstract noun is *courage*, the
concrete noun is *humming-stuff* (alcohol). This type of *zeugma*, he says,
quite rightly, "seems particularly well suited to humour" (475). To push
home this point, Dupriez provides an instance from Ambrose Bierce's
The Devil's Dictionary: "LIGHTHOUSE. A tall building on the sea-
shore in which the government maintains a lamp and the friend of a pol-
itician." Bierce is known to have read Poe and certainly would have
found exemplifications of *zeugma* there, just as the latter may have been
inspired by finding this device in Dickens (see Dupriez).

Another source of humour in Poe depends not on playing with words
but on the amplification of an idea using more words than necessary,
and possibly rather inflated words at that. One type of *amplificatio* is
bomphiologia: bombastic, pompous speech – probably what Mr Blackwood has in mind when recommending "the tone elevated, diffusive" to
Psyche Zenobia in "How to Write a Blackwood Article" (2: 275). In the
following excerpt from "Loss of Breath," Poe's narrator might have said
in plain and simple prose, "two cats fought over my nose," but note the
inappropriately inflated diction, suggesting a grandeur unwarranted by
the subject: "two cats ... alighting opposite one another on my visage,
*betook themselves to indecorous contention for the paltry consideration of my
nose*" (my italics; 2: 159). The saying "less is more" is obviously alien to
this bombastic narrator. Lanham relates the term to *macrologia*, long-
winded speech in which more words are used than necessary (96–7).
Taylor, on the other hand, prefers to see *bomphiologia* as a kind of *hyperbole* similar to *auxesis* (79–80). At any rate, for more instances of pompous speech, see the language of King Pest. Clearly, *bomphiologia* – itself a
pompous-sounding word – may remind us of the linguistic habits of
some of the more pretentious and bloated characters in American situa-
tional comedies, such as Charles Emerson Winchester III in *M*A*S*H*,

or Frasier Crane. Another source of humour is often the *deflation* of the inflated character – essentially the equivalent of a pie in the face Three Stooges style – as the writers of *M*A*S*H* and *Frasier* are clearly aware. In "Loss of Breath," the indignities done to the narrator's body (in this instance, two cats eating away at his nose) obviously comprise a comedic deflation of the narrator's ego. Like some of our professional comic writers, Poe uses *bomphiologia* to establish the pomposity of a character, then delights in having him humiliated – perhaps bringing about in readers a sense of *Schadenfreude*, pleasure in someone else's pain. This is, says Trieber, a "humor of scorn."

Poe, then, wants us to chuckle at the linguistically oversophisticated character, but more frequently he prefers us to chortle at the linguistically vulgar. While *bomphiologia* involves the expansion of an idea through *copia verborum* (an abundance of words), other devices rely on the addition, subtraction, or substitution of units on a more microscopic level – that of letters and syllables. The generic term is *metaplasm*, "a transformation of letters or syllables in single words, contrary to the common fashion of writing or speaking" (Lanham, 101). One type of *metaplasm* is *antistoecon*, which is the classical name for the substitution of one letter or sound for another within a word – a fancy name for a spelling mistake. We may well ask, as Arthur Quinn does at length (23–5), why a writer would deliberately misspell a word. Certainly *antistoecon* can be used to reproduce dialect more accurately (cf *barbarismus*, below) or to suggest the ignorance of uneducated characters – clearly for (albeit crude) comedic purposes. Consider this example from "X-ing a Paragrab": "'*Wery* well,' replied Bob, 'here goes it!' and off he hurried to his case; muttering as he went – 'Considdeble vell, them ere expressions, perticcler for a man as doese n't swar'" (6: 235). Poe's use of *antistoecon* is only one way in which he anticipates the prose of Mark Twain: "Blest if the old Nonesuch ain't a *heppin'* us out *agin*" (*Huck Finn*, 215; my italics).

Another type of *metaplasm* is *epenthesis*, the insertion of a letter, sound, or syllable to the middle of a word (see Dupriez, 166). "The Man that was Used Up: A Tale of the Late Bugaboo and Kickapoo Campaign" offers an instance of this type of Poe's linguistic humour:

"Smith?" said he, in his well-known peculiar way of drawling out his syllables; "Smith? – why, not General John A – B – C.? Savage affair that with the

Kickapo-o-o-os, wasn't it? Say! don't you think so? – perfect *despera-a-ado* – great pity, pon my honor! – wonderfully inventive age! – *pro-o-odigies* of valor! By the by, did you ever hear about Captain *Ma-a-a-n*?" (my italics; 3: 268)

We may wonder why a writer would resort to such a device, but clearly Poe illustrates its comedic potential. As well, a device like this can help us distinguish between Poe's characters, stylistically, for he has enough comedic good sense to limit a device like this to one character – to make it a linguistic idiosyncrasy rather than to overuse it.

Two other types of *metaplasm* are *metathesis* (the transposition of a letter or phonetic element out of normal order in a word) and *prothesis* (adding a letter or syllable at the front of a word without changing its meaning). We find both types in the "Chaplinesque comedy" (Kaufhold, 143) of "Why the Little Frenchman Wears His Hand in a Sling": "And is it ralelly more than the three fut and a bit that there is, inny how, of the little ould furrener Frinchman that lives just over the way, and that's a oggling and a goggling [there is the *prothesis*] the houl day, (and bad luck to him,) at the *purty* [pretty – here is the *metathesis*] widdy Misthress Tracle" (my italics; 4: 115). *Metathesis* on a larger scale – that is, within a sentence – is a spoonerism. Both *metathesis* and *prothesis* help convey a sense of what I might call linguistic *bumpkinism* – such as we find, for instance, in the works of Steinbeck and Mark Twain.

Sometimes Poe's linguistic humour depends on the addition, subtraction, and substitution not of letters or syllables but of words, phrases, and clauses. Consider *parelcon*, redundancy involving unnecessary words – for instance, using two words, as if they were joined, where one should do. In examples from Sonnino (208–9) and Espy (194), the two words actually *are* joined – but it makes no sense to do this in English. In the following example from "Why the Little Frenchman Wears His Hand in a Sling," we have both a noun and a pronoun standing for the subject "widdy" (widow), but the pronoun is hardly necessary after the noun; it is superfluous: "And wid that the *widdy, she* gits up from the sofy, and makes the swatest curtchy nor iver was seen" (my italics; 4: 117). We might also think of this example as a kind of tautology. Clearly, *parelcon* is a stylistic vice and as such should be (but is not) categorized by Lanham under his heading "Ungrammatical, illogical, or unusual uses of language" (195–6). Poe combines it here with *barbarismus* as part of the tale's linguistic comedy, a strategy that (once again) is clearly fore-grounded in the works of Mark Twain: "The *king he* spread his arms, and *Mary Jane she* jumped for them" (*Huck Finn*, 211; my italics).

Barbarismus is the rhetorical term for a mistake in vocabulary, pro-nunciation, or grammar – an illiterate expression that violates the rules of a language due to ignorance or confusion (cf malapropism and *acyrologia*). As such, it is found in Lanham's category, "Ungrammatical, illogi-cal, or unusual uses of language." American writers have had some fun with the dialects of uneducated slaves. Consider Poe's Jupiter: "'Dey aint *no* tin in him, Massa Will, I keep a tellin on you,' here interrupted Jupi-ter; 'de bug is a goole bug, solid, ebery bit of him, inside and all, sep him wing – neber feel half so hebby a bug in my life'" ("The Gold-Bug," 5: 98). Some scholars have criticized Poe for what they see as inaccuracies in Jupiter's dialect. A relatively recent summary of these points of view is Jennifer Dilalla Toner's "The 'Remarkable Effect' of 'Silly Words': Dia-lect and Signature in 'The Gold-Bug'." Following J.L. Dillard, she pro-poses that, *for the most part*, Poe is reproducing the Gullah dialect accurately (3–5). Regardless of the extent to which Poe's powers of dialec-tal mimicry are precise or fall short in this tale, the fact remains that Jupiter's speech comprises *barbarismus*. Elizabeth C. Phillips recognizes the comedic value of the slave's "mirth-provoking dialectal errors" (174) while Killis Campbell also sees Jupiter as having been cast by Poe into the role of "laughing-stock" ("Poe's Treatment of the Negro and of the Negro Dialect," 112).[9]

Campbell maintains that Poe "was never gifted in the management of dialect" (112). Whether this claim is true or not, Poe uses *barbarismus* not only in "The Gold-Bug" but also in "The Angel of the Odd": "'As vor ow I com'd ere,' replied the figure, 'dat iz none ob your pizziness; and as vor vat I be talking apout, I be talk apout vat I tink proper; and as vor who I be, vy dat is de very ting I com'd here for to let you zee for your-zelf'" (6: 106). Stauffer considers this "an outrageous mongrel accent that is a pastiche of German, French, and Southern black" ("The Lan-guage and Style of the Prose," 463). And one has but to glance at "Why the Little Frenchman Wears His Hand in a Sling" to see that the entire tale is told by an Irishman whose grasp of good English pronunciation leaves much to be desired (see above). We also have some *barbarismus* in *Pym*: "'sir! You are a sum'mat mistaken; my name, in the first place, bee'nt nothing at all like Goddin [Gordon], and I'd want you for to know better, you blackguard, than to call my new obercoat a darty one'" (3: 20–1). In "The Spectacles," we get a sample of the bad English of a French lady, Eugénie Lalande:

Monsieur Simpson vill pardonne me for not compose de butefulle tong of his contrée so vell as might. It is only de late dat I am arrive, and not yet ave de opportunité for to – l'étudier.

Vid dis apologie for de manière, I vill now say dat, hélas! – Monsieur Simpson ave guess but de too true. Need I say de more? Hélas! am I not ready speak de too moshe? (5: 191)

Readers who know Poe only by his serious tales may be surprised indeed to find him displaying a comical ability to mimic so many foreign accents – an ability we might normally expect, instead, from that genius of dialects, Mark Twain. Even in his literary criticism, we find him having some fun in this vein at the expense of a poet who incorrectly used *took* instead of *taken*: "why not say *tuk* at once? We have heard of chaps vot vas tuk up for sheep-stealing, and we know of one or two that ought to be tuk up for murder of the Queen's English" (Review of *Wakondah*, 11: 34). Weeks asserts that, "Beginning in the America of the mid-1800s, a certain type of humour came to the fore: dialect humour – in recited or printed form" (81). If Weeks' claim is true, then Poe was clearly an early practitioner of what came to be more popular after his death.

Another example of improper language is represented by the rhetorical term *acyrologia*: the use of an inexact or illogical word. A better known term, though not strictly a rhetorical one, is *malapropism*. That this device has comedic value goes without saying, and we merely have to recall the king of malapropisms, Archie Bunker, for confirmation – he seems to give us at least one per episode. For example, consider when Archie, in one episode of *All in the Family*, refers to gynecology as *groin*ecology, or another in which he says *circumscribed* instead of *circumcised*. Poe, ever sensitive to the comedic potential of language, provides an example of *acyrologia* in "X-ing a Paragrab": "'Oh, goodness, gracious! – what *is* this world coming to? *Oh, tempora! Oh, Moses!*'" (6: 230). The proper Latin saying, of course, is *"O tempora! O mores!"* – "Oh, the times! Oh, the customs!" Let us not forget Mark Twain's love of comedic *acyrologia* – consider Huck's "preforeordestination," for instance.

Our final rhetorical category pertains to the humorous repetition of words. Mooney is the only scholar I have seen so far who identifies two devices of repetition at work in the context of Poe's comedy, though he does not use the classical names for them. Instead, he uses an analogy from music to describe what is going on, linguistically, in certain passages in "The Man that was Used Up":

> Poe's comic means [is] analogous to the suspended tone in music, whereby a note of one chord is held over as the tonal feature of a new chord: the two chords, two contexts of "meaning," have quite different tonal qualities (comparable to contextual meanings) but keep the one note in common. This is of course in music not a device for humor, but Poe exploits it to interesting effect in his story ... His "suspended tone" is the word *man*, an appropriate choice for the general, who is revealed as half a man, and the changing context ... is first a church, then a theater, and last a "salon." ("The Comic in Poe's Fiction," 438–9)

Then Mooney quotes an early passage that repeats the word *man* (meaning Brevet Brigadier General John A.B.C. Smith) as Miss Tabitha T. says the word and is interrupted by the minister, Dr. Drummummupp, who begins his sentence with *man* (as in "man that is born of a woman," 3: 264). Next, at the theatre, Miranda Cognoscenti's "man" is interrupted by an actor's "mandragora" (266). Later, Miss Pirouette's "man" is interrupted by Miss Bas-Bleu's "Man-*Fred*" (267). Mooney might also have quoted the earliest instance of *man* followed by the "Man alive" expression uttered by the general himself (262).

Without knowing it, apparently, Mooney has found instances of *anadiplosis* and *polyptoton*. Had he known these terms, he could have ditched the complicated analogy and provided simple definitions to describe what Poe is doing. *Anadiplosis* refers to the repetition of the last word or words of one line or clause at the beginning of the next (*man* to end one clause; *man* to begin the next). *Polyptoton* involves the repetition of nearby words that have the same roots: "man," then "mandragora" and "Man-*Fred*" (later "Man-Friday"). Poe uses numerous types of linguistic repetition in all his prose for various strategic purposes, not always humour. His comedic use of *polyptoton* is particularly nasty in his review of the novel *Norman Leslie*, a book he feels was unjustifiably puffed by other reviewers and advertisers: "For the sake of everything *puff, puffing* and *puffable*, let us take a peep at its contents" (my italics; 8: 51). Poe ends his scathing review as he began it, with derisive *polyptoton*, in this case laughing at the author's overuse of the word *blistering*. After quoting several sentences containing that word, Poe ends thus: "Here we have a *blistering* detail, a *blistering* truth, a *blistering* story, and a *blistering* brand, to say nothing of innumerable other blisters interspersed throughout the book. But we have done with Norman Leslie, – if ever we saw as silly a thing, may we be----blistered" (8: 62). Although the poor author of *Norman Leslie* was doubtlessly not amused, Poe's *polyptoton* certainly is somewhat amusing for the review's other readers (here is that mean-minded *Schadenfreude* again).[10] *Polyptoton* and *anadiplosis*, like other devices of repetition, are not devices of humour or humorous scorn *per se*, but Poe clearly uses them as such occasionally. Their use amounts to something like derisive chanting, as when a child taunts another by repeating what the second has said, or when hostile hockey fans chant the name of the opposing team's goalie. *Polyptoton* shows more wit than simple repetition (as with *anadiplosis*), and Mooney suggests that, in "The Man that was Used Up," Poe's duplication of *man* "achieves an effect of social vacuity" (439). If we agree with Mooney's interpretation, the devices amount to Trieber's "humor of scorn."[11]

Epanalepsis is another device of repetition, not humorous in itself, which Poe uses as part of the comedy in at least one tale. The second of two definitions of the term is given by Cluett and Kampeas as, "The use of a summarizing subject because of the geographical distance between the beginning of a series of subjects and the main verb" (29). We find this device typically in a long periodic sentence (the rhetorical term for which is *hirmus*) that may also exhibit *hypotaxis* (phrases or clauses arranged in dependent or subordinate relationships). Consider the opening sentence of "The Thousand-and-second Tale of Scheherazade," which shows a combination of *epanalepsis*, *hirmus*, and *hypotaxis*:

Having had occasion, lately, in the course of some oriental investigations, to consult the *Tellmenow Isitsoörnot* [Tell me now, is it so or not], a work which (like the Zohar of Simeon Jochaides) is scarcely known at all, even in Europe, and which has never been quoted to my knowledge, by any American – if we except, perhaps, the author of the "Curiosities of American Literature;" – having had occasion, I say, to turn over some pages of the first-mentioned very remarkable work, I was not a little astonished. (6: 78)

Had this long-winded narrator been more to the point, the sentence would have commenced with the clause that for the most part comprises the *epanalepsis*: "Having had occasion to turn over some pages of the *Tellmenow Isitsoörnot*, I was not a little astonished." The comedic *flakiness* of this narrator, however, is demonstrated by his *inability* to get to the point. He begins firmly on track ("Having had occasion"), but immediately goes *off* track by filling in unnecessary contextual details ("in the course of some oriental investigations") and then getting lost in other syntactical interruptions – dependent clauses. By the time we wade through all the embedded syntax, the point with which he began has been lost, necessitating his use of *epanalepsis*: "having had occasion, I say, to turn over some pages of the first-mentioned very remarkable work." That this humorously annoying linguistic idiosyncrasy on the narrator's part is not accidental or incidental on Poe's part is shown by several other examples:

On the night of the wedding she contrived, upon I forget what specious pretence, to have her sister occupy a couch sufficiently near that of the royal pair to admit of easy conversation from bed to bed; and, a little before cock-crowing, she took care to awaken the good monarch, her husband, (who bore her none the worse will because he intended to wring her neck on the morrow,) – she managed to awaken him, I say, (although, on account of a capital conscience and an easy digestion, he slept well,) by the profound interest of a story (about a rat and a black cat, I think,) which she was narrating (all in an under-tone, of course,) to her sister. (80)

This tale actually has *three* narrators: this linguistically quirky narrator, Scheherazade, and Sinbad, but the combined use of *hirmus*, *hypotaxis*, and *epanalepsis* is absent in the narrations of Scheherazade and Sinbad. The frame narrator's stylistic signature, then, is one way in which Poe differentiates among the three narrators; at the same time, he provides us with some linguistic comedy. As if all this were not enough, once more the narrator makes us shake our heads in amused contempt for his circumlocutions: "the king having been sufficiently pinched, at length ceased snoring, and finally said 'hum!' and then 'hoo!' when the queen understanding these words (which are no doubt Arabic) to signify that he was all attention, and would do his best not to snore any more, – the queen, I say, having arranged these matters to her satisfaction, re-entered thus, at once, into the history of Sinbad the sailor" (82). Here for a third time we have periodic sentence structure with plenty of syntactical embedding, once again necessitating *epanalepsis*, this time more as a scheme of addition than repetition: "the queen, I say, having arranged these matters." That some of our contemporary comedic writers have recognized the humorous potential of linguistic circumlocutions is demonstrated notably by Matt Groening, whose Grandpa Simpson is utterly incapable of telling an anecdote without derailing by way of syntactical interruptions.[12]

In addition to providing humour, *hypotaxis* and *hirmus* seem to be related to theme in "The Thousand-and-second Tale of Scheherazade." Scheherazade, of course, is the legendary queen of Samarkand who delayed her execution for a thousand-and-one nights by telling her husband, Schariar, exotic Eastern tales, anecdotes, and fables, ending each night before the narrative climax and thereby forcing the king to keep her alive in order to hear the conclusion the next night. Scheherazade's technique, then, is the generation of *suspense*, and this technique is mirrored in the largely periodic and hypotactic style of the primary narrator, whose syntactic postponement mirrors Scheherazade's technique of narrative postponement. Like King Schariar, we are kept in suspense until the end. Style relates to theme, here; the linguistic relates to the extra-linguistic. When that is done well, I have always considered it a sign of a master writer. Now and then in his literary reviews Poe expresses his belief, his authorial credo, that style and subject should be one: "The *style* of Mr. Wilmer is not only good in itself, but exceedingly well adapted to his subjects" (Review of *The Confessions of Emilia Harrington*, 8: 236).

A corollary of this credo is that style should reflect, be related to, *characterization*. I have already said that the combination of *epanalepsis*, *hirmus*, and *hypotaxis* shows the flakiness of one narrator; we have also seen that Dupin's use of *asteismus* suggests his urbane sophistication; *bomphiologia* indicates another narrator's pomposity; *antistoecon, metathesis, prothesis, parelcon, acyrologia,* and *barbarismus* often show "lower" character types, just as these devices serve the same function in the works of Mark Twain and, come to think of it, Shakespeare.

A line from "The Literary Life of Thingum Bob, Esq." can be applied to Poe's prose to some extent: "*What* I wrote it is unnecessary to say. The *style!* – that was the thing" (6: 27). That tale *is*, as Stauffer rightly comments, self-consciously about style (*Merry Mood*, 21). As well, consider this line from Poe's "Review of Griswold's *The Poets and Poetry of America*" (3rd ed.), written in the third-person: "This discovery ... was left to Edgar A. Poe, who has spent more time in analyzing the construction of our language than any living grammarian, critic, or essayist" (11: 229). I am inclined to accept Poe's word on that. Certainly he wants to draw our attention to aspects of his *styles*. While he does not engage in a stylistic study, Trieber does mention briefly the "carefully thought out word-plays and wit" in Poe's comedies, and maintains that they are "encased in the concept of the 'superior'" (34). Poe's comedic verbal manipulations are the manifestations of a writer who gloried in his mastery of the English language and perhaps (as Trieber would argue) in his sense of linguistic superiority over his contemporaries. In this sense, his "humor of scorn" is an alienated humour. On the other hand, consider the *dialectal* component of Poe's humour, which so clearly anticipates Mark Twain.[13] Certainly his portrayal of several dialects places Poe clearly in his time and place, as his travels and other personal experiences put him in contact not only with Americanized Africans struggling with the English language but also with European immigrants – such as the Irish, the Germans, the French, and the Scots (remember that his "foster" father, John Allan, was a Scotsman). In this sense, then, attempts to identify Poe's humour with Western or Southwestern locales is too limited, for his dialectal comedy fits into an old tradition in American humour, one not associated exclusively with any particular region (say, the South or Southwest) and even predates Poe's own writing career – recall, for instance, the *barbarismus* of Cooper's Natty Bumppo: the earliest Leatherstocking tale is *The Pioneers* (1823), written when Poe was only about fourteen. One thing is for sure:

along with the traditional terms that have been applied to Poe's comedy –
*hoax, satire, lampoon, farce, burlesque, spoof, parody, bathos, slapstick, black
humour, vaudeville* – we must add a host of words supplied by the ancient
rhetors: *asteismus, antistoecon, epenthesis, metathesis, prothesis, parelcon,
zeugma, barbarismus, acyrologia, bomphiologia, anadiplosis, polyptoton,* and
epanalepsis-hirmus-hypotaxis.

CHAPTER FIVE

The Linguistic Weaponry of the "Tomahawk Man": Poe's Critical Reviews

The laudation of the unworthy is to the worthy the most bitter of all wrong.
Review of *The Poetry of Rufus Dawes*, 11: 147

I have an inveterate habit of speaking the truth.
Letter to Philip Pendleton Cooke (Ostrom, 117)

I have been a critic – and unscrupulously honest and no doubt in many cases a bitter one – that I have uniformly attacked – where I attacked at all – those who stood highest in power and influence – and that, whether in literature or in society, I have seldom refrained from expressing, either directly or indirectly, the pure contempt with which the pretensions of ignorance, arrogance, or imbecility inspire me. – And you who know all this – *you* ask me *why* I have enemies.
Letter to Sarah Helen Whitman (Ostrom, 394)

One year after Poe's death, *The Southern Literary Messenger* published a review essay of his that the editor titled "Poe on Headley and Channing." Appended to the article was the following announcement: "From advance sheets of 'The Literati,' a work in press, by the late Edgar A. Poe, we take the following sketches of Headley and Channing – *as good specimens of the tomahawk-style of criticism of which the author was so great a master.* In the present instances the satire is well-deserved" (13: 202 n1; my italics). Four years earlier, Poe had been engaged to write a series of Literati papers (mentioned above) to *Godey's Lady's Book*. Poe's reputation for critical vituperation was established by then, and the alarm went out. As Harrison reports, the founder of the monthly publication, Louis Antoine Godey, felt compelled "to address a note to the agitated 'Minor Contemporaries'": "We have received several letters from New York, anonymous, and from personal friends, *requesting us to be careful what we allow Mr. Poe to say of the New York authors*" (15: viii; my italics). Some of Poe's more famous contemporaries recognized and commented upon his viciousness: in 1845 Margaret Fuller wrote that, as a professed critic, Poe is "of all the band the most unsparing to others" (*Recognition*, 16); and James Russell Lowell's comment (also of 1845) that Poe "seems sometimes to mistake his phial of prussic-acid for his inkstand" (*Recognition*, 6) is well known. Some of Poe's well-wishers exhorted him to blunt his tomahawk a little: "I did not mean to deny the efficacy of a certain style of criticism in demolishing scribblers," wrote Judge Beverley Tucker, in 1835; "I merely said it was not Judicial. It may make the critic as formidable to the rabble of literary offenders, as Jack Dalgliesh or Jack Portious himself, but it makes him odious too" (17: 23). The praise of Thomas Chivers for Poe's critical writings was qualified, as is clear from an 1844 letter: "There is, in the perspicuous flow of your pure English, a subtle delicacy of expression which always pleases me – *except when you tomahawk people*" (17: 171).

Indeed, Poe's reputation for critical severity had become so widespread that he even found himself being blamed for scathing reviews he did *not* write. In a number for the September issue of *The Broadway Journal*, he notes (using the editorial *we*) that, "Whenever a book is abused, it is taken for granted that it is we who have been abusing it" (12: 244). While he always had sufficient courage to take credit for those harsh reviews he did write, he refused to take the blame for those he did not. Using the rhetorical device *traiectio in alium*, he sometimes found himself shifting responsibility onto another: "Holding these opinions in regard to [Margaret Fuller's] 'Woman in the Nineteenth Century,' I still feel myself called upon to disavow the silly, condemnatory criticism of the work which appeared in one of the earlier numbers of 'The Broadway Journal.' That article was *not* written by myself, and *was* written by my associate Mr. Briggs" (15: 75; see also 15: 195). Still, if one wrote nasty reviews in a time of frequent anonymous reviewing, one had to take the risks.[1]

My purpose here is not to discuss Poe's critical formulae as we find them spread throughout the seven volumes of literary reviews in the Harrison edition; Poe scholars are thoroughly conversant with them. Neither do I intend to consider his strengths and weaknesses as a critic. Much has been written on this subject, including some long explorations

– such as Edd Winfield Parks' *Edgar Allan Poe as Literary Critic* and Robert D. Jacobs' *Poe: Journalist & Critic*. Because of these and other important studies, Poe's pros and cons as a critic are as well understood as his theories (and further evidence can be found in my catalogue for both his powers and his failings – see, for instance, the logical fallacies). I would like, instead, to examine some of the stylistic features of Poe's critical reviews to uncover those aspects of his prose that made him so formidable, so intimidating, so dreaded – even admired – by his contemporary poets, dramatists, and novelists.

Poe's reputation as a literary tomahawk man was founded in part on his love of ridicule when he felt it was called for – such as when he ended reviews with one of the following: a solemn vow to throw the piece reviewed into the fire (8: 205; 9: 191); an expressed wish to toss it out the window (9: 114); a determination to feed it to the pigs (11: 174); a regret that the hero rather than the author of a novel comes to the gallows (10: 219); a desire for a similar fate involving the noose for William Ellery Channing (11: 175), the author of *Stanley Thorne* (11: 13), and "the editor of 'The Dial'" (13: 155); encouragement to a poet to keep his gunpowder fresh to ensure success in blowing his own brains out: "A flash in the pan – and in such a case – were a thing to be lamented" (8: 3). All this is wickedly *funny*, but none of it, of course, depends on linguistic cleverness. Neither does the following: "As for the editor of the 'Jeffersonian Teetotaler' (or whatever it is), we advise her to get drunk, too, as soon as possible – for when sober she is a disgrace to the sex – on account of being so awfully stupid" (13: 8). That is a far cry from Poe's opinion, expressed elsewhere, that no true gentleman, especially a *Southern* one, should ever say anything mean about the "gentler sex," even in a critical review. Typically, it was the *men* whom Poe ridiculed. Writing about a lecturer named Hudson, Poe suggests that this man displays "an elocution that would disgrace a pig, and an odd species of gesticulation of which a baboon would have excellent reason to be ashamed" (13: 27).

The linguistic weaponry that Poe sometimes resorted to entailed much more than merely vulgar name-calling – although he did stoop to *that* now and then. Using the rhetorical device *bdelygma* (an expression of hatred or contempt), he called Carlyle an *ass* (11: 177), Lowell an abolitionist *fanatic* (13: 172), one Miss Walters a *Syren* (13: 8), and the members of Brook Farm, *Crazyites* (13: 27). Sometimes, admittedly, his name-calling is downright humorous: "'Quack' is a word that sounds well only in the mouth of a duck; and upon our honor we feel a scruple in using it: – nevertheless the truth should be told; and the simple fact is, that the author of the 'Sacred Mountains' is the Autocrat of all the Quacks" (13: 208). Evidencing *alleotheta* (substitution of a gender), Poe insulted a male author by referring to him as "an honest woman" (14: 181). When he was not calling other authors names, he was using *tapinosis* (undignified language that debases, belittles, a person or thing) to put down their literary productions as *doggerel* (11: 231, for example) or *twaddle* (15: 260, for example). For the word *poets* he would sometimes substitute *versifiers* or *poetasters* (11: 221). To other critics, he applies the terms *small geniuses, literary Titmice, animalculae* – all in the same review, all in the same *sentence* (11: 39).

Occasionally his satire involved a grotesque parody, as when he ridiculed the bad grammar (*amphibologia*) of the poet Henry B. Hirst by ending a review with this: "My quarrel with him is *not*, in short, that he *did* this thing, but that he *has went and done did it*" (13: 213). Sometimes he would use satirical *hyperbole*: "We are not asserting too much when we say that every second novel since the flood has turned upon some series of hopeless efforts" (10: 166); "The revolution in the character of Tortesa – or rather the final triumph of his innate virtue – is a dramatic point far older than the hills" (13: 51).

These aspects of Poe's critical reviews are nasty and hurtful but not linguistically inventive. My guess is that he inspired not only anger and hatred but even *fear* in his fellow word-artists because his linguistic and rhetorical powers went far beyond mere name-calling, occasional parody, and derisive *hyperbole*. The devices he used that made his reviews so devastating fall into three of the thirteen broad categories outlined by Lanham in his *Handlist of Rhetorical Terms*: vehemence (*ara, optatio, apostrophe, antiphrasis, sarcasmus, bathos, anacoluthon, epiplexis*); argument (*pysma, hypophora, subjectio, paraleipsis, apophasis, amphidiorthosis, peristrophe*); and repetition (*antistasis, antanaclasis, polyptoton, polysyndeton, epimone, epanalepsis*). Some clearly belong to more than one category (*antistasis*, for instance, is both a pun and a figure of repetition; *pysma* can be seen as a figure of emotion as well as a technique of argument). I group them as I do in part to simplify my organizational strategy. What is especially interesting is that Poe now and then uses certain devices in ways not generally associated with them. For example, he expands the usefulness of certain devices of redundancy by giving them a derisive application, and he uses what is supposed to be a *neutral* continuator satirically as well. Maybe I am not going too far in suggesting that only a linguistic genius could amplify, broaden, the applicability of linguistic constructions – give them a legitimate use that, perhaps, no one had thought of before. It is too bad, some may say, that he did so in the name of malice.

Least impressive, rhetorically and linguistically, is Poe's employment of the emotive devices. The first few merit only a brief consideration. *Ara* is a curse, imprecation, malediction. Typically a Gothic convention (recall the famous curse in Hawthorne's *House of the Seven Gables*), we find the device occasionally in Poe's critical reviews. Here it is in the gossipy "Boston and the Bostonians": "The fact is, we despise them and defy them (the transcendental vagabonds!) and they may all go to the devil together" (13: 9). The second, *optatio* (a fervent wish), need not be malicious, but it *is* now and then from Poe's pen. In complaining about the refrain, "Yet I wail!", spoken too often by characters in *The Drama of Exile*, Poe says, "God deliver us from any such wailing again!" (12: 9). To the poet William A. Lord, we get this: "from any farther specimens of your stupidity, good Lord deliver us!" (12: 161). We all know what an *apostrophe* is. Discussing the "poetry" of his nemesis, Rufus Griswold, Poe apostrophizes some of the truly great poets: "We have more of his *poetry* (spirits of Pope, Byron, et al., forgive our desecration of the name!) on hand" (11: 234). In fact, Poe declines to award Griswold the title of *poet*, opting instead for *versifier* (here is *tapinosis* again).

Scarcely more clever, but scarcely less *mean*, are two related devices of vehemence: *antiphrasis* and *sarcasmus*. The first involves the use of a single word ironically – directly opposite to one's real meaning. We look again for what is perhaps the most derisive, most cruel, review Poe ever wrote for an exemplification (consider his use of *modest* in its nominal and adverbial forms):

In the "Prospectus," Mr. Griswold's self-esteem is strangely developed. Here we have him in his capacity of "*author*" of the "Poets and Poetry of America," as thirteenth in the list, and of course superior in rank to Sargent, Benjamin, Simms, Lowell, Thomas, Poe [!], Hill, our own Conrad (one of the sweetest poets of the time), Greeley, &c., &c., who follow him. *Unexampled modesty*! ...

Again, how *modestly* our critic puffs himself in his remarks on the "Editorial
Department." (11: 223–4)

Another of the cruelest reviews Poe wrote was of the novel *Norman
Leslie*, by Theodore S. Fay. Once more we get an ironic twist on a single
word: "there are surely no bounds to Mr. Fay's *excellent* invention" (8: 58;
my italics). Extended *antiphrasis* is called *sarcasm* or *irony*, though not all
rhetors make the distinction. As for *sarcasmus*, Poe believed that "the
principal element of all satire" is sarcasm (13: 167), and sarcastic satire is
certainly how we can categorize some of his critical productions. We find
an instance in Poe's review of *Lafitte: The Pirate of the Gulf*:

Count D' Oyley ... makes his escape from the rendezvous with his mistress and
Juana. In so doing he has *only* [my italics] to dress his mistress as a man, and
himself as a woman, to descend a precipice, to make a sentinel at the mouth of
the cave drunk, and so walk over him – make another drunk in Lafitte's schooner, and so walk over him – walk over some forty or fifty of the crew on deck –
and finally to walk off with the longboat. These things are trifles with a man of
genius – and an author should never let slip an opportunity of displaying his invention. (9: 109–10)

In his "Drake-Halleck" review Poe quotes a writer for the New York
Commercial Advertiser, who condemns Poe's use of *sarcasmus* in previous
reviews: "The critic of the Messenger [Poe himself] has been eulogized
for his scorching and scarifying abilities, and he thinks it incumbent
upon him to keep up his reputation in that line, by sneers, sarcasm, and
downright abuse" (8: 279).

Interestingly, this unnamed writer notes that some have "eulogized"
Poe's critical tomahawkism (if I may coin a word *a la Poe*). One wonders
who did the praising. I suspect the concept of *Schadenfreude*, pleasure in
someone else's pain (see chapter 4), may to some extent be behind those
who cheered on Poe – just as we approve of people of talent today who
satirize those whom many of us love to hate (Bill Gates, England's royal
family, politicians – certainly in Canada). As well, those people who excel in their respective fields but who have not been recognized sufficiently may very likely sympathize with the spirit that animated so much

of Poe's critical reviews. After all, it was he who wrote, "The laudation of the unworthy is to the worthy the most bitter of all wrong" (11: 147). As is so well known to students of Poe, he lived his adult life feeling like a man of genius surrounded by dolts, boors, pretenders, toadies, sycophants. Indeed, such was largely the case, and these unworthies often did get undeserved praise while Poe, whose brilliance deserved so much better, struggled, if not in obscurity, certainly in poverty. There is, then, some psychological explanation – an *etiology* – behind much of Poe's critical mean-mindedness, but that is no new insight to anyone familiar with the Poe biographies.

To this point we have seen several rhetorical devices that Poe used to ridicule the unworthy writers whose productions came across his desk for review. While engendering intense hostility, he did not distinguish himself in his use of these emotive figures. He *does* use two other devices of vehemence in a way that is rather more witty, shrewd, inventive. The first, *anacoluthon*, involves ending a sentence with a different syntactic structure from that with which it commenced. When not used deliberately, it typically indicates heightened emotions (see the catalogue). In one of Poe's most mean-minded reviews, he uses *anacoluthon* deliberately – artificially, if you will – to express his frustration (a heightened emotion) at the Dickensian complexity of secret identities involving the many characters in the novel, *The Swiss Heiress*:

in rushes – Mr. Frederick Mortimer! – It will be seen that he has come back from Philadelphia. He assures the company that the Count Laniski, (that is to say Mr. Theodore Montelieu,) is not the Count Laniski at all, but only Mr. Theodore Montelieu; and moreover, that he himself (Mr. Frederick Mortimer) is not only Mr. Frederick Mortimer, but the bonâ fide Count Laniski into the bargain. And more than this, it is very clearly explained how Miss Laura Montargis is not by any means Miss Laura Montargis, but only the Baroness de Thionville, and how the Baroness de Thionville is the wife of the Baron de Thionville, and how, after all, the Baron De Thionville, is the Count Laniski, or else Mr. Frederick Mortimer, *or else – that is to say – how Mr. Frederick Mortimer is n't* [sic] *altogether the Count Laniski, but – but only the Baron de Thionville, or else the Baroness de Thionville – in short, how everybody concerned in the business is not precisely what he is, and is precisely what he is not.* (9: 190–1; my italics)

Poe might have simply said, "Theodore Montelieu is not the real Count
Laniski; rather, Frederick Mortimer is. He is also known as the Baron de
Thionville, husband of Miss Laura Montargis, who is in reality the baroness." Poe, however, is so disgusted with this labyrinthine plotting that
he uses the resources of language, *anacoluthon* as well as derisive repetition (near-*anadiplosis* – see the catalogue), to dwell on and ridicule the
novelist's strategy. The *anacoluthon* begins to figure near the end of the
excerpt with "or else – that is to say – ." This phrase is not needed and
actually interrupts, *disrupts*, the flow of the sentence; in this way Poe
manifests his exasperation and (pretended) confusion. His syntactical interruption is akin to our saying something like "– no, wait a minute – "
in the middle of a sentence when trying to explain something or tell a
joke or anecdote. We interrupt ourselves, destroy our train of thought,
halt, back up, start again. Poe completes his devastating ridicule with another *anacoluthon* after the final dash: the phrase "in short" summarizes
his point but also interrupts the syntactical flow and sends it off in another direction. It has the emotional impact of Poe saying, "in other
words, after all this rigmarole." We see how Poe takes a figure that is not
associated with satire and invests it with a satirical purpose. That is linguistically clever. It is mean, too, but it is clever.

Bathos, on the other hand, has an older history of deliberate use for
ridicule. Poe was surely aware of that master of deliberate *bathos*, Alexander Pope, and, I think, uses it just as capably. In his review of *The Sacred Mountains*, Poe shows his impatience with the Reverend Headley
for his audacity in presuming to know precisely what went on, in the
physical as well as metaphysical realms of the universe, when Christ was
crucified. The good reverend *does* claim not to know *one* thing:

"How Heaven regarded this disaster, and the Universe felt at the sight, I cannot
tell." Only think of that! *I* cannot! – *I*, Headley, really cannot tell how the Universe
"felt" once upon a time! This is downright bashfulness on the part of Mr. Headley.
He *could* tell if he would only try. Why did he not inquire? Had he demanded of
the Universe how it felt, can any one doubt that the answer would have been –
"Pretty well, I thank you, my dear Headley; how do you feel yourself?" (13: 208)

Poe clearly uses *bathos* derisively in taking us from the sublime ideas of
Christ's crucifixion and a traumatized cosmos to the idea of the universe

engaging in pleasantries with a pompous little reverend. Here is a splendid sample of how Poe, the "Tomahawk Man," uses language as a weapon.

Anyone wanting a demonstration of intensely and consistently used devices of vehemence in Poe's criticism – with foregrounded rhetorical questions – should peruse his stinging review of Griswold's *Poets and Poetry of America*, 3rd edition (11: 220–43). Of the four kinds of rhetorical questions (all of which can be used as emotive devices), perhaps *epiplexis* is the most devastating because it is used not to elicit information but to reproach, rebuke, upbraid. When such questions are accumulated, piled up, they shade off into *pysma* – asking many questions requiring diverse answers. Now, *pysma* does not necessarily have to be used to rebuke, but Poe certainly employs it this way with Griswold, and the device is not any less effective for appearing in written form rather than coming straight from the mouth of Poe during a physical confrontation. Here, Poe grills Griswold for his inclusion of certain poets, the prominence he gives them, and for his exclusion of others:

How comes it that C. Fenno Hoffman is the greatest poet in America, and that his articles figure more than two to one over Bryant, and ten to one over Lowell, Longfellow, &c.? Why were Edward Everett, LL.D., John Quincy Adams, Samuel Woodworth, (the insult might have been spared the dying poet,) Robert M. Bird, M.D., J.K. Mitchell, M.D., Sarah J. Hale, George P. Morris, Rev. William B. Tappan, Catharine H. Esling (or Miss Waterman, as she is better known), Horace Greeley, Seba Smith, Charles West Thompson, Rev. Charles W. Everest, Lieut. G.W. Patten, William Wallace (author of the Star Lyra, &c.), Mrs. Frances S. Osgood (one of our sweetest poetesses), James N. Barker, &c., &c., classed under the head of "various authors," thereby throwing openly the charge of their incompetency to sustain the name of Poets, and implying that they were only occasional scribblers?

Are there no such persons in existence as Anna Cora Mowatt, Lydia J. Pierson, Juliet H. Lewis, Mrs. Harriet Muzzy, Mrs. E.C. Stedman, &c? And if so, have they never written poetry? And if they have, why are they omitted? (241; see also 11: 37; 12: 225)

Sonnino, referring to the use of *pysma* in orations, notes that this device can be used "to underline emotions such as admiration, determination and indignation" (153), and Espy (202) quotes the sixteenth-century rhetor

Henry Peacham, who says that this device makes an oration "sharp and vehement": "Now thus many questions together, are as it were like unto a
courageous fighter, that doth lay strokes upon his enemy so thick and so
hard that he is not able to defend or bear half of them." Indeed, *pysma* can
be used as a wonderfully intimidating device. Some training in classical
rhetoric on Poe's part (see chapter 2) is strongly suggested here.

Two other types of questioning strategies add to the stinging rhetorical
barrage in this review of the Griswold edition. *Hypophora* occurs when
the questioner answers his or her own question. It shows contempt for
the person being addressed – that is, an impatience toward, a lack of interest in, whatever response might be forthcoming. We get two exemplifications in this particularly insulting passage:

Is writing Poetry the exclusive privilege of the *aristocracy* of our country? For we
are so led to imagine by finding no *poor* writers in this work. No! They are all
"descended from ancient and honored families," "the sons of wealthy members
of the Society of Friends," or of "eminent lawyers," or "wealthy merchants,"
"wealthy lawyers," themselves, &c., &c., *ad infinitum*. How comes this? It is
answered in a word. Mr. G. belongs to the class called "toady." (240)

In addition to the *bdelygma* ("toady"), further intensifying the rhetorical
assault is a device similar to *hypophora, subjectio* – the questioner suggests
the answer to his or her own question. I would emphasize the word *suggests*
to distinguish between *subjectio* and *hypophora* (this latter involving a definite assertion as a reply rather than a mere suggestion). *Subjectio*, though
implying more diffidence, can be just as insolent: "Why was Frederick W.
Thomas insulted with a place as the author of *one* song, among the miscellaneous writers, after his having been written to, and 'his biography and
best articles' solicited? Was it not because he did not obey your dictatorial
and impertinent request to write *for you* the biography of Mrs. Welby?"
(240). Poe stops short of making a direct charge, but a rhetorical question,
Corbett affirms, can be more effective than a direct assertion (454). Still,
who is really fooled? It really *is* a "disguised assertion," Bernard Dupriez
insists (370). We might consider Poe's use of rhetorical questions a rather
underhanded way of making assertions, charges, while appearing not to.
Poe's rhetorical underhandedness goes further, as we shall soon see.

While *pysma*, *hypophora*, and *subjectio* can certainly function as emotive devices, Lanham actually lists them as techniques of argument. They can clearly be both, so I shall use them as transitions, then, to this next section on argumentative figures. One of the most obnoxious and offensive of rhetorical devices is *paraleipsis* – pretending not to mention something while mentioning it. Dupriez calls this figure "eminently rhetorical" (353). Lanham, using the synonym *occultatio* (104), and Dupriez, like Arthur Quinn, using the synonym *preterition*, note that this device is a way of *emphasizing* whatever one is pretending to pass over. Quinn thinks this is a particularly nasty linguistic trick: "If I were to declare any figure inherently disreputable ... this would be the one" (71). There is a lack of honesty, a lack of forthrightness, about *paraleipsis*. Here is an instance: "It is needless to call to mind the desperate case of Fay – a case where the pertinacity of the effort to gull, where the obviousness of the attempt at forestalling a judgment, where the wofully over-done be-Mirrorment of that man-of-straw, together with the pitiable platitude of his production, proved a dose somewhat too potent for even the well-prepared stomach of the mob" (10: 186). It may be "needless to call to mind," but Poe not only calls to mind but *amplifies*. *Paraleipsis* appears again in Poe's review of *The Drama of Exile* (12: 23; also 13: 200–1): "Here, saying nothing of the affectation in 'adown;' not alluding to the insoluble paradox of 'far yet near;' not mentioning the inconsistent metaphor involved in the 'sowing of *fiery* echoes," and so on. In this case, amplification is not necessary; it is enough that Poe, by drawing attention to her linguistic foibles, has caused embarrassment to the poetess (after 1846 to be known as Elizabeth Barrett Browning).

Also involving irony and pretence is the device *apophasis* – pretending to deny what is really affirmed. Here Poe quotes Washington Irving – then comments: "'*We may have read poetry more artificially perfect in its structure, but never any more truly divine in its inspiration.*' The nature of inspiration is disputable, and we will not pretend to assert that Mr. Irving is in the wrong. His words, however, in their hyperbole, do wrong to his subject, and would be hyperbole still, if applied to the most exalted poets of all time" (10: 178). While denying it, Poe is clearly *at odds with* his notable contemporary author. Somewhat in between *apophasis* and *paraleipsis* is the following passage from Poe's review of *Poets and Poetry of*

America, 3rd edition: "As to the different degrees of merit allotted to each author [by Griswold], we cannot help thinking it possible, *but we will not say it* [my italics], that *sub rosa* arrangements were made, and a proportionable quantity of fame allotted, in consideration of the *quid pro quo* received" (11: 239–40). This is not exactly *paraleipsis* in that Poe is not pretending to pass over the subject; neither is it exactly *apophasis* in that Poe is not pretending to deny the charge of a conflict of interest on Griswold's part. Still, as with those two figures, Poe is giving us something other than plain dealing – a kind of *linguistic Machiavellianism*. He pretends to want to protect himself by not making the charge explicitly, but it is as good as made. Poe again uses this flimsy self-protective device in his review of *Wakondah*: "We only refrain, however, from declaring, flatly, that the line is not the property of Mr. Mathews, because we have not at hand the volume from which we believe it to be stolen" (11:31). The charge of plagiarism – one of so many that Poe made (aimed most often at poor Longfellow) – is virtually *made*, despite Poe's pretence at avoiding the indiscretion.

What Poe is doing, above, is also similar to another rhetorical figure, *amphidiorthosis* – hedging a charge made in anger by qualifying it either before the charge has been made or (sometimes repeating the charge in other words) after (Lanham, 8). Poe does *hedge*, to be sure. We find a clearer exemplification in Poe's impassioned article, "Achilles' Wrath," where he complains about his ill treatment at the hands of a theatre manager named Dinneford. In this case, Poe hedges the charge *after* he has made it, rather than before: "And the blatherskite ... has the audacity to find fault with us because we *dared* to express an unbiased opinion of his stupidity – *that is to say, of the stupidity of a play gotten up by himself, Mr. Dinneford*" (12: 137; my italics). By qualifying the word *stupidity* after using it, Poe is able to have it both ways: he can suggest that the play is stupid – and so is Dinneford. If pressed, he can always insist that he had in fact corrected himself and withdrawn the charge of stupidity aimed at his adversary (the *ad hominem* attack). In the mean time, he has the satisfaction, nevertheless, of having succeeded in making his opinion of Dinneford known (note also the *bdelygma*: "blatherskite"). As Poe uses the device, here, we see that it can have an underhanded quality about it. Still, he ends the piece with a rather more benign use of *amphidiorthosis* (138).

In the same article, and with the same rude theatre manager as target, Poe employs yet another, though less underhanded, rhetorical technique: *peristrophe* – putting an opponent's argument to one's own use, advantage. (I do not find this device in other rhetorical catalogues; probably *antistrephon* is provided as meaning the same thing; similar is *paromologia*). In his abusive letter, the theatre manager, Dinneford, describes himself as a "caterer for the public amusement" (12: 136). That was all Poe needed: "There is certainly not in New York, at the present moment, any other member of the theatrical profession, who either would have behaved with the gross discourtesy of this gentleman, or who, in inditing the preposterous letter published above, could have proved himself, personally, *so successful a 'caterer for the public amusement'*" (138–9). Poe turns his adversary's own self-description against him, suggesting that, yes indeed, the public has certainly been amused by his silly letter.

In using his adversary's own words against him, Poe has had to repeat them – but in doing so gives them a slightly different meaning. We have now slipped into the third category of rhetorical figures that Poe uses as linguistic weapons in his critical reviews: the devices of repetition. The exemplification, above, of *peristrophe* could also nearly do double duty as an instance of *antistasis*: the duplication of a word in a different or contrary sense. The device figures as part of Poe's satire in one of his nastier critical reviews (concentrate on the word *tried* near the end):

Next we have a preface ... in which ... the author tells us that poetry is a "very great bore, and won't sell" – a thing which cannot be denied in certain cases, but which Mr. Downing denies in his own. "It may be true," he says, "of endless masses of words that are poured forth from the press under the *name* of poetry; but it is not true of *genuine* poetry – of that which is worthy of the name"; in short, we presume he means to say it is not in the least little bit true of "Powhatan," with regard to whose merits he wishes to be tried, not by the critics (we fear, in fact, that here it is the critics who will be tried), "but by the *common* taste of *common* readers." (10: 164)

The first *tried* means *judged*; the second means *subjected to strain* – as of endurance, patience.

Poe's love of wordplay, of punning, is well known to Poe specialists (see chapter 4), and we see his linguistic sportiveness not only in his use

of *antistasis* and *peristrophe*, above, but also in his use of *antanaclasis*.
Lanham provides three distinct definitions: (1) punning *ploce*; (2) homonymic pun; (3) the use of one word in two senses, often contrasting,
usually for comedy. Here is a cruel exemplification: "He [George B.
Cheever] is much better known, however, as the editor of 'the Commonplace Book of American Poetry,' a work which has at least the merit of
not belying its title, and *is* exceedingly commonplace" (15: 32). Dupriez
has a great deal of information on the device (see his index) and provides
yet another definition: "The speaker takes up the words of the interlocutor, or of the adversary, and changes their meaning to the speaker's own
advantage" (43). He has just given us a definition of *peristrophe*, and we
see the extent to which rhetorical figures often overlap in meaning. It
probably did not matter to his victims whether Poe knew these terms because of a formal training in classical techniques of argumentation,
whether he mimicked them from well-established British critics, or
whether he simply had an *instinctive* sense of rhetorical war-play. What
did matter is the anger, the emotional devastation, that his mastery of
linguistic war-play caused many of them.

We have been seeing combinations of punning and repetition, sometimes involving the turning of an adversary's own words against that person. Consider the following example of a pun that Poe uses to deride an
author (poor Reverend Headley, again) who he feels is a quack guilty of
hoaxing the public with a particularly bad book: "He acts upon the principle that if a thing is worth doing at all it is worth doing well: – and the
thing that he 'does' especially well is the public" (13: 209). This time the
repetition is not precisely the same word but forms of it (*doing, does*). That
is the rhetorical figure *polyptoton*. I discuss the comedic value the device
displays in Poe's hands in chapter 4 ("puff, puffing and puffable"), and
how its use can have the effect of derisive *chanting*. Poe puts the device to
satirical use again in his review of *Powhatan*. He is disgusted that the poet,
in a preface, has expressed his desire to be judged by "the *common* taste of
common readers" rather than by the critics, so he seizes upon the word
common in the review's final paragraph and plays with it: "it will not do for
him to appeal from the critic to the *common* readers, because we assure
him that his book is a very *un*common book. We never saw any one so un-
commonly bad, nor one about whose parturition so uncommon a fuss has
been made, so little to the satisfaction of common sense" (10: 166).

Another device of repetition, not in itself typically used in a satirical fashion, is *polysyndeton* – the use of conjunctions (such as *and, or, nor*) in a series of words, phrases, or clauses. Yet again, the Reverend Headley is made the victim: "He explains to us precisely how it all took place – what Noah said, *and* thought, while the ark was building, *and* what the people, who saw him building the ark, said *and* thought about his undertaking such a work; *and* how the beasts, birds, *and* fishes looked, as they came in arm in arm; *and* what the dove did, *and* what the raven did not" (13: 204; my italics). The perceptive reader can readily see that the deliberately monotonous repetition of *and* can suggest several criticisms of Headley's style and/or subject: perhaps Poe's childlike iteration of *and* can be seen to hint at Headley's own puerile style; perhaps it is meant to convey Poe's impatience with the tedium of Headley's catalogues and his amplification of a subject that bores the reader. Perhaps Headley, being a reverend, mimics the tedious biblical repetition of *and*, so Poe is mocking, parodying, his stylistic imitation. Whatever the case, Poe clearly uses language consciously as a *weapon*.

Through a different device of redundancy, another authorial victim felt the pain of Poe's derisive linguistic weaponry in his review of *The Swiss Heiress*. *Epimone* is the rhetorical term for what is more widely known as the *leitmotif*. Lanham defines *epimone* as the "Frequent [choral] repetition of a phrase or question, in order to dwell on a point" (68). The refrain is a device that Poe uses quite often in his prose and poetry, and when it appears in his critical prose, it can be very hurtful. In his nasty review of *The Swiss Heiress*, which stimulated his critical ire even more than usual, he complains about the philosophical/theological discussions that occur too often in the novel – and he makes his displeasure manifest through the use of *epimone*:

she grows melancholy and interesting, patronizes the gipsies, curses the Count Laniski, talks about "fate, fore-knowledge, and free-will." (9: 187)
But, not having forgotten her old bad habits, she perists in talking about "fate, fore-knowledge, and free-will." (188)
and what better can be done than to talk, until Chapter the Fifteenth, about "fate, fore-knowledge, and free-will?" (188)
Now we have no doubt whatever they are discoursing of "fate, fore-knowledge, and free-will." (189)

Mr. Frederick Mortimer ... torments the poor fellow grievously, by grinning at him, and sighing at him, and folding his arms at him [note the derisive *epistrophe*, another device of repetition], and looking at him asquint, and talking him to death about "fate, and fore-knowledge and free-will." (190)

Miss Montargis is very angry and talks about the inexplicable ring, fate, foreknowledge and free-will. (190)

Then Poe ends his review with, "now, in the name of 'fate, foreknowledge and free-will,' we solemnly consign it [*The Swiss Heiress*] to the fire" (191). Poe also uses satirical *epimone* in the review of *Charles O'Malley* in the contemptuous repetition of the author's beloved phrase "devilled kidneys" (11: 92). The reappearance in a poem or novel of certain words and phrases that Poe found annoying he termed "mannerisms," and heaven help the author who evinced any mannerisms.

The final figure of repetition that I have found in Poe's critical reviews is not so much used tauntingly, as with the instances of scornful repetition we have seen, but it is hurtful nonetheless. *Epanalepsis* refers to the duplication at the end of a clause, verse, or sentence of the word or phrase with which it began. The exemplification I am about to provide depends for its effectiveness not so much on the *fact* of a linguistic repetition so much as on the punning twist Poe gives the words repeated (again, recall *antistasis*): "He [Lewis Gaylord Clark] is as smooth as oil or a sermon from Doctor Hawks; *he is noticeable for nothing* in the world except for the markedness by which *he is noticeable for nothing*" (15: 115; my italics). This snide passage appeared in *The Literati of New York City*. Obviously, Mr Godey was not completely able to control what Poe said "of the New York authors."

We have done with the three categories: vehemence, argument, and repetition (sometimes punning). To these I would like to add one more stylistic feature – not really a figure of rhetoric but a device that could very well be included in Lanham's category of amplification. A *continuator* consists of words and phrases that typically come after a catalogue (a list, an inventory) to complete it. Continuators add to the sense of copiousness (wordiness) created by a catalogue; they look back to the list and point ahead, continue it, though without specificity. *Neutral* continuators are words and phrases such as *etc.*, *and so on*, *and so forth*, *and the like*. Here is an example involving a list of names: "To this end we have received ... a variety of aid from the highest sources – Mrs. Sigourney, Miss Sedgwick, Paulding, Flint, Halleck, Cooper, Judge Hopkinson, Dew, Governor Cass, J.Q. Adams, *and many others*" (15: 37; my italics). A *satirical* continuator comprises words that continue a series without specificity but throw a *critical glance* back at it. In the following passage we have two lists, the first ending with a neutral continuator ("and the like"), the second with a satirical continuator: "While the oppositionists, for example, rejoice in the euphonious appellations of Aubrey, Delamere, *and the like*, their foes are called Quirk, Gammon, Snap, Bloodsuck, Rotgut, Silly-Punctilio, *and other more stupid and beastly in-decencies*" (10: 212; my italics). The continuator expands the formula by way of an often-unexpected classifying word or phrase (in this case, "more stupid and beastly indecencies") that throws a new light on the previous members of the list. Louis T. Milic some time ago drew attention to the catalogues and satirical continuators in the clever prose of Jonathan Swift, an author with whom Poe was apparently familiar. One wonders to what extent he may have picked up his habits of linguistic satire from that Irish master.

In his review of *The Swiss Heiress*, however, Poe uses continuators in what seems to be an innovative way. In one passage, they appear but *not* after a series; as well, he employs what normally are neutral continuators rather *satirically*. He clearly was frustrated with the novel – "The Swiss Heiress should be read by all who have nothing better to do" (9: 185) – and quotes: "The Montargis Castle where dwells the young heiress of the Baron de Rheinswald, is neither more nor less than the identical castle 'with the proud battlements' *et cetera*, that 'rises amid the pines and firs' *and so forth*, of the 'Swiss Mountains and the Lake of Geneva' *and all that*" (my italics). The phrases *and so forth*, *and all that*, and *et cetera*, coming where they do, suggest an impatience on Poe's part (cf Seinfeld's "yadda, yadda, yadda") with the prose and comprise a satire on his part directed probably at the novelist's use of clichés (what castle in literary romances *does not* display "proud battlements" or rise "amid the pines and firs"?). Leave it to the "Tomahawk Man" to find a way to turn what in any other writer's hands would be neutral continuators into satirical ones.

We should not suppose, from the avalanche of linguistic/rhetorical nasti-ness just quoted and the comments from Poe's contemporaries with which we began this chapter, that Poe engendered nothing but hostility for his caustic reviews. He became not only *infamous* but also *famous* for them – and he knew it. To gain attention for himself and the magazine for which he happened to be writing, he *made a point* of endeavouring "to kick up a dust," to use his own phrase (Ostrom, 119). By some literary people he was applauded for his critical talents, even by some of those whose works he had reviewed with something other than unqualified praise (to put it lightly). Some, such as Lydia Sigourney (in a letter of 11 June 1836), were high-minded about Poe's negativity regarding their productions. Mind you, her tone of conciliation came *after* he had written – at the request of publisher Thomas Willis White – some letters themselves in the conciliatory manner: "Yours of the 4th was this morning received," she replied, "and I hasten to assure you that your apprehension of having forfeited my good-will, is entirely groundless. – It is surely a hard case, if a critic may not express his opinions, freely, and even severely, in this land of freedom." To cherish vindictiveness, she goes on to say, "forms no part of my creed. There is surely, enough of controversy abroad in our land, without its few literati lifting up the tomahawk, and scalping-knife against each other" (17: 38; see also Jacobs, 105–9). Elizabeth Barrett wrote to R.H. Horne (12 May 1845) asking him to convey her gratitude to Poe for having gone to the trouble of reading her poems so closely for his review, even though his criticisms of them were often harsh (17: 387; also 209). In a letter of 12 September 1839, former editor and novelist James E. Heath manifested a spirit very much like Poe's when he wrote him the following words of encouragement:

The cultivation of such high intellectual powers as you possess cannot fail to earn for you a solid reputation in the literary world. In the department of criticism especially, I know few who can claim to be your superiors in this country. Your dissecting knife, if vigorously employed, would serve to rid us of much of that silly trash and silly *sentimentality* with which puerile and conceited authors, and gain-seeking book sellers are continually poisoning our intellectual food. (17: 48)[2]

Doubtless, praise like that, coupled with his own fearless integrity, encouraged Poe to envision the same critical tone in his projected Philadelphia magazine, *The Penn* (eventually to become the hoped-for *Stylus*). In the prospectus (1840), he wrote, "To those who remember the early days of the Southern periodical in question [*The Southern Literary Messenger*] it will be scarcely necessary to say that its main feature was a somewhat overdone causticity in its department of Critical Notices of new books. The Penn Magazine will retain this trait of severity in so much only as the calmest yet sternest sense of justice will permit" (17: 59).

When adverse criticism, because of *his* adverse criticism, came his way, Poe was capable of defending himself by citing the praise his critical courage had elicited. In his "Drake-Halleck Review" he testifies (again using the editorial first-person plural) that, "We have seen our efforts applauded by men whose applauses we value. From all quarters we have received abundant private as well as public testimonials in favor of our *Critical Notices*" (8: 278). While engaged in the so-called "Longfellow War," he informed his adversary, "Outis," that, while he was writing reviews for the *Messenger*, its subscription list jumped from 700 names to almost 5,000 in a single year, and that, while he was writing for *Graham's*, the list swelled from 5,000 to 52,000 subscribers in just over two years. (He made this boast over and over, and the figures often changed slightly from boast to boast – see also Ostrom, 205, 269, 440, and Jacobs, 72) Poe may be committing the fallacy of false cause, here, but he certainly implies that *his* critical acumen, even when most vicious, was responsible for the surge in popularity of both magazines. "I make no apology for these egotisms," he adds (12: 85).

Furthermore, Poe had a ready answer in the form of a fable that he used several times to introduce his critical credo. It typically came in the form of a digression within a review:

It was by no means my design, however, to expatiate upon the *merits* of what I should read you. These will necessarily speak for themselves. Boccalini, in his "Advertisements from Parnassus," tells us that Zoilus once presented Apollo a very caustic criticism upon a very admirable book: – whereupon the god asked him for the beauties of the work. He replied that he only busied himself about the errors. On hearing this, Apollo, handing him a sack of unwinnowed wheat, bade him pick out *all the chaff* for his reward.

Now this fable answers very well as a hit at the critics – but I am by no means sure that the god was in the right. I am by no means certain that the true limits of the critical duty are not grossly misunderstood. (14: 281; see also 11: 41 and 13: 194)

In other words, it is not the critic's primary duty to point out the merits of a work; they are sufficiently clear. Rather, the critic should point out – independently of friendship, literary cliques, the needs of booksellers, the opinions of other critics, and sectional or nationalistic prejudices – the *defects* of a work so that its author may improve his or her craft. Even so, Poe elsewhere insists that very few of his reviews were entirely negative (see 12: 86, for instance). His typical *modus operandi* is to balance his negative with positive remarks. The rhetorical term for this strategy of compensation is *antanagoge*: ameliorating a fault or difficulty admitted by balancing an unfavourable aspect with a favourable one. Here is but one of numerous examples: "Although Sir Walter Scott is authority for the use of the word in this manner, we have always considered it a decided inelegance. But such blemishes cannot seriously detract from the enduring excellence of the work" (8: 37).

Those who may feel less inclined to sympathize with the linguistic meanness that Poe manifests in his reviews should be reminded that to a very large extent he was part of his *Zeitgeist*. Robert L. Hough says that other reviewers, including Griswold, could be as nasty as Poe, and that a "magazine writer was expected to be witty and tough" (xi). As Parks puts it, "when one compares his criticism with that of some of his journalistic enemies ... Poe seems almost restrained. It was a period of cutthroat criticism, under the rules that might govern a street brawl rather than a duel" (92). Jacobs elaborates by telling us that several critics on both sides of the Atlantic had reputations similar to the one Poe finally attained. Most were British; the only Yankee infamous for his harshness was Robert Walsh of Philadelphia (*Poe: Journalist & Critic*, 65n8). As for the British, Jacobs suggests that Poe learned his "mordant humor" (76), his "tone of jocular contempt" (96), from reading the reviews in *Blackwood's Magazine*. For the twenty-five years before Poe began his tomahawking, the British quarterlies were savaging authors, not just the mediocre nobodies the likes of which so irritated Poe but many of them famous – Keats and Byron, for instance. Poe surely knew the names of the Old World tomahawk men: Sydney Smith, William Gifford, John Wilson (a.k.a. Christopher North), Francis Jeffrey, John Gibson Lockhart (the Scorpion). That he certainly *read* some of them is proved by various things he wrote (see, for instance, Ostrom, 77, for Jeffrey; the review of *Georgia Scenes* for Christopher North [8: 258]).

All of which raises the question: if it was not simply intuitive, to what extent did Poe learn his linguistic weaponry from his rhetorical education or from his British models of the school of critical cutting and slashing? If he *did* learn his verbal nastiness from the likes of Jeffrey, Wilson, et al., we can certainly admire his mimetic abilities. This chapter is not a source study, however, and regardless of *where* or *how* Poe learned his tomahawk style – I suspect it is *both* mimetic and a result of his rhetorical training – it is testimony to his linguistic *brilliance*. This devastating linguistic brilliance, however, not only hurt its victims directly but also *indirectly* hurt Poe's career and, even decades after his death, continued to hurt his reputation. One cannot cut and slash with impunity. Poe's wise friend, Beverley Tucker, commented on the British critics in a letter to him dated 5 December 1835, and warned Poe against tomahawking. After mentioning "the efficacy of a certain style of criticism in demolishing scribblers," he continues:

Jeffrey's nearest approach to it was in his review of Byron's first publication. I am old enough to remember that it provoked a reaction highly favourable to Byron. Nothing else could have given such triumphant success to the English Bards &c. As to Blackwood; I admire Wilson, but he is an offence unto me by the brutal arrogance of his style of criticism. I have no doubt he demolished the poor Tailor. But "who breaks a butterfly upon the wheel?" Supported by the powerful party whose organ he is, he may never feel that he injures himself by such thing; but he does. (17: 23).

Harrison quotes a long letter (27 August 1840) pertaining to "Poe's pungency in criticism" from his friend, Chivers, in which the good doctor gently chastises Poe for laying aside "the pruning-knife for the tomahawk." Using an extended metaphor, Chivers complains that Poe not only lops off unnecessary limbs but also eradicates the entire tree so that it no longer bears any fruit whatsoever. Who knows how many struggling, mediocre authors might have improved their art and flourished in the end had they had encouraging advice rather than devastating criticism, he wonders. A little pruning can be a good thing. He then changes the metaphor slightly but retains the *cutting* imagery: "In surgical operations we always use a sharp knife, and wish to be as expeditious as possible; but we never go so far as to cut away so much of a part as to endanger the vitality of the whole" (1: 190). As Harrison concludes, it would have been wise had Poe taken Chivers' advice to heart – not to mention Tucker's. Both had the best interests of their friend in mind. Poe continued, however, to "fight the good fight" with every linguistic weapon at his command, making Montresors out of authors and editors throughout the eastern seaboard. At *length* they would be avenged.

Catalogue of Rhetorical and Other Literary Terms in Poe's Works

What I wrote it is unnecessary to say. The *style!* – that was the thing.
"The Literary Life of Thingum Bob, Esq.," 6: 27

This discovery ... was left to Edgar A. Poe, who has spent more time in analyzing the construction of our language than any living grammarian, critic, or essayist.
Review of Griswold's *The Poets and Poetry of America*, 11: 229

Most of the 300 terms here are figures of speech and thought – rhetorical devices – such as are found in other catalogues (especially Lanham, Espy, Taylor, Joseph, Sonnino, Quinn, and Dupriez) but I also include certain logical fallacies to show that although Poe could identify errors in argumentation he is occasionally guilty of such himself. The terms are explored here with definitions, exemplifications, and in many cases mini-essays that serve several functions: to offer my own insights on Poe's techniques as a writer; to consider how his styles relate to his themes and characteristic concerns; to inspire further explorations and insights on the part of Poe scholars; to summarize some of the best observations made by others who have examined him as stylist; to uncover some of his own ideas and rules about writing; and, finally, to defend Poe as a deliberate, conscientious, verbal craftsman. Occasionally, where I do *not* provide an exemplification for a term from Poe's prose or poetry, I include the device either to show that Poe has identified it in another writer or to provide Poe's own thoughts on it. Sometimes I provide more than one exemplification of a device – usually to illustrate that it figures in more than one type of literature in which Poe engaged – fiction, literary criticism, personal correspondence, poetry (and in this light, see appendix 1). Some of the exemplifications also appear as part of the chapters; I repeat this material deliberately in the catalogue to prevent the need for cross-referencing.

Following other rhetors (for example, Corbett and Lanham), I provide each term in boldface but in Roman rather than italic lettering; subsequently, within each entry the names of the classical tropes and schemes are italicized according to the conventional treatment of most foreign words and phrases. Often the specific exemplifications within quoted passages are also in boldface for clarity, unless the entire passage is itself the exemplification. The only other scholar I know of who has compiled a rhetorical catalogue devoted to a single author is Sister Miriam Joseph in *Shakespeare's Use of the Arts of Language*. There she divides the terms according to types rather than alphabetically, as I do. I chose this organizational scheme largely for the sake of simplicity and convention; furthermore, some terms fall into several categories at once, which would necessitate either their frequent repetition, had I followed Joseph's strategy, or numerous cross-references. Anyone interested in how the terms fall into and overlap the various categories should consult "The Terms by Type." That approach is particularly helpful when one wants to uncover significant *patterns* in Poe's prose. I believe that I have found some and hope other scholars will discern more.

Finally, it may be asked why I chose some terms and not others for inclusion in this catalogue. If I had expanded my parameters, certainly I could have provided a much larger list – something approaching in length such far more comprehensive works as Dupriez's *Dictionary of Literary Devices*, Cuddon's *Dictionary of Literary Terms and Literary Theory*, or Harmon/Holman's *Handbook to Literature*. For the most part, however, I restricted my search to the figures of speech and thought, the tropes and schemes, found in the rhetorical catalogues – the main design of this book being, after all, to suggest Poe's linguistic and suasive dexterity through either formal or informal rhetorical training.

I cannot pretend to have found examples of *all* the classical figures; doubtless, I missed some, perhaps many. With those I caught, I take certain liberties occasionally in categorizing them. While I follow, for the most part, Lanham's typology, here and there I depart from him: sometimes I add a figure to a category when that figure is not typically considered a proper member there – for instance, I consider all the devices of repetition potentially devices of vehemence as well, so I include them in both categories. As well, to Lanham's fourteen groupings I add three more: "biblical" devices; those that Poe uses for humour ("comedic"); and those he employed for the sake of verisimilitude ("verisimilar"). Despite quibbles about classification, it is my hope that all future students of Poe's writing, especially his prose, will use this catalogue as a *starting point* in their stylistic investigations of his *oeuvre*, and that current scholars will find it stimulating.

ACCUMULATIO: heaping up of praise or accusation; name-calling (Cluett/Kampeas, 17; Lanham, 1); "a figure wherein a rhetor gathers scattered points and lists them together" (Crowley, 333). Both eulogistic (praising) and dyslogistic (condemning) *accumulatio* appear in Poe's literary criticism, the former more likely in his reviews of female writers, the latter in his reviews of male writers. His southern chivalric attitude towards women is displayed particularly in his review of *The Dream, and Other Poems*, by a Mrs Norton (see especially 10: 102–3). It is well known that Poe's critical harshness, on the other hand, earned for him the title of "Tomahawk man," but he could "bury the hatchet" when reviewing the artistic talents and achievements of women:

> As an actress she [Madame Malibran] scarcely ever had an equal, yet her great success arose from the apparent absence of acting. She seemed borne away, and, in a great degree, was so, by an intense enthusiasm. The powerful impression she produced arose from a conviction of her extreme sensibility. It is beyond the reach of art to imbue either air or recitative with more impassioned *expression* than was hers. Her utterance of the romance in "Otello" – the tone with which she occasionally gave the words *Sul mio sasso* in the Capuletti – we may defy any one to forget who ever had the exquisite pleasure of hearing them. (10: 93–4)

Dupriez devotes several pages to a consideration of *accumulatio* (9–12) but he defines it differently from other rhetors cited above. For terms corresponding to his definition, see below under "seriation" and *homoioteleuton*.

Pronunciation: ac cu mu LA ti o
Type: amplification
Type: devices of vehemence

ACRYLOGIA: the use of an inexact or illogical word:

> "Oh, goodness, gracious! – what *is* this world coming to? *Oh, tempora! Oh, Moses!*" ("X-ing a Paragrab," 6: 230)

The proper saying, of course, is "*O tempora! O mores!*": "Oh, the times! Oh, the customs!" – which Poe provides correctly (in the Latin) in his review of *The Poets and Poetry of America* (11: 237). Clearly, *acrylogia* has comedic potential and is part of Poe's linguistic humour. A more well-known term for it is *malapropism* (Poe refers to Mrs Malaprop in "Prospects of the Drama – Mrs Mowatt's Comedy," 12: 125). For more on this subject, see chapter 4.

Pronunciation: a cy ro LO gi a
Type: ungrammatical, illogical, or unusual uses of language

A D H O R T A T I O : exhorting our hearers or readers to do something presumably for their benefit. Some rhetors, such as Lanham and Taylor, refuse to distinguish between *adhortatio* and *protrope*. Espy distinguishes insofar as he separates the two and provides slightly different definitions. I would suggest that we consider *protrope* an exhortation accompanied by threats and/or promises, and *adhortatio* an exhortation accompanied by good reasons short of threats or promises (see also *diatyposis*):

> "If you wish to write forcibly, Miss Zenobia, pay minute attention to the sen-
> sations." ("How to Write a Blackwood Article," 2: 274)

What is delicious about this piece of advice is that, through it, Poe is mocking not only the sensational tales popularized in *Blackwood* maga-zine but also one of his own techniques. Readers of Poe's Gothic tales know how often he relies on the minute description of mental and physical sensations: he employs all types of imagery (see under that term). Perhaps the most intense sensation tale is "The Pit and the Pen-dulum" (a tale, after all, about physical and mental torment), but Poe makes fun of the reporting of sensations in the companion piece to "How to Write a Blackwood Article" – "A Predicament: The Scythe of Time." That he is capable of parodying his own literary tricks (see Joseph R. McElrath's "Poe's Conscious Prose Technique") is one answer to those critics who consider Poe a sloppy writer; he was instead a care-ful, conscientious, self-conscious literary technician. On this point, see also *soraismus*. We may not be surprised to find *adhortatio* figuring in Poe's critical reviews:

> In general it may be boldly asserted that the clapping of hands and the
> rattling of canes are no tokens of the *success* of any play – such success as
> the dramatist should desire: – let him watch the *countenances* of his audi-
> ence, and remodel his points by these. Better still – let him "look into his
> own heart and write" – again better still (if he have the capacity) let him
> work out his purposes *à priori* from the infallible principles of a Natural
> Art. ("Prospects of the Drama – Mrs. Mowatt's Comedy," 12: 126; see also
> 11: 122)

Adhortatio also shows up in Poe's correspondence. In a letter of 4 January 1848, he advises someone about Margaret Fuller:

> she is an ill-tempered and very inconsistent old maid – **avoid her.** (Ostrom, 355)

Pronunciation: ad hor TA ti o
Type: devices of vehemence
Type: techniques of argument
Type: "biblical"

ADIANOETA: "An expression that has an obvious meaning and an unsuspected secret one beneath" (Lanham, 2):

> "Enough," he said; "the cough is a mere nothing; it will not kill me. I shall not die of a cough."
> "**True – true**," I replied. ("The Cask of Amontillado," 6: 170)

It is indeed true that the intended victim, Fortunato, will not die of a cough, as Montresor suggests, for he has planned another fate for Fortunato: he will wall him up alive, to die eventually by fear, or starvation, or suffocation, or dehydration, deep within the vaults of the Montresor catacombs. Montresor's concession, "True – true," is Poe's way of winking at the reader, who suspects that the unsuspecting Fortunato will certainly not die *of a cough*.

Pronunciation: a di a no E ta
Type: metaphorical substitutions and puns

ADYNATA: exaggeration that involves the magnification of an event by reference to the impossible (Dupriez, 18); sometimes, a confession that words fail us (Lanham, 3). This device figures often enough in Poe's tales of the fantastic; although Poe claimed to be able to express *any* thought verbally, it is not unusual for a Poe narrator to be unable to express some apects of his incredible experiences. They are *ineffable*:

> The night was as dark as it could possibly be, and the horrible shrieking din and confusion which surrounded us **it is useless to attempt describing**. (*The Narrative of Arthur Gordon Pym of Nantucket*, 3: 99)
> Of a sudden, and all at once, there came wafted over the ocean from the strange vessel (which was now close upon us) a smell, a stench, **such as the whole world has no name for – no conception of – hellish – utterly suffocating – insufferable, inconceivable**. (111)
> **I am at a loss to give a distinct idea of the nature of this liquid.** (186)

The device figures four times in "Ligeia," too, and five times in "The Fall of the House of Usher." Poe's use of *adynata* is part of his hyperbolic style, one that many scholars abhor. He is, indeed, the king of superlatives, of exaggeration (see also *hyperbole*).

Adynata is related to more than simply the exaggeration of Poe's overwrought narrators, however; he also relates it to epistemology – how we know what we know about ultimate truths of the universe, natural and supernatural, physical and metaphysical. Poe felt that people are only open to absolute insights during the fleeting state between waking and sleeping. While Poe had great faith in the power of human language to express thoughts, it is not adequate to convey those "psychal impressions" of the hypnagogic state:

> How very commonly we hear it remarked, that such and such thoughts are beyond the compass of words! I do not believe that any thought, properly so called, is out of the reach of language … For my own part, I have never had a thought which I could not set down in words, with even more distinctness than that with which I conceived it …
>
> There is, however, a class of fancies, of exquisite delicacy, which are not thoughts, and to which, *as yet*, I have found it absolutely impossible to adapt language … They arise in the soul (alas, how rarely!) only at its epochs of most intense tranquility – when the bodily and mental health are in perfection – and at those mere points of time where the confines of the waking world blend with those of the world of dreams. I am aware of these "fancies" only when I am upon the very brink of sleep, with the consciousness that I am so …
>
> These "fancies" [are] of a character supernal to the Human Nature – [they are] a glimpse of the spirit's outer world. (Marginalia, 16: 88–9)

If we can take him at his word, then, Poe himself claimed to be able to express any mere *thought* (as distinct from "psychal impressions") through words, but his own narrators often confess an *inability* to convey verbally *some* thoughts related to their own extraordinary experiences. This discrepancy between Poe's linguistic facility and that of his narrators suggests the objective *distance* that Poe keeps in relation to them. That is to say, the issue of *adynata* helps support Gargano's assertion – with which I agree fully, as does Stauffer – that the stylistic excesses sometimes found in Poe's works cannot be blamed on Poe (as they often are) but are the responsibility of his narrators, who therefore speak their own thoughts (or cannot, as the case may be): "Poe's narrators possess a character and consciousness distinct from those of their creator" (Gargano, "The Question of Poe's Narrators," 165).

It is interesting to note that Poe even wrote a poem on the subject of *adynata*. It begins with a reference to the statements quoted above from the Marginalia:

Not long ago, the writer of these lines,
In the mad pride of intellectuality,
Maintained "the power of words" – denied that ever
A thought arose within the human brain
Beyond the utterance of the human tongue:
And now, as if in mockery of that boast,
Two words – two foreign soft dissyllables ...
Have stirred from out the abysses of his heart,
Unthought-like thoughts that are the souls of thought,
Richer, far wilder, far diviner visions
Than even the seraph harper, Israfel ...
Could hope to utter. And I! my spells are broken.
The pen falls powerless from my shivering hand. ("To – – ," 7: 106)

If we continue to believe Poe's claim that he could express any thought in words – and I, for one, insist on believing it still – then we surely recognize the romantic *hyperbole*, the "mere rhetoric," in the above lines, as we must also in the following from an impassioned epistolary plea to Poe's Aunt Maria Clemm:

I cannot express in words the fervent devotion I feel towards my dear little cousin – my own darling [Virginia]. (Ostrom, 69; see also 399)

Pronunciation: a DY na ta
Type: devices of vehemence
Type: techniques of argument

AETIOLOGIA (*etiologia*; etiology): giving a reason or cause for having said or done something, or for saying or doing something, or for wanting to do something. In "The Literary Life of Thingum Bob, Esq.," Thingum relates how he broke the news to his father that he did not want to follow his father's trade of merchant-barber:

"Father," I said, "pardon me! – but I have a soul above lather. It is my firm intention to cut the shop. I would be an editor – I would be a poet – I would pen stanzas to the 'Oil of Bob'." (6: 2–3)

Cf *dicaeologia, proecthesis, praeparatio,* and *praemunitio.* Sonnino (145) considers *aetiologia* synonymous with *praeparatio* – preparing an audience, readers, or interlocutors before telling them of something done. The following example of *aetiologia*, however, does not seem to fit the definition of *praeparatio*:

> I made the night tempestuous, first, to account for the Raven's seeking admission, and secondly, for the effect of contrast with the (physical) serenity within the chamber. ("The Philosophy of Composition," 14: 205)

"The Philosophy of Composition," Poe's explanation of how he wrote "The Raven," is an *extended* instance of *aetiologia* (that some scholars do not credit Poe's explanation is irrelevant to the application of this label). Pronunciation: ae ti o LO gi a

Type: amplification

Type: techniques of argument

ALLEGORIA (allegory): a rhetorical trope – "a narrative in which the agents and action, and sometimes the setting as well, are contrived so as to make coherent sense on the 'literal,' or primary, level of signification, and also to signify a second, correlated order of agents, concepts, and events" (Abrams, 4); an extended analogy, a continued metaphor (cf parable). There are two kinds of allegory: (a) the *allegory of ideas* in which one concrete thing represents an abstraction, an idea; (b) for want of a better name, we can call the other kind the *allegory of things* – one concrete thing represents itself as well as another concrete thing.

The allegorical dimension of some of Hawthorne's tales was too obvious to Poe, who wrote in a review of *Twice-Told Tales*, "In defense of allegory, (however, or for whatever object, employed,) there is scarcely one respectable word to be said" (13: 148). In his review of *Undine: A Miniature Romance*, Poe says, "Although, in this case, the plan is essentially distinct from Allegory, yet it has too close an affinity to that most indefensible species of writing – a species whose gross demerits we cannot now pause to examine" (10: 37). Essentially, Poe disliked tales in which the allegory was too clear, too obvious. He insisted that one should have to dig for the suggested meaning; it should not lie on the surface of the tale: "Where the suggested meaning runs through the obvious one in a *very* profound under-current so as never to interfere with the upper one without our own volition, so as never to show itself unless *called* to the surface, there only, for the proper uses of fictitious narrative, is it [allegory] available at all" (see also 12: 174). Perhaps this is what

Dupriez means when he says that, in allegory, "the tenor [the thing being suggested] may be suppressed" (21). That Poe himself did write allegories is pretty much universally accepted among Poe scholars. In "The
Masque of the Red Death," as well, Poe gives us both an allegory of ideas
and one of things. On the level of abstractions,

  (vehicle) the Phantom = the plague (tenor),
  (vehicle) Prospero = Everyman (tenor);
on the level of things,
  (vehicle) the Phantom = hour hand (tenor),
  (vehicle) Prospero = minute hand (tenor),
  (vehicle) the abbey = half of a clock's face (tenor).

Dupriez says "Allegory is a feature of the 'sublime' or 'high style' of expression" (23). For extended considerations of the device, see Lanham
(4–6) and Abrams (4–7). For an extended consideration of the use of *allegoria* in "The Masque of the Red Death," see chapter 3. In a letter to
Griswold, Poe mentions his poem "The Haunted Palace," by which he
means "to imply a mind haunted by phantoms – a disordered brain,"
then admits to the poem's "allegorical conduct" (Ostrom, 161). Finally,
let us not forget that in the concluding stanzas of "The Raven" Poe, by
his own admission, converts the bird "into an allegorical emblem of personification [sic] of Mournful Remembrance" (12: 75).
Type: metaphorical substitutions and puns

ALLEOTHETA (*allotheta*; *alloeosis*): the substitution of one gender,
number, case, mood, or tense for another. This is a type of *enallage* (see
below). Obviously, *alleotheta* can indicate a vice, an error; otherwise, we
may wonder why anyone would deliberately make such a substitution.
In the following example, Poe substitutes genders – clearly as an insult:

  Mr. A — is frequently spoken of as "one of our most industrious writers;"
  and, in fact, when we consider how much he has written, we perceive, at
  once, that he *must* have been industrious, or he could never (like an honest
  woman as he is) have so thoroughly succeeded in keeping himself from being
  "talked about." ("Fifty Suggestions," 14: 181)
Pronunciation: al le o THE ta
Type: addition, subtraction, and substitution: words, phrases, and clauses
Type: ungrammatical, illogical, or unusual uses of language

ALLITERATION: repetition of initial or middle consonants in nearby or adjacent words. The following example also employs *consonance*, a kind of reverse alliteration that involves the repetition of terminal consonants in nearby words:

> Then a rushing revival of soul and a successful effort to move. And now a full memory of the trial, of the judges, of the sable draperies, of the sentence, of the sickness, of the swoon. ("The Pit and the Pendulum," 5: 70)

The many *s* sounds here anticipate the *hiss* of the murderously sharp pendulum that the prisoner of the Spanish Inquisition is soon to encounter. Like Melville, Poe is known among his readers and scholarly devotees as a writer who had a good ear for the auditory qualities of prose. In this context, see also *onomatopoeia* and *assonance*. For Poe's own definition and discussion of alliteration, see "The Rationale of Verse" (14: 228–9). He did believe that one could do too much with this device, however: in his review of *The Coming of the Mammoth*, Poe quotes a stanza ending with the line "Dark was the desolate desert before us, but darker the depth of our shame," then comments: "Here the alliteration is too obvious – quite overdone, – and is an instance of the hyperism to which we alluded in the beginning of our notice" (12: 179).

We encounter alliteration now and then in Poe's critical reviews, not just in his prose fiction and poetry:

> The silliest thing of this kind ever penned, perhaps, was an elaborate attack of his on Thomas Babington Macaulay, published in "The Democratic Review;" – the force of folly could no farther go. (*The Literati of New York City*, Charles F. Briggs, 15: 22)

Pronunciation: al lit er A tion

Type: repetition: sounds

AMPHIBOLOGIA (*amphibology* or *amphiboly*): intended or accidental ambiguity arising from an ambivalence of grammatical structure, sometimes by mispunctuation, vague pronoun reference, or dangling modifiers (see the hilarious examples in Espy [48]). This term appears not only in rhetorical catalogues but also in inventories of logical fallacies – for instance, *Introduction to Logic* (151), by Cohen and Copi. As well, Engel, in *With Good Reason: An Introduction to Informal Fallacies*, has several pages discussing *amphiboly*, with several very funny exemplifications (82–5). Harmon and Holman suggest that, in literature, *"amphibology* is usually intentional when it occurs" (18), and they offer as a well-known example Fedallah's ambiguous assurances to Ahab in Melville's *Moby-Dick*. In his literary criticism, Poe occasionally complains about instances of *amphibologia*. He quotes some pasages from *The Swiss Heiress*:

> The Baron de Rheinswald is a "Catholic of high repute" who "early in life marries a lady of great wealth, a member of his own church, actuated by ambition" – that is to say, there was either something or somebody "actuated by ambition," but we shall *not* say whether it was a lady or a church. (9: 185; see also 9: 11–12; 262; 13: 140)

The ambiguity, as Poe rightly figures, arises in the order of the clauses. A clearer syntactical arrangement would be this: "The Baron, a Catholic of high repute, early in life marries a member of his own church, a lady of great wealth, who is actuated by ambition." Or the sentence might end with, "a wealthy lady actuated by ambition." Poe came under attack by some of his contemporaries for his close attention to matters of grammar in his role as book reviewer: Griswold said Poe was *"little better than a carping grammarian"* (*Recognition*, 35). Elsewhere Poe calls attention to faulty punctuation:

> Again, at page 59, Vol. I., – "Women, who are very foolish, are apt to be very cruel." In this equivocal sentence, Mr. S., no doubt, intended to assert that very foolish women are apt to be very cruel. His words, as they stand, however, convey a really serious charge of stupidity against the gentle sex at large. (Review of *The Damsel of Darien*, 10: 55)

Quite right: the problem lies with the incorrect placement of both commas when no commas are required: "Women who are very foolish are apt to be very cruel." We do *not* want commas around the restrictive clause "who are very foolish" (see also 12: 151). Elsewhere, after correcting the faulty punctuation of a poetess (especially commas and semicolons), Poe says, "These seeming *minutiæ* are of real importance" (Review of *The Poetical Writings of Elizabeth Oakes Smith*, 13: 83). Finally, Poe draws our attention to some faulty pronoun reference in his review of *Life of Petrarch*:

> What are we to make of such phraseology as this, occurring in the very second sentence of the work? "It was known that the Rev. Archdeacon Coxe had bequeathed to the Library of the British Museum a Ms. 'Life of the Poet'

which *he* had written" [Poe's italics]. Here "*he*" implies the poet, but is intended to imply the Archdeacon. Such misconstructions are abundant.
(10: 205; see also 8: 184; 10: 211; 11: 37, 218)

Here is how Poe scoffs at Henry B. Hirst's bad grammar: "My quarrel with him is *not*, in short, that he *did* this thing, but that he *has went and done did it*" (13: 213).

Pronunciation: am phi bo LO gi a

Type: ungrammatical, illogical, or unusual uses of language

AMPHIDIORTHOSIS: "To hedge a charge made in anger by qualifying it either before the charge has been made or (sometimes repeating the charge in other words) after" (Lanham, 8). In Poe's "Mystification," Baron Von Jung has just offered opinions on the subject of duels, opinions that he knows will offend the expert on the subject, Johan Hermann. Hermann is angered but wary of expressing this anger too vehemently to the Baron, his host. He qualifies his charge at the outset:

"Your opinions, allow me to say, Baron Von Jung, **although in the main correct**, are, in many nice points, discreditable to yourself and to the university of which you are a member. In a few respects they are even unworthy of serious refutation. I would say more than this, sir, were it not for the fear of giving you offense (here the speaker smiled blandly,) I would say, sir, that your opinions are not the opinions to be expected from a gentleman." (4: 107)

For another instance (a rather nasty one), see chapter 5.

Pronunciation: am phi di or THO sis

Type: devices of vehemence

Type: techniques of argument

AMPLIFICATIO (amplification): the expansion, elaboration, extension, of an idea, a sentence. Dupriez defines the term as "The grandiloquent development of ideas so as to make them more richly ornamented, broader in scope, or more forceful" (32; see also Lanham, 8–9 and Harmon/Holman, 19). I cannot pretend to like the derogatory definition of amplification supplied by Crowley: "the ancient art of saying a great deal about very little" (333). In the following passage, Poe's narrator is breaking open coffins in a vault and has just come across an obese corpse; he soliloquizes about the difficulties the man must have had moving around:

"this has been, no doubt … an unfortunate man. It has been his terrible lot
not to walk, but to waddle – to pass through life not like a human being, but
like an elephant – not like a man, but like a rhinoceros.

"His attempts at getting on have been mere abortions, and his circumgyra-
tory proceedings a palpable failure. Taking a step forward, it has been his
misfortune to take two towards the right, and three towards the left. His
studies have been confined to the poetry of Crabbe [i.e., sideways walking].
He can have had no idea of the wonder of a *pirouette*. To him a *pas de papil-
lon* has been an abstract conception." ("Loss of Breath," 2: 161–2)

Amplification can involve, for instance, *divisio*, apposition, lists (seriation), the heaping up of *exempla* (examples) or authorities (quotations),
or the repetition of ideas or statements in different words (*accumulatio,
commoratio, cohortatio, disjunctio*, the pleonastic doublet, *tautologia, exergasia, periergia, epexegesis*). Obviously, it is the opposite of any devices involving brevity. For other rhetorical devices that involve amplification,
see those listed on pages 183–4 of Lanham's *Handlist*; as well, see his catalogue of devices involving the repetition of ideas (190–1).

Under the heading of "other definitions," Dupriez offers the following:
Classical rhetoricians applied the term to the treatment of the whole discourse.
Amplification to them implied the art of finding the best arguments and of ex-
ploiting them in accordance with a logical and persuasive plan, preferably based
on their mounting intensity. Such a process of reasoning demanded description, comparison, examples, a discussion of motives, pathetic elements, reminiscences, quotations elicited from prominent citizens or from poets,
explanation, and justification. In short, discursive amplification would employ
an accumulation of arguments, of facts, or of sentences or synonyms. (33)

Pronunciation: am pli fi CA ti o

ANACOENOSIS: see under *communicatio*.
Pronunciation: an a coe NO sis

ANACOLUTHON: ending a sentence with a different syntactic structure from that with which it began:
This, then, was the smile which had cheered us on to hope! this the – **but I
forbear.** (*The Narrative of Arthur Gordon Pym of Nantucket*, 3: 113)

Anacoluthon is a device of vehemence, of heightened emotions. Pym is
reporting with bitter despair the shocking discovery that the apparent

smile of a friendly sailor seen from a distance is that not of Pym's rescuers but of a skeletal corpse on a death ship. Even in relating the event years later, Pym is overcome with emotion and cannot bring himself to finish the sentence the way he intended. Here is an instance of *anacoluthon* from Poe's reply to Thomas Dunn English and others who had attacked him publicly in print:

> Much is he to be pitied for his countenance (that of a fat sheep in a reverie) – for his *Providential* escapes – for the unwavering conjugal chivalry which, in a public theatre – **but I pause.** Not even in taking vengeance on a Fuller can I stoop to become a Fuller myself. (17: 252–3)

For a satirical or parodic use of the device, see chapter 5.

Pronunciation: an a co LU thon

Type: devices of vehemence

Type: ungrammatical, illogical, or unusual uses of language

ANADIPLOSIS: this is *not* the name of one of Poe's romantic interests ("Anna Diplosis") but refers to the repetition of the last word or words of one line or clause at the beginning of the next:

> Yes, he had been trying to comfort himself with these suppositions: but he had found **all in vain.** *All in vain.* ("The Tell-Tale Heart," 5: 91)

Since, like other devices of repetition, *anadiplosis* can express emotion, we see how the repetitiousness here emphasizes the narrator's mounting frenzy, a frenzy quite at odds with the calmness with which he had promised to tell the story. *Anadiplosis* and near-*anadiplosis* seem to have another function in "The Conversation of Eiros and Charmion," for this time it enables the statements of one of these angelic beings to dovetail into those of the other – perhaps suggesting a linguistic and emotional harmony impossible to any other than metaphysical beings in Aidenn, the interstellar, ethereal region:

Charmion

Let us converse of familiar things, in the old familiar language of the world which has so **fearfully** perished.

Eiros

Most **fearfully,** fearfully! – this is indeed no **dream.**

Charmion

Dreams are no more. Was I much **mourned,** my Eiros?

Eiros

Mourned, Charmion? – oh deeply. To that **last hour** of all, there hung a
cloud of intense gloom and devout sorrow over your household.

Charmion

And that **last hour** – speak of it. Remember that, beyond the naked fact of
the catastrophe itself, I know nothing. When, coming out from among mankind, I passed into Night through the Grave – at that period, if I remember
aright, the **calamity** which overwhelmed you was utterly **unanticipated**. But,
indeed, I knew little of the speculative philosophy of the day.

Eiros

The individual **calamity** was, as you say, entirely **unanticipated**. (4: 2–3)

That the repetitive nature of angelic dialogue is not accidental on Poe's
part is shown by the opening lines of another supernatural conversation:

Una. "**Born again?**"

Monos. Yes, fairest and best-beloved Una, "**born again**." These were the
words upon whose mystical meaning I had so long pondered, rejecting the
explanations of the priesthood, until **Death** himself resolved for me the secret.

Una. **Death!**

Monos. How strangely, sweet Una, you echo my words! ("The Colloquy
of Monos and Una," 4: 200)

The near-*anadiplosis* is less noticeable in the third angelic dialogue, but is
present:

Oinos. – I clearly perceive that the infinity of matter is no **dream**.

Agathos. – There are no **dreams** in Aidenn – but it is here whispered that,
of this infinity of matter, the sole purpose is to afford infinite springs. ("The
Power of Words," 6: 140)

Repetition is easily one of the foregrounded features of Poe's prose and
he uses all the devices of verbal duplication listed by Lanham (see below
for the various terms; and see Stauffer's "The Language and Style of the
Prose"). They can be figures of vehemence but can function in other
ways as well. Stauffer says, "Repetition, like the use of certain rhythmic
patterns, gives [Poe's] style an incantatory quality" ("Style and Meaning," 321). McElrath holds that Poe's prose sometimes embodies "a controlled repetition of words that appeal directly to the reader's audial and
visual senses" (40). Forrest also considers the devices of repetition that
Poe and the Bible have in common: despite Poe's love of stylistic brevity,
"outside the Bible it would be hard to find one who used the repetend

[sic] more than he" (96). For a comedic use of the device, see chapter 4; for a satirical use, see chapter 5.

Pronunciation: an a di PLO sis

Type: repetition: words, phrases, clauses

ANALOGY: reasoning or arguing from cases that are alike in certain important respects, often when a less familiar object or idea is explained by comparing it to a more familiar object or idea. In the following example, however, the reverse is true, as Poe uses a rather esoteric idea to explain a simpler one:

> "Vidocq, for example, was a good guesser, and a persevering man. But, without educated thought, he erred continually by the very intensity of his investigations. He impaired his vision by holding the object too close. He might see, perhaps, one or two points with unusual clearness, but in so doing he, necessarily, lost sight of the matter as a whole. Thus there is such a thing as being too profound. Truth is not always in a well. In fact, as regards the more important knowledge, I do believe that she is invariably superficial … **The modes and sources of this kind of error are well typified in the contemplation of the heavenly bodies. To look at a star by glances – to view it in a side-long way, by turning toward it the exterior portions of the *retina* (more susceptible of feeble impressions of light than the interior), is to behold the star distinctly – is to have the best appreciation of its lustre – a lustre which grows dim just in proportion as we turn our vision *fully* upon it. A greater number of rays actually fall upon the eye in the latter case, but, in the former, there is the more refined capacity for comprehension. By undue profundity we perplex and enfeeble thought; and it is possible to make even Venus herself** [the brightest object in the sky after the moon and sun] **vanish from the firmament by a scrutiny too sustained, too concentrated, or too direct."** ("The Murders in the Rue Morgue," 4: 166)

Poe's detective, Dupin, shows himself to have a mind of a poet – "I have been guilty of certain doggerel myself" ("The Purloined Letter," 6: 34) – for his frequent use of analogies shows his ability to see connections, correspondences, similarities between various things. Likewise, Dupin demonstrates his scientific mind; specifically, his knowledge of astronomy is also evident in the analogy he uses: he is describing what astronomers call "averted vision" (the analogy – Poe's favourite – also appears in "Letter to B – " [7: xxxix], his review of *The American in England* [8: 215], and *Eureka* [16: 190]). This idea – that it is possible to miss seeing the truth by examining something too closely – is one that Poe critics have too often neglected in their interpretations of his work.

The idea of analogy also figures in "Ligeia" when the narrator admits to his inability to express the nebulous sentiment, the vague idea, he feels when scrutinizing the mysterious expression in Ligeia's eyes. In other words, here is another instance of *adynata* (see above), and he uses the idea of analogy to deal with this *adynata*: "I found, in the commonest objects of the universe, a circle of analogies to that expression" (2: 252). Considering the objects he goes on to name, we can guess that the analogous phenomena he lists suggest the idea of changeability, eclipse, transcendence, transformation – metempsychosis (the theme of the tale).

In one place Poe states that "The analogies of Nature are universal" (review of *Poetical Remains of the Late Lucretia Maria Davidson*, 10: 222), and this view was very much a part of his epistemology. The concept of analogy is important in "Mellonta Tauta" as a practical guide for everything from politics to cosmology. After sneering at the predominant Western ways of discovering Truth – Aristotelian logic (the epistemology of the medieval and Renaissance scholastic philosophers) and Baconian empiricism – the futuristic narrator offers intuition (imagination) and analogy in their place. As for cosmology, he complains about certain astronomical theories concerning the structure of the universe because "analogy was suddenly let fall" (6: 210; see *Eureka*, below). As for politics, condemning the "ancient" (nineteenth-century) unnatural and erroneous political philosophies of America, he speaks in disparaging terms of the democratic Mob that "taught mankind a lesson which to this day it is in no danger of forgetting: never to run directly contrary to the natural analogies. As for Republicanism, no analogy could be found for it upon the face of the earth – unless we except the case of 'prairie dogs,' an exception which seems to demonstrate, if anything, that democracy is a very admirable form of government – for dogs" (209). A similar condemnation of this "unnatural" form of politics figures as well in "The Colloquy of Monos and Una": after insisting that only the imagination could discover Truth through analogy, Monos informs Una that, on earth before the cataclysm, the idea "of universal equality gained ground; and in the face of analogy and of God – in despite of the loud warning voice of the laws of gradation so visibly pervading all things in Earth and Heaven – wild attempts at an omni-prevalent Democracy were made" (4: 203). The aristocratic-minded Poe seems, then, to have believed in something like the medieval and Renaissance notion of the Great Chain of Being, a system of metaphysical and physical forms ranging from God at the top (the *ens perfectissimum*) through the various orders of angels and archangels, through to *humanum genus* in the middle, with its secular and ecclesiastical heads, down through the animal and plant kingdoms, ending with nothingness at the bottom of the Chain. Just as the natural and metaphysical worlds are based on the idea of gradation, so, by analogy, should be the human socio-political world. Poe also uses "Some Words with a Mummy" as a vehicle to attack democracy and the "usurping tyrant" to which it gives rise: Mob (6: 136 [cf Tocqueville's concept of the "tyranny of the majority"]) – or what he often refers to in his critical reviews as "the rabble."

Anyone who has managed successfully to wade through *Eureka* knows how important the concept of analogy is to that work. Poe provides ideas that were to reappear in "Mellonta Tauta" (1849) and uses analogy to argue his ideas about the structure of the universe at the level of galactic clusters:

And now we have reached a point at which the intellect is forced, again, to struggle against its propensity for analogical inference – against its monomaniac grasping at the infinite. Moons have been seen *revolving* about planets; planets about stars; and the poetical instinct of humanity – its instinct of the symmetrical ... which the Soul, not only of Man but of all created beings, took up, in the beginning, from the *geometrical* basis of the Universal radiation – impels us to the fancy of an endless extension of this system of *cycles*. Closing our eyes equally to *de*duction and *in*duction, we insist upon imagining a *revolution* of all the orbs of the Galaxy about some gigantic globe which we take to be the central pivot of the whole. Each cluster in the great cluster of clusters is imagined, of course, to be similarly supplied and constructed; while, that the "analogy" may be wanting at no point, we go on to conceive these clusters themselves, again, as *revolving* about some still more august sphere; – this latter, still again, *with* its encircling clusters, as but one of a yet more magnificent series of agglomerations, *gyrating* about yet another orb central *to them* – some orb still more unspeakably sublime – some orb, let us rather say, of infinite sublimity endlessly multiplied by the infinitely sublime. Such are the conditions, continued in perpetuity, which the voice of what some people term "analogy" calls upon the Fancy to depict and the Reason to contemplate, if possible, without becoming dissatisfied with the picture. (16: 292–3)

Later Poe mentions the theory that our galaxy's supposed central orb cannot be seen because of its nonluminosity, a theory he desires to refute because "analogy is suddenly let fall" (295). An alternative theory – that the Milky Way has at its core not a gigantic orb but an immaterial centre of gravity – is equally unattractive because, again, "analogy is let fall" (296). Several pages later, Poe employs analogy to predict the destiny of the cosmos: "Of the still more awful Future a not irrational analogy may guide us in framing an hypothesis" (307).

That some of the central ideas of *Eureka* (1848) had occurred to Poe years before is shown in his review of Macaulay's *Critical and Miscellaneous Essays* (1841), where he employs analogy to argue the soul's immortality on the basis of Laplace's nebular hypothesis:

> That we know no more to-day of the nature of Deity, of its purposes – and thus of man himself – than we did even a dozen years ago, is a proposition disgracefully absurd; and of this any astronomer could assure Mr. Macaulay. Indeed, to our own mind, the *only* irrefutable argument in support of the soul's immortality – or, rather, the only conclusive proof of man's alternate dissolution and rejuvenescence *ad infinitum* – is to be found in analogies deduced from the modern established theory of the nebular cosmogony. (10: 160)

Poe then provides an explanatory footnote: "This cosmogony *demonstrates* that all existing bodies in the universe are formed of a nebular matter, a rare ethereal medium, pervading space; shows the mode and laws of formation, and *proves* that all things are in a perpetual state of progress; that nothing in nature is *perfected*." Next, Poe at least admits that analogical evidence cannot be considered direct, empirical proof, and I doubt that any logician or empiricist would be impressed by Poe's insistence on analogy as an epistemology. We may also question its usefulness more generally in argumentation. Dupriez says this: "distrust of the argument by analogy appears in the adage 'Analogic is not logic.' And yet, in certain cases there is nothing more expressive or convincing than a comparison" (380).

We do not very often hear Poe's views on "the women question," but even when we do, he insists on arguing by analogy. Writing of Margaret Fuller's *Woman in the Nineteenth Century*, he says,

> The conclusions reached are only in part my own ... in their attainment too many premises have been distorted and too many analogical inferences left

altogether out of sight. I mean to say that the intention of the Deity as re-
gards sexual differences – an intention which can be distinctly compre-
hended only by throwing the exterior (more sensitive) portions of the mental
retina *casually* over the wide field of universal *analogy* [averted vision again!]
– I mean to say that this *intention* has not been sufficiently considered.
(*The Literati of New York City,* 15: 74–5)
Type: metaphorical substitutions and puns
Type: techniques of argument

ANAMNESIS: recalling matters of the past – ideas, events, persons:
> Time was when we imported our critical decisions from the mother country.
> For many years we enacted a perfect farce of subserviency to the *dicta* of
> Great Britain. At last a revulsion of feeling, with self-disgust, necessarily en-
> sued. Urged by these, we plunged into the opposite extreme. In throwing
> *totally* off that "authority," whose voice had so long been so sacred, we even
> surpassed, and by much, our original folly. But the watchword now was, "A
> national literature!" ... We became, suddenly, the merest and maddest *parti-
> zans* in letters. (11: 1–2)

Often matters recalled are of woes or injuries:
> The thousand injuries of Fortunato I had borne as I best could, but when he
> ventured upon insult I vowed revenge. ("The Cask of Amontillado," 6: 167)

All of Poe's tales of homicide are, obviously, extended examples of *anamnesis*.
Pronunciation: an am NE sis
Type: devices of vehemence
Type: example, allusion, and citation of authority

ANAPHORA: repetition of the same word or group of words at the
beginning of successive clauses or verses, usually in a parallel series:
> **I knew that** the fit was over. **I knew that** the crisis of my disorder had long
> passed. **I knew that** I had now fully recovered the use of my visual faculties.
> ("The Premature Burial," 5: 270)

The intensive use of *anaphora* is called *epanaphora* (see below). Corbett
maintains that "This scheme is usually reserved for those passages where
the author wants to produce a strong emotional effect" (438). Stauffer
maintains that *anaphora* is typically part of what he terms Poe's "parabolic style" ("The Language and Style of the Prose," 459).

Pronunciation: a NA pho ra
Type: repetition: words, phrases, and clauses
Type: devices of vehemence

ANEMOGRAPHIA: a type of *enargia* (see below) – description of the
wind:

> It was blowing almost a gale, and the weather was very cold – it being late in
> October ... The wind, as I said before, blew freshly from the south-west.
> (*The Narrative of Arthur Gordon Pym of Nantucket*, 3: 7)

Pronunciation: a ne mo GRA phi a
Type: description

ANOICONOMETON: badly arranged words. In his review of *The
Conquest of Florida*, Poe is not at his best. He not only provides mostly
plot summary rather than penetrating literary observations but he also
gives his readership this difficult-to-read passage:

> Hence, although the imagination is not dazzled in the conquest of Florida,
> with descriptions of boundless wealth and regal magnificence – although
> the chiefs are not decked in "barbaric pearls and gold" – their sturdy resis-
> tance, and the varied vicissitudes created by the obstacles which nature pre-
> sented to the conqueror's march, afford numberless details of great interest.
> (8: 39)

What begins the confusion is the second comma that Poe inserts; we
might think it should be omitted – and he often placed commas where
they do not belong (at least by *our* standards of usage). Then, adding to
the difficulty of the passage is the parenthetical clause "although the
chiefs are not decked in 'barbaric pearls and gold'," and the following
pronoun "their" should actually refer to something *before* the inserted
clause, I would think. We might rewrite it omitting the second comma
and replacing the dashes with commas. The excerpt's very left-branching
structure increases its unreadability.

Neither Taylor nor Sonnino provides exemplifications of this device
from the ancients; it is not even mentioned by Dupriez. Lanham's example is from Kingsley Amis (12). Taylor (69) and Lanham both quote
Sherry's definition: "when there is no good disposicion of the woordes,
but all are confused up and down and set without order." I would not

say the excerpt from Poe is *that* bad; we might look to quotations from schizophrenic patients in the throes of the active phase of that disease for sad instances of *anoiconometon* (see note 5, chapter 1). The device compares with *hyperbaton* and *synchisis* (*synchysis*; *confusio*), confused word order in a sentence, sometimes by parenthetical additions. Poets, clearly, may fall into this stylistic vice in their attempts to maintain metre or rhyme – see Dupriez's comments on *synchisis* (445).

As a literary critic, Poe often caught the grammatical blunders of the authors whose works he was reviewing. While commenting on William Gilmore Simms' novel *The Partisan*, Poe complains that "Mr. Simms' English is bad – shockingly bad"; the language is "exceedingly confused, ill-arranged, and ungrammatical" (8: 152). He offers a few examples:

> "He was under the guidance of an elderly, drinking sort of person – one of the fat, beefy class, whose worship of the belly-god has given an unhappy distension to that ambitious, though most erring member." By the 'most erring member' Mr. S. means to say *the belly* – but the sentence implies the *belly-god* ... "That need not surprise you, Miss Walton; you remember that ours are British soldiers' – smiling, and with a bow was the response of the Colonel." We have no great difficulty here in *guessing* what Mr. Simms wishes to say – his actual words convey no meaning whatever. (153)

In his review of *Night and Morning*, Poe complains – without using the phrase – of Bulwer's dangling participles, which we might also consider *anoiconometon* (10: 127). Even Poe *nods* in this regard, now and then:

> Earthquake ... is of opinion that the Indians have been murdering some emigrant family. **While deliberating**, a light is discovered on the Illinois bank of the river. (Review of *Elkswatawa*, 9: 117)

The participle *deliberating* is meant to be coupled with the proper name *Earthquake*, but it would seem to go with *a light*, the first noun after the participle.

Pronunciation: a noi co no ME ton

Type: ungrammatical, illogical, or unusual uses of language

ANTANACLASIS: Lanham provides three distinct definitions: (1) punning *ploce*; (2) homonymic pun; (3) the use of one word in two senses, often contrasting, usually for comedy. It is obviously a type of pun (see below). Here is an exemplification (a nasty one) that Poe uses in more than one place:

He is much better known, however, as the editor of "the **Commonplace**
Book of American Poetry," a work which has at least the merit of not belying
its title, and *is* exceedingly **commonplace**. (*The Literati of New York City*,
George B. Cheever, 15: 32)

See chapter 4 for more on Poe's love of punning. Lanham (110) and Taylor (69) compare *antanaclasis* with *paronomasia*, punning on the sounds
and meanings of words that sound similar but not, as with *antanaclasis*,
precisely the same. Dupriez has a great deal of information on the device
(see his index) and provides yet another definition: "The speaker takes
up the words of the interlocutor, or of the adversary, and changes their
meaning to the speaker's own advantage" (43). In this sense, *antanaclasis*
compares with *antistrephon* (below) and *peristrophe* (below).

Pronunciation: an ta NA cla sis
Type: metaphorical substitutions and puns
Type: repetition: words

ANTANOGOGE: ameliorating a fault or difficulty admitted by balancing an unfavourable aspect with a favourable one. Although Poe (the
"Tomahawk man") was notorious in his day as a scathing literary critic
and reviewer, frequently in his reviews when he does provide a negative
comment, he balances it with a positive one:

> The censures of her book, are doubtless, in the main, well deserved; but in
> their excess, the merits which the "Journal" unquestionably possesses in great
> abundance and of a high order, have in many cases been passed by unheeded
> by her indignant critics. (Review of Frances Anne Butler's *Journal*, 8: 24; see
> also 37; 9: 192–3)

Poe's review of *The Drama of Exile* is an *extended* exemplification of
antanagoge (12: 1–35). This device can be compared to two others, *antisagoge* and *compensatio*, which involve a weighing, a balancing, a compen-
satory antithesis. See also Dupriez on *compensatio* (105–6).

One wonders what the opposite of *antanagoge* is – providing a *negative* comment after praise. Poe does this in his reviews as well:

> Of the numerous personages who figure in the book, some are really excellent
> – some horrible. (Review of *The Partisan*, 8: 149)

Pronunciation: an ta na GO ge
Type: balance, antithesis, and paradox
Type: techniques of argument

ANTHIMERIA: a type of *enallage* (see below) involving the exchange of one part of speech for another. Quinn feels that *anthimeria* is the "most important type of *enallage*," and that "the most important parts of speech are the most commonly substituted for" (50). In his comments on the poetry of William Ellery Channing, Poe criticizes this feature:

> The affectations – the Tennysonisms of Mr. Channing – pervade his book at all points, and are not easily particularized. He employs, for example, the word "delight" for "delighted;" as at page 2:
>
> > Delight to trace the mountain-brook's descent.
>
> (Review of *Our Amateur Poets*, No. III, 11: 181)

It is interesting that Poe considers Channing's use of *anthimeria* a deliberate affectation rather than an error.
Pronunciation: an thi MER i a
Type: addition, subtraction, and substitutions: words, phrases, and clauses
Type: ungrammatical, illogical, or unusual uses of language

ANTICATEGORIA: "Mutual accusation or recrimination" (Lanham, 13). Whereas *categoria* (see below) involves a charge of wickedness from one person to another (one accuser, one accused), *anticategoria* involves charge and countercharge; the people involved are both accusers and accused. I take the following exemplification from the notorious Poe-English correspondence. Thomas Dunn English had accused Poe among other things of being a coward. Here is Poe's reply:

> I shall not think it necessary to maintain that I am *no* "coward." On a point such as this a man should speak only through the acts, moral and physical, of his whole private life and his whole public career. But it is a matter of common observation that your *real* coward never fails to make it a primary point to accuse all his enemies of cowardice. (17: 243)

Pronunciation: an ti ca te GO ri a
Type: balance
Type: devices of vehemence

ANTIMETABOLE: see under *chiasmos*.
Pronunciation: an ti me TA bo le
Type: balance
Type: repetition

ANTIPHRASIS (adjective: antiphrastic): the use of a single word ironically – 180 degrees opposite to one's real meaning:

> "Oh, yes! – Oh, we perceive! Oh, no doubt! The editor over the way is a **ge-nius** – O, my!" ("X-ing a Paragrab," 6: 230)

The context from which this quote is taken makes it clear that the writer of these words has nothing but contempt for the "editor over the way," however, so the term *genius* is clearly ironic. Those Poe scholars who have read his critical reviews know he is capable of cruel and brutal invective and they may not be surprised to find *antiphrasis* figuring there as part of that tone and strategy. We have but to look into one of his angriest reviews, that of Griswold's *The Poets and Poetry of America*, for exemplifications (11: 223–4; see chapter 5).

Extended *antiphrasis* is called *sarcasm* or *irony*, although not all rhetors make the distinction. For a more detailed discussion of this trope, see Dupriez (49–50).

Pronunciation: an TI phra sis
Type: balance, antithesis, paradox
Type: devices of vehemence

ANTIRRHESIS: rejecting an argument or opinion because of its error, wickedness, or insignificance (cf *apodioxis*):

> True! – nervous – very, very dreadfully nervous I had been and am; but why *will* you say that I am mad? The disease had sharpened my senses – not destroyed – not dulled them. Above all was the sense of hearing acute. I heard all things in the heaven and in the earth. I heard many things in hell. How, then, am I mad? ("The Tell-Tale Heart," 5: 88)

Here the clearly insane narrator in Poe's tale rejects as erroneous the argument that he is mad. *Antirrhesis* is only one of several rhetorical devices, stances, adopted by Poe's homicidal criminals but used by him with conscious ironic intent (see below).

Stauffer, in "The Language and Style of the Prose," suggests that emotionalism characterizes Poe's "arabesque" tales – and he is quite right, of course – but that it is for the most part lacking in his critical prose. While this *may* be true as a tendency, it is nevertheless fairly easy to find examples of devices of vehemence in Poe's criticism. Here is only one of many instances of *antirrhesis*:

The ordinary talk about "continuous and sustained effort" is pure twaddle
and nothing more. Perseverance is one thing and genius is another, – whatever Buffon or Hogarth may assert to the contrary. (Review of *Night and
Morning*, 10: 122)

Pronunciation: an tir RHE sis

Type: devices of vehemence

Type: techniques of argument

ANTISAGOGE: assuring a reward to those who possess a virtue and/
or a punishment to those who hold it in contempt or lack it. In Poe's
drama review, he says this of a young actress with whom he was quite
smitten:

> In taking leave of Mrs. Mowatt for the present, we have only again to record
> our opinion that, if she be true to herself, she is destined to attain a very high
> threatrical rank. (12: 211)

Sometimes rhetors provide a second definition – "Stating first one side
of a proposition, then the other, with equal vigor" (Lanham, 15) – but
this would seem to be a definition of *antanagoge* (see above).

Pronunciation: an ti sa GO ge

Type: balance

Type: techniques of argument

ANTISTASIS: repetition of a word in a different or contrary sense:

> I made no doubt that I could readily displace the bricks at this point, insert
> the corpse, and **wall** the whole up as before, so that no eye could detect any-
> thing suspicious.
>
> And in this calculation I was not deceived. By means of a crow-bar I easily
> dislodged the bricks, and, having carefully deposited the body against the in-
> ner **wall**, I propped it in that position. ("The Black Cat," 5: 153)

Here *wall* is used both as a verb and as a noun; as such, it functions as a
kind of pun (see under "pun"). For more on this device, see chapter 5
and compare with Poe's punning on *doing* and *does* in his review of *The
Sacred Mountains* (13: 209).

Pronunciation: an TI sta sis

Type: repetition: words

Type: metaphorical substitutions and puns

ANTISTOECON (also *antisthecon*): the substitution of one letter or sound for another within a word – a fancy name for a spelling mistake. We may well ask, as Quinn does at length (*Figures of Speech*, 23–5), why a writer would deliberately misspell a word. Certainly *antistoecon* can be used to reproduce dialect more accurately (cf *barbarismus*) or to suggest the ignorance of uneducated characters:

> "*Wery* well," replied Bob, "here goes it!" and off he hurried to his case; mut-
> tering as he went – "Considdeble vell, them ere expressions, perticcler for a
> man as doese n't swar." ("X-ing a Paragrab," 6: 235)

The device also has a comedic function, although it is a rather crude at-
tempt at humour. For more on this subject, see chapter 4.
Pronunciation: an ti STO e con
Type: addition, subtraction, and substitution: letters and syllables

ANTISTREPHON: arguing such that you turn your opponent's arguments or proofs to your own advantage – a very clever rhetorical strategy
indeed. In an editorial reply to his critics – specifically the editor of the
Newbern *Spectator* – who complained about Poe's "literary hypercriti-
cism" (8: 335), Poe demonstrates what a shrewd rhetorician he could be:

> The paper is in error – we refer it to any decent school-boy in Newbern – in
> relation to the only sentence in our Magazine upon which it has thought
> proper to comment specifically, viz. the sentence above (by Lieutenant
> Slidell) … The *Spectator* says, "We would ask if it never entered into the
> critic's mind [Poe's] that 'slouched hat' and 'embroidered jacket' are here used
> as generic terms? Lieutenant Slidell evidently intended that they should be so
> received; but that he entertained the same intention respecting 'horsemen,'
> the whole context disproves." **We reply, (and the Spectator should imagine
> us smiling as we reply) that it is precisely because "slouched hat" and "em-
> broidered jacket" *are* used as generic terms, while the word "horsemen" *is
> not*, that we have been induced to wish the sentence amended.** (8: 337)

Poe does it again in his very mean review of *Powhatan*:

> The leading fault of "Powhatan," then, is precisely what its author supposes to
> be its principal merit. "It would be difficult," he says … "to find a poem that
> embodies more truly the spirit of history, or indeed that follows out more
> faithfully many of its details." **It would indeed; and we are very sorry to say
> it** … But he gets them all in, every one of them – the facts we mean. Powhatan
> never did anything in his life, we are sure, that Mr. Downing has not given in

his poem. He begins at the beginning, and goes on steadily to the end, painting away at his story, just as a sign-painter at a sign; beginning at the left-hand side of his board, and plastering through to the right. (10: 165)

And we know that *antistrephon* is about to appear in Poe's review of Hugh A. Pue's *A Grammar of the English Language* when Poe says, "We are only taking the liberty of condemning Mr. P. by the words of his own mouth" (10: 169). We also find him using the device against John Stuart Mill in *Eureka* (16: 194). Cf *paromologia* and *peristrope.*

Pronunciation: an TI stre phon

Type: techniques of argument

A N T I S T R O P H E : rhetors usually define this term as the repetition of a word or words at the end of successive lines of verse or clauses, but then there would be no difference between *antistrophe* and *epistrophe* (below). However, Lanham (16) and Taylor (72), on the authority of the Elizabethan rhetor George Puttenham, provide the definition of *antistrophe* that I prefer – medial repetition:

"Bête!" **said the** first.

"Fool!" **said the** second.

"Dolt!" **said the** third.

"Ass!" **said the** fourth.

"Ninny!" **said the** fifth.

"Noodle!" **said the** sixth.

"Be off!" **said the** seventh. ("Lionizing," 2: 41)

Clearly the device helps to ensure parallel syntactic structure, *isocolon* (see below).

Pronunciation: an TI stro phe

Type: repetition: words

A N T I T H E S I S : joining contrasting ideas:

In the glare of noon – at the dead hour of night – in sickness or in health – in calm or in tempest – the young Metzengerstein seemed riveted to the saddle of that colossal horse, whose intractable audacities so well accorded with his own spirit. ("Metzengerstein," 2: 193–4)

Quinn suggests (*Figures of Speech*, 67) that *antithesis* involves denying the contrary of something, then asserting it: Such-and-such is not A, but B. However, this very narrow definition is not insisted on by other rhetors as the only definition of the device (see also *syncrisis*). Poe shows his awareness of antithesis as an aspect of style when he mentions "antitheses" in a discussion of Macaulay's style ("About Critics and Criticism," 13: 195).

Pronunciation: an TI the sis

Type: balance, antithesis, paradox

ANTITHETICAL DOUBLET: a word-pair or short phrase-pair of opposed terms, usually coordinated by conjunctions such as *and* or *or* (cf pleonastic, range, and simple doublets):

> Mimes, in the form of God on high,
>> Mutter and mumble low,
> And **hither and thither** fly –
>> Mere puppets they, who **come and go**
> At bidding of vast formless things
>> That shift the scenery **to and fro**,
> Flapping from out their Condor wings
>> Invisible Wo! ("Ligeia," 2: 256)

Type: balance, antithesis, paradox

ANTITHETICAL PARALLELISM: see *syncrisis.*

ANTONOMASIA (adjective: antonomastic): a trope that involves the substitution of an epithet, a descriptive word or phrase, for a proper name or any common noun – or vice versa:

> I suggest the idea, nevertheless, because of a certain species of austere **Merry-Andrewism** which seemed to beset my poor friend, and caused him to make quite a **Tom-Fool** of himself. ("Never Bet the Devil Your Head," 4: 220)

The noun *Merry-Andrewism* is a substitute for *buffoonery,* and the proper name *Tom Fool* stands in for *fool, clown,* or *buffoon.* Dupriez calls *antonomasia* "a stylistic embellishment" (52), and Crowley says this: "The rhetorical effects of this trope are obvious. It not only suggests that someone is so well known that her name need not be used, thus cementing group loyalty [see *her* examples]; it also provides a rhetor with an opportunity to characterize the person spoken of or written about in either positive or negative terms" (215). Clearly, Poe's narrator uses "Merry-Andrewism" and "Tom-Fool" negatively to characterize his friend Toby Dammit as a silly ass. The device figures often in "Four Beasts in One; The Homo-Cameleopard," in which Antiochus Epiphanes, King of Syria, is also called "Prince of Poets," "Glory of the East," "Delight of the Universe," and "most Remarkable of Cameleopards" (2: 211; see also 5: 40, "Lothario"; 11: 148, "Homers" and "Jeremy Benthams"). Perhaps his favourite *antonomasia* is the word *Zoilus* to stand in for *critic* (see, for instance, 15: 227).

Poe liked to coin new words, as his use of *antonomasia* suggests (see 12: 218 for "Boswellism"); these new words are often based on the titles of books he reviewed negatively. In his review of *Life on the Lakes*, he mentions "Paul Ulricism" (9: 77); in his comments on *The Drama of Exile*, he gives us "Nat-Leeism" (12: 23; see 169, as well). Now and then, however, Poe stays with conventional instances of *antonomasia*, as in his letter of 4 June 1842, where he refers to Baltimore as "the Monumental City" (Ostrom, 201).

See also Holman/Harmon (33) and Baldick (13). Rhetors compare this figure of speech with *synecdoche* and *metonomy* (for both, see below).
Pronunciation: an to no MA si a
Type: metaphorical substitutions and puns

APHAERESIS (*aphoresis*): a type of *metaplasm*, the omission of a syllable or letter from the beginning of a word:
> "great pity, [u]pon my honor! – wonderfully inventive age!" ("The Man that was Used Up: A Tale of the Late Bugaboo and Kickapoo Campaign," 3: 268)

Of course, perhaps the most frequently occurring instance of *aphaeresis* in poetry is ' *T is*, and it surely appears in Poe's verse:
> "'T is some visiter," I muttered, "tapping at my chamber door –
> Only this and nothing more." ("The Raven," 7: 94)

The device figures several times in "The Raven." Still, in his review of *The Drama of Exile*, Poe complains about the frequency of *aphaeresis* there:
> What can be well said in defence of the unnecessary nonsense of "'ware" for "aware" – of "'bide," for "abide" – of "'gin," for "begins" – of "'las" for "alas" …? That there is *authority* for the mere words proves nothing; those who employed them in their day would not employ them if writing *now*.
> (12: 19–20)

This attack on the fallacy known as the "appeal to tradition" may remind us of the debate about archaic language in Castiglione's *The Book of the*

Courtier. We see here, as we see elsewhere fairly often, Poe's willingness to use stylistic features that he condemns in the productions of other writers. He would no doubt ingeniously defend his own use of said features and roundly abuse me for my impertinence in committing the fallacy of *tu quoque* – charging him with advocating a position not consistent with his own practice (hypocrisy).

Pronunciation: a PHAE re sis

Type: addition, subtraction, and substitution: letters and syllables

APHELIA: plainness in writing or speech. The so-called "plain" style supposedly refers to prose that is unadorned (lacking in poetic and oratorical devices), to relatively short sentences without or with very little expansion, pleonasm, or amplification. We might also expect to find a lot of *parataxis* – phrases or independent clauses set one after the other without subordination and often without coordinating conjunctions (such as *and, but, or*); as well, we might find a lot of *asyndeton* – a scheme of omission involving unlinked independent clauses side by side without subordination or interlinking conjunctions. Certainly we can find some *asyndeton* and *parataxis* in "The Tell-Tale Heart":

> A shriek had been heard by a neighbour during the night; suspicion of foul play had been aroused; information had been lodged at the police office. (5: 93).

Here is another paratactic piece from "The Premature Burial":

> She presented all the ordinary appearances of death. The face assumed the usual pinched and sunken outline. The lips were of the usual marble pallor. The eyes were lustreless. There was no warmth. Pulsation had ceased. (5: 257)

Note that paratactic sentences are also linear (they depend on the normal word order of subject-verb-object). The "plain" style might also display a predominantly right-branching sentence structure – namely, one that begins with a main (independent) followed by at least one dependent clause. This type of sentence, also referred to as "loose" or "unsuspended," is complete grammatically well before the end; the material that follows in the dependent clause(s) seems incidental. The following quote from "The Tell-Tale Heart" exemplifies this type of syntax:

> I knew what the old man felt; and pitied him, although I chuckled at heart. (5: 90)

Of course, it is possible for sentences to be short but left-branching and hypotactic, or short but full of ornamental figures, so the features of the "plain style" are not necessarily found together at all times. Nevertheless, the passages I have provided above do demonstrate both shortness in sentence length *and* a lack of poetic or rhetorical adornment, illustrating *aphelia* very nicely. Critics who condemn Poe for his overwrought "style" should take the above into consideration (see chapter 1). As well, they should read his *Literati of New York City*, which exemplifies almost consistently and at length a relatively plain style of writing. Nowhere else do I find Poe so easy to read – unless we consider his business letters, which are straightforward throughout (F.W. Thomas, interestingly, wrote to Poe saying "your letter is just as you talk" [17: 67]).

Historically, it has been argued that, rather than to entertain, to move, to gain sympathy, or to persuade, the plain style should be used to explain, to teach. As such, we might expect to find Poe using *aphelia* often in his literary criticism – not so much when he is merely paraphrasing the plot of a novel (and he does that a lot) but when he is expounding his critical principles. I will not venture to argue that such is always the case, however. Indeed, in "The Language and Style of the Prose," Stauffer argues that Poe's critical "style" involves features that we would not expect to find in the "plain" style. Excerpts elsewhere in this catalogue substantiate that claim.

It is certain, however, that Poe had a definite idea about the plain style: it is to teach *Truth*. Perhaps he means *moral* Truth, and this is the basis of his hatred of the didactic in poetry. In his well-known review of Longfellow's *Ballads and Other Poems*, he criticizes that poet's effusions because of "the too obtrusive nature of their *didacticism*" (11: 68). To inculcate moral truths, one must use prose – and a certain style of prose:

> The demands of truth are severe. She has no sympathy with the myrtles. All that is indispensable in song is all with which she has nothing to do. To deck her in gay robes is to render her a harlot. It is but making her a flaunting paradox to wreathe her in gems and flowers. Even in stating this our present proposition, we verify our own words – we feel the necessity, in enforcing this *truth*, of descending from metaphor. Let us then be simple and distinct. To convey "the true" we are required to dismiss from the attention all inessentials. We must be perspicuous, precise, terse. (70)

Also related to the issue of stylistic plainness is J. Lasley Dameron's essay, "Poe, 'Simplicity,' and *Blackwood's Magazine*." Dameron argues that Poe, along with the critics who wrote for *Blackwood's*, adopted their definition of *simplicity* ultimately from Hugh Blair (*Lectures on Rhetoric and Belles Lettres*): "Opposed to too much ornament, or 'pomp of language' ['affectation'], a simplicity of style manifests an 'easy and natural manner' of expression" (quoted by Dameron, 233). This was an "all-encompassing critical standard" from 1830 to 1840, says Dameron, and in Poe's reviews and critical essays it "becomes a major critical standard in judging the works of others" (235). Simplicity should avoid "verboseness, turgidity, bombast, complexity, abstruseness, floridity, and 'too much ornament and pomp'" (236). Dameron then quotes a long excerpt from Poe's review of *Horse-Shoe Robinson*, in which Poe praises simplicity of style but apparently distinguishes between it and what has traditionally been called the "plain" style: "Nor is it to be supposed that by simplicity we imply a rejection of ornament, or of a proper use of those advantages afforded by metaphorical illustration"; Kennedy's style, he says, displays simplicity but also is "richly figurative and poetical" (236). The "simple" style, then, is not without ornamentation, but it must be "lucid, accurate, and appropriately concise" (239). Perhaps Poe and his fellow critics are describing what has traditionally been called the "middle" style, the main purpose of which is not to teach (as with the "plain") or to move (as with the "grand") but to delight, to please (*delectare*). Dameron notes that Poe's attitude toward the style of "simplicity" is hard to pin down: in an 1835 letter to Thomas White, Poe disparages simplicity as "the cant of the day" (234) – recall Thoreau's complaint in *Walden* that "It is a ridiculous demand which England and America make, that you shall speak so that they can understand you" – but apparently describes himself at the end of his life as a writer of "distinctness and simplicity" (241; see also Jacobs, *Journalist & Critic*, 79, 82). "To what extent, if at all, did Poe adhere to his own standard of simplicity in composing his own poems and fiction?", Dameron asks (241). It is hoped that this book, particularly this catalogue, will enable us to answer that question definitively. Certainly in one review Poe states that "Simplicity is, indeed, a very lofty and very effective feature in all true Art" ("The Antigone at Palmo's," 12: 131–2).

Related to *aphelia* is the device *aschematiston*, which refers to the absence of ornamental or figured language, "a healthy sign of the plain style" (Lanham, 23). At worst, the term means an unskillful use of rhetorical figures.

Pronunciation: a PHE li a

APHORISM: a figure of thought: a concise, witty statement full of meaning and often moralistic:

> it is precisely at that time when men are most anxious to throw off the burden of their own calamities that they feel the least desirous of relieving them in others. ("Loss of Breath," 2: 165)

We do not find a lot of aphorisms in Poe, but here is another:

> Enlightened liberality is the truest economy. (Review of *Report of the Committee on Naval Affairs*, 9: 87)

Here is yet another:

> Time, not fire, is the trier of verse. (Review of *The Poems of Alfred Lord Tennyson*, 11: 127)

In his review of *Plato Contra Atheos*, we get one quoted in French from Poe:

> It would be as well, however, to bear in mind the aphoristic sentence of Leibnitz – "La plupart des sectes ont raison en beaucoup de ce qu'elles avancent, mais non pas en ce qu'elles nient." (12: 165)

Pronunciation: APH or is im

APOCARTERESIS: giving up one hope and turning to another, or giving up all hope. I borrow from Lanham, here, who provides both definitions. That there is more than one illustrates the disagreement and confusion on the part of rhetors with regard to some of the rhetorical tropes and schemes. The device (first definition) is foregrounded in "The Man that was Used Up," as the frustrated narrator goes from one person to another trying (in vain) to discover more about the enigmatic General Smith:

> There was no chance of hearing anything farther that evening in regard to Brevet Brigadier General John A.B.C. Smith.
>
> Still I consoled myself with the reflection that the tide of ill luck would not run against me forever, and so determined to make a bold push for information at the rout of that bewitching little angel, the graceful Mrs. Pirouette. (3: 267)

Pronunciation: a po car te RE sis
Type: devices of vehemence

APOCOPE: omitting a syllable or letter from the end of a word – a type of *elision* (see below). The device figures in informal speech:

> "Hillo! hillo, there!" said a gruff voice in reply.
>
> "What the devil's the matter now?" said a second.
>
> "Get out o' that!" said a third. ("The Premature Burial," 5: 271)

Pronunciation: a PO co pe
Type: addition, subtraction, and substitution: letters and syllables

APODIOXIS: rejecting an argument indignantly as impertinent or absurdly false. This device is frequently found in Poe's literary criticism:

> That we know no more to-day of the nature of Deity, of its purposes – and thus of man himself – than we did even a dozen years ago, is a proposition disgracefully absurd; and of this any astronomer could assure Mr. Macaulay. (Review of *Critical and Miscellaneous Essays*, 10: 159)

"The Longfellow War," in which Poe answers the friends of Longfellow, who have defended him against Poe's charge of plagiarism, is extended *apodioxis* – Poe at his most polemical. We may wonder how *apodioxis* differs from *antirrhesis*. *Apodioxis* can involve the rejection of an argument *without* addressing it, the assumption being that to attempt a rebuttal of such a childish point of view would be a waste of time. If we go with this definition, the excerpt, above, placed back into its context, would not quite be an exemplification of the device because Poe does go on at some length to refute Macaulay's point. Espy gives a precise definition: "when we reject the objections of adversaries as trifles, or scorn them as absurdities, to which it is hard to answer, either saying they pertain not to the purpose, or feigning them to be foolish with laughing at them, or else promise to answer them at some more fit time, and so shake them off, with bringing in other matters" (156).
Pronunciation: a po di OX is
Type: devices of vehemence
Type: techniques of argument

APODIXIS: "Confirming a statement by reference to generally accepted principles or experience" (Lanham, 18):

> Was I aware – was I fully aware of the discrepancy between us? **That the age of the husband should surpass by a few years – even by fifteen or twenty – the age of the wife, was regarded by the world as admissible, and, indeed, as even proper**; but she had always entertained the belief that the years of the wife should never exceed in number those of the husband. ("The Spectacles," 5: 194)

Given Poe's contempt for the "rabble," the democratic "mob," it is perhaps surprising to find him using *apodixis* now and then in his literary reviews and essays:

we object to our contemporary's appropriation in its behalf, of a term to which we, **in common with a large majority of mankind**, have been accustomed to attach a certain and very definite idea. ("Exordium," 11: 6; see also 10: 187)

Clearly, Poe was not averse to siding with the "rabble" when it gave him a rhetorical edge.

This definition of *apodixis*, as given by Lanham and Taylor, differs from that given by Sonnino (160).

Pronunciation: a po DIX is

Type: example, allusion, and citation of authority

Type: techniques of argument

Type: "verisimilar"

A P O M N E M O N Y S I S : quoting an approved authority from memory:
"He is well acquainted with my MS., and I just copied into the middle of the blank sheet the words –

– Un dessein si funeste,
S'il n'est digne d'Atrée, est digne de Thyeste.

They are to be found in Crébillon's 'Atrée.'" ("The Purloined Letter," 6: 52)

Consider *apomnemonysis* as part of what Poe called the "plausible or verisimilar style" in some of his hoaxes (see under *epicrisis*).

Pronunciation: a po mne mo NY sis

Type: example, allusion, and citation of authority

Type: techniques of argument

Type: "verisimilar"

A P O P H A S I S (adjective: apophantic): pretending to deny what is really affirmed (a type of irony); mentioning something that you pretend you have no intention of mentioning. As for affirming what one pretends to deny, perhaps the following passage exemplifies this eminently rhetorical device. Poe is quoting Washington Irving:

" *We may have read poetry more artificially perfect in its structure, but never any more truly divine in its inspiration.*" The nature of inspiration is disputable, **and we will not pretend to assert that Mr. Irving is in the wrong. His words, however, in their hyperbole, do wrong to his subject, and would be hyperbole still, if applied to the most exalted poets of all time.** (Review of Irving's *Biography and Poetical Remains of the Late Margaret Miller Davidson*, 10: 178)

Here is a somewhat more snide instance: after quoting from the *Poems* of William A. Lord the lines, "I poured a hymn/ Of 'praise and gratulation' like the noise/ Of banded angels when they shout to wake/ Empyreal echoes!", Poe says that Lord

> may have enemies (*very* little men!) who will pretend to deny that the "hymn of praise and gratulation" (if *this* is the hymn) bears at all points more than a partial resemblance to the "noise of banded angels when they shout to wake empyreal echoes." Not that *we* intend to deny it – but *they* will: – they are *very* little people and they *will*. (12: 155)

This device is quite similar to *paraleipsis* (see below). Taylor provides some different definitions as well as this one (74–5). Another term is *negatio*.
Pronunciation: a PO pha sis
Type: techniques of argument

APORIA (adjective: aporetic): true or pretended doubt or deliberation about an issue. Dupriez lists several similar terms: under *dubitatio*, he says "The speaker hesitates, appearing not to know which word or line or argument to take, or which meaning to attach to an action" (144). Sometimes the speaker's indecision is genuine; other times it may be fake. When phony, this irresolution is called *deliberatio* by Dupriez: "The pretense that one is weighing the arguments with respect to a decision which has already been taken" (123). Poe provides an example of an aporetic display in "The Murders in the Rue Morgue":

> "I don't mean that you should be at all this trouble for nothing, sir," said the man. "Couldn't expect it. Am very willing to pay a reward for the finding of the animal – that is to say, anything in reason."
>
> "Well," replied my friend, "that is all very fair, to be sure. **Let me think! – what should I have? Oh! I will tell you. My reward shall be this.** You shall give me all the information in your power about these murders in the Rue Morgue." (4: 186)

Dupin's deliberation about his reward is not spontaneous, is phony, for he has lured the sailor into his apartment with the *express purpose* of getting him to confess his knowledge of the Rue Morgue tragedy. In other words, he has already determined what "reward" he wants and so hardly needs to deliberate the question.
Pronunciation: a po RI a
Type: devices of vehemence
Type: techniques of argument

APOSIOPESIS: stopping suddenly in midcourse; leaving a statement unfinished as if unable or unwilling to continue. Here is an exemplification from "Hop-Frog":

"Drink, I say!" shouted the monster, "**or by the fiends** – "
The dwarf hesitated. (6: 221)

Aposiopesis sometimes also suggests hesitation, distractedness, as in Poe's drama, "Politian" (7: 72–3). If used deliberately, it can convey an indirect (implied) threat (as above, in "Hop-Frog"). As Quinn says, however, "An aposiopesis does not always have to be used for the expressing of deep emotion. Sometimes it can be used to convey casualness, spontaneity" (*Figures of Speech*, 36).
Pronunciation: a po si o PE sis
Type: devices of vehemence
Type: techniques of argument

APOSTROPHE: address to or invocation of absent persons (sometimes the reader) or inanimate things (see also *ecphonesis*):

Science! true daughter of Old Time thou art!
  Who alterest all things with thy peering eyes.
Why preyest thou thus upon the poet's heart,
  Vulture, whose wings are dull realities? ("Sonnet – To Science," 7: 22)

We even encounter an apostrophe where we might not expect to find it – in a specimen of Poe's literary criticism:

We have more of his *poetry* (**spirits of Pope, Byron, *et al.*, forgive our desecration of the name!**) on hand. (Review of Griswold's *Poets and Poetry of America*, 11: 234)

Pronunciation: a POS tro phe
Type: devices of vehemence

APPOSITIO (apposition): a scheme of addition that involves placing beside a noun or pronoun, without hypotactic linkage, another (possibly synonymous) noun or noun phrase that explains, modifies, describes, specifies, or otherwise comments upon the first:

Pascal, **a philosopher whom we both love**, has said, how truly! – "que tout notre raisonnement se réduit à céder au sentiment." ("The Colloquy of Monos and Una," 4: 204)

The first line *with* hypotactic linkage would begin with "Pascal, **who is** a philosopher whom we both love." Poe discusses apposition in a devastating review of Hugh A. Pue's *A Grammar of the English Language*. He quotes several sentence fragments from the book's Preface, then demonstrates how Pue should have avoided them with the correct use of punctuation: "This would have been the proper method of punctuation. 'A mode' is placed in apposition with 'a series of letters.' But it is evident that it is *not* the 'series of letters' which is the 'mode.' It is *the writing of the lessons in a series* which is so. Yet, in order that the noun 'mode' can be properly placed in apposition with what precedes it, this latter must be either a noun, or a sentence, which, taken collectively, can serve as one" (10: 169).

See the lengthy commentaries on this figure in Corbett (433) and Dupriez (61–2). Lanham lists it as *epexegesis* (67). Compare with *peristasis*.
Pronunciation: ap po SI ti o
Type: addition, subtraction, and substitution: words, phrases, and clauses
Type: amplification

ARA: a curse, imprecation, malediction. We might expect to find this device in some of Poe's emotionally overwrought Gothic tales, but we find a low-key, even comedic, instance in his literary criticism – specifically, his remarks about a handbook of etiquette:

> As for its author ... we wish him no worse fate than to be condemned to its
> perpetual perusal until such time as he shall succeed in describing with his
> hat one of his own very funny circles – one of those circles of just ninety de-
> grees. (Review of *The Canons of Good Breeding*, 10: 49)

Here is a less humorous one:

> The fact is, we despise them and defy them (the transcendental vagabonds!)
> and they may all go to the devil together. ("Boston and the Bostonians," 13: 9)

Espy discusses this device under the term *imprecatio* (185), and Sonnino under *execratio* (89).
Pronunciation: A ra
Type: devices of vehemence

ARGUMENTUM AD ABSURDUM: see *Reductio ad absurdum*.

ASCHEMATISTON: most rhetors define this as (1) the absence of or-namental or figured language. Some consider it a vice, "whereas we are more likely to see it as a healthy sign of the plain style," says Lanham (23; see *aphelia*). He provides a second definition, however: (2) "Unskillful use of figures" (24). Joseph notes that we cannot find *aschematiston* anywhere in the Shakespeare canon (304 n12) – though we can certainly imagine its *comedic* use – and I like to think the same is true of the Poe canon. We *do* find him now and then accusing other writers of the vice (second definition). In considering the merits of a fellow critic, Whipple, Poe gives us this:

> In a review of "The Drama of Exile and other Poems," by Miss Barrett, (now Mrs. Browning,) he speaks of the following passage as "in every respect faultless – sublime:"
>
>> Hear the steep generations how they fall
>> Adown the visionary stairs of Time,
>> Like supernatural thunders – far yet near,
>> Sowing their fiery echoes through the hills!
>
> Now here, saying nothing of the affectation in "adown;" [note Poe's extended *paraleipsis*] not alluding to the insoluble paradox of "far yet near;" not mentioning the inconsistent metaphor involved in the sowing of fiery echoes; adverting but slightly to the misusage of "like" in place of "as;" and to the impropriety of making anything fall like *thunder*, which has never been known to fall at all; merely hinting, too, at the misapplication of "steep" to the "generations" instead of to the "stairs" – (a perversion in no degree justified by the fact that so preposterous a figure as *synecdoche* exists in the school-books) – letting these things pass, we shall still find it difficult to understand how Mrs. Browning should have been led to think the principle idea itself … the idea of *tumbling down stairs*, in any shape, or under any circumstance – either a poetical or a decorous conception. And yet Mr. Whipple speaks of it as "sublime." That the lines narrowly *missed* sublimity, I grant: – that they came within a step of it, I admit; but, unhappily, the step is that *one* step which, time out of mind, has intervened between the sublime and the ridiculous. ("About Critics and Criticism," 13: 200–1)

Then Poe presumes to rewrite the passage, displaying a more skillful use of figures and eliminating the *bathos* (201–2).

Sonnino provides two alternate terms: *aschematismus* and *sicca* (220), and only the first definition given, above.

Pronunciation: a sche ma TIS ton

Type: ungrammatical, illogical, or unusual uses of language

ASPHALIA: offering oneself as surety for a bond (Lanham, 24) – that is, making oneself responsible, legally and sometimes financially, for the obligation, the conduct, even the debt, of another person. In "Thou Art the Man" Old Charley Goodfellow offers to pay the bail of Mr Pennifeather:

> the examining magistrate refused to listen to any farther testimony, and immediately committed the prisoner for trial – declining resolutely to take any bail in the case, although against this severity Mr. Goodfellow very warmly remonstrated, and offered to become surety in whatever amount might be required. (5: 302–3)

This generous use of *asphalia* is part of Goodfellow's appeal to *ethos*, his attempt to come across as a man of good character. This appeal anticipates what would become a convention in detective fiction: the least likely suspect (apparently the most ethical and likeable) turning out to be the culprit.

Pronunciation: as pha LI a

Type: devices of vehemence

ASSONANCE: a scheme of repetition involving a resemblance or similarity between internal vowel sounds in neighbouring words:

> I found myself emerging from total unconsciousness into the first feeble and indefinite sense of existence. ("The Premature Burial," 5: 269)
>
> One night, near the closing in of September, she pressed this distressing subject with more than usual emphasis upon my attention. ("Ligeia," 2: 262)

Cf *consonance* and alliteration. Poe, of course, is famous for his sensitivity to the sounds of words, especially in his poetry – recall his discussion of the "long *o* as the most sonorous vowel, in connection with *r* as the most producible consonant" for the refrain "Nevermore" in "The Raven" ("The Philosophy of Composition," 14: 200). Poe displays his sensitivity to sound not only in his fiction and poetry but even in his literary criticism. Note (again) the repetition of the short *e* sound in this passage from "The Philosophy of Composition":

> We commence, then, with this intention.
>
> The initial consideration was that of extent. If any literary work is too long to be read at one sitting, we must be content to dispense with the immensely important effect derivable from unity of impression. (196)

Perhaps Poe's noticeable use of this appeal to the reader's ear, even in a work of literary criticism, relates to his suggestion in his review of *Peter Snook* that a critique might be "a work of art in itself" (14: 74) – and his complaint that, typically in America, at least, such is not the case.

Pronunciation: AS so nance
Type: repetition: letters and sounds

ASTEISMUS: "Facetious or mocking answer that plays on a word" (Lanham, 25); "A contrived turning or twisting of the meaning of something said so that it implies something else" (Cuddon, 64):

> "a certain rich miser conceived the design of spunging upon this Abernethy for a medical opinion. Getting up, for this purpose, an ordinary conversation in a private company, he insinuated his case to the physician, as that of an imaginary individual.
>
> "'We will suppose,' said the miser, 'that his symptoms are such and such; now, doctor, what would *you* have directed him to **take?**'
>
> "'**Take!**' said Abernethy, 'why, **take** *advice*, to be sure'." ("The Purloined Letter," 4: 38)

Rhetors (see especially those quoted by Sonnino [188]) stress that *asteismus* does not involve sarcasm or rudeness; it is an inoffensive "civil jest," a "merry scoff" the likes of which has come to be associated with the urbane wit of the sophisticated city-dweller. And who is a more sophisticated city-dweller than Dupin, whose wit is evident here? *Asteismus* is clearly associated with the pun (see chapter 4).

Another definition of *asteismus* is this: (2) delicate, clever banter or badinage that praises while appearing to reproach or blames while appearing to flatter (cf *antiphrasis*). As such, it is "a form of social irony" and is "eminently rhetorical," says Dupriez; it "is used mostly between friends" (73).
Pronunciation: as te IS mus
Type: pun
Type: repetition: words

ASTROTHESIA: the description of a star. Frequently, Poe's astronomical allusions are quite esoteric, and only those readers whose understanding of the science is comparable to Poe's can make sense of his astronomical symbolism and imagery. The following excerpt from "Ligeia" is a case in point. There, the narrator is wonderstruck as he contemplates the mysterious eyes of his beloved Ligeia. He is unable to express the ineffable meaning they may have (*adynata*); he can only suggest through symbols what the expression in her eyes may mean, and the strange feeling he gets when he ponders them:

And there are one or two stars in heaven – (one especially, a star of the sixth
magnitude, double and changeable, to be found near the large star in Lyra
[Vega]) in a telescopic scrutiny of which I have been made aware of the feeling. (2: 252)

Although the editors of the Mabbott edition of Poe's works suggest
that this star is the double binary Epsilon Lyrae (2: 252), I think Poe is
more likely referring to Beta Lyrae (Sheliak), which is "changeable" in
brightness because it is really composed of two stars, one eclipsing the
other regularly and bringing about periodic changes in the system's magnitude as seen from Earth. When we consider the events of "Ligeia," the
stellar symbolism becomes clear: Ligeia can be said to "eclipse" the Lady
Rowena, as if they were the two stars of the Sheliak system. Thus, Poe's
use of astronomy in "Ligeia" is not merely ornamental but is related cen-
trally to the story's theme, metempsychosis – the passage of the soul
from one body to another, thus usurping, "eclipsing," that body's original soul.

Even in one of his literary reviews, Poe shows his knowledge of astronomy – specifically, uranography (celestial geometry – the map of the
nighttime sky). Complaining of certain blunders in *The Damsel of
Darien*, he says this:

At page 161 of the same volume, we find these words, – "And how natural, in
an age so fanciful, to believe that the stars and starry groups beheld in the
new world, for the first time by the native of the old, were especially assigned
for its government and protection!" Now if by the old world be meant the
East, and by the new world the West, we are quite at a loss to know what *are*
the stars seen in the one, which cannot be equally seen in the other. (10: 56)

Indeed: if the same hemisphere – say, the northern – is meant, the stars
seen in the old world are the same ones seen in the new. The night sky
changes only when moving from the northern to the southern hemisphere, or vice versa, not from the eastern to the western.

Poe scholars are well aware of Poe's interest in, and literary employment
of, astronomy largely because of his mystical-cosmological work, *Eureka*
(1848). Harold Beaver reminds us that "Poe had been a keen astronomer
since earliest youth. When John Allan, his step-father, in 1825 bought a
house with a two-storey portico extending along one side, the sixteen-year-
old Edgar had set up his telescope on the upstairs porch to study the stars
and beckoning mystery of the moon" (340). Perhaps it is no surprise,
therefore, that the nebular hypothesis, the moon, planets, constellations,

comets, and stars figure in his essays, short stories, and poems, also. We even find Poe's knowledge of astronomy – specifically, the moon – in *The Literati of New York City* (15: 127–35), where he is discussing Richard Adams Locke (he of the famous moon hoax). He also demonstrates certain inaccuracies in Locke's account by arguing from analogy, a rhetorical strategy employed frequently by Galileo, especially in his *Starry Messenger* (see under "analogy"). As well, in a letter (30 October 1845) to Poe, Thomas Chivers mentions "the '*Star of Tycho Brache*,' which you delivered in Boston" (17: 220). This star is the famous Cassiopeia supernova, which is Poe's "Al Aaraaf." Poe gives the following note to his poem explaining the celestial object: "A star was discovered by Tycho Brahe [sic] which appeared suddenly in the heavens – attained, in a few days, a brilliancy surpassing that of Jupiter – then as suddenly disappeared, and has never been seen since" (7: 23n; see also Ostrom, 18, 33). Finally, in a letter to Sarah Helen Whitman (24 November 1848), Poe discusses her poem "To Arcturus," a name for the brightest star in the constellation Boötes as well as the magazine of the Duyckincks. Poe shows that he to some extent had kept abreast of relatively recent developments in astronomy by telling Sarah that "61 Cygni has been proved *nearer* than Arcturus & Alpha Lyrae is presumably so. Bessel, also, has shown 6 other stars to be *nearer* than the brighter ones of this hemisphere" (Ostrom, 408). Indeed, the double star 61 Cygni is so close to Earth that it has a large "proper motion" – it was once dubbed the "Flying Star" – and the German astronomer Friedrich Wilhelm Bessel calculated its distance at about 10 light years, close to today's estimate of 11.2. That star was the first to have its distance measured accurately, which Bessel did in 1838, just ten years before Poe displayed his knowledge of this astronomical development to Sarah Whitman. As for Arcturus, its distance from Earth is 36 light years, and Alpha Lyrae (Vega) is 26.5. Thus, Poe was right in stating that both Vega and 61 Cygni are closer to us than Arcturus.

Several studies, long and short, have been written on Poe and astronomy, including the unpublished dissertation of Elva Baer Kremenliev, "The Literary Uses of Astronomy in the Writings of Edgar Allan Poe," and Frederick W. Connor's article "Poe and John Nichol: Notes on a Source of *Eureka*." Much useful information is also found in the Commentary to Beaver's *The Science Fiction of Edgar Allan Poe.*

Pronunciation: as tro THE si a

Type: description

ASYNDETON: unlinked independent clauses side by side without subordination or interlinking conjunctions; a scheme of omission:

> A shriek had been heard by a neighbour during the night; suspicion of foul play had been aroused; information had been lodged at the police office.
> ("The Tell-Tale Heart," 5: 93)

Corbett says, quite rightly, "The principal effect of asyndeton is to produce a hurried rhythm in the sentence" (435; and cf *epitrochasmus*). Consider how the addition of conjunctions and other connectors would have slowed the passage: "A shriek had been heard by a neighbour during the night, and suspicion of foul play had been aroused; then information had been lodged at the police office." *Asyndeton* is the opposite of *polysyndeton* but compares with *parataxis* (see below). That Poe can use both *asyndeton* (and other devices of brevity and omission) and devices involving verbosity and amplification suggests his stylistic versatility. Quinn has several pages of examples and insights on *asyndeton* (*Figures of Speech*, 7–11).
Pronunciation: a SYN de ton
Type: addition, subtraction, and substitution: words, phrases, and clauses
Type: brevity
Type: "biblical"

AUXESIS: (1) use of a heightened word in place of an ordinary one (Lanham, 26); magnifying the importance of something by referring to it with a disproportionate name (Corbett, 452). We can see how this figure is similar to *hyperbole* (see below) and the opposite of *meiosis* (see below). In Melville's "The Paradise of Bachelors," the narrator refers to a mere waiter as a "field-marshal" and then as "Socrates." We might consider Poe's name for the former slave in "The Gold-Bug" – *Jupiter* – as an instance of *auxesis* according to this first definition.
(2) words or clauses placed in a climactic order – that is, of increasing importance:

> Was it possible they heard not? Almighty God! – no, no! They heard! – they suspected! – they *knew!* ("The Tell-Tale Heart," 5: 94)

> The school-room was the largest in the house – I could not help thinking, in the world. ("William Wilson," 3: 303)

The climactic arrangement becomes a perfect way to express the idea of cosmic *hierarchy* at the core of Poe's vision of the universe in *Eureka*:

A **man**, in this view, becomes **mankind**; **mankind** a member of the **cosmical family of Intelligences**. (16: 187)

The Galaxy ... interests man chiefly, although less immediately, on account of its being his home; the home of the **Earth** on which he exists; the home of the **Sun** about which this Earth revolves; the home of that "**system**" **of orbs** of which the Sun is the centre and primary. (270)

This is the second of four definitions of *auxesis* that Lanham provides for this slippery term, and it clearly puts us in mind of climax (see below). Lanham suggests a way to distinguish: "The difference between the auxesis and climax clusters seems to be that in the climax cluster, the climactic series is realized through linked pairs of terms" (27). *Anadiplosis* (see above), therefore, would seem to be necessary for climax, and in the third quote I give to illustrate *auxesis*, *anadiplosis* is present at least in the middle: "mankind; mankind."

Pronunciation: aux E sis

Type: amplification (2)

BARBARISMUS: a mistake in vocabulary, pronunciation, or grammar – an illiterate expression that violates the rules of a language due to ignorance or confusion (cf malapropism and *acyrologia*). American writers have had some fun with the dialects of uneducated slaves – witness Poe's Jupiter:

"Claws enuff, massa, and mouff too. I nebber did see sich a d – d bug – he kick and he bite ebery ting what cum near him. Massa Will cotch him fuss, but had for to let him go gin mighty quick, I tell you – den was de time he must ha got de bite. I didn't like de look ob de bug mouff, myself, no how, so I wouldn't take hold ob him wid my finger, but I cotch him wid a piece ob paper dat I found. I rap him up in de paper and stuff piece ob it in he mouff – dat was de way." ("The Gold-Bug," 5: 102–3)

Poe is not the only American writer to use *barbarismus* to depict the language of American blacks: consider the racist portrayals of Jim in Mark Twain's *Huckleberry Finn*, Fleece in Melville's *Moby-Dick*, and most of Harriet Beecher Stowe's slaves in *Uncle Tom's Cabin*, for example.

Clearly, *barbarismus* has comedic potential. Poe uses it as such not only in "The Gold-Bug" but also in "The Angel of the Odd":

"I was always under the impression that an angel had wings."

"Te wing!" he cried, highly incensed, "vat I pe do mit te wing? Mein Gott! do you take me vor a shicken?" (6: 107)

Stauffer considers this "an outrageous mongrel accent that is a pastiche of German, French, and Southern black" ("The Language and Style of the Prose," 463). And consider "Why the Little Frenchman Wears His Hand in a Sling":

> And shud ye be wantin to diskiver who is the pink of purliteness quite, and the laider of the hot tun in the houl city o' Lonon – why it's jist mesilf. And fait that same is no wonder at all at all, (so be plased to stop curlin your nose,) for every inch o' the six wakes that I've been a gintleman, and left aff wid the bog-throthing to take up wid the Barronissy, it's Pathrick that's been living like a houly imperor, and gitting the iddication and the graces. Och! (4: 114)

We have some (deceptive) *barbarismus* in *Pym*:

> "sir! You are a sum'mat mistaken; my name, in the first place, bee'nt nothing at all like Goddin [Gordon], and I'd want you for to know better, you black-guard, than to call my new obercoat a darty one." (3: 20–1)

Readers who know Poe only by his serious tales may be surprised indeed to find him displaying a comical ability to mimic so many foreign accents – an ability we might normally expect, instead, from that much abler genius of dialects, Mark Twain. For more on this subject, see chapter 4.

Poe complains of *barbarismus* (without using the term) in his review of *Sketches of Conspicuous Living Characters of France*:

> So far as mere translation goes, the volume now before us is, in some respects, not very well done. Too little care has been taken in rendering the French idioms by English equivalents ... Mr. Walsh is always too literal, although sufficiently correct. He should not employ, however, even in translation, such queer words as "to legitimate," meaning "to legitimatize," or "to fulmine," meaning "to fulminate." (10: 138)

Pronunciation: bar ba RIS mus
Type: ungrammatical, illogical, or unusual uses of language
Type: "comedic"

BATHOS: the Greek word for *depth* and referring to an unintentional descent in literature when, attempting to be sublime, elevated, or passionate, a writer overshoots the mark and drops into the insignificant, the ridiculous. (Poe may have been familiar with Alexander Pope's essay on the bathetic, *Peri Bathous, or, Of the Art of Sinking in Poetry* [Campbell, "Poe's Reading," 175n20]). Poe the literary critic was on the lookout for *bathos* and takes a contemporary poetess to task for this blunder. He begins by quoting excerpts:

> Through the *breast*
> Of that fair vale the Susquehannah roam'd
> Wearing its *robe of silver* like a bride.
> Now with a noiseless current gliding slow,
> 'Mid the rich *velvet* of its *curtaining* banks
> It seemed to sleep. [Poe's italics]

Poe comments thus:

> when the noble river is bedizened out in *robes of silver*, and made to wash
> with its bright waters nothing better than *curtains of velvet*, we feel a very sen-
> sible and a very righteous indignation. We might have expected such lan-
> guage from an upholsterer, or a *marchande des modes*, but it is utterly out of
> place upon the lips of Mrs. Sigourney. To liken the glorious objects of natural
> loveliness to the trappings and tinsel of artificiality, is one of the lowest, and
> at the same time, one of the most ordinary exemplifications of the *bathos*.
> (Review of *Zinzendorff, and Other Poems*, etc., 8: 129)

A few pages later, he quotes another stanza and comments that "The
conclusion of this is *bathetic* to a degree bordering upon the grotesque"
(132). He makes the same complaint about the bathetic in his review of
Drake's poem *The Culprit Fay* (8: 296–7; 299; see also 306); it becomes a
clear aspect of Poe's literary credo that one should never compare the
picturesque or the natural sublime with artificial objects for, in his opinion, the bathetic is always the result (304; see also 11: 21; 12: 23–4;
13: 201). For a satirical use of *bathos*, see chapter 5.

The term is sometimes interchangeable with *anticlimax*, but *bathos*
can appear *intentionally* when a writer uses it for comical or satirical purposes (as we see from the Headley excerpt in chapter 5). Most of "The
Premature Burial" is devoted to preparing the readers for the climactic
ending in which the narrator himself is finally buried alive – but Poe deliberately surprises us with a rather comical anticlimactic ending (quoted
at length in chapter 4).

Pronunciation: BA thos

Type: devices of vehemence

Type: "comedic"

BDELYGMA: an expression, usually short, of hatred or disgust for a
person or thing:

> "Thou wretch! – thou vixen! – thou shrew!" said I to my wife on the morn-
> ing after our wedding, "thou witch! – thou hag! – thou whipper-snapper! –

thou sink of iniquity! – thou fiery-faced quintessence of all that is abominable!" ("Loss of Breath," 2: 151)

This passage can also be considered *accumulatio* (see above). Here is a
shorter one from one of Poe's magazine pieces:

P.S. Miss Walters (**the Syren!**) has seen cause, we find, to recant all the ill-
natured little insinuations she has been making against us. ("Boston and the
Bostonians," 13: 8)

Pronunciation: del YG ma
Type: devices of vehemence

BOMPHIOLOGIA: bombastic, pompous speech. In the following
excerpt, Poe's narrator might have written, simply, "two cats fought over
my nose":

two cats ... alighting opposite one another on my visage, **betook themselves
to indecorous contention for the paltry consideration of my nose.** ("Loss of
Breath," 2: 159)

Bomphiologia, as here, has obvious comedic potential (see chapter 5).
Some people (especially English teachers) would consider it a stylistic
vice, and those readers who deplore Poe's "style" may argue that *bomphiologia* is a vice that characterizes much of his prose and is generally *not*
something he uses intentionally for comedic (or any other justifiable) effect. Now and then, yes, we do find instances:

Meantime Angelo is absent from home, attempting to get access to the cathe-
dral; and his servant Tomaso, takes the opportunity of absenting himself also,
and of **indulging his bibulous propensities while perambulating the town.**
("The American Drama," 13: 41)

Lanham relates the term to *macrologia* – long-winded speech in which more
words are used than necessary (96–7; see below). Taylor, on the other hand,
prefers to see *bomphiologia* as a kind of *hyperbole* similar to *auxesis* (79–80).
For more instances of pompous speech, see the language of King Pest, in the
tale of that name. Poe complains about the *bomphiologia* in Bulwer's novel
Zanoni: "His language was always inflated, often bombastic" (11: 123).

Pronunciation: bom phi o LO gi a
Type: amplification
Type: "comedic"

BRACHYLOGIA: excessive brevity of diction, often with words omitted (minus additioning). We find the device now and then in Poe's

Literati of New York City, especially at the end of each section where he seems suddenly impatient and desirous of wrapping up quickly:

> The hair curls, and is of a dark brown, interspersed with gray. He wears full whiskers. **Is about forty years of age. Unmarried.** (Charles Fenno Hoffman, 15: 122)

Here is a newspaper report concerning the murders in the Rue Morgue:

> "*William Bird,* tailor, deposes that he was one of the party who entered the house. **Is an Englishman. Has lived in Paris two years. Was one of the first to ascend the stairs. Heard the voices in contention.** The gruff voice was that of a Frenchman. **Could make out several words, but cannot now remember all. Heard distinctly 'sacré' and 'mon Dieu.'** There was a sound at the moment as if of several persons struggling – a scraping and scuffling sound. The shrill voice was very loud – louder than the gruff one. **Is sure that it was not the voice of an Englishman. Appeared to be that of a German. Might have been a woman's voice. Does not understand German.**" ("The Murders in the Rue Morgue," 4: 161–2)

The minus additioning, above, involves *ellipsis* – here, the omission of the pronouns *He* and *It*. Poe parodies the curtness that this device entails in his satirical piece "How to Write a Blackwood Article": "there is the tone laconic, or curt, which has lately come much into use. It consists in short sentences. Somehow thus. Can't be too brief. Can't be too snappish. Always a full stop. And never a paragraph" (2: 275). McElrath suggests that "Poe seems to have been one of the few Americans to effectively use the 'curt' tone" (39) – a rather sweeping observation, but one supported by William Mentzel Forrest in his chapter on Poe's use of the "biblical" style: despite his deliberate use of repetition and expansion on occasion, "No man ever hated verbosity more than he. None other ever so appreciated the value of brevity – stories must be short; poems must be short. For him the Homeric virtue of length was not a virtue. Hence no words could be wasted" (95–6). Herbert Marshall McLuhan puts it this way: "he had the craftsman's contempt for verbiage masquerading as expression" (25). Sometimes *brachylogia* can indicate a stylistic vice, certainly when it leads to obscurity (see Dupriez, 82–4), so Poe is careful to avoid that pitfall; Forrest (96) quotes him in *Eureka*: "On important topics it is better to be a good deal prolix than even a very little obscure" (16: 199). In his early criticism, Poe suggests a *via media*: "The cant of verbiage is bad enough – but the cant of laconism is equally as bad" (Review of *The Partisan*, 8: 143). The middle way is exemplified, he believes, in *Maury's Navigation*: "Its style is concise without being obscure" (9: 49). In his 1837 review of *Poems by William Cullen Bryant*, Poe complains about "an objectionable ellipsis in the expression 'I behold them from the first'," because the poet means to say "I behold them from the first *time*" (9: 282). Poe clearly feels that the omission of *time* makes a little for obscurity. See under *brevitas*.

Pronunciation: bra chy LO gi a

Type: addition, subtraction, and substitution: words, phrases, and clauses

Type: brevity

BREVITAS: concise expression. What is expressive concision good for, according to Poe? For one thing, "In enforcing a truth, we need severity rather than efflorescence of language. We must be simple, precise, terse" ("The Poetic Principle," 14: 272; also, see under *aphelia*). One must not be *too* brief, however, or one can become obscure. In his review of James Fenimore Cooper's novel *Wyandotté*, Poe says this: "In endeavoring to compel his meaning within the compass of a brief sentence, Mr. Cooper has completely sacrificed its intelligibility" (11: 219). As well, see under *brachylogia*. While some scholars have praised Poe for his alleged concision, he could be rather wordy at times. See under *macrologia*.

Pronunciation: BRE vi tas

Type: brevity

CACEMPHATON (also called *aischrologia*): a scurrilous jest, lewd allusion, or double entendre (Lanham, 30). I list this device to suggest the *unlikelihood* of ever finding an exemplification in Poe (but see chapter 4). Consider his censorious words in the review of *The Quacks of Helicon*:

> We are also sure that the gross obscenity, the filth – we can use no gentler name – which disgraces the "Quacks of Helicon," cannot be the result of innate impurity in the mind of the writer. It is but a part of the slavish and indiscriminating imitation of the Swift and Rochester school. It has done the book an irreparable injury, both in a moral and pecuniary view, without effecting anything whatever on the score of sarcasm, vigour, or wit. "Let what is to be said, be said plainly." True; but let nothing vulgar be *ever* said, or conceived. (10: 184)

In his review of *The Damsel of Darien*, Poe condemns the author for using *cacemphaton*: "amid a passage of great beauty, he pauses to quote from the 'Seige of Corinth' the well-known image about 'peeling the fig when the fruit is fresh' – an image whose disgusting application where it originally stands has been often made the subject of severe and very justifiable censure" (10: 54). Look for the device here and there in Melville, particularly *Moby-Dick*.

A second definition of *cacemphaton*, provided by Lanham (30) and Taylor (80), is synonymous with the definition of *cacophonia* (see below). Pronunciation: cac EM pha ton
Type: ungrammatical, illogical, or unusual uses of language

CACOPHONIA (adjective: cacophonous or cacaphonic): a combination of vowels, consonants, or syllables that sounds disagreeable, inharmonious, harsh, jarring. Sometimes this effect is brought about by a too-frequent use of the same letters or syllables, as in excessive alliteration in tongue-twisters. *Cacophony* may be done deliberately for effect but, when done accidentally, it is clearly a vice and the opposite of *euphony.*

Poe had a good ear for sound, especially in poetry, and in his "Drake-Halleck" review he supplies an instance of *cacaphonia* from the poetry of Halleck: "Not unfrequently, too, we meet with lines such as this, 'Like torn branch from death's leafless tree,' in which the multiplicity of consonants renders the pronunciation of the words at all, a matter of no inconsiderable difficulty" (8: 318). In his review of the third edition of Griswold's *Poets and Poetry of America*, Poe analyses Griswold's bad poetry, commenting on the lines, "The summer sun has sunk to rest/ Below the green clad hills," thus: "'Green clad hills' is as harsh as the grating of a coffee-mill" (11: 230; see also 11: 247; 13: 138). Reviewing the poetry of Mary E. Hewitt, Poe complains about her

excessive use of difficult consonants. Such a line as
"And back, repressed, they coldly shrink"
is scarcely pronounceable; and this merely on account of the union of such letters as *n d b, c k r, d t h,* and *l d l* followed immediately by *s h r.*
"It feels the warm sun's seldom ray,"
is quite as bad, if not worse. In repeating it rapidly once or twice we find as much embarrassment as in the schoolboy stumbling-block about "the cat that ran up the ladder with a lump of raw liver in his mouth." (13: 103–4)

Dupriez has an extended discussion of the device (86–7). Both Lanham (30) and Taylor (80), without providing the term *cacophony,* give its definition as the second meaning of *cacemphaton.*
Pronunciation: cac O pho ny

Pronunciation: cac EM pha ton
Type: repetition: letters, syllables, and sounds
Type: ungrammatical, illogical, or unusual uses of language

CACOSISTATON: a badly constructed argument because it can serve as well on either side of a question. I find this term only in Lanham (30). It may not surprise us that Poe's detective Dupin can recognize this sort of argument in the newspaper reports of crimes, given his superior acumen and ability to see things from a different angle than the common run of reporters and police officers. We know he is about to announce *cacosistaton* when, referring to a journalist, he tells the narrator, "Nor is this the sole instance, even in this division of his subject, where our reasoner unwittingly reasons against himself" ("The Mystery of Marie Rogêt," 5: 30). He later seizes on certain details of the crime that have led the newspapers to suspect that a gang was involved in the murder of Marie, but takes the same evidence to come up with an antithetical conclusion:

> "Let us reflect now upon 'the traces of a struggle;' and let me ask what these traces have been supposed to demonstrate. A gang. But do they not rather demonstrate the absence of a gang?" (54)

Pronunciation: ca co SIS ta ton
Type: techniques of argument

CACOZELIA: studied affectation of style; "affected diction made up of adaptation of Latin words or inkhorn terms" (Lanham, 31). An "inkhorn term" is an obscure, affectedly erudite borrowing from another language, especially Latin or Greek. Lanham reminds us, quite rightly, to look up *soraismus* in this connection as well (see below). Poe's prose abounds in foreignisms, but in a couple of book reviews he surprises us with a term that we have encountered before in the Middle English of Chaucer – and to most of us, Middle English is as good as another language:

> Accident delays the ceremony until night, when, just as the lady is hesitating whether she shall say *yes*, or *no*, the tall gentleman **ycleped** Sterling [etc.].
> (Review of *The Hawks of Hawk-Hollow*, 8: 69)

The term *ycleped* means *called, named*, and we can certainly consider it "an obscure, affectedly erudite borrowing." Poe uses the word again in his review of *A Pleasant Peregrination* (9: 40); however, in the review of *Zinzendorff, and Other Poems*, Poe says, "We [this is the editorial *we*]

dislike the use made by the poetess of antique modes of expression"
(8: 129). Elsewhere he complains about a poet's use of "the obsolete terminations of verbs in the third person singular present tense [*eth*]" (*The
Literati of New York City*, Christopher Pease Cranch, 15: 71). We can only
guess that he could therefore justify his own use of the antique mode of
expression – I sense for the sake of humour.

Espy spells the term as *cacozelon* and relates it to *cacosyntheton* and
malapropism (158). Sonnino provides as a synonym the term *ambitio*
(214).

Pronunciation: ca co ZE li a

Type: ungrammatical, illogical, or unusual uses of language

CATACHRESIS (adjective: catachretic): (1) the wrong use of one
word for another – a type of substitution, clumsy or deliberate; (2) a
strained, farfetched, mixed, illogical, or extreme metaphor; "Implied
metaphor, using words wrenched from common usage" (Lanham, 31). In
the following example, one wonders whether Poe had in mind Hamlet's
"I will speak daggers to her":

> "No, sir! the soul is no such thing!" (Here, the philosopher **looking daggers**,
> took occasion to make an end, upon the spot, of his third bottle of Chamber-
> tin.) ("Bon-Bon," 2: 141)

Cf the metaphysical conceit (below). Espy says "Experts can make catachresis into a powerful figure" (75) but advises caution in employing
this figure. Quinn emphasizes the term's deliberate rather than accidental use – when a writer makes "a substitution of a word which, far from
having an easily definable connection with the substitutee, seems to have
been chosen precisely because of its inappropriateness" – arguing the
possibility that "the highest function of language is to reveal to us inde-
finable connections, those moments when we understand but know not
why" (*Figures of Speech*, 55–6).

While I have provided two definitions of the term, if we see a mixed
metaphor as bungled *because* of the inappropriate use of a word, then
there really is no difference between the definitions. To complicate matters, Dupriez insists that *catachresis* involves using a name in an unusual
sense to label something that previously had no name, but that now demands one (92–3). See also Crowley (217). *Catachresis* is also known as
abusio or *audacia*.

Pronunciation: ca ta CHRE sis
Type: metaphorical substitutions and puns
Type: ungrammatical, illogical, or unusual uses of language

CATACOSMESIS: ordering words in descending importance; anticlimax. Taylor and Sonnino suggest that this scheme can involve as few as two words – a doublet: "sun and moon," "life and death." A larger series of words and phrases intensifies the sense of diminishing:

> Indeed, in America generally, the traveller who would behold the finest landscapes, must seek them **not by the railroad, nor by the steamboat, nor by the stage-coach, nor in his private carriage, nor yet even on horseback – but on foot.** ("The Elk," 5: 158)

This device is obviously the opposite of climax (see below). In his "Drake-Halleck" review, Poe combines climax with *catacosmesis*: "to be sentimentally droll is a thing intolerable to **men, and Gods, and columns**" (8: 310; see also 9: 168).
Pronunciation: ca ta cos ME sis

CATAPLEXIS: a threatening of misfortune, disaster, or punishment:

> *"You have conquered, and I yield. Yet, henceforward art thou also dead – dead to the World, to Heaven and to Hope! In me didst thou exist – and, in my death, see by this image, which is thine own, how utterly thou hast murdered thyself."* ("William Wilson," 3: 325)

Most exemplifications of this device that I have seen in the rhetorical handbooks involve a threat uttered to someone, such as this, from the same tale:

> "Follow me, or I stab you where you stand!" (324)

The first instance, however, is more of a *prophecy*, a warning of impending misfortune. As such, it illustrates another device, *ominatio* (from which we get our words *omen* and *ominous*). Compare also with *paraenesis*.
Pronunciation: ca ta PLEX is
Type: devices of vehemence

CATEGORIA: reproaching a person with wickedness to his or her face; accusation:

> "Scoundrel!" I said, in a voice husky with rage, while every syllable I uttered seemed as new fuel to my fury, "scoundrel! impostor! accursed villain! You shall not – you *shall not* dog me unto death!" ("William Wilson," 3: 324)

We can also consider this passage as illustrating *bdelygma* (see above). The irony in the passage is clear to anyone familiar with this allegory: it is the *speaker*, the narrator, who has been acting as a scoundrel, a villain, while he who stands accused is in fact Wilson's *conscience*.

Pronunciation: ca te go RI a

Type: devices of vehemence

CHARACTERISMUS (a type of *enargia*): description of the body or mind. Perhaps this description of Ligeia's intellectual abilities and accomplishments works as an instance of *characterismus*:

> In the classical tongues was she deeply proficient, and as far as my own acquaintance extended in regard to the modern dialects of Europe, I have never known her at fault. Indeed upon any theme of the most admired, because simply the most abstruse of the boasted erudition of the academy, have I *ever* found Ligeia at fault? ... I said her knowledge was such as I have never known in woman – but where breathes the man who has traversed, and successfully, *all* the wide areas of moral, physical, and mathematical science? ("Ligeia," 2: 253–4)

We might also consider as examples of this device the descriptions of Dupin's mental abilities in "The Murders in the Rue Morgue":

> I often dwelt meditatively upon the old philosophy of the **Bi-Part Soul**, and amused myself with the fancy of a **double Dupin – the creative and the resolvent.** (4: 152)

Characterismus is foregrounded in Poe's gossipy *Literati of New York City.*

Pronunciation: cha rac ter IS mus

Type: description

CHARIENTISMUS: a type of irony involving the glossing over of a disagreeable subject with more agreeable language (see the example in Harmon/Holman, 90); "soothing over a difficulty, or turning aside antagonism with a joke" (Lanham, 33; see also Sonnino, 198–9). Dupriez lists this term under *persiflage*, "Light banter or raillery; a frivolous manner of treating any subject" (339). Depending on his friends and connections to get him a government job as an inspector, Poe showed up in Washington and, that evening, drank too much at a party. "Later he insisted on wearing his cloak inside out, and at another party became embroiled in an argument with a heavily whiskered Spaniard whose

mustaches he found comic" (Symons, 83). In a letter to Frederick
Thomas and Jesse Dow (16 March 1843), we certainly find Poe smoothing over his serious social blunders with agreeable language and humour
– *charientismus*:

> Thank you a thousand times for your kindness & great forbearance, and
> don't say a word about the cloak turned inside out, or other peccadilloes of
> that nature. Also, express to your wife my deep regret for the vexation I must
> have occasioned her … Remember me most kindly to Dr Lacey – also to the
> don, whose mustachios I *do* admire after all, and who has about the finest fig-
> ure I ever beheld – also to Dr Frailey. Please express my regret to Mr Fuller
> for making such a fool of myself in his house, and say to him (if you think it
> necessary) that I should not have got half so drunk on his excellent Port wine
> but for the rummy coffee with which I was forced to wash it down. (Ostrom,
> 229)

This is a fine use of *charientismus* but, as his friend Thomas wrote at the
end of this epistle, "there is a great deal of heartache in the jestings of this
letter" (Ostrom, 230).

Pronunciation: cha ri en TIS mus

Type: techniques of argument

CHIASMOS (sometimes spelled *chiasmus*): reversing the arrangement
of subject and complement, and occasionally other clausal components,
in successive clauses (AB:BA):

> At each intersection of these paths the nest of an albatross is constructed,
> and a penguin's nest in the centre of each square – thus every **penguin** is
> surrounded by four **albatrosses**, and each **albatross** by a like number of
> **penguins**. (*The Narrative of Arthur Gordon Pym of Nantucket*, 3: 156)

While some rhetors make no distinction between *antimetabole* and *chiasmos*, I would insist on differentiating: in *antimetabole* the exact same two
words are reversed in order:

> He observed that all **fools** were **philosophers**, and that all **philosophers** were
> **fools**. ("Lionizing," 2: 38)

We have an AB:BA reversal of precise words: fools/philosophers: philos-
ophers/fools. Here is a double helping of the AB:BA syntactic pattern
from Poe's review of Macaulay's *Critical and Miscellaneous Essays*:

> The error is exactly analogous with that which leads the immature poet to
> think himself **sublime** wherever he is **obscure**, because **obscurity** is a source

of the **sublime**, thus confounding **obscurity** of **expression** with the **expression** of **obscurity**. (10: 156)

In *chiasmos* the words reversed are not entirely the same and up to four different words or phrases can be used, and I provide several examples to illustrate how much Poe, like John F. Kennedy, liked the device:

All **men of genius** have their **detractors**; but it is merely a *non distributio medii* to argue, thence, that **all men who have their detractors** are **men of genius**. ("A Chapter of Suggestions," 14: 189)

As a matter of course, my enemies referred the **insanity** to the **drink**, rather than the **drink** to the **insanity**. (Letter of 4 January 1848 [Ostrom, 356])

The shrill **voice** was very **loud** – **louder** than the gruff **one**. ("The Murders in the Rue Morgue," 4: 162)

In *chiasmos* it is not the words so much as the order of the parts of speech that reverse – in the "Rue Morgue" example: noun, adjective; adjective, (pro)noun. Still, both devices can, but do not always, function similarly to suggest ironic reversal (see instances in Thoreau's *Walden*, for example). Lanham suggests other functions: "Chiasmus seems to set up a natural internal dynamic that draws the parts closer together, as if the second element wanted to flip over and back over the first, condensing the assertion back toward the compression of **Oxymoron** and **Pun**. The AB:BA form seems to exhaust the possibilities of argument" (33).

Quinn provides another distinction between *antimetabole* and *chiasmos*, suggesting that larger groups of words can constitute *chiasmos*: not just sentences, but entire paragraphs, even entire books, can be arranged with the first half reversed in the second half, as if each half is a mirror image of the other (*Figures of Speech*, 95). Indeed, some scholars have seen a chiasmatic structure in several of Poe's prose works, and this certainly seems true of *Pym*, for instance. Max Nänny has detected the structure as well in "The Masque of the Red Death," *Eureka*, and "The Fall of the House of Usher." Richard Kopely sees it in "The Tell-Tale Heart": "The story comprises two halves, each of them featuring nine paragraphs, with the second half reversing the order of phrase in the first. Together, the halves yield chiasmus – the pattern ABCDEEDCBA. Thus the beginning's 'You fancy me mad' … is answered by the ending's 'If you still think me mad' … At the close of the ninth paragraph, at the center of the symmetrical phrasing, is the central phrase of the tale, 'damned spot'" (235).

In "Mesmeric Revelation," Poe uses several instances of *antimetabole* and *chiasmos* in a discussion of the essential pantheistic oneness, indivisibility, of God and the universe, particled matter and "unparticled" matter, motion and thinking:

> "But there are *gradations* of matter of which man knows nothing; the **grosser** impelling the **finer**, the **finer** pervading the **grosser**. The **atmosphere**, for example, impels the **electric principle**, while the **electric principle** permeates the **atmosphere**." [*antimetabole*] (5: 245)

> "The metaphysicians maintain that all **action** is reducible to **motion and thinking**, and that the **latter** is the origin of the **former**." [*chiasmos*] (246)

The AB:BA structure of the sentences suggests that their components are mirror images of one another – in other words, the same; simultaneously, the "A" components *envelop* the "B" components, suggesting an enclosed, self-contained universe of which the components are all-pervasive and ultimately indivisible (cf Einstein's E = mc²: matter and energy are essentially two forms of the same thing). In other words, the very *syntax* of the sentences reinforces Poe's theme.

Pronunciation: chi AS mos

Type: balance, antithesis, paradox

CHOROGRAPHIA: a type of *enargia* – the description of a country, a nation. Here Poe anticipates Thorstein Veblen's concept of "conspicuous consumption" (*The Theory of the Leisure Class*):

> The Yankees alone are preposterous [regarding interior decorating].
>
> How this happens, it is not difficult to see. We have no aristocracy of blood, and having therefore as a natural, and indeed as an inevitable thing, fashioned for ourselves an aristocracy of dollars, the *display of wealth* has here to take the place and perform the office of the heraldic display in monarchical countries. By a transition readily understood, and which might have been as readily foreseen, we have been brought to merge in simple *show* our notions of taste itself. ("The Philosophy of Furniture," 14: 101)

Pronunciation: cho ro GRA phi a

Type: description

CHREIA: (1) "a short exposition of a deed or saying of a person whose name is mentioned," which saying or deed may be regarded as useful for living; (2) "a short rhetorical exercise that develops and varies a moral

observation" (Lanham, 188). We find an exemplification of the first definition in a letter (26 June 1849) from Poe to George Eveleth:

> Touching "The Stylus": – Monk Lewis once was asked how he came, in one
> of his acted plays, to introduce *black* banditti, when, in the country where
> the scene was laid, black people were quite unknown. His answer was: –
> "I introduced them because I truly anticipated that blacks would have more
> *effect* on my audience than whites – and if I had taken it into my head that,
> by making them sky-blue, the *effect* would have been greater, why sky-blue
> they should have been." To apply this idea to "The Stylus" – I am awaiting
> the *best opportunity* for its issue. (Ostrom, 449–50)

Here are two more examples from a letter dated 10 September 1849:

> I would endeavor to explain to you what I really meant – or what I really
> fancied I meant by the poem ["Ulalume"], if it were not that I remember
> Dr. Johnson's bitter and rather just remarks about the folly of explaining
> what, if worth explanation, should explain itself. He has a happy witticism,
> too, about some book which he calls "as obscure as an explanatory note."
> (Ostrom, 460)

We find the term spelled *chria* in Dupriez (266), Joseph (103, 311), and
Taylor (82).

Pronunciation: CHREI a

Type: example, allusion, and citation of authority

Type: techniques of argument

CHRONOGRAPHIA: a type of *enargia* (see below) – the description
of time:

> It was in this apartment, also, that there stood against the western wall, a gi-
> gantic clock of ebony. Its pendulum swung to and fro with a dull, heavy, mo-
> notonous clang; and when the minute-hand made the circuit of the face, and
> the hour was to be stricken, there came from the brazen lungs of the clock a
> sound which was clear and loud and deep and exceedingly musical, but of so
> peculiar a note and emphasis that, at each lapse of an hour, the musicians of
> the orchestra were constrained to pause ... and then, after the lapse of sixty
> minutes, (which embrace three thousand and six hundred seconds of the
> Time that flies,) there came yet another chiming of the clock. ("The Masque
> of the Red Death," 4: 252–3)

As Gargano has shown, though without using the term, *chronographia* is
also foregrounded in "The Tell-Tale Heart" ("The Theme of Time

in …"). I have counted the references to time passing and time pieces there: in this five-page short story, Poe provides *twenty-nine* references, an impressive *notional set* (see below) that suggests what the monomaniacal narrator's central obsession truly is (see chapter 1). As other scholars have shown (see chapter 3), the theme of time figures significantly in many of Poe's tales. Poe has been called "the maniac of time" by Jean-Paul Weber ("Edgar Poe or the Theme of the Clock"). Dennis W. Eddings, in his monograph *Poe's Tell-Tale Clocks*, insists, rather, that

the true maniacs of time are Poe's characters, not their creator. Poe uses clocks and clock imagery to delineate and judge his characters' attitudes toward life and its possibilities, their treatment of the clock being what tells the tale. Those who depend upon the clock would impose reliability and predictability upon a universe that is, for Poe, anything but reliable and predictable. Such characters are almost invariably the victims of their own clockwork mentality. On the other hand, those who beat the clock through a transcendent conversion of the physical world enter a new realm of possibility, an imaginative world "Out of Space – out of Time." (1)

In "The Colloquy of Monos and Una" we get a description of time passing that is somewhat different than in Poe's other tales and made possible by a sixth sense. After transcending what we think of as "death," Monos attempts to describe, with some difficulty (*adynata*), his new, unearthly sense of time going by:

Let me term it a mental pendulous pulsation. It was the moral [mental] embodiment of man's abstract idea of Time. By the absolute equalization of this movement – or of such as this – had the cycles of the firmamental orbs themselves been adjusted. By its aid I measured the irregularities of the clock upon the mantel, and of the watches of the attendants. Their tickings came sonorously to my ears. The slightest deviations from the true proportion – and these deviations were omni-prævalent – affected me just as violations of abstract truth were wont, on earth, to affect the moral sense. Although no two of the time-pieces in the chamber struck the individual seconds accurately together, yet I had no difficulty in holding steadily in mind the tones and the respective momentary errors of each. And this – this keen, perfect, self-existing sentiment of duration – this sentiment existing … independently of any succession of events – this idea – this sixth sense, upspringing from the ashes of the rest, was the first obvious and certain step of the intemporal soul upon the threshold of the temporal Eternity. (4: 209–10)

(Cf Melville's horologicals and chronometricals in *Pierre*.) After a year, the sense of time passing gives way to "that of mere locality" (211). In his engaging essay, "Poe and Phrenology," Hungerford says,

> The association of these two concepts in Poe's mind [the "idea of Time" and "that of mere locality"] is startlingly suggestive when one finds that [they] were represented in phrenology by definite, primary organs. Was Poe's analysis of these psychical states caught from the science of mind? Of the organ of *Time* Gall had written: "We see persons who find amusement in a collection of watches and clocks, and must have them all go with the greatest exactness." (13)

This organ of time is located slightly above the eye just forward of the temple. Poe himself had been examined by phrenologists and he may have believed himself to have had a well-developed organ of time – consider, after all, just how expansive Poe's famous forehead is! That causes me to wonder if the many references to time and time passing in his tales are there because Poe felt obliged to put them there, thus giving free rein to the workings of his own temporal organ. At any rate, that he did is our gain. For more on phrenology, see under *effictio* and especially *enargia*.
Pronunciation: chro no GRA phi a
Type: description

CLICHÉ: a trite, banal, commonplace, worn-out expression that was once striking, cleverly original, but has been used so often that it suggests rather a poverty of originality, of imagination, on the part of the user. This is not a rhetorical term, strictly speaking, and from the French rather than the Greek or Latin. In French, *cliché* refers to the stereotype plate used in printing – hence, a cliché is a stereotyped expression. Except for deliberate satire or comedy, all good writers avoid clichés. As Dupriez argues, however, a cliché can be revived by the substitution of terms (see Thoreau's *Walden* for some examples). In his review of *Elkswatawa*, Poe simply denies the truth of a certain cliché:

> And to a man of genius the world of invention is *never* shut. **There is always something new under the sun** – a fact susceptible of positive demonstration, in spite of a thousand dogmas to the contrary. (9: 123; cf "Oh, there is '*nothing* new under the sun' & Solomon is right – for once" [Ostrom, 427])

He adopts the same strategy elsewhere:

> With *him*, at least, a little learning is *no* dangerous thing. (*The Literati of New York City*, N.P. Willis, 15: 11)

We find several instances of the device in "The Literary Life of Thingum Bob, Esq.," a satirical look at writing and publishing in Poe's day, and Thingum himself is the object of satire as a poor writer and plagiarist. As the first, he indeed uses the occasional cliché:

> The result of my experiment with the old books [Dante, Homer, and Milton, from which he plagiarized], convinced me, in the first place, that **"honesty is the best policy."** (6: 8)

Thingum uses another, later, when he mentions how he used to "consume the midnight oil" (27). His father uses a cliché, too:

> "the trade of editor is best: – and if you can be a poet at the same time, – as most of the editors are, by the by, – why you will **kill two birds with one stone.**" (3; see also Stauffer's *The Merry Mood*, 20–1)

When Poe uses a cliché while speaking (writing) in his own voice, he typically does so *to comment* on the cliché (when he is not denying it outright):

> that **time *is* money** – to an American at least – is a proposition not for an instant to be disputed. ("Street Paving," 14: 166)

Compare with this, from a letter to Chivers (15 November 1845):

> Time with me now, is money & money more than time. (Ostrom, 302)

In a letter to "Annie" (19 February 1849), we find this:

> It is true, that **"Hell hath no fury like a woman scorned,"** but I have encountered such vengeance before, on far lighter grounds – that is to say, for a far less holy purpose, than I feel the defence of your good name to be. (Ostrom, 431)

Still, Poe begins several letters by apologizing for tardy responses with a cliché – as in this one of 4 December 1848:

> On the principle of **"better late than never"** I seize the first opportunity afforded me … to write you a few words of cordial thanks. (Ostrom, 411)

Finally, in a letter of 19 July 1849, we have "the darkest hour is just before daylight" (Ostrom, 455). For more on clichés, see Abrams (27), Harmon/Holman (99), and Dupriez (98–100). Cuddon (152) recommends Eric Partridge's *A Dictionary of Clichés*.
Pronunciation: clee SHAE

CLIMAX: the arrangement of words, phrases, or clauses in order of increasing importance. Lanham (27) suggests that a true climactic cluster must involve linked pairs of terms, by which I suppose he means *anadiplosis* (see above). I take the following passage as exemplifying climax, then, as Poe moves us gradually from stellar rotation, through in-rushing atoms, through the law of gravity, through atomic tendency toward unity, through, finally, to the act of God that set the whole process in motion. In other words, we move from stars to the most important entity in the universe:

> I consider this force as originating in the **rotation** of the stars: – this **rotation** as brought about by the **in-rushing** of the primary atoms, towards their respective centres of aggregation: – this **in-rushing** as the consequences of the **law** of Gravity: – this **law** as but the mode in which is necessarily manifested the **tendency** of the atoms to return into imparticularity: – this **tendency** to return as but the inevitable rëaction of the first and most sublime of **Acts** – that **act** by which a **God**, self-existing and alone existing, became all things at once, through dint of his volition, while all things were thus constituted a portion of God. (16: 255)

Here is another climactic passage from *Eureka*:

> Neither are we to consider the paths through which these different spheroids move – the moons about the **planets**, the **planets** about the **Sun**, or the **Sun** about the common centre – as circles in an accurate sense. (277)

This is the opposite kind of arrangement to *catacosmesis* (see above). It compares with one definition (the second) given by Lanham of *auxesis* (see above) and, like it, becomes a wonderful way of suggesting the idea of cosmic *hierarchy* important to Poe's vision of the universe. John P. Hussey suggests that the structure of *Eureka* in its entirety is climactic (39).

Poe shows his awareness of the climactic arrangement as an aspect of style in his discussion of Macaulay: "For his short sentences, for his antitheses, for his modulations, for his climaxes – for every thing that he does – a very slight analysis suffices to show a distinct reason" ("About Critics and Criticism," 13: 195). Poe clearly loved the climactic arrangement, and we find it now and then in his criticism, too:

> upon the prejudice of *caste* exemplified in the case of a **Catholic**, and this **Catholic** a **Spaniard**, and this **Spaniard** a **student**, and this **student** loving a **Gipsy**, and this **Gipsy** a **dancing-girl**, and this **dancing-girl** bearing the name Preciosa. ("The American Drama," 13: 60; see also 15: 110)

Type: amplification
Type: balance, antithesis, and paradox
Type: repetition: words

COHORTATIO: amplifying a point to arouse the hearers' indignation, as when the alleged crimes of an enemy or, in court, a defendant, are dwelt upon. Naturally, this device can figure in literature, not just oratory, and can be applied to one's readers. In his "Drake-Halleck" review, Poe dwells on what he considers the ridiculous literary patriotism of his fellow Americans – hoping, perhaps, to arouse the indignation of his readers into playing a role in reversing this partisan trend:

> We are becoming boisterous and arrogant in the pride of a too speedily assumed literary freedom. We throw off, with the most presumptuous and unmeaning hauteur, *all* deference whatever to foreign opinion – we forget, in the puerile inflation of vanity, that *the world* is the true theatre of the biblical histrio – we get up a hue and cry about the necessity of encouraging native writers of merit – we blindly fancy that we can accomplish this by indiscriminate puffing of good, bad, and indifferent, without taking the trouble to consider that what we choose to denominate encouragement is thus, by its general application, rendered precisely the reverse. In a word, so far from being ashamed of the many disgraceful literary failures to which our own inordinate vanities and misapplied patriotism have lately given birth, and so far from deeply lamenting that these daily puerilities are of home manufacture, we adhere pertinaciously to our original blindly conceived idea, and thus often find ourselves involved in the gross paradox of liking a stupid book the better, because, sure enough, its stupidity is American. (8: 277)

Cohortatio figures typically in Poe's most scathing critical reviews, although the body of his reviews – I mean their *tone* – is far more moderate than his contemporaries recognized (on this point, see also *antanagoge*).
Pronunciation: co hor TA ti o
Type: amplification
Type: devices of vehemence
Type: techniques of argument

COMMISERATIO: evoking pity in the audience for oneself or for someone else. Consider Poe's remarks about the author of *The Dream, and Other Poems*:

> There is, in reading these poems, an abiding sense of the desolation that has fallen on the heart of the writer – a desolation which only adds to the mournful music of her lyre, like the approach of death fabled to give music to the swan. We have studiously avoided, heretofore, touching upon this

subject, as we would not, by awakening pity, blind the judgment of the public; but we cannot avoid the remark that every page of this volume bears evidence that the heart of the authoress, like that of Rachel, will not be comforted. The arrow has entered deep into her soul. Like Mrs. Hemans, unfortunate in her domestic life … she "seeks, as the stricken deer, to weep in silence and loneliness." Hers is a hard lot: deserted by the one who has sworn to love her, and maligned by the unfeeling world, she has not even the consolation of weeping with her children, and finding some relief in their caresses for her broken heart. Hear her once more – we have almost wept as we read – hear her, when gazing in the twilight at the pictures of her absent children [here follows a quotation]. (10: 103–4)

Poe's rhetorical powers of *pathos* are evident, and that he is aware of his use of *commiseratio* is clear by his remark that he has attempted to avoid "awakening pity" in the readers of the review. That he immediately goes on to do so, after having stated his desire not to "blind the judgment of the public," amounts to *paraleipsis* (see below).

Pronunciation: com mi se RA ti o

Type: devices of vehemence

COMMORATIO: emphasizing a strong point by repeating it several times in different words. This device appears in Poe's definition of the psychological theory he dubbed the "imp of the perverse":

> It was this unfathomable longing of the soul *to vex itself* – to offer violence to its own nature – to do wrong for the wrong's sake only – that urged me to continue and finally to consummate the injury I had inflicted upon the unoffending brute. ("The Black Cat," 5: 146)

That the device figures in Poe's impassioned lectures and critical reviews will not likely surprise anyone:

> There neither exists nor *can* exist any work more thoroughly dignified – more supremely noble than this very poem – **this poem *per se* – this poem which is a poem and nothing more – this poem written solely for the poem's sake.** ("The Poetic Principle," 14: 272; see also 273)

Compare with Dupriez's definition of *metabole* (274) and see under *amplificatio*. As well, compare with *synonymia, iteratio,* and *disjunctio*.

Pronunciation: com mo RA ti o

Type: amplification

Type: repetition: clauses, phrases, and ideas

COMMUNICATIO: appearing to consult one's audience for their advice or opinions. In his "Drake-Halleck" review, Poe quotes the criticism of his editorial tendencies from one Col. Stone, of the New York *Commercial Advertiser*; he complains that Stone has provided mere assertions without supporting his case with examples. Knowing that Stone will no doubt read Poe's response, Poe replies thus:

> We call upon the Colonel for assistance in this dilemma. We wish to be
> shown our blunders that we may correct them – to be made aware of our
> flippancy, that we may avoid it hereafter – and above all to have our person-
> alities pointed out that we may proceed forthwith with a repentant spirit, to
> make the *amende honorable.* (8: 280)

This debating trick is part of the appeal to *ethos*, for one flatters one's audience in asking their opinion, the better to persuade them and gain their approval (that Poe is very likely being *ironic* here does not disqualify the passage from being categorized as *communicatio*). Taylor discusses this device under the term *anacoenosis* (67), as does Lanham (9–10).
Pronunciation: com mu ni CA ti o
Type: emotional appeals
Type: techniques of argument

COMPROBATIO: complimenting one's judges or hearers to gain their confidence, their favour; showing approval of the good traits belonging to one's auditors:

> "My *dear* uncle," said I, closing the door gently, and approaching him with
> the blandest of smiles, "you are always so *very* kind and considerate, and have
> evinced your benevolence in so many – so *very* many ways – that – that I feel
> I have only to suggest this little point to you once more to make sure of your
> full acquiescence." ("Three Sundays in a Week," 4: 227)

Pronunciation: com pro BA ti o
Type: devices of vehemence
Type: techniques of argument

CONGERIES: a multiplication or heaping up of many words. For examples, see under "seriation" and *synathroesmus*. Sometimes *congeries* is considered synonymous with *accumulatio* and is discussed by rhetors under that term.

CONSOLATIO: "Consoling one who grieves; a stylized letter or essay of condolence" (Lanham, 40). In Poe's drama, "Politian," Lalage has been betrayed by her lover, Castiglione. Politian, who is in love with Lalage, shows up and attempts to diminish her sorrow:

> *Lalage.* And dost thou speak of love
> To *me*, Politian? – doest thou speak of love
> To Lalage? – ah wo – ah wo is me!
> This mockery is most cruel – most cruel indeed!
> *Politian.* **Weep not! Oh, sob not thus! – thy bitter tears**
> Will madden me. Oh mourn not, Lalage –
> Be comforted! I know – I know it all,
> **And *still* I speak of love.** (7: 71)

A synonymous term is *paramythia*.
Pronunciation: con so LA ti o
Type: devices of vehemence

CONSONANCE: a kind of reverse alliteration, similarity of consonant sounds, especially when they come at the end of nearby words. Given Poe's sensitivity to the auditory qualities of language, we would expect this device to figure in his poetry and even, perhaps, in his prose fiction; when we find it in his literary criticism, we may wonder to what extent it may be accidental. In the following exemplification, note the repetition of the *s* sounds, most of them in the middle or at the end of words:

> In contrast between the artless, thoughtless, and careless character of Undine
> before possessing a soul. (Review of *Undine: A Miniature Romance*, 10: 36)

Cluett and Kampeas remind us that prose employing auditory agreeableness – devices of sound – is characteristic of the Ciceronian high style (21–2).
Pronunciation: CON so nance
Type: repetition: letters, syllables, and sounds

CONTINUATOR: words and phrases that typically come after a catalogue (see under "seriation") to complete it. *Neutral* continuators are words and phrases such as *etc.*, *and so on*, *and so forth*, *and the like*. Continuators add to the sense of copiousness (wordiness) created by seriation; they look back to the list and point ahead, continue it, though without specificity. Here is an example from *Pym* involving a list of nouns:

He planted onions, potatoes, cabbages, **and a great many other vegetables.**
(3: 161)

The example illustrating nominal seriation (see below) also ends with a
neutral continuator.

A *satirical* continuator comprises words that continue a series without
specificity but throw a critical glance back at it. In the following example, Poe cannot help showing off his Latin, as he does so often (*"et id genus omne"* means "and all that sort"):

He was great in dreams, portents, **et id genus omne** of rigmarole. ("Three
Sundays in a Week," 4: 231–2)

The continuator expands the formula by way of an often-unexpected
classifying word (in this case, *rigmarole*) that throws a new light on the
previous members of the list (see also 10: 212).

And what about continuators that are neither neutral nor satirical but
positive? We might call the following a *eulogistic continuator*:

Mr. Irving in his vivid account of the primitive French Canadian Merchant,
his jovial establishments and dependents – of the licensed traders, missionar-
ies, *voyageurs*, and *coureurs des bois* – of the British Canadian Fur Merchant –
of the rise of the great Company of the "North-West," its constitution and
internal trade; its parliamentary hall and banquetting room; its boating, its
huntings, its wassailings, **and other magnificent feudal doings in the wilder-
ness.** (Review of *Astoria*, 9: 208)

See chapter 5 for Poe's interesting use of neutral continuators for satire.
Type: addition, subtraction, and substitution: words, phrases, and clauses
Type: amplification

CONTRARIUM: "One of two opposite statements is used to prove
the other" (Lanham, 41):

As far as I can understand the "loving our enemies," it implies the hating our
friends. ("Fifty Suggestions," 14: 171)

We like to think Poe was merely being facetious, here, rather than that
he was actually looking for the authority to hate his friends. Let us say,
then, that this is a facetious exemplification of *contrarium*.

A supposedly synonymous term is *enantiosis* – but see Dupriez (51).
Complicating matters further is Sonnino's definition of *contrarium* as
enthymeme (an incomplete syllogism), but he also relates it to *antithesis*
(62). Certainly it is a kind of antithesis, and Lanham stresses an argu-

mentative function for it rather than seeing it merely as verbal wit involving opposites. Espy, using *enantiosis* rather than *contrarium*, considers it merely as a kind of irony – "A negative statement of what is to be understood affirmatively, or vice versa" (91); Taylor also sees the term as involving irony. Clearly, rhetors cannot agree on a single definition.

Pronunciation: con TRA ri um
Type: balance, antithesis, and paradox
Type: techniques of argument

CORRECTIO: see under *epanorthosis*.
Pronunciation: cor REC ti o

DEESIS: an emotional entreaty, supplication, either of gods or humans. Here is a vehement entreaty to Poe's good friend, John Kennedy, written (in a letter of 11 September 1835) when the former was in one of his black moods – evidence supporting (in part) the theory that Poe was a manic depressive (see also Ostrom, 404, 437):

> I am wretched, and know not why. Console me – for you can. But let it be quickly – or it will be too late. Write me immediately. Convince me that it is worth one's while – that it is at all necessary to live, and you will prove yourself indeed my friend. Persuade me to do what is right. (Ostrom, 73)

The term is also known as *deisis*, *obsecratio*, and *obtestatio*. See also Dupriez on *supplication* (434–5).
Pronunciation: de E sis
Type: devices of vehemence

DEHORTATIO: dissuasion; advice to the contrary. Old Charley Goodfellow practises this device on his fellow Rattleburghers:

> the people of Rattleborough, principally through the persuasion of Mr. Pennifeather, came at length to the determination of dispersing over the adjacent country in search of the missing Mr. Shuttleworthy … I forget, however, by what ingenious train of reasoning it was that "Old Charley" finally convinced the assembly that this was the most injudicious plan that could be pursued. Convince them, however, he did – all except Mr. Pennifeather; and, in the end, it was arranged that a search should be instituted carefully and very thoroughly by the burghers *en masse*. ("Thou Art the Man," 5: 295)

We even find *dehortatio* – coupled with an apostrophe – in Poe's literary criticism:

> Now, we do not object to the introduction of these personages if they are necessary to the plot; but, for heaven's sake, Mr. Bulwer, give us something more than mere automatons! **Don't ask us in to a second Mrs. Jarley's wax-works!** (Review of *Zanoni*, 11: 122)

Taylor prefers to define the term as an attempt "to dissuade one's hearers from approaching danger" (86). Compare this term with *adhortatio* (above) and *protrope* (urging hearers to act by threats or promises).

Pronunciation: de hor TA ti o
Type: devices of vehemence
Type: techniques of argument
Type: "biblical"

DELIBERATIO: weighing arguments or courses of action. In *The Narrative of Arthur Gordon Pym of Nantucket*, Pym finds himself facing quite a dilemma. Severe deprivations have put his dog, Tiger, on the verge of going mad and attacking him. Pym deliberates what to do:

> I was at a loss what course to pursue. I could not endure the thought of killing him, yet it seemed absolutely necessary for my own safety.

Deliberatio implies hesitation while struggling to decide, but Pym's safety requires that he not hesitate for too long: "At last I could endure my terrible situation no longer, and determined to make my way from the box at all hazards, and dispatch him" (3: 43).

Instances of *deliberatio* often involve asking oneself questions as to the appropriate argument or action. Dupriez suggests that this device can also entail a *pretence* to weighing arguments rather than sincere deliberation, but then how would it differ from *aporia* (above)? Another term for *deliberatio* is *dubitatio*, which Sonnino considers synonymous with *aporia* (82–3).

Pronunciation: de li be RA ti o
Type: techniques of argument

DENDROGRAPHIA: a type of *enargia* (see below) – the description of trees. The figure abounds in "Landor's Cottage":

> beyond all question the most magnificent tree I have ever seen ... It was a triple-stemmed tulip tree – the *Liriodendron Tulipiferum* – one of the natural

order of magnolias. Its three trunks separated from the parent at about three feet from the soil, and diverging very slightly and gradually, were not more than four feet apart at the point where the largest stem shot out into foliage: this was at an elevation of about eighty feet. The whole height of the principal division was one hundred and twenty feet. Nothing can surpass in beauty the form, or the glossy, vivid green of the leaves of the tulip tree. In the present instance they were fully eight inches wide; but their glory was altogether eclipsed by the gorgeous splendor of the profuse blossoms. Conceive, closely congregated, a million of the largest and most resplendent tulips! Only thus can the reader get any idea of the picture I would convey. And then the stately grace of the clean, delicately-granulated columnar stems, the largest four feet in diameter, at twenty from the ground. The innumerable blossoms, mingling with those of other trees scarcely less beautiful, although infinitely less majestic, filled the valley with more than Arabian perfumes. (6: 260–1)

Pronunciation: den dro GRA phi a

Type: description

D I A C O P E : repetition of a word with one or a few words between:
   "We careered **round** and **round** for perhaps an hour, flying rather than float-
   ing, getting gradually **more** and **more** into the middle of the surge, and
   then **nearer** and **nearer** to its horrible inner edge." ("A Descent into the
   Maelström," 2: 240–1)

Like other devices of repetition, *diacope* is a good device for emphasis and can also suggest heightened emotion, as in this excerpt from a letter:
   Could I believe in the efficiency of prayers to the God of Heaven, I would in-
   deed **kneel** – humbly **kneel** – at this the most earnest epoch of my life –
   kneel in entreaty for words. (Ostrom, 382–3)

We find *diacope* used, though more calmly, here and there in Poe's criticism, too:
   About everything she writes we perceive this indescribable and incomprehensible **charm** – a **charm** of which the elements are, perhaps, a vivid fancy and a
   keen sense of the proportionate. (Review of *A Wreath of Wild Flowers from
   New England*, 13: 114)

Pronunciation: di A co pe

Type: repetition: words

DIAERESIS: (1) dividing a larger component into its constituent smaller ones in order to explore the idea more fully – a way of taking a general statement and amplifying, enlarging it, by examining its details; (2) dividing one syllable into two, pronouncing each. Poe's "The Domain of Arnheim" provides an instance of the first definition – actually, we find *diaeresis* within *diaeresis* here (the second elementary condition of bliss is subdivided into examples given of healthy people):

> He admitted but four elementary principles, or, more strictly, conditions, of bliss. That which he considered chief was (strange to say!) the simple and purely physical one of free exercise in the open air. "The health," he said, "attainable by other means is scarcely worth the name." He instanced the ecstasies of the fox-hunter, and pointed to the tillers of the earth, the only people who, as a class, can be fairly considered happier than others. His second condition was the love of woman. His third, and most difficult of realization, was the contempt of ambition. His fourth was an object of unceasing pursuit; and he held that, other things being equal, the extent of attainable happiness was in proportion to the spirituality of this object. (6: 177; see also 13: 59)

This is also one definition of *dinumeratio*, says Lanham (50; 55), following other rhetors. Sometimes, he tells us, the amplification can involve the "division of subject into adjuncts, cause into effects, antecedent into consequents." The device is similar to *divisio*; it would be synonymous with *epanodos* except that, with this latter device, the terms used in the general statement are repeated in the discussion of the particulars. For instance, if the words in the phrase "elementary principles, or, more strictly, conditions, of bliss" were repeated with each of the four particulars, we would have *epanodos*.

Pronunciation: di AE re sis
Pronunciation: di nu me RA ti o
Type: amplification
Type: techniques of argument

DIALLAGE: bringing in several arguments tending to the same conclusion; a summing up. In the Gothic detective tale "The Murders in the Rue Morgue," Dupin employs this device to summarize the *outré* (bizarre, unusual, excessive, extreme) features of the mystery and to make his case that the killer of the L'Espanaye women is not human:

"If now, in addition to all these things, you have properly reflected upon the odd disorder of the chamber, we have gone so far as to combine the ideas of an agility astounding, a strength superhuman, a ferocity brutal, a butchery without motive, a *grotesquerie* in horror absolutely alien from humanity, and a voice foreign in tone to the ears of men of many nations, and devoid of all distinct or intelligible syllabification. What result, then, has ensued?" (4: 180–1)
Cf *dinumeratio*, a recapitulation, summary.
Pronunciation: di AL la ge
Type: amplification
Type: techniques of argument

DIALOGISMUS: speaking in another person's character (a type of *enargia*). In "The Murders in the Rue Morgue," the Watson-like narrator has told us that one of Dupin's methods of detection is to achieve identification with the mind of his opponent – whoever is involved in the crime under question. Like the analytical draughts player, Dupin as analyst "throws himself into the spirit of his opponent, identifies himself therewith" (4: 147). Dupin does this very thing in determining what actions the sailor will take, and thus provides an instance of *dialogismus*:
"He will reason thus: – 'I am innocent; I am poor; my Ourang-Outang is of great value – to one in my circumstances a fortune of itself – why should I lose it through idle apprehensions of danger? Here it is, within my grasp'."
(184)
We have it again in "The Mystery of Marie Rogêt," when Dupin attempts to identify with the thought processes of Marie:
"We may imagine her thinking thus – 'I am to meet a certain person for the purpose of elopement, or for certain other purposes known only to myself. It is necessary that there be no chance of interruption'." (5: 44)
We also find an extended instance of the device in "The Longfellow War" (12: 58), where Poe attempts to reduce his opponent's argument – that there is no such thing as plagiarism – to absurdity by imagining what an attorney might say in court making the same point about petty larceny (that there is no such thing). See also 11: 39, 252–3.
Pronunciation: di a log IS mus
Type: description
Type: techniques of argument

DIALOGUE TAG: words preceding or following dialogue that indicate who is speaking: "Dupin replied," "she said, laughingly," "he answered." The omission of dialogue tags can increase the pace of a story. In the following passage from "Bon-Bon," the first line has a dialogue tag but the following lines do not:

"The – hiccup! – soul," **replied the metaphysician**, referring to his MS.,
"is undoubtedly" —
　　"No, sir!"
　　"Indubitably" —
　　"No, sir!"
　　"Indisputably" —
　　"No, sir!"
　　"Evidently" —
　　"No, sir!"
　　"Incontrovertibly" —
　　"No, sir!"
　　"Hiccup!" —
　　"No, sir!"
　　"And beyond all question, a" — (2: 141)

DIALYSIS: (1) a method of analysis whereby one argues from a series of compound hypothetical propositions, in favour of or against something, to a conclusion (either this, or that, therefore …; either this, in which case … or that, in which case …; if … then, if … then). If I understand this term correctly, I would offer this bit of reasoning from Dupin as an instance:

"our agreement has been arranged with the Prefect. We both know this gentleman well. It will not do to trust him too far. **If, dating our inquiries from the body found, and thence tracing a murderer, we yet discover this body to be that of some other individual than Marie; or, if starting from the living Marie, we find her, yet find her unassassinated – in either case we lose our labor; since it is Monsieur G — with whom we have to deal. For our own purpose, therefore, if not for the purpose of justice, it is indispensable that our first step should be the determination of the identity of the corpse with the Marie Rogêt who is missing.**" ("The Mystery of Marie Rogêt," 5: 20–1) Compare with "dilemma."

Lanham offers a second definition: "A statement of a problem followed by particularization of the alternatives" (52). Perhaps the opening of a letter (16 January 1845) provides an exemplification:

> Dear Griswold – if you will permit me to call you so – Your letter occasioned me first pain and then pleasure: – pain because it gave me to see that I had lost, through my own folly, an honorable friend: – pleasure, because I saw in it a hope of reconciliation. (Ostrom, 275)

Pronunciation: di A ly sis
Type: balance, antithesis, and paradox
Type: techniques of argument

DIALYTON: sometimes used as a synonym for *asyndeton* (see above), but can also mean "emphasizing a word by setting it off from the rest of the sentence in other ways besides asyndeton" (Lanham, 52) – with dashes, for example:

> The inscription commemorates the surrender of – what? – why, "of Lord
> Cornwallis." ("Mellonta Tauta," 6: 215; see also 9: 188)

Readers of Poe know that he frequently uses dashes to separate words from the rest of the sentence in which they are found. Typically he does so to emphasize heightened emotions on the part of his narrators.
Pronunciation: di A ly ton

DIASTOLE: a type of *metaplasm*, lengthening a short syllable or vowel, or stressing a normally unstressed syllable. We should certainly expect to find this device in poetry for the sake of metre:

> Above the closed and **fringéd** lid. ("The Sleeper," 7: 51)

With the accent, Poe has stressed the final *ed* in *fringed*. He uses the device several more times in his poetry: wingéd, damnéd, hornéd, Accurséd, tunéd. See also Espy (165). Synonymous terms are *eciasis* (Joseph, 294) and *ectasis* (Lanham, 52).
Pronunciation: di A sto le
Type: addition, subtraction, and substitution: letters and syllables

DIATYPOSIS: recommending useful precepts, rules of conduct, to someone. "How to Write a Blackwood Article" in a sense constitutes an extended instance of *diatyposis* since it involves largely the advice given

by Mr Blackwood to an inspiring writer, the narrator Psyche Zenobia.
Here is an excerpt of the advice:

> "The matter stands thus. In the first place, your writer of intensities must
> have very black ink, and a very big pen, with a very blunt nib. And, mark me,
> Miss Psyche Zenobia!" he continued … "mark me! – *that pen – must – never
> be mended!* Herein, madam, lies the secret, the soul, of intensity." (2: 272)

Pronunciation: di a ty PO sis
Type: devices of vehemence
Type: example, allusion, and citation of authority
Type: techniques of argument
Type: "biblical"

DIAZEUGMA: one subject with many verbs. Here are two instances
from "The Black Cat":

> Upon my touching him, **he** [subject] immediately **arose** [verb], **purred** [verb]
> loudly, **rubbed** [verb] against my hand, and **appeared** [verb] delighted with
> my notice. This, then, was the very creature of which I was in search. I at
> once offered to purchase it of the landlord; but this **person** [noun] **made**
> [verb] no claim to it – **knew** [verb] nothing of it – **had never seen** [verb
> phrase] it before. (5: 149)

Clearly, *ellipsis* (see below) is used with this device, and the combined
use of *ellipsis* and *diazeugma* is a splendid way to emphasize action and
to help ensure a swift pace to the narrative – a sense of many things happening, and quickly. The device figures several times in the tale of detection, "Thou Art the Man." I indicate the missing subject-pronoun *he*
with a caret (∧):

> He followed his victim to the vicinity of the pool; there ∧ **shot** his horse with
> a pistol; ∧ **despatched** the rider with its butt end; ∧ **possessed** himself of the
> pocket-book; and, supposing the horse dead, ∧ **dragged** it with great labour
> to the brambles by the pond. (5: 307)

Pronunciation: di a ZEUG ma
Type: addition, subtraction, and substitution: words, phrases, and clauses
Type: brevity

DICAEOLOGIA: (sometimes spelled *dichologia*) defending one's words
or acts with reasonable excuses; defending briefly the justice of one's cause.
We might expect this device to figure in Poe's first-person confessional

tales. Here is an instance from "The Black Cat" describing the psychological phenomenon that Poe called the "imp of the perverse":

> And then came, as if to my final and irrevocable overthrow, the spirit of PER-
> VERSENESS. Of this spirit philosophy takes no account. Yet I am not more
> sure that my soul lives, than I am that perverseness is one of the primitive im-
> pulses of the human heart – one of the indivisible primary faculties, or senti-
> ments, which give direction to the character of Man. Who has not, a
> hundred times, found himself committing a vile or a silly action, for no other
> reason than because he knows he should *not*? ... It was this unfathomable
> longing of the soul *to vex itself* – to offer violence to its own nature – to do
> wrong for the wrong's sake only – that urged me to continue and finally to
> consummate the injury I had inflicted upon the unoffending brute. One
> morning, in cool blood, I slipped a noose about its neck and hung it to the
> limb of a tree. (5: 146)

What gives an interesting twist to the use of *dicaeologia* in Poe's tales is
the extent to which we, the readers, may find the defence, the excuse,
outrageously unconvincing and bizarre. Poe maintains an objective distance with us – certainly in "The Tell-Tale Heart" – and watches the
ironic dicaeologia.

See also *praemunitio*. We may also wonder how *dicaeologia* differs
from *proecthesis* – defending what one has done or said by giving reasons
and circumstances (Lanham, 119). Similar are *aetiologia* and *pareuresis*.
Pronunciation: di cae o LO gi a
Type: devices of vehemence
Type: techniques of argument

DIGESTION: an orderly listing of points to be discussed:

> My object is simply, in the first place, to say a few words of Von Kempelen
> himself (with whom, some years ago, I had the honor of a slight personal ac-
> quaintance,) since every thing which concerns him must necessarily, at this
> moment, be of interest; and, in the second place, to look in a general way,
> and speculatively, at the results of the discovery. ("Von Kempelen and His
> Discovery," 6: 245)

The device figures at the beginning of *Eureka* – as it should, given that *di-
gestion* compares with *division* (the third part of a classical oration), and that
Eureka can be read as following the structure of this kind of speech, as John
P. Hussey argues ("Narrative Voice and Classical Rhetoric in *Eureka*"):

I design to speak of the *Physical, Metaphysical and Mathematical – of the Material and Spiritual Universe: – of its Essence, its Origin, its Creation, its Present Condition and its Destiny.* (16: 185)

Type: amplification

Type: techniques of argument

DIGRESSIO (digression): any digressive tale or interpolated anecdote, especially one prepared in advance on a commonplace subject, and inserted at the appropriate time (Lanham, 54). While Lanham suggests digressing as a deliberate and planned ploy, Sonnino (73) quotes some rhetors who suggest that the digression is spontaneous, unplanned. Either way, the digression, which must be pertinent and useful, can be inserted to praise, condemn, adorn, charm, or prepare for what follows. It can come at the beginning of a speech or prose passage or at the end, but "Quintilian thinks the position of the anecdote is not crucial" (Lanham). Sonnino quotes Peacham as saying that "Digressions are taken either from the declaration of deeds, the descriptions of persons, places and times, the reporting of apologies [fables] and similitudes" (74). We all know that a badly used digression can destroy the unity of the work in which it figures, but the following exemplification shows that Poe could use it well to illustrate a point about the critic's function:

It was by no means my design, however, to expatiate upon the *merits* of what I should read you. These will necessarily speak for themselves. **Boccalini, in his "Advertisements from Parnassus," tells us that Zoilus once presented Apollo a very caustic criticism upon a very admirable book: – whereupon the god asked him for the beauties of the work. He replied that he only busied himself about the errors. On hearing this, Apollo, handing him a sack of unwinnowed wheat, bade him pick out *all the chaff* for his reward.**

Now this fable answers very well as a hit at the critics – but I am by no means sure that the god was in the right. I am by no means certain that the true limits of the critical duty are not grossly misunderstood. ("The Poetic Principle," 14: 281)

The digression makes possible, makes necessary, the *reditus ad propositum* – the return to the subject after a digression (see below). Harmon and Holman have some useful observations on the term (154); see also Dupriez (135–6). (See also *fable* and *paradiegesis.*)

Pronunciation: di GRES si o

Type: techniques of argument

DILEMMA: any technique of argument that offers an opponent a choice, or a series of choices, all of which are unacceptable to the opponent. I now and then try this out on my students: "Why didn't you follow my instructions when you wrote your essays? Either you're too cocky to do what you're told, or you're too ignorant! Either way, it doesn't look good on you!" That is certainly a nasty way of arguing, a rhetorical trap. It may not surprise us that Poe, who could be pretty nasty himself, rhetorically, offers a dilemma to an opponent occasionally:

> it is Outis' design to impose the idea of similarity between my lines and those of Coleridge, upon some one or two grossly ignorant individuals: at the same time, whoever attempts such an imposition is rendered liable at least to the suspicion of very gross ignorance himself. **The ignorance or the knavery are the two uncomfortable horns of his dilemma.** ("The Longfellow War," 12: 70)

On the next page Poe says, "If Outis will now take a seat upon one of the horns of his dilemma, I will proceed to the third variation of the charges *insinuated* through the medium of the 'snarling critic'." Elsewhere, he provides another dilemma:

> those who write *after* Macaulay have to choose between the two horns of a dilemma: – **they must be weak and original, or imitative and strong.** ("About Critics and Criticism," 13: 196)

To be weak is unacceptable – or should be; to be imitative is also unacceptable – or should be. Both choices are problematic.

Rhetors typically relate dilemma to *divisio* and *dialysis* (see above). Dupriez mentions dilemma frequently; see his index.

Type: balance, antithesis, and paradox

Type: techniques of argument

DINUMERATIO: (1) a summary that refreshes the hearer's or reader's memory. Near the end of Suggestion XXIII (23) of his "Fifty Suggestions," Poe begins thus:

> To sum up our results in respect to this very simple, but much *vexata quæstio*: – (14: 177)

We know we have an example of *dinumeratio*. Consider also the passage in "The Mystery of Marie Rogêt" where Dupin begins with, "Let us sum up now the meagre yet certain fruits of our long analysis" (5: 60; see also *Eureka*, 16: 241–2). Lanham reminds us, quite rightly, that this meaning of the term can be related to the summing-up stage of a speech, the *peroration* (56). But *dinumeratio* has another meaning: (2) "Dividing a subject into subheadings; amplifying a general fact or idea by giving all of its details" (Lanham, 55). Whereas the first meaning of the term describes an act "going" (summarizing and recalling – cf *anamnesis*), the second meaning describes the act "coming," "when one is opening out the matter to be discussed." As such, it compares with *divisio*, "the stage of an oration where one opens out one's argument" (Lanham, 56). Other rhetors provide the definition of *dinumeratio* as simply amplification, not necessarily coming at the opening of a speech or passage of literature. For another good example, see "The Poetic Principle" (14: 275).

Pronunciation: di nu me RA ti o

Type: amplification

Type: techniques of argument

DISJUNCTIO: the use of different verbs in parallel structure to express similar ideas in successive clauses (Lanham, 57) – a kind of *commoratio* (see above):

> You **dispel** its dream-like luxury: – you **dissolve** the atmosphere of the mystic in which its whole nature is bound up: – you **exhaust** it of its breath of faëry. (Review of *George P. Morris*, 10: 42)

Pronunciation: dis JUNC ti o

Type: balance, antithesis, and paradox

Type: repetition: clauses, phrases, and ideas

DISTINCTIO: reference to various meanings of a word in order to remove ambiguities:

> And here, lest I be misunderstood, permit me to digress for one moment merely to observe that the exceedingly brief and simple Latin phrase which I have employed, is invariably mistranslated and misconceived. *"Cui bono?"* in all the crack novels and elsewhere [is] rendered "to what purpose," or (as if *quo bono*) "to what good." Their true meaning, nevertheless, is "for whose advantage". *Cui*, to whom; *bono*, is it for a benefit. It is a purely legal phrase, and applicable precisely in cases such as we have now under consideration, where the probability of the doer of a deed hinges upon the probability of the benefit accruing to this individual or to that from the deed's accomplishment. ("Thou Art the Man," 5: 299; see also 15: 260)

Poe's knowledge of Latin, in which he excelled at the University of Virginia, is evident here. It may not surprise us that we find occasional instances of *distinctio* in Poe's literary criticism:

The word *plot*, as commonly accepted, conveys but an indefinite meaning. Most persons think of it as a simple *complexity* … But the greatest involution of incident will not result in plot; which, properly defined, is *that in which no part can be displaced without ruin to the whole.* (Review of *Night and Morning*, 10: 116–17)

The device is also significant in *Eureka* (see, for example, 16: 186)

Pronunciation: dis TINC ti o

Type: amplification

Type: techniques of argument

DOUBLETS: pairs of grammatical items joined by coordinators such as *and* or *or*. We should distinguish between:

- simple doublet (words connected by a coordinator but not by meaning)
- pleonastic doublet (words so connected that overlap in meaning largely or entirely)
- antithetical doublet (words so connected that are opposite in meaning – see above)
- range doublet (a word-pair in which the members refer to the range of a group – see below)

The following passage from *Pym* contains six doublets, two of which are pleonastic, or nearly so:

> It is strange, too, that he most strongly enlisted my feelings in behalf of the life of a seaman, when he depicted his more terrible moments of **suffering and despair** … My visions were of **shipwreck and famine**; of **death or captivity** among barbarian hordes; of a lifetime dragged out in **sorrow and tears**, upon **some gray and desolate** rock, in an ocean **unapproachable and unknown**. (3: 17)

Poe quotes a well-known pleonastic doublet in "Mellonta Tauta":

> a corner-stone being cautiously laid by itself **"solitary and alone"** (excuse me for quoting the great Amriccan [sic] poet Benton!) as a guarantee of the magnanimous intention. (6: 214)

Harold Beaver tells us that this "pompous pleonasm became a national byword" (422n30). In his essay on "The American Drama," Poe complains about the use in a play of a pleonastic doublet, *"attired/ And garmented,"* calling it a tautology (see *tautologia*).

ECPHONESIS: vehement exclamation expressing emotion (sometimes equivalent to *apostrophe* – see above):

> Ill-fated and mysterious man! – bewildered in the brilliancy of thine own imag-
> ination, and fallen in the flames of thine own youth! Again in fancy I behold
> thee! Once more thy form hath risen before me! ("The Assignation," 2: 109)

Compare with *augendi causa*. Poe's frequent use of *ecphonesis* is surely responsible to a large degree for the charge that he wrote in an overwrought style, and those who deplore his prose must surely wince when
they force their way through the opening paragraph of "The Assignation." Such critics, however, must ask themselves to what extent Poe really is to blame; they should consider that Poe's *narrators* are themselves
responsible for their own stylistic excesses, Poe himself maintaining an
objective distance from them as a craftsman in complete and conscious
control (see chapter 1). This is Gargano's thesis in "The Question of
Poe's Narrators," and other scholars (for instance, Stauffer and Vitanza)
have come to the same conclusion.

Pronunciation: ec pho NE sis

Type: devices of vehemence

EFFICTIO: the description of a person's outward appearance:

> It was with difficulty that I could bring myself to admit the identity of the
> wan being before me with the companion of my early boyhood. Yet the char-
> acter of his face had been at all times remarkable. A cadaverousness of com-
> plexion; an eye large, liquid, and luminous beyond comparison; lips
> somewhat thin and very pallid, but of a surpassingly beautiful curve; a nose
> of a delicate Hebrew model, but with a breadth of nostril unusual in similar
> formations; a finely moulded chin, speaking, in its want of prominence, of a
> want of moral energy; hair of a more than web-like softness and tenuity;
> these features, with an inordinate expansion above the regions of the temple
> [like Poe's], made up altogether a countenance not easily to be forgotten.
> ("The Fall of the House of Usher," 3: 278–9)

This description of Roderick Usher has a basis in phrenology (see under
enargia and *chronographia*) and a related pseudoscience, physiognomy
(anthroposcopy). Occasionally we get some *effictio* in Poe's reviews; here
he describes the actress, Mrs Mowatt – and note the physiognomic eval-
uation again:

> Her face is a remarkably fine one, and of that precise character best adapted
> to the stage. The forehead is the least prepossessing feature, although it is by
> no means an unintellectual one. The eyes are grey, brilliant and expressive,

without being full. The nose is well formed, with the Roman curve, and strongly indicative of energy; this quality is also shown in the prominence of the chin. (12: 187)

In modern criticism we tend not to name this device, *effictio*, using instead the broader term *characterization*. Another term for *effictio* might be *prosopographia* (Lanham, 123).

Pronunciation: ef FIC ti o

Type: description

E I D O L O P O E I A : putting words in the mouth of someone who has died, or the speech thus assigned. It should come as no surprise that we find this device in some of Poe's works:

> the graves were closed with a sudden violence, while from out them arose a tumult of despairing cries, saying again – "Is it not – O God! is it *not* a very pitiful sight?" ("The Premature Burial," 5: 268)

In this Gothic passage, Poe literally has the dead speaking, but this device also refers to words that the deceased is *imagined* as saying – see Lanham's example (62). As such, *eidolopoeia* compares with *dialogismus*. Crowley notes that the term can also refer to a rhetorical exercise for students "wherein the character of a spirit or an image is depicted" (336).

Pronunciation: ei do lo po EI a

Type: techniques of argument

E L I S I O N : the omission of a vowel, consonant, or syllable in pronunciation. Rhetorical terms for the subtraction of letters and syllables are the following:

- *aphaeresis*: omitting a syllable from the beginning of a word (see above)
- *syncope*: omitting a syllable or letter from the middle of a word (see below)
- *apocope*: omitting a syllable or letter from the end of a word (see above)
- *synalepha*: omitting letters so that two words are fused into one (see below)

Poe did not like elisions, although he used them now and then in his poetry. Still, he believed (quite correctly) that they are artificial and that, in poetry as in prose, the most natural language is preferable. Consider his condemnation of Amelia Welby's poetry:

> Neath ... is an awkward contraction [*aphaeresis*]. *All* contractions are awkward. It is no paradox, that the more prosaic the construction of verse, the better ... Mrs. Welby owes three-fourths of her power (so far as style is concerned), to her freedom from these vulgar, and particularly English errors – elision and inversion. *O'er* is, however, too often used by her in place of *over* [*syncope*], and *'t was* for *it was* [*synalepha*]. (11: 279–80; see also Marginalia, 16: 58).

Pronunciation: e LEE shun
Type: addition, subtraction, and substitution: letters and syllables
Type: ungrammatical, illogical, or unusual uses of language

ELLIPSIS: a kind of "minus additioning" – the omission of a word or words in a clause that would be necessary for full grammatical completeness but not for understanding of meaning. In the following quote I place in square brackets and bold the words that Poe omitted:

> In all that I endured there was no physical suffering, but of moral distress **[there was]** an infinitude ... The ghastly Danger to which I was subjected, haunted me day and night. In the former, the torture of meditation was excessive – in the latter, **[the torture of meditation was]** supreme. ("The Premature Burial," 5: 266)

Schemes of omission often indicate heightened, even increasing, emotional agitation because of the economy of expression involved (cf *prozeugma*). Quinn calls ellipsis "an extremely important stylistic device" (*Figures of Speech*, 28). Certainly its frequency in Poe's prose fiction tells us how much he loved brevity (although he did not always practice it). See *brevitas*, *brachylogia*, and all figures involving minus additioning. We encounter the device often in Poe's criticism as well. In the following passage, the missing phrase is *this work* or the pronoun *it* (indicated by a caret):

> This work appeared in 1834, Λ went through several editions, Λ was reprinted in London, Λ was very popular, and Λ deserved its popularity. (*The Literati of New York City*, Charles Fenno Hoffman, 15: 118)

We do find one place, however (the review of *Ideals and Other Poems*), where Poe complains about a poet's use of *ellipsis*:

> He is endeavoring too, and very literally, to render confusion worse confounded by the introduction into poetry of Carlyle's hyper-ridiculous elisions

[Poe means *ellipsis*] in prose. Here, for example, where the pronoun "he" is left to be understood:

> Now the fervent preacher rises,
>> And his theme is heavenly love,
> *Tells* how once the blessed Saviour
>> Left his throne above. (11: 115)

Clearly, Poe insists that, if one must use a figure of omission, the sense must remain intact. Obscurity is unacceptable. In the examples from "The Premature Burial," we are meant to repeat, mentally, words already supplied earlier in the sentence ("there was" and "the torture of meditation was"); in the verses Poe ridicules, however, the pronoun *he* has not appeared earlier. (The noun *preacher* has appeared earlier, though, and Poe is perhaps being unfair in disqualifying it as the item for mental repetition.)

Pronunciation: el LIP sis

Type: addition, subtraction, and substitution: words, phrases, and clauses

Type: brevity

ENALLAGE: when we substitute, exchange, one gender, number, case, person, mood, tense, or part of speech for another. When done deliberately, this is a figure of language; when done accidentally through ignorance, it is a vice of language. In English it is difficult to understand why a speaker or writer would want to use *enallage* except for ridicule (calling a man *she*, for example). Normally we would expect *enallage* as a vice of language in English, such as a breakdown in grammatical agreement between subjects and verbs, nouns and pronouns, or pronouns and pronouns:

Now, the **Day-Book** is a thing that **don't** lie. ("The Business Man," 4: 128)

In this example, we have a breakdown in subject-verb agreement: the singular subject "Day-Book" should be paired with the verb phrase "does [not]" rather than "do [not]." That instance is clearly used for comedic effect – but Poe, while quite good at catching instances of *enallage* in the prose of others in his capacity as literary critic (see, for example, 11: 216), occasionally made a blunder of his own:

None of these "Sketches" **have** the merit of an equal number of pages in that very fine novel. (Review of *Tales and Sketches* by Miss Sedgwick, 8: 162)

None should be paired with *has* rather than *have*. Here is another:

> and **neither** of these selections **embrace** any of the matter now issued. (Review of *The Critical and Miscellaneous Writings of Henry Lord Brougham*, 11: 100; see also 15: 115)

Enallage is the most general of a cluster of similar figures:

- *alleotheta* (also *allotheta* or *alloeosis*): another more general term but narrower than *enallage*, it means the substitution of one gender, number, case, mood, or tense for another (see above)
- *solecismus* (sometimes *solecismos* or *solecisme*): the ignorant misuse – presumably rather than a deliberate substitution – of genders, cases, and tenses
- *anthimeria*: using one part of speech for another – an adjective for an adverb, for example (see above); Joseph refers to this as "perhaps the most exciting" scheme of grammar, certainly as it figures in Shakespeare (62)
- *anthypallage*: changing grammatical case (possessives, subjects, objects) for emphasis
- *antiptosis*: substituting one case for another

Pronunciation: en AL la ge

Type: ungrammatical, illogical, or unusual uses of language

ENANTIOSIS: (1) irony; (2) *contrarium*. See under *contrarium*.

Pronunciation: en an ti O sis

ENARGIA: "A generic term for visually powerful, vivid description which recreates something or someone, as several theorists say, 'before your very eyes'"; "vigorous ocular demonstration" (Lanham, 64–5):

> I examined the contour of the lofty and pale forehead – it was faultless – how cold indeed that word when applied to a majesty so divine! – the skin rivalling the purest ivory, the commanding extent and repose, the gentle prominence of the regions above the temples; and then the raven-black, the glossy, the luxuriant and naturally-curling tresses, setting forth the full force of the Homeric epithet, "hyacinthine!" I looked at the delicate outlines of the nose – and nowhere but in the graceful medallions of the Hebrews had I beheld a similar perfection. There were the same luxurious smoothness of surface, the same scarcely perceptible tendency to the aquiline, the same harmoniously curved nostrils speaking the free spirit. I regarded the sweet mouth. Here was

indeed the triumph of all things heavenly – the magnificent turn of the short
upper lip – the soft, voluptuous slumber of the under – the dimples which
sported, and the color which spoke – the teeth glancing back, with a brilliancy almost startling, every ray of the holy light which fell upon them in her
serene and placid, yet most exultingly radiant of all smiles. I scrutinized the
formation of the chin – and here, too, I found the gentleness of breadth, the
softness and the majesty, the fullness and the spirituality, of the Greek.

("Ligeia," 2: 250–1)

Poe's belief in physiognomy is evident here – elsewhere (15: 43) he mentions the Swiss physiognomist Lavater – and Hungerford shows that the
detailed descriptions of the cranial and facial features of Poe's characters
often have a solid basis in another pseudoscience, phrenology, a system
of thought in which Poe very much believed ("Poe and Phrenology"). In
a *Southern Literary Messenger* book review on Mrs L. Miles's *Phrenology,
and the Moral Influence of Phrenology*, Poe writes that phrenology "has assumed the majesty of a science; and as a science, ranks among the most
important which can engage the attention of thinking beings" (13: 252).
He was himself examined by phrenologists, as he wrote to his friend
Frederick William Thomas (27 October 1841): "Speaking of heads – my
own *has been* examined by several phrenologists – all of whom spoke of
me in a species of extravaganza which I should be ashamed to repeat"
(Ostrom, 185). Poe's interest in phrenology explains why he provides
such notable instances of *enargia*, for the very appearance of characters
such as Ligeia and Roderick Usher contributes to the themes of their respective stories (see also *effictio*). Phrenology also figures in, for instance,
"The Business Man" and "The Imp of the Perverse." References to this
silly pseudoscience appear many times in Poe's *Literati of New York City*
(15: 7, 18, 60, 72, 91, 116, 118), and Poe should have recognized it as sheer
nonsense when it *failed*: "the forehead [of Charles Fenno Hoffman], *to
my surprise*, although high, gives no indication, in the region of the tem-
ples, of that ideality (or love of the beautiful) which is the distinguishing
trait of his moral nature" (my italics; 15: 122).

Enargia was used by several of Poe's contemporaries to describe *him*,
and in each vivid description of his remarkable head we find references
to phrenology. The editor of the *Aristidean*, Thomas Dunn English, describes Poe thus: "His face is a fine one, and well gifted with intellectual
beauty. Ideality, with the power of analysis, is shown in his very broad,

high and massive forehead – a forehead which would have delighted GALL [one of the founders of phrenology] beyond measure" (Thomas and Jackson, 529). Author and editor Charles Frederick Briggs describes Poe in even greater detail and in a vein of animosity:

> Mr. Poe is about 39 … In height he is about 5 feet 1 or two inches, perhaps 2 inches and a half [actually 5 ft. 8 in.]. His face is pale and rather thin; eyes gray, watery, and always dull; nose rather prominent, pointed and sharp; nostrils wide; hair thin and cropped short; mouth not very well chiselled, nor very sweet; his tongue shows itself unpleasantly when he speaks earnestly, and seems too large for his mouth; teeth indifferent; forehead rather broad, and in the region of ideality [above the temples where Poe had a large protuberance on each side of his head] decidedly large, but low, and in that part where phrenology places conscientiousness and the group of moral sentiments [the top of the head] it is quite flat; chin narrow and pointed, which gives his head, upon the whole, a balloonish appearance. (Thomas and Jackson, 643; see also 693)

Four days before Poe's death, Joseph Evans Snodgrass encountered him: "the broad, capacious forehead of the author of "The Raven" … was still there, with a width, in the region of ideality, such as few men have ever possessed" (Thomas and Jackson, 844).

Several types of *enargia* have been classified:

- *anemographia*: description of the wind (see above)
- *astrothesia*: description of a star (see above)
- *characterismus*: description of the body or mind (see above)
- *chorographia*: description of a country, a nation (see above)
- *chronographia*: description of time (see above)
- *dendrographia*: description of trees (see above)
- *geographia*: description of the earth (see below)
- *hydrographia*: description of water (see below)
- *pragmatographia*: description of an action or event (see below)
- *prosopographia*: description of the appearance of a person, imaginary or real, alive or dead (see below)
- *topographia*: description of a real place (see below)
- *topothesia*: description of an imaginary place (see below)

Some Poe tales are almost all *enargia*; "The Man of the Crowd" displays heavily foregrounded *prosopographia*. When Poe was not using *enargia* to describe his characters in vivid detail, he would use it to describe *events* vividly. In a letter of 6 November 1839, Washington Irving even criticized Poe for laying on the *enargia* too heavily in "The Fall of the House of Usher": "you have been too anxious to present your picture vividly to the eye, or too distrustful of your effect, and have laid on too much coloring. It is erring on the best side – the side of luxuriance. That tale might be improved by relieving the style from some of the epithets" (17: 54). In his review of *Lafitte: The Pirate of the Gulf*, Poe himself condemns another writer for too much *enargia*: "The novelist is too minutely, and by far too frequently *descriptive*. We are surfeited with unnecessary detail. Every little figure in the picture is invested with all the dignities of light and shadow, and chiaroscuro. Of mere outlines there are none" (9: 114).

That Poe approved of *enargia* in the works of others *when it is not overdone*, and when it is *appropriate*, is shown by his comments on Robert Montgomery Bird's novel *The Infidel*:

> The details of the seige are given in the same powerful style as characterised the combats in Calavar. Indeed it is in descriptions of battles, that we think the author excels, and is transcendently superior to any modern writer. When his armies meet, he causes us to feel the shock, and to realize each turn of fortune by a minuteness of description, which is never confused. When his heroes engage hand to hand, we see each blow, each parry, each advantage, each vicissitude, with a thrilling distinctness. (8: 34)

A careful description of things and events is part of Poe's stylistic credo where his Gothic tales are concerned. To facilitate what Coleridge called "the willing suspension of disbelief," *enargia* becomes for Poe part of his "versimilar" or "plausible" style. In his review of *Sheppard Lee*, Poe considers as part of that style "minuteness of detail, especially upon points which have no immediate bearing upon the general story ... in short, by making use of the infinity of arts which give verisimilitude to a narration" (9: 139). (See under "verisimilar" in "The Terms by Type" for a list of the "infinity of arts" that Poe employs for verisimilitude.)

That Poe sometimes succeeded in fooling even intelligent people with his "verisimilar" style is attested to by Robert Carter in a letter of 19 June 1843:

> Within a week I have read for the first time, Pym's Narrative. I lent it to a friend who lives in the house with me, and who is a lawyer, a graduate of Harvard, and a brother of Dr. O.W. Holmes, yet he is so completely deceived by *the minute accuracy of some of the details*, the remarks about the statements

of the press, the names of people at new Bedford, &c. that, though an intelligent and shrewd man he will not be persuaded that it is a fictitious work, by any arguments drawn from the book itself. (17: 147; my italics)

In a letter to Poe (April 1846), Elizabeth Barrett (Browning) praised "The Case of M. Valdemar," alluding to Poe's "versimilar" techniques: "The certain thing in the tale in question is the power of the writer, and the faculty he has of making horrible improbabilities seem near and familiar" (17: 229).

Dupriez discusses *enargia* under the synonymous term *hypotyposis* (219–20) and Lanham distinguishes between it and *energia*. Crowley points out that *enargia* is useful rhetorically to orators to stir the emotions of an audience, often empathy with a person being described (126). See also under "Imagery" and the term *ekphrasis*, under *topothesia*.
Pronunciation: en AR gi a
Type: description

ENCOMIUM: praise of a person or thing by extolling inherent qualities:

> I have spoken of the learning of Ligeia: it was immense – such as I have never known in woman. In the classical tongues was she deeply proficient, and as far as my own acquaintance extended in regard to the modern dialects of Europe, I have never known her at fault. Indeed upon any theme of the most admired, because simply the most abstruse of the boasted erudition of the academy, have I *ever* found Ligeia at fault? ... I said her knowledge was such as I have never known in woman – but where breathes the man who has traversed, and successfully, *all* the wide areas of moral, physical, and mathematical science? I saw not then what I now clearly perceive, that the acquisitions of Ligeia were gigantic, were astounding. ("Ligeia," 2: 253–4)

Although in his own day Poe was notorious as a cruel literary critic (see chapter 5), he was not incapable of praising some of the literature he reviewed:

> The work has been accomplished in a masterly manner – the modesty of the title affording no indication of the fulness, comprehensiveness, and beauty, with which a long and entangled series of detail, collected, necessarily, from a mass of vague and imperfect data, has been wrought into completeness and unity. (Review of *Astoria*, 9: 207–8)

Pronunciation: en CO mee um
Type: description
Type: devices of vehemence

END-LINK/END-LINKAGE: a stylistic term referring to a way of linking clauses that depends not on conjunctions (as with *polysyndeton* – see below) but on a noun or pronoun that refers to the terminal word or idea in the preceding clause:

> "In my situation it is really a great relief to be able to open one's mouth – to be able to expatiate – to be able to communicate with a person like **yourself, who** do not think yourself called upon at every period to interrupt the thread of a gentleman's discourse." ("Loss of Breath," 2: 163–4)

Compare with Dupriez's definition of "staircase": "The text reproduces several times a subordinating syntactic link. The simplest case is that of a noun governed by a relative pronoun, which in its turn is governed by a second relative pronoun, and so on" (429).

ENTHYMEME: a rhetorical term the equivalent of a syllogism in logic and science, but an *enthymeme* is an abbreviated syllogism. As Poe, the inventor of the literary detective, would know, a syllogism is a deductive argument consisting of a major premise, a minor premise, and a conclusion derived from the premises. An *enthymeme*, however, leaves out one of the premises but it is implied. In the following example, two major premises are actually involved:

> If you ever perceive a man setting up as a merchant, or a manufacturer; or ... anything out of the usual way – **you may set him down at once as a genius, and then, according to the rule-of-three, he's an ass.** ("The Business Man," 4: 123)

In mathematics, the "rule-of-three" is the method of finding the fourth term in a proportion when three terms are given. Here Poe's narrator provides three of the terms: one major premise, the minor premise (the specific idea), and the conclusion; missing is one of the major premises, one of the general ideas. Several lines earlier, at the beginning of the paragraph, we get the missing major premise. So, putting them all together, we have the following bit of deductive reasoning (syllogism):

> *Major premise #1*: men who set up businesses "out of the usual way" are geniuses
> *Major premise #2*: "genuises are all arrant asses" (123)

Minor premise: that particular businessman who is setting up a business out of
the usual way is a genius

Conclusion: "he's an ass"

The Poe character most known for his abilities in deductive and inductive reasoning is, of course, the detective C. Auguste Dupin.

Pronunciation: EN thy meme

Type: techniques of argument

EPANALEPSIS: (1) the repetition at the end of a clause, verse, or sentence of the word or phrase with which it began:

The poet in Arcady is, in Kamschatka, **the poet** still. ("Mr. Griswold and the Poets," 11: 148)

Evil thoughts became my sole intimates – the darkest and most **evil of thoughts**. ("The Black Cat," 5: 151)

Quinn suggests that "epanalepsis tends to make the sentence or clause in which it occurs stand apart from its surroundings" (*Figures of Speech*, 89). Certainly the repeated words seem to create walls enclosing the words in between and perhaps to draw attention to them. In the example from "The Black Cat," Poe seems to use the device to create the sense that evil was the beginning and the end of the narrator's vision of things; that is, the syntactical arrangement of the sentence, starting and ending as it does with the phrase "evil thoughts," suggests that evil was the very alpha and omega of the narrator's view of the world – that he would always begin with and come around again inevitably to malevolence. Like all devices of repetition, *epanalepsis* is a splendid way to emphasize, to reinforce.

(2) The device, however, can also refer to the use of a summarizing phrase (below, "this consideration") because of the distance between the beginning of a sentence and the independent clause (below, "we have …") that finishes the thought. It is often necessary in long, periodic (left-branching) sentences such as this:

Apart, however, from the inevitable conclusion, *à priori*, that such causes must produce such effects – that the well known occurrence of such cases of suspended animation must naturally give rise, now and then, to premature interments – **apart from this consideration**, we have the direct testimony of medical and ordinary experience, to prove that a vast number of such interments have actually taken place. ("The Premature Burial," 5: 256)

Epanalepsis seems to serve a comedic function in "The Thousand-and-second Tale of Scheherazade." There we have *three* narrators: the primary narrator, who tells us about Scheherazade; Scheherazade herself, who relates the thousand-and-second tale of the Arabian Nights; and Sinbad the Sailor, who tells his own story (the thousand-and-second tale). Poe is able to differentiate the primary narrator's style from those of Scheherazade and Sinbad in part through a foregrounded use of *epanalepsis* (and embedded syntax):

> the king having been sufficiently pinched, at length ceased snoring, and finally said "hum!" and then "hoo!" when the queen understanding these words (which are no doubt Arabic) to signify that he was all attention, and would do his best not to snore any more, – **the queen, I say, having arranged these matters to her satisfaction**, re-entered thus, at once, into the history of Sinbad the sailor. (6: 82)

This passage typifies the primary narrator's long-windedness: he is unable simply to *get to the point* (the queen awoke the king) without inserting a lot of parenthetical observations (see under *hypotaxis* and "parenthesis"). This nested syntax in turn necessitates the use of *epanalepsis*, which device is absent in the narrative styles of Scheherazade and Sinbad. At the same time, the frequent use of *epanalepsis* (I count four instances in only about four pages of narrative) reveals, somewhat comically for the frustrated reader, the primary narrator's flaky personality (see chapter 4). (For two more instances of *epanalepsis*, see under "left-branching sentence.")

The frequently left-branching and embedded (hypotactic) structure of Poe's sentences caused him to use *epanalepsis* now and then or a device *something like it* fairly often – the repetition of a phrase in the middle of a long sentence of the phrase with which it began:

> But **in the case of the terminating *m*,** which is the most readily pronounced of all consonants, (as the infantile *mama* will testify,) and the most impossible to cheat the ear of by any system of sliding – **in the case of the *m*,** I should be driven to reply that [etc.]. ("The Rationale of Verse," 14: 259)

I would not call this *epanalepsis* precisely, because the phrase in the middle is not really a *summarizing* phrase of what has gone before; it is merely a repetition (*diacope*). Yet it does serve the same function as *epanalepsis* – to remind the reader of how the passage began, necessary because of the several embedded (parenthetical) interruptions. I have noticed this stylistic feature independently of Stauffer, who also comments on it in "The Language and Style of the Prose"; there he prefers to classify it as *anaphora*. This combination of *anaphora* with an "interrupting or qualifying parenthetical expression" produces "the double effect of interrupting narrative flow and emphasizing the key word" – or *phrase*, I might add (463). Dupriez uses the term *restart* for this repetition and provides an exemplification from Poe (396).

Pronunciation: e pa na LEP sis

Type: repetition: words and phrases

EPANAPHORA: intensive *anaphora* (see above):

> I love to regard these as themselves but the colossal members of one vast animate and sentient whole – a whole whose form (that of the sphere) is the most perfect and most inclusive of all; **whose** path is among associate planets; **whose** meek handmaiden is the moon; **whose** mediate sovereign is the sun; **whose** life is eternity; **whose** thought is that of a God; **whose** enjoyment is knowledge; **whose** destinies are lost in immensity; **whose** cognizance of ourselves is akin with our own cognizance of the *animalculæ* which infest the brain. ("The Island of the Fay," 4: 194)

See also "The Poetic Principle" (14: 291) for a splendid exemplification. Although Stauffer says that *anaphora* is typically part of Poe's "parabolic style" ("The Language and Style of the Prose," 459), we find it now and then in Poe's criticism, too. Here is an excerpt from his article on a contemporary actress:

> **Her** conceptions of character are good. **Her** elocution is excellent, although still susceptible of improvement. **Her** beauty is of the richest and most impressive character. **Her** countenance is wonderfully expressive. **Her** self-possession is marvellous. **Her** step is queenly. **Her** general grace of manner has never, in our opinion been equalled on the stage. (12: 211–12)

Pronunciation: e pa NA pho ra

Type: repetition: words

Type: devices of vehemence

EPANORTHOSIS: a return to something already said, either to reinforce, soften, qualify, or retract it completely; often a kind of self-correction (Dupriez, 165); or correcting a word after it is uttered (Lanham). We find Poe's narrator using the device in an attempt to define the "imp of the perverse":

> Through its promptings we act without comprehensible object; **or, if this shall be understood as a contradiction in terms, we may so far modify the proposition as to say, that through its promptings we act, for the reason that we should *not*.** ("The Imp of the Perverse," 6: 146–7)

Epanorthosis figures quite frequently in Poe's reviews; here is only one of many instances:

> There are two kinds of popular reputation, – **or rather there are two roads by which such reputation may be attained.** (Review of *Zinzendorff, and Other Poems*, etc., 8: 122)

Poe seems anxious to express himself in the most precise way possible, and we can find no fault with that. He could have simply omitted the first expression, however, and used only the corrected or qualified version in the name of brevity. That Poe decided to keep *both* suggests that he apparently wants his readers to consider not just one but each of the expressions as valid or at least worthy of consideration. While the frequent use of *epanorthorsis* might suggest diffidence in a writer, in Poe's case I am more inclined to think it suggests a writer so enamored of his own powers of expression that he refuses to discard the first version of a statement even in light of a second, possibly better, one.

Lanham's name for this device is *correctio* (42). See also *metanoia*.
Pronunciation: e pa nor THO sis
Type: techniques of argument

EPENTHESIS: a type of *metaplasm*, the insertion of a letter, sound, or syllable to the middle of a word (see Dupriez, 166):

> "Smith?" said he, in his well-known peculiar way of drawling out his syllables; "Smith? – why, not General John A – B – C.? Savage affair that with the **Kickapo-o-o-os**, wasn't it? Say! don't you think so? – perfect **despera-a-ado** – great pity, pon my honor! – wonderfully inventive age! – **pro-o-odigies** of valor! By the by, did you ever hear about Captain **Ma-a-a-n?**" ("The Man that was Used Up: A Tale of the Late Bugaboo and Kickapoo Campaign," 3: 268)

We may wonder why a writer would resort to such a device but clearly Poe illustrates its comedic potential. For more on this subject, see chapter 4.
Pronunciation: e PEN the sis
Type: addition, subtraction, and substitution: letters and syllables
Type: "comedic"

EPEXEGESIS: adding words to clarify, explain, or specify a statement; or adding interpretation:

> This epoch – **these later years** – took unto themselves a sudden elevation in turpitude, whose origin alone it is my present purpose to assign. ("William Wilson," 3: 299)

Dupriez prefers to discuss this term as apposition (61–2), and certainly it is a form of *appositio* (see above); compare also with "parenthesis." Note, also, Poe's use of dashes here to enclose the *epexegesis* and consider his remarks about the proper use of the dash (see chapter 1). I love this next example from Poe's comments on Amelia Welby:

> Nothing is more clear than this proposition – although denied by the chlorine critics (**the grass green**). (11: 277)

Pronunciation: e pex e GE sis

Type: addition, subtraction, and substitution: words, phrases, and clauses

Type: amplification

EPIC SIMILE: an elaborated comparison differing from the ordinary simile (see below) in being more involved, more ornate, and often beginning with *As* followed eventually by *so*. In the following passage, Poe uses a double epic simile with bathetic intent – part of his comedic technique:

> But, **as** the loss of his ears proved the means of elevating to the throne of Cyrus, the Magian or Mige-Gush of Persia, and **as** the cutting off his nose gave Zopyrus possession of Babylon, **so** the loss of a few ounces of my countenance proved the salvation of my body. ("Loss of Breath," 2: 159)

We find another double epic simile in a specimen of Poe's criticism:

> The analogies of Nature are universal [see "analogy,"]; and just **as** the most rapidly growing herbage is the most speedy in its decay, – just **as** the ephemera struggles to perfection in a day only to perish in that day's decline, – **so** the mind is early matured only to be early in its decadence. (Review of *Poetical Remains of the Late Lucretia Maria Davidson*, 10: 222)

This type of comparison is also called an "Homeric simile" after its first practitioner, and it is imitated by Virgil, Milton, and other writers of epics in part to enhance the wide range of reference of the epic style (Abrams, 53). We find another instance in *Eureka*, where it is appropriate, given the epic scope of that work:

> He who from the top of Ætna casts his eyes leisurely around, is affected chiefly by the *extent* and *diversity* of the scene. Only by a rapid whirling on his heel could he hope to comprehend the panorama in the sublimity of its

oneness. But **as**, on the summit of Ætna, *no* man has thought of whirling on his heel, **so** no man has ever taken into his brain the full uniqueness of the prospect. (16: 186)

Type: description

Type: metaphorical substitutions and puns

EPICRISIS: quoting a passage from authority and commenting, either agreeing, disagreeing, or qualifying it:

> These particulars being made known to the Royal Geographical Society of London, the conclusion was drawn by that body **"that there is a continuous tract of land extending from 47° 30' E. to 69° 29' W. longitude, running the parallel of from sixty-six to sixty-seven degrees south latitude."** ... My own experience will be found to testify most directly to the falsity of the conclusion arrived at by the society. *(The Narrative of Arthur Gordon Pym of Nantucket,* 3: 170–1)

Like Pym's catalogues of nouns and his use of *martyria* (below), *epicrisis* adds to the sense of verisimilitude in *Pym* – the impression that Pym's Antarctic voyage was fact and not fiction, and that Pym, with the crew of the *Jane Guy,* really did go beyond previous explorers towards the south pole.

In a letter to Evert A. Duyckinck (8 March 1849), Poe refers to "Von Kempelen and His Discovery" as written "in the plausible or verisimilar style" (Ostrom, 433). In "The Language and Style of the Prose," Stauffer suggests that the "plausible style itself is more easily illustrated than described" (458). This is a surprising and disappointing statement coming from a scholar who has displayed an impressive ability to describe stylistic features. We can describe the components of the "verisimilar" style quite readily. Referring to Lanham's list of rhetorical devices of "Example, allusion, and citation of authority," we might note that several of those figures might be part of Poe's "verisimilar style": in addition to nominal seriation (below), *martyria,* and *epicrisis,* we could suggest, for instance, *apodixis, apomnemonysis* (above), and *exemplum* (below). Look for these especially in his literary *hoaxes,* wherein he would "deceive by verisimilitude" (Ostrom, 433; see also 15: 128). Elizabeth Barrett (Browning) seemed to testify to Poe's powers of the verisimilar when she wrote about his "Facts in the Case of M. Valdemar" that "The *certain* thing in the tale in question is the *power* of the writer and the faculty he has of making horrible improbabilities seem near & familiar" (Ostrom, 320).

Although not used for verisimilitude, *epicrisis* figures frequently in Poe's literary criticism as well as in his fiction. Furthermore, it is central to "The Mystery of Marie Rogêt," as much of this detective tale is made up of Dupin's comments on the many newspaper accounts of the murder.
Pronunciation: e PI cri sis
Type: example, allusion, and citation of authority
Type: techniques of argument
Type: "verisimilar"

EPILOGOS (epilogue): inferring what will follow based on what has been said or done previously:

> *As yet*, they have not *insisted* on our estimating Lamartine by the cubic foot, or Pollok by the pound – but what else are we to *infer* from their continual prating about "sustained effort"? ("The Poetic Principle," 14: 268)

Another name for this device is *conclusio*, and it is also defined as the sixth and last part of a classical oration, the *peroration*. Presumably, however, the device does not necessarily have to conclude an oration or essay. The example from Poe comes three pages into a twenty-six-page lecture.
Pronunciation: e pi LO gos
Type: techniques of argument

EPIMONE: see *leitmotif.*
Pronunciation: e PI mo ne

EPIPHONEMA: a moral note expressing disapproval or admiration on the part of the writer, narrator, or speaker; or an epigrammatic or sententious statement that summarizes and concludes a passage of prose or poetry, or a speech:

> There are moments when, even to the sober eye of Reason, the world of our sad Humanity may assume the semblance of a Hell – but the imagination of man is no Carathis, to explore with impunity its every cavern. Alas! the grim legion of sepulchral terrors cannot be regarded as altogether fanciful – but, like the Demons in whose company Afrasiab made his voyage down the Oxus, they must sleep, or they will devour us – they must be suffered to slumber, or we perish. ("The Premature Burial," 5: 273)

Some rhetors insist that the *epiphonema* must be an exclamation (that is, must include *ecphonesis*). Dupriez, for instance, cites (168) this passage from Poe as an example:

Against the new masonry I re-erected the old rampart of bones. For the half
of a century no mortal has disturbed them. *In pace requiescat!* ("The Cask of
Amontillado," 6: 175)

As for *epiphonema* expressing a moral note, Poe's contempt for moral didacticism in literature is well known to Poe scholars and we would therefore
not expect to find the device often in his writings; look for it, instead, in
Hawthorne and Stowe, for instance. For a story that satirizes the didactic in
literature, see "Never Bet the Devil Your Head: A Tale with a Moral."
Pronunciation: e pi pho NE ma
Type: devices of vehemence

EPIPLEXIS: a type of rhetorical question asked not to elicit information but to reproach, upbraid, rebuke. Poe uses the device sometimes in
his sternest literary reviews:

We will dismiss the "Editor of the Mirror" [Theodore S. Fay] with a few
questions. **When did you ever know, Mr. Fay, of any prosecuting attorney**
behaving so much like a bear as *your* prosecuting attorney in the novel of
Norman Leslie? When did you ever hear of an American court of Justice
objecting to the testimony of a witness on the ground that the said witness
had an interest in the cause at issue? (Review of *Norman Leslie*, 8: 61–2)

Stauffer, in his highly stimulating essay, "The Language and Style of the
Prose", maintains that the "ratiocinative style" of Poe's critical reviews
largely lacks the highly charged emotional words that characterize his
Gothic tales and parables (see appendix 1). That is not to say, however,
that Poe's so-called "ratiocinative style" is without rhetorical devices of
vehemence – as the heavy-handed use of *epiplexis*, above, suggests. Anyone wanting a demonstration of intensely and consistently used devices
of vehemence in Poe's criticism, including numerous instances of *epiplexis*, should simply peruse his stinging review of Griswold's *Poets and
Poetry of America*, 3rd edition (11: 220–43).
Pronunciation: e pi PLEX is
Type: devices of vehemence

EPISTROPHE: the use of the same terminal word or phrase in successive clauses or verses, generally for emphasis:

As I put a portion of it within my lips, there rushed to my mind a half
formed thought of joy – of **hope**. Yet what business had *I* with **hope**?
("The Pit and the Pendulum," 5: 80)

Pronunciation: e PI stro phe
Type: devices of vehemence
Type: repetition: words
Type: repetition: clauses, phrases, and ideas

EPITHETON (epithet): qualifying a subject with an appropriate adjective or adjectival phrase. Poe undoubtedly loved the adjective, and Washington Irving once advised him to cut down on his use of epithets (see under *enargia*); even in his criticism, Poe now and then overuses them in a fit of rhetorical passion (see under *synathroesmus*). In his review of *Powhatan*, Poe even draws attention to the epithet he uses to describe the work:

> In truth, a more absurdly *flat* affair – for flat is the only epithet which applies
> in this case – was never before paraded to the world with so grotesque an air
> of bombast and assumption. (10: 163)

The epithet can follow the noun as well, as when Lincoln is termed "the Emancipator." Sonnino (31) quotes Quintilian, who comments on the usefulness of the device: to adorn and enhance the style, to add to the meaning (amplify), to express indignation, admiration, contempt. Negative epithets are called dyslogistic; positive epithets are called eulogistic. Lanham adds that the adjective involved can frequently or habitually accompany its noun: I think of "senseless murder," for instance (see "cliché," and consider the stock and Homeric epithet – "rosy-fingered dawn"). Sonnino quotes Quintilian as saying, "If [the epithet is] separated from the word to which it belongs[,] it has a significance of its own and becomes an antonomasia" (see above). See also Baldick (74), Harmon/Holman (194), Abrams (56), and especially Dupriez (170–1).
Pronunciation: e PI the ton
Type: amplification
Type: description

EPITROCHASMUS: a rapid succession of concise statements often involving an accumulation of short, expressive words; a quick movement from statement to statement, swiftly touching on several different points:

> Object there was none. Passion there was none. I loved the old man. He had
> never wronged me. He had never given me insult. For his gold I had no desire.
> I think it was his eye! ... Now this is the point. You fancy me mad. Madmen
> know nothing. But you should have seen *me*. ("The Tell-Tale Heart," 5: 88)

This example of *epitrochasmus* also happens to be *asyndetonic*, but *epitrochasmus* is not necessarily so, as the example provided by Lanham shows (70). *Epitrochasmus* also compares with *brachylogia* in its ability to increase the pace of a narrative (see *brevitas*). When combined with *ecphonesis*, as at the end of "The Tell-Tale Heart" (see above), it suggests heightened emotional agitation on the part of the narrator.

The following instance from a gossipy magazine piece called "Boston and the Bostonians," shows just how terse and concise Poe could be when he desired it. The short, simple sentences here convey the impression that Poe finds his subject distasteful (he truly *does*) and that he wants to finish as quickly as possible:

> The Bostonians are very well in their way. Their hotels are bad. Their pumpkin pies are delicious. Their poetry is not so good. (13: 11)

Pronunciation: e pi tro CHAS mus
Type: brevity

EPITROPE: granting agreement or permission to an opponent, often ironically. When ironic, it involves pretending to grant something that we would forbid or with which we disagree. Surely at some time or another we have all encountered this device in conversation, especially as an expression of frustration after arguing in vain: "You want to go and play outside in the pouring rain? Sure, go ahead! Get soaking wet! Catch your death of pneumonia!" We see how one's original use of *dehortatio* can change to its opposite, *adhortatio* (see above). Dupriez equates *epitrope* with *permissio* – pretending to allow what we would prefer to prevent (338).

In his notes on "The Longfellow War," we find Poe at his most rhetorical, his most polemical. Three friends of the American poet Longfellow had written Poe's friend, N.P. Willis, "to publish an explicit declaration of his disagreement with '*all* the disparagement of Longfellow'" that Poe had published (12: 43). Poe imagined the subtext of Willis' concession in an ironic light, and surely this passage, therefore, passes as *epitrope*:

> "My dear Sir, or Sirs, what will you have? You are an insatiable set of cormorants, it is true; but if you will only let me know what you desire, I will satisfy you, if I die for it. Be quick! – merely say what it is you wish me to admit, and (for the sake of getting rid of you) I will admit it upon the spot. Come! I will grant at once that Mr. Longfellow is Jupiter Tonans, and that his three friends are the Graces, or the Furies, whichever you please. As for a fault to be

found with either of you, *that* is impossible, and I say so. I disagree with *all* –
with every syllable of the disparagement that ever has been whispered against
you up to this date, and (not to stand upon trifles) with all that ever *shall* be
whispered against you henceforward, forever and forever. May I hope at
length that these assurances will be sufficient?" (43–4)

Compare with *paromologia.*

Pronunciation: e PI tro pe

Type: devices of vehemence

Type: techniques of argument

EPIZEUXIS: emphatic repetition of a word with no other words between:

"By the bye, gentlemen, **this** – **this** is a very well constructed house." ("The
Black Cat," 5: 155)

Espy (92) reminds us that Poe's poem "The Bells" employs *epizeuxis*
quite intensively: "the bells, bells, bells, bells, bells, bells, bells." Probably
Daniel Hoffman had Poe's use of *epizeuxis* in mind when he gave his
critical book on that author the rather obnoxious title *Poe Poe Poe Poe
Poe Poe Poe.* Forrest sees it as a figure that Poe may have borrowed from
the Bible: "In epizeuxis emphasis is sought by the repetition of a word, a
favorite device with biblical writers" (91); he then offers examples from
"Silence," "The Premature Burial," and "Ligeia." Stauffer cites an instance from "The Oval Portrait" –

Long – **long** I read – and devoutly, devotedly I gazed

– then suggests that "Poe achieves the incantatory quality of such passages by combining rhythmical and rhetorical patterns of repetition"
("The Language and Style of the Prose," 463). We find the device used
in a satirical vein in Poe's criticism:

And **this** – *this* is the *work*, in respect to which its author, aping the airs of intellect [etc.]. (Review of *Charles O'Malley,* 11: 98)

Epizeuxis figures quite vehemently in a passionate letter to Sarah Helen
Whitman:

During our walk in the cemetery I said to you, while the **bitter, bitter** tears
sprang into my eyes – "Helen, I love **now** – **now** – for the first and only
time." (Ostrom, 383)

Pronunciation: e pi ZEUX is

Type: repetition: words

E R O T E S I S (*erotema*): a rhetorical question implying strong affirmation or denial:

> Who has not, a hundred times, found himself committing a vile or a silly action, for no other reason than because he knows he should *not*? Have we not a perpetual inclination, in the teeth of our best judgment, to violate that which is *Law*, merely because we understand it to be such? ("The Black Cat," 5: 146)

The subject of the narrator's rhetorical questions here is what Poe called the "imp of the perverse," the uncontrollable desire that sometimes comes upon us to act against our own best interests by harming ourselves or breaking the law. He provides this psychological theory to explain what drove him to hang his beloved cat, Pluto. Not all scholars find this explanation acceptable, however, and some maintain instead that the theory of perversity is simply the narrator's rationalization, a conscious or unconscious attempt to hide the *real* motive for his crime (see chapter 2). The narrator's use of *erotema* would seem to be a frantic rhetorical attempt to encourage acceptance in his audience of the theory of perversity. Through *erotema* he is asking his auditors to think deductively (to move from the general to the specific) by saying something like this: "Look, everyone has succumbed to perverse impulses now and then, right? – so you'll believe me when I tell you that perversity overcame *me*, too, on the occasion when I hanged my poor cat." Poe must have known what Corbett confirms, that this type of rhetorical question "can be an effective persuasive device, subtly influencing the kind of response one wants to get from an audience … By inducing the audience to make the appropriate response, the rhetorical question can often be more effective as a persuasive device than a direct assertion would be" (454).

We find the device occasionally in Poe's criticism:

> We possess, as a people, the mental elasticity which liberal institutions inspire, and a treasury which can afford to remunerate scientific research. **Ought we not, therefore, to be foremost in the race of philanthropic discovery, in every department embraced by this comprehensive term?** Our national honor and glory which, be it remembered, are to be "transmitted as well as enjoyed," are involved. (Review of *Report of the Committee on Naval Affairs*, 9: 89)

Pronunciation: e ro TE sis
Pronunciation: e ro TE ma
Type: devices of vehemence
Type: techniques of argument

ETHOPOEIA: (1) a figure of thought that involves the "description of natural propensities, manners, affections, virtues and vices in order to flatter or reproach; character portrayal generally" (Lanham, 71). For examples, see under *characterismus*, *effictio*, and *enargia*. See also Dupriez under "portrait" (350–1) and Crowley's interesting discussions (84, 86, 210, 212, 315–21). This device is foregrounded in Poe's gossipy *Literati of New York City*.

(2) Lanham provides a second definition missing from the catalogues of other rhetors: "Putting oneself in place of another, so as to both understand and express that person's feelings more vividly." We seem to have instances of this device in Poe's literary criticism:

> One might almost picture to the mind's eye the exact air and attitude of the writer as he indited the whole thing. Probably he compressed his lips – possibly he ran his fingers through his hair … Let us then imagine the author of "The Partisan" presenting a copy of that work to "Richard Yeadon, Jr. Esq. of South Carolina," and let us, from the indications afforded by the printed Dedication, endeavor to form some idea of the author's demeanor upon an occasion so highly interesting. We may suppose Mr. Yeadon, in South Carolina, at home, and in his study. By and bye [sic] with a solemn step, downcast eyes, and impressive earnestness of manner, enters the author of "The Yemassee." He advances towards Mr. Yeadon, and, without uttering a syllable takes that gentleman affectionately, but firmly, by the hand. Mr. Y. has his suspicions, as well he may have, but says nothing. Mr. S. commences as above.
>
> (Review of *The Partisan*, 8: 144)

Poe's detective, Dupin, employs both *dialogismus* and *ethopoeia* (second definition) to understand the motives of the various criminals and strangers with whom he deals. Here he attempts to place himself in the position of the murderer of Marie Rogêt:

> "Let us see. An individual has committed the murder. He is alone with the ghost of the departed. He is appalled by what lies motionless before him. The fury of his passion is over, and there is abundant room in his heart for the natural awe of the deed. His is none of that confidence which the presence of numbers inevitably inspires. He is *alone* with the dead. He trembles and is bewildered. Yet there is a necessity for disposing of the corpse. He bears it to the river, but leaves behind him the other evidences of guilt; for it is difficult, if not impossible, to carry all the burthen at once, and it will be easy to return for what is left. But in his toilsome journey to the water his fears redouble

within him. The sounds of life encompass his path. A dozen times he hears or fancies the step of an observer. Even the very lights from the city bewilder him. Yet, in time, and by long and frequent pauses of deep agony, he reaches the river's brink, and disposes of his ghastly charge ... But *now* what treasure does the world hold – what threat of vengeance could it hold out – which would have power to urge the return of that lonely murderer over that toil-some and perilous path, to the thicket and its blood-chilling recollections? He returns *not*, let the consequences be what they may. He *could* not return if he would. His sole thought is immediate escape. He turns his back *forever* upon those dreadful shrubberies, and flees as from the wrath to come." (5: 54–5)

Pronunciation: e tho po EI a

Type: description

Type: techniques of argument

E U C H E : (1) a vow or oath to keep a promise, to follow a definite course; (2) a prayer for evil, a curse (cf *ara*). Here is an example of the first definition:

"You will understand me to say, then, that I wish you to wear spectacles ..."

"It is done!" I cried, with all the enthusiasm that I could muster at the moment. "It is done – it is most cheerfully agreed. I sacrifice every feeling for your sake. To-night I wear this dear eye-glass, as an eye-glass, and upon my heart; but with the earliest dawn of that morning which gives me the pleasure of calling you wife, I will place it upon my – upon my nose – and there wear it ever afterwards, in the less romantic, and less fashionable, but certainly in the more serviceable form which you desire." ("The Spectacles," 5: 200)

I give a somewhat light-hearted instance of the second definition:

And is it ralelly more than the three fut and a bit that there is, inny how, of the little ould furrener Frinchman that lives just over the way, and that's a oggling and a goggling the houl day, (and **bad luck to him**,) at the purty widdy Mis-thress Tracle. ("Why the Little Frenchman Wears His Hand in a Sling," 4: 115)

The first definition compares with *eustathia*, below.

Pronunciation: EU che

Type: devices of vehemence

E U L O G I A : commending or blessing a person or thing. After quoting with great approval a passage of poetry from the hand of Mrs Caroline Norton, Poe concludes,

God bless her who has written this. (Review of *The Dream, and Other Poems*,
10: 103)

This *eulogia* helps to substantiate the justifiable charge of occasional partiality on Poe's part when it came to reviewing the written work of *women*
– the *eulogia* coming in the midst, by the way, of mawkishly sentimental
reflections upon womanhood in the good old southern tradition.

Pronunciation: eu LO gi a

Type: devices of vehemence

EUPHEMISMUS (euphemism): (1) to avoid bluntness, the use of a
pleasant term for an unpleasant term or fact (cf *paradiastole*). In his
harsh review of *Paul Ulric*, Poe accuses the author, Morris Mattson, of
plagiarism:

> His doings in this cavern, as related by Mr. Mattson, we must be allowed to
> consider the most laughable piece of plagiarism on record ... The *imitations*
> (let us be courteous!) from Pelham are not so palpable as those from the other
> two novels. (8: 196)

By the end of his career as a critic (in other words, near the end of his
life), Poe had become notorious for the number of times he had accused
other authors of plagiarism. Perhaps that is why he decides to use a *euphemism* for *stolen* in the above, and the following, passages (doubtless,
though, the *euphemisms* are ironic):

> Now my objection to all this is not that Mr. Hirst has *appropriated* my prop-
> erty – (I am fond of a *nice* phrase) – but that he has not done it so cleverly as
> I could wish. ("Henry B. Hirst," 13: 213)

See also the discussions in Harmon/Holman (200–1), Cuddon (313),
Abrams (57), and Dupriez (177–9). Espy (95) furnishes several examples
and draws our attention to Hugh Rawson's *Dictionary of Euphemisms
and Other Double Talk* (1981).

(2) prognostication of good (opposite of *ominatio*). Some rhetors (for example, Sonnino and Taylor) give this as the only meaning of the term.
Certainly it is less well known. Sonnino provides other terms: *euphemis-
mos* (the Greek) and *boni ominis captatio* (26). Cf *meiosis*.

Pronunciation: eu phe MIS mus

Type: devices of vehemence

Type: metaphorical substitutions and puns

Type: techniques of argument

E U S TAT H I A : pledging constancy concerning something "in attitude or endeavor" (Taylor, 99); "To declare the firm and unremovable purpose of the mind" (Sonnino, 59):

> I pledge you, before God, the solemn word of a gentleman, that I am temperate even to rigor. From the hour in which I first saw this basest of calumniators to the hour in which I retired from his office in uncontrollable disgust at his chicanery, arrogance, ignorance and brutality, *nothing stronger than water ever passed my lips.*
>
> I have now only to repeat to you, in general, my solemn assurance that my habits are as far removed from intemperance as the day from the night. My sole drink is water. (Letter to Dr J.E. Snodgrass, 1 April 1841 [1: 160–1])

The device is also called *constantia*. Cf *euche*, first definition.
Pronunciation: eu sta THI a
Type: devices of vehemence

E X E M P L U M (plural: *exempla*): a cited example that may be either true or mythical; a story or anecdote cited to illustrate a moral or doctrine. As shown by "The Imp of the Perverse," "The Premature Burial," and "Diddling Considered as One of the Exact Sciences," Poe's technique is sometimes to begin with a concept, a proposition, and then provide several examples to illustrate it. In "Never Bet the Devil Your Head: A Tale with a Moral," Poe satirizes the aesthetic didacticism advocated by so many of the writers and literary critics of his time, especially the Transcendentalists. He commences with a proposition and then furnishes *exempla*:

> Every fiction should have a moral; and, what is more to the purpose, the critics have discovered that every fiction has. Philip Melancthon, some time ago, wrote a commentary upon the "Batrachomyomachia" and proved that the poet's object was to excite a distaste for sedition. Pierre La Seine, going a step farther, shows that the intention was to recommend to young men temperance in eating and drinking. Just so, too, Jacobus Hugo has satisfied himself that, by Euenis, Homer meant to insinuate John Calvin; by Antinous, Martin Luther; by the Lotophagi, Protestants in general; and, by the Harpies, the Dutch. Our more modern Scholiasts are equally acute. These fellows demonstrate a hidden meaning in "The Antediluvians," a parable in "Powhatan," new views in "Cock Robin" and transcendentalism in "Hop O' My Thumb." In short, it has been shown that no man can sit down to write without a very profound design. (4: 213–14)

Pronunciation: ex EM plum
Type: example, allusion, and citation of authority
Type: techniques of argument
Type: "verisimilar"

EXERGASIA: repeating the same thought in many figures (cf *commoratio*, above).

> In building up the fabric of our commercial prosperity, let us not filch the corner-stone. Let it not be said of us, in future ages, that we ingloriously availed ourselves of a stock of scientific knowledge, to which we had not contributed our quota – that we shunned as a people to put our shoulder to the wheel – that we reaped where we had never sown. (Review of *Report on Naval Affairs*, 9: 89)

I would not expect to find too many instances of *exergasia* involving metaphors in Poe's prose, given that he did not approve of an injudicious overuse of that figure (see *metaphora*). Note, by the way, Poe's use of the dash in the excerpt, above, and see his explanation of its proper use in chapter 1 and compare with his use of *metanoia*.

Pronunciation: ex er GA si a
Type: amplification
Type: repetition: clauses, phrases, and ideas

EXPANSION: an increase in syllabic count of the phrases or clauses placed nearest the end of a sentence:

> I grew, day by day, **more moody, more irritable, more regardless of the feelings of others**. ("The Black Cat," 5: 145)

The phrase *more moody* has three syllables; the phrase *more irritable* has five; the final phrase, *more regardless of the feelings of others*, has eleven. Cluett and Kampeas tell us that "Expansion was for a long time taught, in English as in Latin, as an aspect of rhetoric and was considered a necessary part of the repertory of any writer who wanted to attain 'pleasing sound' in his sentences" (31). Poe appears to have known this, and his instances of expansion very frequently involve tricolonic arrangements (see *tricolon*), especially, perhaps, in his criticism:

> As far as he appreciates her loveliness or her augustness, no appreciation can be **more ardent, more full of heart, more replete with the glowing soul of adoration**. (1837 Review of *Poems by William Cullen Bryant*, 9: 304)

Type: addition, subtraction, and substitution: letters and syllables
Type: amplification

EXPEDITIO: "Rejection of all but one of various alternatives" (Lanham, 75). If we can accept the term as meaning not just the rejection of all but one of various reasons why something should be done but also of why something was done, then the following excerpt from "The Tell-Tale Heart" works splendidly as an exemplification:

> Object there was none. Passion there was none. I loved the old man. He had never wronged me. He had never given me insult. For his gold I had no desire. I think it was his eye! yes, it was this! He had the eye of a vulture – a pale blue eye, with a film over it. Whenever it fell upon me, my blood ran cold; and so by degrees – very gradually – I made up my mind to take the life of the old man, and thus rid myself of the eye forever. (5: 88)

Taylor discusses this term under the heading *apophasis* (70).
Pronunciation: ex pe DI ti o
Type: techniques of argument

EXUSCITATIO: an emotional utterance that seeks to move the audience to a like feeling. The following pathetic plea was part of Poe's epistolary response when he learned of plans for his aunt, Maria Clemm, and his cousin, Virginia, to move away to live with Neilson Poe:

> You both have tender hearts – and you will always have the reflection that my agony is more than I can bear – that you have driven me to the grave – for love like mine can never be gotten over. It is useless to disguise the truth that when Virginia goes with N.P. that I shall never behold her again – that is absolutely sure. Pity me, my dear Aunty, pity me. I have no one now to fly to – I am among strangers, and my wretchedness is more than I can bear. (Ostrom, 70)

Pronunciation: ex us ci TA ti o
Type: devices of vehemence
Type: techniques of argument

FABLE (adjectives: fabular, fabulous): a "short allegorical story that points a lesson or moral" (Lanham, 77). In his posthumously published magazine piece, "About Critics and Criticism," Poe presents us with a fable he repeated several times before in earlier critical essays – the moral of which he does not entirely condone:

> Zoilus once presented Apollo with a very caustic review of a very admirable
> poem. The god asked to be shown the beauties of the work; but the critic
> replied that he troubled himself only about the errors. Hereupon Apollo
> gave him a sack of unwinnowed wheat – bidding him pick out all the chaff
> for his pains.
>
>   Now this fable does very well as a hit at the critics. (13: 194; see also 11: 41;
> 14: 281)

Lanham tells us, as do other rhetors, that the characters in fables are often – in fact, typically – animals (beast fables such as Aesop's). Another
term is *apologia* or *apologue* (see Dupriez, 55–6); see also *allegoria*. See
also Sonnino, who lists it under the term *fabella* (97–8); Baldick (80);
Cuddon (322); Harmon/Holman (207). This fable also appears under
digressio and under *paradiegesis*.
Type: example, allusion, and citation of authority
Type: metaphorical substitutions and puns
Type: techniques of argument

FALLACY OF THE APPEAL TO IGNORANCE (*argumentum
ad ignorantium*): not a rhetorical device but the name of a logical fallacy;
as a fallacy of argumentation, it is therefore a fallacy of rhetoric. Someone committing this error argues that, because an opponent cannot *disprove* a thesis or conclusion, it must therefore be sound (a proposition is
true because it has never been proved false). Presumably, however, the reverse can occur: because an opponent cannot *prove* a thesis or conclusion, it must therefore be unsound (a proposition is false because it has
never been proved true). Poe seems to commit this fallacy in *Eureka* in
arguing against those who believe that the universe of stars is infinite:

> No astronomical fallacy is more untenable, and none has been more pertina-
> ciously adhered to, than that of the absolute *illimitation* of the Universe of
> Stars ... Were the succession of stars endless, then the background of the sky
> would present us an uniform luminosity, like that displayed by the Galaxy –
> *since there could be absolutely no point, in all that background, at which would
> not exist a star.* (16: 273–4)

Poe, in other words, drags out Olbers' Paradox, phrased by the German
physician and astronomer, Heinrich M.W. Olbers, in 1826, to refute the
idea of the infinity of the stellar universe. If the universe of stars went on
forever, then the entire sky would be bright – but such is clearly not the

case, as we see voids of blackness between stellar objects. But Poe then acknowledges a possible explanation:

> The only mode ... in which, under such a state of affairs, we could comprehend the *voids* which our telescopes find in innumerable directions, would be by supposing the distance of the invisible background so immense that no ray from it has yet been able to reach us at all. That this *may* be so, who shall venture to deny? **I maintain, simply, that we have not even the shadow of a reason for believing that it *is* so.** (274)

His opponents cannot absolutely *prove* their solution to Olbers' Paradox, and therefore the illimitation of the universe, so Poe concludes that they are wrong. That is, they cannot prove their propositions true, so Poe assumes them to be false ("No astronomical fallacy is more untenable ... than that of the absolute *illimitation* of the Universe of Stars"). Therein lies the fallacy of ignorance, and Poe as a logician should have known better. Type: techniques of argument

FALLACY OF ASSERTION: this is one of the "fallacies of relevance" (under the subheading, "appeals to authority") and entails a bold assertion given without any substantiating proof; the communicator, acting as "authority," asks us to take his or her word as fact rather than as mere opinion. We might look for this fallacy in Poe's literary criticism, and indeed we find occasional (unsubstantiated) magisterial pronouncements:

> No human being exists, over the age of fifteen, who has not, in his heart of hearts, a ready echo for all here so pathetically expressed. (Review of *The Child of the Sea and Other Poems*, 13: 160)

In another place he does admit to the fallacy because of page limits: "We have had to content ourselves chiefly with assertion, where our original purpose was to demonstrate" (Review of *Orion*, 11: 275). In the introduction to *The Literati of New York City*, he confesses that, because of required brevity, he must provide "simple *opinion*, with little of either argument or detail" (15: 5). Poe's method, however – especially when engaged in a close textual analysis – is typically to avoid that error; normally he backs up any point he wants to make with relevant examples (see also 8: 152). If he accuses a writer, for instance, of poor grammar (and he does frequently), he cites textual evidence.

He certainly can recognize when someone *else* commits the fallacy of assertion. In "The Longfellow War," Poe accuses his opponent, "Outis,"

of this error: "One of the most amazing things I have yet seen, is the complacency with which Outis throws to the right and left his anonymous assertions, taking it for granted that because he (Nobody) asserts them, I must believe them as a matter of course" (12: 64). Poe then writes of his opponent's *"ipse dixit"* – "he himself said it." Here Poe conflates two logical errors: the fallacy of assertion and the fallacy of the appeal to "expert" opinion. With this latter, we attempt to support our case by appealing to expert opinion – he himself (the great expert) said it (therefore it must be true!) – but experts can be wrong or actuated by unworthy motives. Poe is suggesting that "Outis" is putting himself forth as the expert whose mere assertions are reliable enough as not to need to be questioned or challenged. Elsewhere, Poe quotes from the preface to Rufus Griswold's *The Poets and Poetry of America* to demonstrate that Griswold is committing the fallacy of assertion: *"'It is said that the principles of our fathers are beginning to be regarded with indifference.'* Who has said this, Mr. G.?" (11: 238).
Type: techniques of argument

FALLACY OF FALSE CAUSE: this is one of the "fallacies of presumption" (distorting or overlooking the facts) and is also known as the "Questionable Cause" or *"Post Hoc, Ergo Propter Hoc"* ("after this, therefore because of this"). This fallacy occurs when one concludes without proof that a previous event or phenomenon explains or gave rise to a subsequent event or phenomenon. In his comments pertaining to "The Longfellow War," Poe accuses his opponent, "Outis," of committing this fallacy. Responding to Poe's charge that the poet Longfellow stole certain ideas from "The Raven," "Outis" attempts to turn the tables in suggesting that Poe, in "The Raven," committed plagiarism in mimicking a refrain previously appearing in one of Longfellow's poems. Here is Poe's response:

> The repetition in question is assuredly not claimed by myself as original –
> I should therefore be wary how I charged Mr. Longfellow with imitating it
> from myself. It is, in fact, a musical effect, which is the common property of
> all mankind, and has been their common property for ages. (12: 88)

Poe's point is a good one – that the refrain in question was not purloined by him from Longfellow or by Longfellow from him, but that both poets borrowed the idea of the refrain from the public domain.
Type: techniques of argument

FALLACY OF HASTY GENERALIZATION ("HASTY CONCLUSION"): one of the "fallacies of presumption" (distorting or overlooking the facts), this logical error depends on a particular case being used as the basis for an (unwarranted) generalization or rule.

Poe criticizes Margaret Fuller's feminist assumptions in *Woman in the Nineteenth Century* by accusing her of committing the fallacy of hasty generalization: "Miss Fuller has erred – through her own excessive objectiveness. She judges *woman* by the heart and intellect of Miss Fuller, but there are not more than one or two dozen Miss Fullers on the whole face of the earth" (*The Literati of New York City*, 15: 75).
Type: techniques of argument

FALLACY OF IRRELEVANT THESIS: also called the "fallacy of irrelevant conclusion," this is one of the fallacies of presumption (distorting the facts) and involves an attempt to prove something that is not the point being discussed or debated. When B does this to A, B is trying to attribute a position to A that A has not, in fact, advocated. Person B may do this because s/he thinks it will be easier to refute A's imagined argument than A's actual argument; or, more honestly, B may simply have misunderstood A's position. Whether a person commits the fallacy of irrelevant thesis deliberately or by accident, it nevertheless is a *diversion* from the real point being discussed; at worst, it ignores the issue completely. Another term that describes this fallacy is *straw man*: B sets up a straw man (A's imagined argument) that can be knocked down easily.

In the articles known collectively as "The Longfellow War," Poe commits the fallacy of irrelevant thesis. In a debate over plagiarism, his opponent, "Outis," has hinted that Poe has borrowed fifteen ideas, themes, from another poem for "The Raven,"

"and that, too, without a word of rhythm, metre, or stanza, which should never form a part of such comparison" – by which of course we are to understand that *with* the rhythm, metre, and stanza … he would have succeeded in establishing eighteen. Now I insist that rhythm, metre, and stanza, *should* form and *must* form a part of the comparison, and I will presently demonstrate what I say. I also insist therefore, since he *could* find me guilty if he *would* upon these points, that guilty he *must* and *shall* find me upon the spot. He then, distinctly, has established eighteen identities – and I proceed to examine them one by one. (12: 73)

Poe then refutes all but two minor points, and included in those easily refuted are the additional three that Poe has added, imagining that "Outis" should have argued them. Poe is hardly being fair, however: his opponent has *not* argued the items relating to rhythm, metre, and stanza, and should not have been imagined as having done so. Poe has set up a "straw man" to increase his rhetorical advantage: it is more impressive to refute sixteen points than the thirteen that he did abolish. Surely Poe should have felt strong enough, rhetorically, in being able to demolish most of his opponent's points; he did not have to debate items that "Outis" never argued to prove that he (Poe) did not commit plagiarism regarding his choice of rhythm, metre, and stanza in "The Raven." Poe was a keen enough logician to have recognized a fallacy when he saw one, and his vaunted honour, his boasted integrity, should have kept him from deliberately committing one. He reminds me of the young Benjamin Franklin, who learned the art of disputation and got so good at it that he often, as he says, obtained "victories that neither myself nor my cause always deserved."

A few pages later, Poe seems to accuse "Outis" himself of committing the fallacy of irrelevant thesis: "to prove me or any body else an imitator, is no mode of showing that Mr. Aldrich or Mr. Longfellow is *not*" (78). That is a point well taken: to accuse Poe of being a plagiarist is not the issue that he raised initially – whether Aldrich and Longfellow are plagiarists. The argument made by "Outis" is *irrelevant*. Poe might also have accused his adversary of committing the fallacy of *tu quoque*, which is essentially a charge of hypocrisy. To Poe's charge that Aldrich and Longfellow are plagiarists, "Outis" essentially tried to argue that Poe himself might be charged with the same thing. Whether Poe is also guilty of something he accuses others of, literary borrowing, does not invalidate his argument that that practice is unconscionable.

Type: techniques of argument

FALLACY OF POISONING THE WELL: a somewhat underhanded trick Poe employs occasionally, most often in his literary criticism. When we "poison the well of discourse," we make it impossible for our opponents to reply without incriminating themselves; "that is perhaps what such unfair tactics ultimately are designed to do: by discrediting in advance the only source from which evidence either for or against a particular position can arise, they seek to avoid opposition by precluding discussion" (Engel, *With Good Reason*, 197). When Poe employs this strategy, he typically is not arguing against any *particular* opponent but he forces anyone who *might* disagree with him into an embarrassing position. Poe poisons the well of discourse in "The Poetic Principle":

> I make Beauty the province of the poem, simply because it is an obvious rule of Art that effects should be made to spring as directly as possible from their causes: – **no one as yet having been weak enough to deny that the peculiar elevation in question is at least *most readily* attainable in the poem**. (14: 275)

Poe might have said, "no one as yet having denied that ... ", but he inserted what amounts to an *ad hominem* attack against anyone who disagrees with his position; that is, anyone who *does* deny "that the peculiar elevation in question is at least *most readily* attainable in the poem" has already been dismissed, *unfairly*, as being "weak." Poe poisons the well again in the introduction to his *Autography*:

> that a strong analogy *does* generally and naturally exist between every man's chirography and character, will be denied **by none but the unreflecting**. (15: 178)

Anyone who *did* have the audacity to challenge this mystical (and absurd) connection between one's written signature and mental characteristics would damn himself (or herself) from the outset of the debate as "unreflecting." Here is Poe in his review of *The Linwoods*:

> we are acquainted with few persons **of sound and accurate discrimination** who would hesitate in placing her [Catherine Sedgwick] upon a level with the best of our native novelists. (8: 95; see also 11: 98, 194, 275; 15: 51; 16: 254)

Once more, the person who disagrees with Poe's position has been prejudged to be lacking in "sound and accurate discrimination." Poe's arrogance is showing (nothing new), and he clearly demonstrates one way in which a knowledge of logic – and its attendant fallacies – can be useful: one can win arguments, or at least appear to win arguments, without deserving such victories. I am sure that, given his critical acumen, he knew very well when he was using this unfair rhetorical tactic, and his arrogant conviction of his intellectual superiority over most of his fellows convinced him that they would probably not notice the fallacy being perpetrated on them.

Type: techniques of argument

FALLACY OF SPECIAL PLEADING: one of the fallacies of presumption (evading the facts) – applying a double standard, one for ourself and another for other people; presenting only one side of a case, the one favourable to ourself. Poe makes his awareness of this fallacy manifest in his reply to "Outis": "No gentleman should degrade himself, on any grounds, to the paltriness of *ex-parte* argument; and I shall not insult Outis at the outset, by assuming for a moment that he (Outis) is weak enough, to suppose me (Poe) silly enough, to look upon all this abominable rigmarole as anything better than a very respectable specimen of special pleading" (12: 53). In typically providing *balanced* critical reviews – arguing for the merits *and* demerits of a work – Poe attempted to avoid the "*ex-parte* argument" – that is, arguing only one side of a case (see *antanagoge*). He finds fault with those critics who do *not* provide balanced reviews: "I have read nothing finer in its way than his [Whipple's] eulogy on Tennyson. I say 'eulogy' – for the essay in question is unhappily little more: – and Mr. Whipple's paper on Miss Barrett, was *nothing more*" (13: 193). Still, sometimes Poe felt himself compelled, for reasons of either chivalry (toward female writers) or friendship, to change the rules a bit to avoid censuring an author whom he did not want to offend. So averse was Poe to finding fault with the poetry of his friend Chivers that he provides the following startling remark:

> The poems of Dr. Chivers abound in what must undoubtedly be considered as gross demerit, if we admit the prevalent canons of criticism. But it may safely be maintained that these prevalent canons have, in great part, no surer foundation than arrant conventionality. (12: 206)

If *that* is not the fallacy of special pleading, then I do not understand the term. Poe prided himself on his integrity as a critical reviewer, but in the case of Chivers he was willing to suspend current standards of criticism. Of course, there is some question as to the extent to which the current standards were *Poe's*, but Symons even suggests that, in applying his *own* philosophy of composition to the prose and poetry of other writers, "there is an element of special pleading for his own work" (184).
Type: techniques of argument

FICTIO: attributing rational actions and speech to nonrational creatures (Lanham, 78). This would seem to be a foregrounded device in "The Raven":

"Prophet!" said I, "thing of evil! – prophet still, if bird or devil!
By the Heaven that bends above us – by that God we both adore –
Tell this soul with sorrow laden if, within the distant Aidenn,
It shall clasp a sainted maiden whom the angels name Lenore –
Clasp a rare and radiant maiden whom the angels name Lenore."
Quoth the Raven "Nevermore." (7: 99)

We may wonder how *fictio* differs from personification (see under *proso-popoeia*), but Lanham does not offer the two terms as synonymous.
Pronunciation: FIC ti o
Type: techniques of argument

GEOGRAPHIA: a type of *enargia* (see above) – a description of the earth. In "The Unparalleled Adventure of One Hans Pfaall" we get a description of Earth from a balloon 7,254 miles up:

at length [I] beheld what there could be no hesitation in supposing the northern Pole itself … At all events I undoubtedly beheld the whole of the earth's major diameter; the entire northern hemisphere lay beneath me like a chart orthographically projected; and the great circle of the equator itself formed the boundary line of my horizon … Northwardly from the huge rim before mentioned, and which, with slight qualification, may be called the limit of human discovery in these regions, one unbroken, or nearly unbroken sheet of ice continues to extend. In the first few degrees of this its progress, its surface is very sensibly flattened, farther on depressed into a plane, and finally, becoming not a little concave, it terminates, at the Pole itself, in a circular centre, sharply defined, whose apparent diameter subtended at the balloon an angle of about sixty-five seconds, and whose dusky hue, varying in intensity, was at all times darker than any other spot upon the visible hemisphere, and occasionally deepened into the most absolute blackness …

April 8th. Found a sensible diminution in the earth's apparent diameter, besides a material alteration in its general color and appearance. The whole visible area partook in different degrees of a tint of pale yellow, and in some portions had acquired a brilliancy even painful to the eye. (2: 87–9)

As Beaver reminds us, "This aeronaut view of the North Pole as a black concave circle can only refer to John Cleves Symmes's theory of gigantic whirlpools, or holes at the Poles" (349n29). At the end of *Pym* we get a vivid description of the Symmes's hole at the southern pole, into which Pym and Peters descend.

Pronunciation: ge o GRA phi a
Type: description

GRAECISMUS: "Use of a Greek idiom or grammatical or ortho-
graphical features in writing or speaking English" (Lanham, 81). Not being fluent in Greek, I cannot easily supply an example from the Poe
canon. I have, however, found a place where Poe chastises another writer
for *graecismus*. In his review of James Fenimore Cooper's *Wyandotté*, Poe
says "the Greek 'pseudo' is objectionable, since its exact equivalent is to
be found in the English 'false'" (11: 220). In other words, Cooper should
simply have stuck to the English rather than show off with the Greek.
This implied advice is in keeping with Poe's praise of "an unambitious,
unadulterated Saxon" in Washington Irving's productions (11: 106).
Given his apparent preference for plain English, it is strange that Poe's
own prose is loaded with foreignisms (see under *soraismus*), and given
that his own prose *is* loaded with foreignisms, it is odd that he should
condemn another writer for the same thing.
Pronunciation: grae CIS mus
Type: ungrammatical, illogical, or unusual uses of language

HENDIADYS: (1) separating two words by the conjunction *and* when
those words should follow one after the other, such as an adjective then
its noun, or a verb then its adverb, or a verb then an infinitive; (2) replacing an adjective with a substantive. Here is an exemplification of the
first definition from a letter to Maria Clemm, 29 August 1835:
   Try and convince my dear Virg^a how devotedly I love her. (Ostrom, 71)
The two words *try* and *convince* are connected by *and* but, strictly speaking, *try* should be followed instead by the infinitive form of *convince* –
"try *to* convince." This is a common error in undergraduate writing and
here it shows that even Poe committed the occasional grammatical blunder. In another letter (7 April 1844) to Maria Clemm, Poe lets his grammatical guard down again:
   Be sure and go to the P. O. & have my letters forwarded. (Ostrom, 252)
The conjunction *and* appears instead of the infinitive verb *to go*.
   Sonnino discusses the term under its alternate spelling, *endiadis*, and
all rhetors mentioned in this text furnish illustrations of the other defini-

tion. Harmon and Holman provide *hendiadys* as one of the tropes that involves *and* or another coordinating conjunction and that fall under the general term *sleight of "and"* (486).
Pronunciation: hen DI a dys
Type: ungrammatical, illogical, or unusual uses of language

HIRMUS: the name in rhetoric for what linguists call the "left-branching" sentence (see below) and what everyone else calls the "periodic" or "suspended" sentence.
Pronunciation: HIR mus

HOMIOLOGIA: a tedious, uniform, repetitive style. In the following passage, Poe is demonstrating what he takes to be plagiarism by closely comparing two poems. He deliberately writes in a tedious, repetitive style to *reinforce* the parallelisms, the duplication, of certain themes in the poems in question. The repetition, combined with his clever use of syllabic expansion, has the effect of gradually but indubitably forcing the conviction on us that borrowing has indeed occurred:

> In the first place, then, the subject in both pieces is *death*. In the second it is the death of a woman. In the third, it is the death of a woman *tranquilly* dying. In the fourth, it is the death of a woman who lies tranquilly *throughout the night*. In the fifth it is the death of a woman whose "*breathing* soft and low is watched through the night" in the one instance and who "*breathed* the long long night away in statue-like repose" in the other. In the sixth place, in both poems this woman dies just at daybreak. In the seventh place, dying just at daybreak, this woman, in both cases, steps directly into Paradise. In the eighth place all these identities of circumstance are related in identical rhythms. In the ninth place these identical rhythms are arranged in identical metres; and, in the tenth place, these identical rhythms and metres are constructed into identical stanzas. ("The Longfellow War," 12: 45–6; see also 81)

Leave it to that master stylist, Poe, to be able to take what is normally a vice of style – cf *macrologia* – and use it strategically (that is, in a positive sense) to reinforce his argument. Once again, as we see so often in Poe, style is related to theme.
Pronunciation: ho mi o LO gi a
Type: repetition: clauses, phrases, and ideas

HOMOIOPTOTON: placing near one another in a sentence or verse various words in the same case and with similar case endings:

> It is not to be supposed, however, that in the delivery of such passages I was found at all deficient in the loo**king** asquint – the show**ing** my teeth – the work**ing** my knees – the shuff**ling** my feet – or in any of those unmention-able graces which are now justly considered the characteristics of a popular performer. ("Loss of Breath," 2: 155–6)

I adopt Lanham's and Taylor's distinction between *homoioptoton* and another term often confused with it: *homoioteleuton* (see below). While the latter refers to the similar closing of several clauses, phrases, verses, or sentences, *homoioptoton* means the similar termination of a pair or series of words that do not end but come in the middle of clauses, phrases, verses, or sentences (Lanham, 85). Some scholars may simply refer to *homoioptoton* as internal rhyme. Here is another example, a very clever one, from Poe's review of *Georgia Scenes*:

> This book has reached us **anonymously** – not to say **anomalously** – yet it is most heartily welcome. (8: 257)

We see that *assonance* can be involved with *homoioptoton*. See also "morphological set" and "phonological set."

Pronunciation: ho moi OP to ton

Type: repetition: letters, syllables, and sounds

HOMOIOTELEUTON: the placement of words having the same final syllable(s) at the end of clauses, phrases, verses, or sentences:

> but which Mr. Coleridge would have called myst**ical**, Mr. Kant panthe**istical**, Mr. Carlyle twist**ical**, and Mr. Emerson hyperquizzit**istical**. ("Never Bet the Devil Your Head," 4: 218)

We can find an instance in Poe's criticism as well:

> There is nothing more rich**ly** – more vivid**ly** – more chaste**ly** – more sub-lime**ly** imaginative – in the wide realm of poetical literature. (Review of *Orion*, 11: 268)

The next is from his remarks on Hawthorne:

> But is there any one of these qualities which should prevent his doing doubly as well in a career of honest, upright, **sensible**, prehen**sible** and comprehen**sible** things? (13: 155)

See also "morphological set" and "phonological set," *homoioptoton*, and *assonance*.

Pronunciation: ho moi o te LEU ton
Type: repetition: letters, syllables, and sounds

H O R I S M U S : a clear, brief, pithy definition (sometimes antithetical). The following definition of *music*, from a letter to Lowell (2 July 1844), will not surprise anyone familiar with Poe's musical poetry:

Music is the perfection of the soul, or idea, of Poetry. (Ostrom, 258)

Sometimes the definition in question functions to distinguish between the meaning of two words; sometimes, as in the *rhetorical* definition, the subject is defined by its opposite(s). *Horismus* is variously spelled as *horysmos* (Espy, 180) and *orismos* (Sonnino, 67). A synonymous term is *definitio* (see Dupriez, 121–3).
Pronunciation: ho RIS mus
Type: balance, antithesis, and paradox

H Y D R O G R A P H I A : a type of *enargia* (see above) – the vivid description of water:

On account of the singular character of the water, we refused to taste it, supposing it to be polluted; and it was not until some time afterward we came to understand that such was the appearance of the streams throughout the whole group. I am at a loss to give a distinct idea of the nature of this liquid, and cannot do so without many words [here is more of Poe's *adynata*]. Although it flowed with rapidity in all declivities where common water would do so, yet never, except when falling in a cascade, had it the customary appearance of limpidity. It was, nevertheless, in point of fact, as perfectly limpid as any limestone water in existence, the difference being only in appearance. At first sight, and especially in cases where little declivity was found, it bore resemblance, as regards consistency, to a thick infusion of gum Arabic in common water. But this was only the least remarkable of its extraordinary qualities. It was not colourless, nor was it of any one uniform colour – presenting to the eye, as it flowed, every possible shade of purple, like the hues of a changeable silk. (*The Narrative of Arthur Gordon Pym of Nantucket*, 3: 186)

In his biography of Poe, Harrison suggests that "No one has depicted ... water in its infinite diversities of color and motion, more graphically than the author of 'Arthur Gordon Pym,' 'A MS. found in a Bottle,' and 'The Fall of the House of Usher'" (1: 20).
Pronunciation: hy dro GRA phi a
Type: description

HYPERBATON: the rearrangement or inversion of normal word order (subject-verb-object) usually for a specific effect, often emphasis:

Object there was none. Passion there was none. ("The Tell-Tale Heart," 5: 88)

This word order allows the narrator to emphasize the usual motives for crime (object, passion) and to stress that they were completely absent through the repetition of the word *none* (*epistrophe*). Moreover, his syntax is more emphatic and attention-grabbing than "I had no motive, such as passion, for committing the crime." The important words *motive* and *passion* get lost in the middle of this sentence and so are deemphasized rather than emphasized. The mad narrator then follows with another instance of *hyperbaton*, "For his gold I had no desire," instead of "I had no desire for his gold." *Hyperbaton* can be used as another figure of vehemence; indeed, Dupriez says that "Most theorists ... have been content to return to the definition of hyperbaton as an inversion which expresses 'a violent movement of the soul' (Littré)" (214). That the narrator in "The Tell-Tale Heart" displays this and other devices of emotion undermines his claim that he can relate the entire story "calmly"; in other words, the only thing he proves is that he is yet another of Poe's many self-deluded narrators.

Stauffer has some intelligent suggestions to make about Poe's use of *hyperbaton* in "Ligeia," saying that the device "gives the style a distant, archaic, otherworldly tone" ("Style and Meaning," 321). He then offers a few instances:

In the classical tongues was she deeply proficient. (2: 253)

Yet not until the last instance, amid the most convulsive writhings of her fierce spirit, was shaken the external placidity of her demeanor. (255)

For long hours, detaining my hand, would she pour out before me the overflowing of a heart. (255)

In his essay published thirty years later, Stauffer remarks again on Poe's use of *hyperbaton* (which Stauffer labels *anastrophe*), saying that Poe "tends to use more than the usual number of inversions of normal word order ... Most of Poe's inversions produce a poetic effect or provide emphasis, and sometimes both. His most frequently used poetic inversion is the rearrangement of the verb and its negative. For example, instead of 'did not move' he writes 'moved not'" ("The Language and Style of the Prose," 464).

Perhaps surprisingly, considering what we have just seen, in a review of the work of Amelia Welby, Poe expresses his distaste for *hyperbaton* in poetry: "the more prosaic the construction of verse, the better. Inversions [*hyperbaton*] should be dismissed. The most forcible lines are the most direct. Mrs. Welby owes three-fourths of her power (so far as style is concerned), to her freedom from these vulgar and particularly English errors" (16: 58). The closer the syntax of poetic lines is to that of normal English, the better – the more natural it is, Poe believed. He has the same complaint about Drake's poem *Niagara*, complaining about its "frequent inversions of language" (8: 305; see also 10: 76; 11: 183). In his review of *The Songs of Our Land, and Other Poems*, Poe amplifies his reasons for advising against *hyperbaton*:

> The putting the adjective after the noun is an inexcusable Gallicism, but the putting the *preposition* after the noun is not only *not* a Gallicism, but is alien to all languages, and in opposition to all the principles of language. Such things serve no other purpose than to betray the versifier's poverty of resource. Inversions are ranked among the poetic licenses; but the true poet will avail himself of no license whatever that does not aid his intended effect. When an inversion occurs, we say at once, "here the poet had not sufficient skill to make out his line without distorting the language." Nothing so much tends to render verse feeble, ineffective. In ninety-nine cases out of a hundred where a line is spoken of as unusually forcible, it will be found that the *force* is attributable to the *directness* of its expression. Nearly all the passages which have become household through frequent quotation, owe their popularity either to this directness, or, in general, to the scorn of poetic license. In short, as regards verbal construction, the more prosaic a poetical style is, the better. No modern poet is more remarkable for this species of prosaicism than Moore, and to this his unusual point and force are mainly attributable. It will be observed that he is the most *quotable* of poets. (13: 103)

Given his attitude toward inversions in poetry, that Poe himself is known to revert to *hyperbaton* in his own poetry probably will surprise many:

> Not the least obeisance made he; not a moment stopped or stayed he. ("The Raven," 7: 96)

We have *three* instances of syntactical inversions here. Written in the normal word order, we would have, "He made not the least obeisance," "he stopped not a moment" and "he stayed not a moment."

As the lines from "The Tell-Tale Heart" show, Poe recognized the usefulness of *hyperbaton* (in prose) to express emotional frenzy in a mad narrator. Forrest, perhaps committing the fallacy of false cause, holds that this device is one of several that Poe learned from the Bible (98). Stauffer suggests that it is part of Poe's "parabolic" and "arabesque" styles ("The Language and Style of the Prose," 459–60). Lanham tells us that *hyperbaton* is the generic name for various forms of departure from normal word order, including *anastrophe, cacosyntheton, epergesis, hypallage, hysterologia, hysteron proteron,* parenthesis, and *tmesis* (86).

Pronunciation: hy PER ba ton

Type: ungrammatical, illogical, or unusual uses of language

HYPERBOLE: exaggeration, overstatement, often used for emphasis or for comical effect. The use of comic *hyperbole* is appropriate for a uniquely American type of humour, the tall tale, which often depends on gross exaggeration. When using it seriously, however, a writer must not let it become excessive – as it sometimes is in the works of Poe, who is often denounced for his frequent use of superlatives, *adynata* (see above), and other forms of *hyperbole*:

> suddenly, a loud and long scream or yell, as if from the throats of a thousand demons, seemed to pervade the whole atmosphere around and above the boat. (*The Narrative of Arthur Gordon Pym of Nantucket,* 3: 10)

> he found himself beneath the surface, whirling round and round with inconceivable rapidity. (15)

> I felt, I am sure, more than ten thousand times the agonies of death itself. (45)

Since Poe typically retains an ironic detachment from his narrators, however, we may conjecture that he was well aware of Pym's use of *hyperbole* here and that, by this absurd level of exaggeration, Poe wants us to question Pym's reliability as a narrator. Or we may consider Poe's *hyperbole* a deliberate clue to the attentive reader that *Pym* is in fact a hoax (Poe loved hoaxing the American public) – that *Pym* itself can be seen within the tall-tale tradition. That the novel may indeed be a deception on Poe's part is suggested in part by the centrality of deceit as a theme in that work. Largely a story about ocean mishaps, *Pym* introduces one of three main characters, Augustus Barnard, who loved to relate his own stories of the ocean, "one half of which I [Pym] now suspect to have been sheer fabrications." Thus, Augustus himself appears to be a teller of tall tales marked by *hyperbole*.

In his sometimes-scathing literary reviews, Poe occasionally uses *hyperbole* rather cruelly:

In all this balderdash about the stage, there is not one original incident or idea. The same anecdotes are told, but in **infinitely** better language, **in every book of dramatic reminiscences since the flood.** (Review of *Paul Ulric*, 8: 184–5; see also 10: 116; 13: 51, 70)

Now and then he uses it to praise:

> There can be no doubt that Lady Dacre is a writer of **infinite genius.** (Review of *Tales of the Peerage and the Peasantry*, 8: 75; see also 12: 31)

In "The Language and Style of the Prose," Stauffer uses the term *hyperbolic* in a broader sense to describe one *type* of style to which Poe has recourse. As Stauffer uses the term, it covers several stylistic features, "those many tricks of rhetoric – puns, rhyming words, parody, burlesque – that Poe found irresistible" (459). I would refer the reader to Stauffer's paragraph on "the hyperbolic style."

Pronunciation: hy PER bo le

Type: metaphorical substitutions and puns

HYPOPHORA: a type of rhetorical question that involves a speaker or writer raising a question then answering it him- or herself:

> "Let us now transport ourselves, in fancy, to this chamber. **What shall we first seek here? The means of egress employed by the murderers.**" ("The Murders in the Rue Morgue," 4: 172)

This handling of rhetorical questions suggests that the speaker is not open to anyone else's opinions. *Hypophora*, therefore, can suggest narrow-mindedness or impatience on the part of the person who employs it. We should not be surprised that Poe's brilliant detective, Dupin, uses this device now and then: since no one can keep up with his acute deductive and inductive reasoning, it becomes necessary for him to explain his reasoning processes – "this is what I asked myself; this was my answer" (see also "The Mystery of Marie Rogêt," 5: 55, 61).

The device appears now and then in Poe's literary criticism, too:

> What connection has the name of Lieutenant Upshur with the present Spanish Adventures of Lieutenant Slidell? None. (Review of *Spain Revisited*, 9: 2; see also 10: 102)

Pronunciation: hy PO phor a

Type: devices of vehemence

Type: techniques of argument

HYPOTAXIS: (adjective: hypotactic) a complicated type of writing style involving phrases or clauses arranged in dependent or subordinate relationships:

> From the paintings over which his elaborate fancy brooded, and which grew, touch by touch, into vagueness at which I shuddered the more thrillingly, because I shuddered knowing not why; – from these paintings (vivid as their images now are before me) I would in vain endeavour to educe more than a small portion which should lie within the compass of merely written words.
> ("The Fall of the House of Usher," 3: 283)

The main idea in this long-winded and complicated passage is, "From the paintings I would in vain endeavour to educe ..."; however, note all the phrases and clauses that intervene between the beginning and the end of the excerpt. Obviously, a hypotactic sentence structure can be very difficult to read. Another relevant term that applies in discussions of *hypotaxis* is *nested syntax*, which Cluett and Kampeas define as "Multiple inclusion, or the placing of subordinate and relative clauses inside other subordinate and/or relative clauses" (42). Interestingly, in his Marginalia Poe himself uses this nest metaphor in a condemnation of Sir Edward Bulwer-Lytton's style, which he calls "atrociously involute": "He wraps one sentence [clause?] in another ad infinitum – very much in the fashion of those 'nests' of boxes sold in our wooden-ware shops, or like the islands within lakes, within islands within lakes, within islands within lakes" (16: 66). That Poe could even make such an observation shows his sensitivity to issues of style; for his parody of the hypotactic style see an extreme instance on the first page of "A Predicament: The Scythe of Time" (2: 283). Poe's critical reviews sometimes display an annoyingly hypotactic structure and those who deplore his "style" may well cite his embedded passages as difficult reading. *Hypotaxis* is the opposite of *parataxis* and tends to slow the pace of a passage because of the syntactic interruption. As the largely paratactic style of "The Cask of Amontillado" (for instance) shows, Poe could write in both the simple paratactic and the difficult hypotactic styles.

Perhaps the most unreadable hypotactic passages in the Poe canon are to be found in *Eureka* – this is Poe at his most impenetrable. My guess is that Poe, because he was writing about a sublime subject (the most sublime of all), decided to write in the high, the grandiloquent, style as suitable for the grandeur of his theme – and one aspect of the high style is syntactic embedding, especially in combination with periodicity:

Unless we are to conceive that the appetite for Unity among the atoms is doomed to be satisfied *never*; – unless we are to conceive that what had a beginning is to have no end – a conception which cannot *really* be entertained, however much we may talk or dream of entertaining it – we are forced to conclude that the repulsive influence imagined, will, finally – under pressure of the *Uni-tendency collectively* applied, but never and in no degree *until*, on fulfilment of the Divine purposes, such collective application shall be naturally made – yield to a force which, at that ultimate epoch, shall be the superior force precisely to the extent required, and thus permit the universal subsidence into the inevitable, because original and therefore normal, *One*. (16: 211)

Poe can write much more simply and clearly than this. I suspect that he decided to relate style to subject matter by writing in a difficult style to reflect the difficulty of his theme.

Hypotaxis seems to be related to theme in "The Thousand-and-second Tale of Scheherazade." Scheherazade, of course, is the legendary queen of Samarkand who delayed her execution for a thousand-and-one nights by telling her husband, Schariar, exotic Eastern tales, anecdotes, and fables, ending each night before the narrative climax and thereby forcing the king to keep her alive in order to hear the conclusion the next night. Scheherazade's technique is the generation of *suspense*, and this technique is mirrored in the largely left-branching and hypotactic style of the primary narrator:

Having had occasion, lately, in the course of some oriental investigations, to consult the *Tellmenow Isitsoörnot*, a work which (like the Zohar of Simeon Jochaides) is scarcely known at all, even in Europe, and which has never been quoted to my knowledge, by any American – if we except, perhaps, the author of the "Curiosities of American Literature;" – having had occasion, I say, to turn over some pages of the first-mentioned very remarkable work, I was not a little astonished. (6: 78)

As the comments from his Marginalia, above, show, Poe is conscious of the hypotactic style. He knows exactly what he is doing. In the passage from "The Thousand-and-second Tale," the syntactic postponement mirrors Scheherazade's technique of narrative postponement. We, like King Schariar, are kept in suspense until the end. Style relates to theme, here; the linguistic relates to the extralinguistic. When that is done well, I have always considered it a sign of a master writer (see, also, *epanalepsis* and "parenthesis"). Now and then in his literary reviews Poe expresses his belief, his authorial

credo, that style and subject should be one: "The *style* of Mr. Wilmer is not only good in itself, but exceedingly well adapted to his subjects" (Review of *The Confessions of Emilia Harrington*, 8: 236).
Pronunciation: hy po TAX is

HYPOZEUGMA: the last clause of a sentence provides the verb that is missing in the previous ones:

> The waver, the jostle, and the hum **increased** in a tenfold degree. ("The Man of the Crowd," 4: 141)

This device compares obviously with other types of minus additioning, such as *ellipsis* (above), *zeugma*, *prozeugma*, and *mesozeugma* (see below for all three).
Pronunciation: hy po ZEUG ma
Type: addition, subtraction, and substitution: words, phrases, and clauses
Type: brevity

HYPOZEUXIS: when each clause in a sentence has its own subject and verb (in other words, when each clause is independent):

> He **eats** your dinner, he **drinks** your wine, he **borrows** your money, he **pulls** your nose, he **kicks** your poodle, and he **kisses** your wife. ("Diddling Considered as One of the Exact Sciences," 5: 213)

Cf *asyndeton* and *parataxis*. This example from "Diddling" also illustrates *parison*, or *isocolon* (see below); thus, *hypozeuxis* can involve a kind of balance (though it does not necessarily have to).
Pronunciation: hy po ZEUX is
Type: balance, antithesis, paradox

IMAGERY: classified as a literary rather than a strictly rhetorical term, but, as Lanham puts it, "The pictorial (visual image-making) part of its meaning was expressed by the various subdivisions of Enargia" (89; see above). In literature, an image can be a representation of a scene or object (a castle, for instance), a mental picture evoked by a descriptive passage in a poem or prose. "Imagery," however, also refers to qualities of sense perception in addition to the visual. There are thus different kinds of images, each of which refers to one of our senses. (A use of imagery with a "twist" can be found in "The Colloquy of Monos and Una," where Poe's Monos describes the confusion of his senses after "death" –

synesthesia.) A writer may use imagery to report sensations in a tale to provide a realistic presentation of a character's predicament. Poe was further concerned with the response of a reader – the way s/he reacts to the events in a story. The reader is more likely to identify with the protagonist if the writer is effective in portraying the sensations that the character experiences. Poe relies heavily on this experiential identification on the part of the reader – empathy.

The following instances of imagery are all taken deliberately from "The Pit and the Pendulum"; that tale, after all, is one of torture, which involves the cruellest attack on the senses. Poe's prisoner is being tormented by the sadistic monks of the Spanish Inquisition, and Poe therefore provides descriptions of every kind of sensation – each type of imagery. Occasionally, however, we also witness the absence of sensory stimulation, Edmund Burke's idea of "privation." In *A Philosophical Enquiry into the Origin of our Ideas of the Sublime and Beautiful*, Burke states, "All *general* privations are great, because they are all terrible; *Vacuity, Darkness, Solitude* and *Silence*" (65). Poe's prisoner experiences all of these most of the time, so, when his senses are not being overwhelmed, resulting in physical torment, they are being deprived, resulting in mental torment.

- **auditory imagery**: appealing to our sense of hearing. Auditory imagery can involve soft as well as loud sounds. In this example, Poe's prisoner-narrator describes the sound of the huge, razor-sharp pendulum swinging above him (and in this connection, see *onomatopoeia*, below):
  It was appended to a weighty rod of brass, and the whole hissed as it swung through the air. (5: 78)
- **gustatory imagery**: appealing to our sense of taste:
  This thirst it appeared to be the design of my persecutors to stimulate: for the food in the dish was meat pungently seasoned. (77)
- **kinesthetic imagery**: sensations of movement:
  These shadows of memory tell, indistinctly, of tall figures that lifted and bore me in silence down – down – still down – till a hideous dizziness oppressed me at the mere idea of the interminableness of the descent ... Then comes a sense of sudden motionlessness throughout all things. (70)
- **olfactory imagery**: appealing to our sense of smell:
  Even while I breathed there came to my nostrils the breath of the vapor of heated iron! A suffocating odour pervaded the prison! (85)

- **tactile imagery**: appealing to our sense of touch:
  Then again sound, and motion, and touch – a tingling sensation pervading my frame. (70)
- **thermal imagery**: appealing to our sense of hot and/or cold:
  I shrank from the glowing metal to the centre of the cell. Amid the thought of the fiery destruction that impended, the idea of the coolness of the well came over my soul like balm. (85)
- **visual imagery**: appealing to our sense of sight.

This kind of imagery can be related to *enargia* and its various subtypes (see above). It includes chromatic imagery – descriptions of colours. Poe is a very "colourful" writer, and red (16.5 per cent) joins black (28 per cent) and white (and gray – 28.6 per cent) as a predominant colour in his canon. Yellow is fourth most frequent (10.2 per cent); other colours appear under 6 per cent. These figures are from a notable study of the frequency of colours in Poe's works: Clough's "The Use of Color Words by Edgar Allen [*sic*] Poe." His most polychromatic tale is, of course, "The Masque of the Red Death" (see chapter 3).

Type: description

INCLUSIO: a scheme of repetition using *epanalepsis* (see above) to mark off not merely a sentence or clause but an entire passage – that is, beginning and ending a poem, paragraph, story, play, or even novel with the same word or group of words. "The Man of the Crowd" exhibits *inclusio* insofar as it begins and ends with the same phrase:

It is well said of a certain German book that *"es lässt sich nicht lesen"* – it does not permit itself to be read. (4: 134)

The worst heart of the world is a grosser book than the "Hortulus Animæ," and perhaps it is but one of the great mercies of God that *"es lässt sich nicht lesen."* (145)

Just as the tale begins and ends the same way, stylistically, so it does geographically: the narrator follows the mysterious stranger from the street of the D— Hotel and back again over the course of the night. In terms of style and geography, Poe takes us in a circle, and the linguistic and the extralinguistic come together. "William Wilson" also exhibits *inclusio* insofar as one of its paragraphs begins and ends with the same short clause: *"I fled in vain"* (3: 321).

In his discussion of the resemblances of Poe's poetry to that of the Bible, Forrest uses a different term from *inclusio*: "What is known as envelope structure is the use of an initial refrain repeated at the end of the poem instead of in the opening of its middle stanza. As so used it encloses the thought which should be read in the light of the refrain" (112); he then offers Poe's "I saw thee on thy bridal day" as an exemplification of the device:

I saw thee on thy bridal day –
  When a burning blush came o'er thee,
Though happiness around thee lay,
  The world all love before thee:
And in thine eye a kindling light
  (Whatever it might be)
Was all on Earth my aching sight
  Of Loveliness could see.

That blush, perhaps, was maiden shame –
  As such it well may pass –
Though its glow hath raised a fiercer flame
  In the breast of him, alas!

Who saw thee on that bridal day,
  When that deep blush *would* come o'er thee,
Though happiness around thee lay,
  The world all love before thee. (7: 10; see also 74)

Clearly, *inclusio* gives a sense of circularity to a passage or work, a sense of closure, a sense of "what goes around comes around"; but sometimes, as Anthony Caputi suggests, the second instance of the repeated lines can involve "very subtle shadings in emotional complexity" (95). Poe discusses a type of repetition, the refrain, in "The Rationale of Verse," noting that its use can be improved "by relieving its monotone in slightly varying the phrase at each repetition, or, (as I have attempted to do in 'The Raven,') in retaining the phrase and varying its application" (14: 229). See "The Philosophy of Composition" (14: 199–202). Oddly, perhaps, we find Poe elsewhere condemning a poet for his use of *inclusio*: "In his continuous and absolutely uniform repetition of the first line in the last of each stanza, he has by much exceeded the legitimate limits of the quaint, and impinged upon the simply ludicrous" (Review of *A Chaunt of Life and Other Poems*, 12: 195). I suspect that Poe disapproves of the absolute *uniformity* of the duplicated lines – that is, in the poet's inability or unwillingness to vary, even slightly, the repeated line or its application.

Caputi has devoted an entire essay to the use of the refrain in Poe's poetry, for he believes that Poe's "use of the refrain constitutes a valuable index to his literary practice and to the relation between his practice and theory" (92), and that "His use of the refrain in the final years of his life almost amounted to a dependence" (94). Caputi's essay is valuable, if a little condescending, and the term *refrain* as he uses it actually refers to several types of rhetorical repetition (such as *ploce*), not just to *inclusio*. Caputi concludes thus: "Poe viewed the refrain largely as a device, even a kind of trick, by which to produce emotional excitement"; "That he was frequently successful with the refrain suggests that he probably understood it better than he understood the other devices. At his worst his use of the refrain descends to sheer rhetoric [whatever that means]. At his best the refrain is integral in his poetic conception, though frequently submerged in rhetoric of other kinds" (101).

Pronunciation: in CLU si o

Type: repetition: clauses, phrases, and ideas

Type: "biblical"

INDIGNATIO: arousing the audience's scorn and indignation. This device is more typically found in oratory, but perhaps Poe is attempting to encourage his readers to feel the same disgust as he does in the following excerpt from his review of *Life on the Lakes*:

> We have other faults to find with the work. It contains some ill-mannered and grossly ignorant sneers at Daniel O'Connell, calling him "the great pensioner on the poverty of his countrymen," and making him speak in a brogue only used by the lowest of the Irish, about *"the finest pisantry in the world."* (Poe's italics; 9: 77)

Lanham makes additional remarks regarding this device (90). He also relates it, quite rightly, to *commiseratio*, "a part of an oration intended to excite compassion" (37), and *pathopoeia*, "a general term for arousing passion or emotion" (111). Another term for the device is *aganactesis*.

Pronunciation: in dig NA ti o
Type: devices of vehemence
Type: techniques of argument

INTENTIONAL FALLACY: not a term from rhetoric or logic but a well known one from literary criticism, it describes the error of criticizing and judging a work according to whether it fulfills its author's stated or implied intentions for that work. One also commits the fallacy if one *surmises* what the author's intentions were. Poe does this in his review of the novel *Zanoni*:

> Many even of the leading incidents have no bearing on the *dénouement*. The compact betwixt Zanoni and the EVIL EYE, at Venice, is of this character. **The author's original intention was to make the condition exacted from the husband play a prominent part at the crisis**; but he subsequently changed his mind, and brought about the *dénouement* by other means, forgetting, however, to rewrite this scene, so as to adapt it to the altered aspect of the story. (11: 118)

One should concentrate solely on the work itself for its value and meaning, rather than on surmises about an author's intentions, or on his or her stated intentions, for a work often grows beyond its creator's control and lends itself to meanings that s/he did not intend. Once it leaves the author's hands, it becomes part of the public domain. Thus, to be safe, the critic should concentrate simply on what the work *says*. Poe, as a superb practitioner of New Criticism, would likely approve of that doctrine, despite his commission of the fallacy of intent.

The term is covered – and elaborated on – in any good dictionary of literary terms: Abrams (84–5), Baldick (110–11), Cuddon (452), Gray (149–50), Harmon/Holman (271–2).
Type: techniques of argument

ISOCOLON: the repetition of phrases or clauses of equal or roughly equal syllabic length and usually corresponding structure; sometimes there are similar sounds in the parallel phrases or clauses:

> She partly arose, and spoke, in an earnest low whisper,
> **of sounds which she *then* heard, but which I could not hear –**
> **of motions which she *then* saw, but which I could not perceive.** ("Ligeia," 2: 262)

I have stacked the clauses the better to show the corresponding syntactical structure. Note, also, that the first two clauses have twelve syllables between them, while the second two have nearly the same: fourteen. *Isocolon* can, but does not always, involve *anaphora* (initial repetition) and seriation (listing, cataloguing). Clearly a scheme of parallelistic balance, *isocolon* "contributes greatly to the rhythm of sentences" (Corbett, 429). For another good example of the device, see the second-last paragraph of "The Poetic Principle" (14: 291). Sometimes *isocolon* is called *parison* (cf expansion). See also "parallelism" and *syncrisis*.

Pronunciation: i so CO lon

Type: balance, antithesis, paradox

Type: repetition: clauses, phrases, and ideas

ITERATIO: repetition of the same idea, sometimes in different words, for vehemence or fullness:

> we most easily and immediately comprehend the subsequent most feasible carrying out to completion of any such design as that which I have suggested **– the design of variety out of unity – diversity out of sameness – heterogeneity out of homogeneity – complexity out of simplicity.** (*Eureka*, 16: 208)

This example also illustrates parallel structure, reinforced by *antistrophe* (see above) and *homoioteleuton* (see above). *Iteratio* is variously defined. Lanham considers it synonymous with *anaphora*, but then why not equate it with any of the other many devices of repetition? Sonnino cites certain ancient and Renaissance rhetors who see it as a summary of points made (124). It compares with one definition of *palilogia* (which is synonymous), *commoratio* (above), and *synonymia* (below). These terms all seem to mean the same, and that we find them all in Poe shows how much he liked devices of repetition, amplification.

Pronunciation: i te RA ti o

Type: amplification

Type: devices of vehemence

Type: repetition: clauses, phrases, and ideas

LEFT-BRANCHING SENTENCE: called a *periodic* or *suspended* sentence by most English teachers and *hirmus* by rhetors, a left-branching sentence is one in which full grammatical completeness is left until the end. It begins with a phrase or at least one dependent rather than independent clause (contrast with the "right-branching sentence" – see below). Sometimes the left-branching sentence is hypotactic, with many phrases and clauses embedded into it. Here is an extremely long left-branching sentence describing quite vividly the horrors of premature burial:

> **The unendurable oppression of the lung – the stifling fumes from the damp earth – the clinging of the death garments – the rigid embrace of the narrow house – the blackness of the absolute Night – the silence like a sea that overwhelms – the unseen but palpable presence of the Conqueror Worm – these things, with thoughts of the air and grass above, with memory of dear friends who would fly to save us if but informed of our fate, and with consciousness that of this fate they can never be informed – that our hopeless portion is that of the really dead** – these considerations, I say, carry into the heart, which still palpitates, a degree of appalling and intolerable horror from which the most daring imagination must recoil. ("The Premature Burial," 5: 263)

The main thought in this long structure is at the very end but we must wade through twelve dependent clauses before we get there. Afraid that we would lose the sense of his meaning long before he concludes the sentence, Poe must employ not one but two summarizing phrases (see *epanalepsis* #2) to help carry the sentence along: "these things" and "these considerations." Clearly, long left-branching sentences can slow the pace of a passage; Poe does so deliberately and thus forces us to consider at torturous length the horrors of being buried alive. Premature burials of various kinds occur several times in Poe's fiction, and he himself may have suffered from *taphephobia* – fear of premature interment.

Stauffer submits that complex sentence structure characterizes Poe's "ratiocinative" style, which includes his critical prose, and although we do find instances of simple sentences there, extremely hypotactic and left-branching ones such as the following abound:

> Now if the author of "Ernest Maltravers," implicitly following authority like *les moutons de Panurge, will* persist in writing long romances because long romances have been written before, – if, in short, he cannot be satisfied with the brief tale (a species of composition which admits of the highest development of artistical power in alliance with the wildest vigour of imagination), – he must then content himself, perforce, with a more simply and more rigidly narrative form. (Review of *Night and Morning,* 10: 122–3)

LEITMOTIF: not a rhetorical term but worth mentioning here for its similarity to the rhetorical device *epimone*, which Lanham defines as the "Frequent [choral] repetition of a phrase or question, in order to dwell on a point" (68). Some may consider the two terms synonymous. *Epimone* can be especially effective in oratory; preachers like to use it, too. "Leitmotif" refers to the frequent intentional repetition of a word, phrase, sentence, or complex of images in a single work. A leitmotif can function to unify a work by reminding the reader of its earlier occurrences (see Abrams, 110–11; Harmon/Holman, 288). Poe employs the device seven times in "Eleonora"; here are two instances:

> We had always dwelled together, beneath a tropical sun, in **the Valley of the Many-Colored Grass** ... The passions which had for centuries distinguished our race, came thronging with the fancies for which they had been equally noted, and together breathed a delirious bliss **over the Valley of the Many-Colored Grass.** (4: 237, 239)

Forrest gives this device as partial proof that Poe sometimes attempted to duplicate the "biblical" style. He then cites passages from "Silence" to show the refrain at work again and concludes that "Poe's use of the refrain in prose is especially noteworthy because he spoke of it in one of his lectures as a thing restricted to poetry alone, and as commonly limited to lyric poetry ["The Philosophy of Composition"]. But where used by him and the biblical writers outside of poetry the writings are highly poetic and not infrequently lyrical" (93). "Silence" exhibits several instances of the leitmotif:

> But there is no wind throughout the heaven. [repeated twice]
> And I lay close within my covert and observed the actions of the man. And the man trembled in the solitude; – but the night waned, and he sat upon the rock. [repeated four times]

The refrain, like other devices Forrest discusses, is not restricted solely to the Bible, however, and Forrest frequently commits the fallacy of *post hoc, ergo propter hoc* ("after this, therefore because of this" – see above) in attempting to prove the Bible as a stylistic source of inspiration. Still, cumulatively he does make a good enough case, and anyone familiar with Poe's prose should not have trouble accepting the Bible as one of his sources for rhetorical figures. Killis Campbell believes that Poe read

> some parts of it fairly closely. He quotes from the Bible, by my count, forty-five times; and he echoes passages from the Bible or alludes to persons or

places or incidents mentioned in it seventy-four times. Thirty-one of his direct quotations are from the Old Testament and fourteen from the New Testament; and fifteen of the twenty-two Scriptural passages that he echoes are from the Old Testament. Most of his allusions, too, are to characters or places or happenings spoken of in the Old Testament. The books that he appears to have known best are Psalms, Isaiah, and Ezekiel in the Old Testament, and the Gospels of Matthew and John in the New Testament. He refers once to the Apocryphal book of Judith. ("Poe's Reading," 193)

Elsewhere, Poe shows his approval of a poet's use of the leitmotif: "the poet has preserved a thorough monotone throughout, and renders its effect more impressive by the repetition (gradually increasing in frequency towards the *finale*) of one of the most pregnant and effective of the stanzas" (Review of *Wiley and Putnam's Library of Choice Reading*. No. XIX. Prose and Verse, 12: 236). See chapter 5 for material on how Poe uses the leitmotif satirically.

Pronunciation: LITE mo teef

Type: amplification

Type: repetition: words

Type: repetition: clauses, phrases, and ideas

Type: "biblical"

LITOTES: ironical understatement; denial of the contrary often using *no* or *not*:

> In speaking of his [the cat's] intelligence, my wife, who at heart was **not a little** tinctured with superstition, made frequent allusion to the ancient popular notion, which regarded all black cats as witches in disguise. ("The Black Cat," 5: 144)

Corbett proposes that *litotes* can be employed "to enhance the impressiveness of what we say" (452), though I am not sure it always functions that way in Poe's prose (wherein *litotes* is quite frequent); occasionally it even makes for awkwardness of expression:

> I have had **no little** to do, in my day, with the trade of Aristarchus. ("Literary Small Talk," 14: 90)

In his criticism, Poe sometimes uses *litotes* to damn with faint praise:

> The play is **not without merit**. (*The Literati of New York City*, Anna Cora Mowatt, 15: 29)

In a letter (22 January 1841) to a prominent citizen of Philadelphia, Poe solicits his help using *litotes* for the sake of modesty:

I have been induced to hope that you would **not be altogether unwilling** to aid me. (Ostrom, 154)

Annoyed that some "Student of Theology" had attacked *Eureka*, Poe wrote the editor of *The Literary World* to offer some words in his own defence. In his letter of 20 September 1848, Poe's use of *litotes* is rather biting:

> our young students of Theology do not seem to be aware that in defence ... of Christianity, there is anything wrong in such **gentlemanly peccadillos** as the deliberate perversion of an author's text – to say nothing of the **minor *indecora*** of reviewing a book without reading it and without having the faintest suspicion of what is it about. (Ostrom, 379–80)

Pronunciation: LI to tes

MACROLOGIA (macrology): using more words than necessary; being long-winded. In his literary criticism, Poe complains now and then of this vice – sometimes called *copia verborum* – in the works under consideration. For instance, in his review of *The American in England*, he quotes an instance of wordiness from the book and then comments (*epicrisis*): "The absence of intellectual and moral culture, in occupations which rendered it unnecessary for those who worked only to administer food to themselves and profit or luxury to the class of masters, could only account for the absence of forehead, of the ornamental parts of that face which was moulded after a divine model [note the allusion to phrenology]." Poe says this:

> We perused this sentence more than once before we could fathom its meaning. Mr. Slidell wishes to say, that *narrowness of forehead in the rabble is owing to want of mental exercise – they being laborers not thinkers* ... the entire passage is overloaded with verbiage. A rigid scrutiny will show that all essential portions of the intended idea are embodied in the lines Italicised. In the original sentence are *fifty-four* words – in our own *eighteen* – or precisely one third. (8: 219–20; see also 11: 216; 13: 199)

Poe himself, however, is sometimes verbose:

> In fact, it will be seen at once, that **what we have said has a tendency directly the reverse of any such accusation.** ("The Magazine Prison-House," 14: 161)

Poe might simply have said, "In fact, the reverse is true." While I have found *many* proofs of Poe's love of stylistic brevity throughout his prose (see under *brachylogia* and *brevitas*; note as well all devices of minus additioning), frequently he is guilty of *bomphiologia* and *macrologia* – and

these no doubt have partly engendered the *contempt* for Poe's prose on the part of other writers and scholars. Lanham has an extended discussion of *macrologia* (96–7).
Pronunciation: ma cro LO gi a
Type: amplification

MARTYRIA: confirming something by one's own experience:

> I have given his ideas respecting these matters somewhat at length, that the reader may have an opportunity of seeing how far they were borne out by my own subsequent experience. (*The Narrative of Arthur Gordon Pym of Nantucket,* 3: 170)

Martyria joins with *epicrisis* (see above) and nominal seriation (see below) to create a sense of verisimilitude in *Pym*, and it compares with *orcos* – swearing that one is telling the truth. It is part of what Poe called the "plausible or verisimilar style."
Pronunciation: mar TYR i a
Type: example, allusion, and citation of authority
Type: techniques of argument

MEDELA: apologizing for the undeniable offences of a friend. Anyone who was a friend of Poe more likely found him- or herself apologizing for Poe rather than the other way around, especially if he had been persuaded to drink alcohol on some occasion. Thus, instead of providing an exemplification of *medela* from Poe, I give one from his friend Frederick W. Thomas. After the famous incident of the "inside-out cloak" (see *charientismus*), Thomas wrote the following explanation of and apology for Poe's occasionally intemperate behaviour:

> I have seen a great deal of Poe, and it was his excessive, and at times marked sensibility which forced him into his "frolics", rather than any mere marked appetite for drink, but if he took but one glass of week [*sic*] wine or beer or cider the Rubicon of the cup was passed with him, and it almost always ended in excess and sickness. But he fought against the propensity as hard as ever Coleridge fought against it. (Ostrom, 230)

Medela clearly compares with *charientismus*, which also involves smoothing over a difficulty with pleasing language – healing an indefensible offence with conciliatory words. Compare also with *philophronesis*.
Pronunciation: me DEL a
Type: techniques of argument

MEIOSIS (adjective: meiotic): a lessening, sometimes belittling a thing or person, possibly with a degrading epithet, or with the substitution of a word:

> My immediate purpose is to place before the world, plainly, succinctly, and without comment, a series of **mere** household events. (5: 143)

Anyone who has read "The Black Cat" knows that the mutilation and hanging of a cat, the murder of a wife with an axe, and the attempt to hide the corpse behind a brick wall in a basement are anything but mere household events! The narrator in that tale obviously wants to downplay, to deemphasize, the enormity of his crimes. His use of *meiosis* functions in another way that is even more important to him: while "The Tell-Tale Heart" is an extended example of *antirrhesis* – rejecting an argument as erroneous (the argument of his captors that the narrator is mad) – in "The Black Cat" the narrator seems more concerned with convincing not so much his readers but *himself* that he has *not* witnessed supernatural events or will suffer the eschatological consequences – that he is *not* doomed by an angry God to eternal punishment, that he has *not* been duped by a witch-cat into murder or exposed for that murder by a witch-cat. He wants desperately to believe that the narrative he is about to relate is not one of supernatural vengeance on the part of demonic cats and punishing gods; rather, he calls it – again using *meiosis* – a **homely** narrative. By *homely* he means ordinary. Through *meiosis* he attempts to downplay the events and their possible implications for his soul. When he mentions the apparent shape of the white fur on the second cat as resembling a gallows, he again tries to deemphasize the significance of the phenomenon by referring to it as "one of the **merest** chimaeras it would be possible to conceive." He frantically wants to believe that the gallows on the cat's fur is a mere trick of the imagination and *not* a supernatural portent of his doom (see chapter 2).

The term obviously compares with *litotes* (above) and *tapinosis* (below), and is the opposite of *hyperbole* (above) and *auxesis* (#1, above). See Lanham (98), Corbett (453), Abrams (80–1), Cuddon (536), Baldick (131), Dupriez (273), Joseph (151–2), Sonnino (95–6), Espy (186). *Meiosis* can be used for modesty, as when Poe refers to his poems as "trifles" in the preface to the 1845 edition of his poetry (7: xlvii).

Pronunciation: mei O sis

Type: metaphorical substitutions and puns

Type: techniques of argument

M E M P S I S : complaining against injuries and pleading for help. We have a truly pathetic exemplification in a letter to John Allan, dated 12 April 1833:

> It has now been more than two years since you have assisted me, and more than three since you have spoken to me. I feel little hope that you will pay any regard to this letter, but still I cannot refrain from making one more attempt to interest you in my behalf. If you will only consider in what a situation I am placed you will surely pity me – without friends, without any means, consequently of obtaining employment, I am perishing – absolutely perishing for want of aid. And yet I am not idle – nor addicted to any vice – nor have I committed any offence against society which would render me deserving of so hard a fate. For God's sake pity me, and save me from destruction. (Ostrom, 49–50)

Clearly, *mempsis* can be used as part of the appeal to pity (*pathos*). Cf *exuscitatio*, and *commiseratio*.
Pronunciation: MEMP sis
Type: devices of vehemence

M E S O Z E U G M A : a type of *zeugma* involving a verb in the middle of a construction that governs clauses before and after it:

> "The will **may assent** – the soul – the intellect, never." ("Mesmeric Revelation," 5: 243)

The verb phrase "may assent" (consisting of an auxiliary and its main verb) governs both "The will" before it and "the soul" and "the intellect" after it. The sentence might have been written otherwise: "The will may assent; the soul and intellect will never assent." *Mesozeugma* is a kind of minus additioning (see below), a trope of brevity.
Pronunciation: me so ZEUG ma
Type: addition, subtraction, and substitution: words, phrases, and clauses
Type: brevity

M E T A B A S I S : a brief statement recalling what has just been said and linking it to what will follow; a transition (*transitio*):

> We have hitherto spoken of poetry in the abstract; we come now to speak of it in its every-day acceptation – that is to say, of the practical result arising from the sentiment we have considered. ("Drake-Halleck" Review, 8: 283–4)

The things that have been discussed and those about to be discussed may be equal, unequal, contrary, diverse, similar, or based on consequents and relatives (Espy, 186; Sonnino, 181). The use of the device possibly "gives emphasis to our argument and makes it more memorable" (Sonnino, 180).

Pronunciation: me TA ba sis

METANOIA: qualifying a recalled statement by expressing it in a better way, often by using a negative (Lanham, 100):

> I finally concluded that my senses were impressed by a certain air of gravity, sadness, **or still more properly, of weariness.** ("The Spectacles," 5: 183)

While this exemplification does not use a negative, the narrator is clearly qualifying an earlier statement to express it more accurately. Still, it is difficult to distinguish between *metanoia* and *epanorthosis*, sometimes called *correctio* (see above).

Poe's overuse of the dash has been noticed by some critics (Levin, for instance) and, according to Poe's understanding of how that punctuational mark should be used, it is apparent that he often employs the dash to stand in for *metanoia* or *epanorthosis*. In his Marginalia, Poe states that the dash is exploited to represent "*a second thought – an emendation*" (and Poe in these words illustrates its use); "The dash gives the reader a choice between two, or among three or more expressions, one of which may be more forcible than another, but all of which help out the idea. It stands, in general, for these words – '*or, to make my meaning more distinct*'" (16: 131). In "The Spectacles," for example, we find numerous instances of dashes used in just this way:

> my Christian name is Napoleon Buonaparte – or, more properly, these are my first and middle appellations. (5: 177)

> This extraordinary behaviour, by throwing me into a perfect fever of excitement – into an absolute delirium of love – served rather to embolden than to disconcert me. (185–6)

> It is useless, of course, to dwell upon my joy – upon my transport – upon my illimitable ecstasy of heart. (186)

Munson suggests, quite rightly, that the use of the dash and *metanoia* (he does not use the term) is part of "Poe's characteristic sentence structure," certainly in his literary criticism: "He was very skilled in the use of the emendation, the afterthought, the additional clarification ... His fondness for the emendation was consistent with his habit of parallelism in sentence building. Notice how in the quoted paragraph on Imagination he makes a statement, and then extends it in another parallel statement, and then advances it still further in a third parallel arrangement – all terminating in a short triumphant demonstrated conclusion." This habit, says Munson, is quite "pronounced in Poe's cosmological treatise, *Eureka*" (35). Of course, Poe does not use the dash exclusively for this purpose. For more on this subject, see chapter 1.

Pronunciation: me ta NOI a

Type: amplification

Type: techniques of argument

METAPHORA (metaphor): a trope wherein one word is substituted for another; a comparison that differs from simile in that it does not use *like* or *as* and, as Cluett and Kampeas suggest, is "stated as a fact would be stated" (40):

> Most writers – poets in especial – prefer having it understood that they compose by a species of fine frenzy – an ecstatic intuition – and would positively shudder at letting the public take a peep behind the scenes … at the wheels and pinions – the tackle for scene-shifting – the step-ladders and demontraps – the cock's feathers, the red paint and the black patches, which, in ninety-nine cases out of the hundred, constitute the properties of the literary *histrio*. ("The Philosophy of Composition," 14: 194–5)

This is a striking comparison between the minds of writers, poets especially, and the stage machinery of a theatre (a metaphor started at the phrase "behind the scenes"). By implication, the *poem* is likened to the stage production, the play, which goes on in front of the scenes and is presented to the world.

I have not found a *great deal* of metaphors in Poe's prose – perhaps because of a certain item in his authorial credo stipulating that one must use this device sparingly. In his review of *Night and Morning*, he complains that Bulwer overuses metaphor: "the predominant and most important failing of the author of 'Devereux,' in point of style, is an absolute mania of metaphor – metaphor always running into allegory … Metaphor, its softened image, has indisputable force when sparingly and skilfully employed. Vigorous writers use it rarely indeed" (10: 130). Elsewhere, Poe complains that a Miss Landon "showered her metaphors too indiscriminately around her" (10: 195). Referring to Thomas Holley Chivers, Poe gripes that "His figures of speech are metaphor run mad"

(*Autography,* 15: 242). Now and then, Poe draws attention to a *mixed* metaphor – he cites "the inconsistent metaphor involved in the 'sowing of *fiery* echoes'," for instance, in his review of *The Drama of Exile*, 12: 23; see also 194). Jacobs insists that Poe adopted his rules for metaphors from the rhetorician Hugh Blair; see Jacobs' long footnote on these dicta in *Poe: Journalist and Critic* (198–9). This argument helps my case (in chapter 2) that Poe did indeed receive training in rhetoric, either formally or otherwise.

The term *metaphor* is so important and well known that it seems superfluous to provide a definition but, not surprisingly, it has attracted a great deal of critical attention. For some extended discussions of the trope, see, for instance, Baldick (134), Corbett (444–5), Lanham (100–1), and Espy (108–9). Sonnino quotes several ancient rhetors who write of the metaphor with enthusiasm (181–3). For the related terms *tenor* and *vehicle*, see Dupriez (276–9) and Harmon/Holman (315–16). Another term for *metaphora* is *translatio*.
Type: metaphorical substitutions and puns

METAPHYSICAL CONCEIT: a highly ingenious comparison, an unusual analogy that links two really dissimilar things. I do not recall encountering any in Poe's prose, and I do not think it likely we will find one, given the attitude Poe had toward the metaphysical conceit: "He [Christopher Pearse Cranch] is as full of absurd conceits as Cowley or Donne … the conceits of these latter are Euphuisms beyond redemption – flat, irremediable, self-contented nonsensicalities" (*The Literati of New York City,* 15: 69–70). Cf the definition of the rhetorical term *catachresis*.
Type: metaphorical substitutions and puns
Type: ungrammatical, illogical, or unusual uses of language

METAPHYSICAL STYLISTICS: a term coined by Louis T. Milic in his 1967 essay, "Metaphysical Criticism of Style." By way of explaining what Milic means by this term, let me first provide an example. In an 1853 book review of Melville's *Moby-Dick*, the British editor and novelist William Harrison Ainsworth – a writer whose works Poe himself reviewed (10: 214ff) – describes the style of that work as "maniacal – mad as a March hare – mowing, gibbering, screaming, like an incurable Bedlamite [lunatic], reckless of keeper or strait-waistcoat" (620). This bizarre statement tells us something, perhaps, about the behaviour of a lunatic in an insane asylum but what does it really tell us about Melville's style? Nothing. Later descriptions he applies to Melville's style remind us more about human physiology than about literature: "maundering, drivelling, subject to paroxysms, cramps, and total collapse" (620). Obviously, Ainsworth never took a course on style and stylistics. The language he uses is not literary at all – all the more surprising given that Ainsworth was a man of literature.

This kind of nonliterary language used to describe style is exactly what Milic considers "metaphysical" – an unfortunate term because it is already used in literary criticism to describe a type of far-fetched comparison made mostly by certain writers of the English Renaissance, such as John Donne (see "metaphysical conceit"), but Milic uses it to describe "any criticism of style that is not usefully quantitative" and any critical statement that is not verifiable (163n). Also, a "metaphysical" judgment tells us more about the reader than the writing, as Cluett and Kampeas say (*Grossly Speaking*, 40–1).

Poe himself could be guilty of "metaphysical stylistics" occasionally. He describes Elizabeth Barrett's *The Drama of Exile* as having, despite its blemishes, "an exceedingly chaste, vigorous and comprehensive style" (12: 27). Milic would ask, quite rightly, how a style can be "chaste," "vigorous" (see also 10: 147), or "comprehensive." Elsewhere, Poe calls Charles J. Ingersoll's style "hard but honest" (12: 253). He says the "style of Mr. Hawthorne is purity itself" (11: 103). He likens the euphony of Lord Bolingbroke's style to "the liquid flow of a river" (10: 173). He terms Kennedy's style "nervous" and "forcible" (8: 9); that of "Peregrine Prolix" is "witty-pedantic" (9: 36); that of David B. Edward is "*overabundant*" (9: 78); that of Sir N.W. Wraxall is "very minute and prosy" (9: 177); that of Charles Anthon is "beautiful" (9: 267). Frances Anne Butler's *Journal* is characterized by "the vivacity of its style" (8: 21); Sarah Stickney's *The Poetry of Life* by its "neatness" (8: 173). In the novel *George Balcombe* we find a style that is "bold, vigorous, and rich" (9: 262).

I am confident that Poe could undoubtedly justify his use of these impressionistic terms and in doing so he would have to adopt a more precise, more analytical, more "scientifically" quantitative critical vocabulary. As most of his literary criticism shows and as this very catalogue demonstrates, he normally *did*: consider his discussions of metre, rhyme, rhythm, grammar, diction, imagery, rhetorical devices, syntax, punctuation, spelling, and logical fallacies. In his time and place, Poe succeeded in doing what Milic urges literary critics to do – put criticism on a surer footing by employing quantitative rather than impressionistic, intuitive, language. Although he now and then uses figurative terms such as *chaste, vigorous,* and *comprehensive* to describe style, Poe's precise and detailed critical pronouncements are typically verifiable by close reference to the texts; his normal practice is to justify, to prove, to demonstrate, his pronouncements – whether about metre, rhyme, rhythm, grammar, diction, imagery, rhetorical devices, syntax, punctuation, spelling, or logic – by providing substantiating quotes. While he made enemies because of his critical bluntness, and was accused by some of being a "mere" grammarian, Poe brought a refreshing integrity, a new respectability, to American literary criticism, largely *because* of his microscopic precision at the level of style. In his emphasis on the *technical* in prose and poetry, and in his critical versatility, he strikes me as being a nineteenth-century Aristotle.

METASTASIS: (1) passing over an issue quickly as if it were of no importance; moving rapidly from one point to another:

> There have been many attempts at solving the mystery of the Automaton ...
> Of the first of these opinions we shall say nothing at present more than we
> have already said. In relation to the second it is only necessary to repeat what
> we have before stated. ("Maelzel's Chess Player," 14: 18)

(2) turning back an insult or objection against the person who made it. While a student at the University of Virginia, Poe got into debt because his foster-father, John Allan, would not furnish Poe with the necessary finances; then he and Poe quarrelled over the debts incurred. Poe's response, in a letter dated 3 January 1831, illustrates definition #2 of *metastasis*:

> You would not let me return because bills were presented you for payment
> which I never wished nor desired you to pay. Had you let me return ... you
> would never have heard more of my extravagances. But I am not about to
> proclaim myself guilty of all that has been alledged against me ... I will
> boldly say that it was wholly and entirely your own mistaken parsimony that
> caused all the difficulties in which I was involved while at Charlotte[s]ville.
> The expenses of the institution at the lowest estimate were $350 per annum.
> You sent me there with $110. (Ostrom, 39–40)

The device of *metastasis* really defines the stormy relationship that Poe had with his rather cold-hearted foster-father. Another term for this device is *transmissio* or *transmotio*. Cf *anticategoria*.
Pronunciation: me TA sta sis
Type: devices of vehemence
Type: techniques of argument

M E TAT H E S I S : a type of *metaplasm*, this refers to the transposition of a letter or phonetic element out of normal order in a word. In "Why the Little Frenchman Wears His Hand in a Sling," it is part of the Irishman's more general *barbarismus*:

> And is it ralelly more than the three fut and a bit that there is, inny how, of the little ould furrener Frinchman that lives just over the way, and that's a oggling and a goggling the houl day, (and bad luck to him,) at the **purty** [pretty] widdy Misthress Tracle. (4: 115)

Metathesis on a larger scale – that is, within a sentence – is a spoonerism. It clearly can have a comedic application. For more on this subject, see chapter 4.
Pronunciation: me TA the sis
Type: addition, subtraction, and substitution: letters and syllables
Type: ungrammatical, illogical, or unusual uses of language
Type: "comedic"

M E T O N Y M Y : substitution for what is actually meant by some term or phrase associated closely with it – sometimes (1) a cause for its effect, (2) an effect for its cause, (3) a proper name for one of its qualities, or (4) a quality for its proper name:

> in less than a minute afterward his corpse had all the stern rigidity of stone. His brow was of the coldness of ice. Thus, ordinarily, should it have appeared, only after **long pressure from Azrael's hand**. ("Mesmeric Revelation," 5: 254)

Azrael, in Hebrew and Muslim lore, is the Angel of Death. Thus, the phrase "long pressure from Azrael's hand" is a metaphorical substitution for "dead a long time" or "death." The advantage of the substituted words or phrases is that they sometimes provide visual images for the abstractions that might otherwise have been employed. Poe's use of *metonymy* here hardly seems accidental, as he clearly knew the word and what it means – as he shows in his "Drake-Halleck" review: "The metonymy involved in 'There should a wreath be woven/ To *tell* the world their worth,' is unjust" (8: 317).

Some rhetors have refused to distinguish between *metonymy* and a similar figure of speech, *synecdoche* (see below and cf *antonomasia*). For those with heads for theory and abstractions, see Dupriez's lengthy discussion on these two tropes (280–3).
Pronunciation: me TO ny my
Type: metaphorical substitutions

MINUS ADDITIONING: the grammatical term pertaining to rhetorical devices that involve schemes of omission – clauses missing subjects, predicators (verb phrases), or both (for example, *ellipsis, prozeugma, diazeugma, zeugma, syllepsis*). See under those terms.

MORPHOLOGICAL SET: a term from linguistics referring to a set of words linked on the basis of identity or similarity of shape. The shapes of words are often determined by groups of letters called "morphemes" – frequently prefixes and suffixes (groups of letters added to the beginnning or end of words). In the following excerpt, notice how often Poe uses words that either begin or end with the morpheme *in*. Add these to the frequent appearance of the preposition *in* and we get an emphatic sense of the intense *depth* of the catacombs into which Montresor leads his victim, Fortunato: they go farther and farther *in* until they reach an extremity so remote that Fortunato is beyond all assistance from outside sources. He is profoundly deep within the catacombs and utterly isolated – a stock situation in Gothic literature:

> We had passed through long walls of piled skeletons, with casks and puncheons intermingling, into the inmost recesses of the catacombs ...
>
> At the most remote end of the crypt there appeared another less spacious ... Three sides of this interior crypt were still ornamented in this manner ... Within the wall thus exposed by the displacing of the bones, we perceived a still interior crypt or recess, in depth about four feet, in width three, in height six or seven. It seemed to have been constructed for no especial use within itself, but formed merely the interval between two of the colossal supports. ("The Cask of Amontillado," 6: 171–2)

In his short book, *The Merry Mood: Poe's Uses of Humor,* Stauffer provides quite a few examples of Poe's wordplay involving

> words and names that rhymed, as in the line of descent of Mr. Simpson in "The Spectacles": his mother Mademoiselle Croissart, his father, M. Froissart, his grandfather, Mr. Croissart, his grandmother, Mademoiselle Voissart, his great-grandfather, M. Voissart, and his great-grandmother Mademoiselle Moissart. He also uses repetition and rhyme in "'His Grace the Arch Duke Pest-Iferous' – 'His Grace the Duke Pest-Ilential' – 'His Grace the Duke Ten-Pest' – and 'Her Serene Highness the Arch Duchess Ana-Pest'" from "King Pest"; "'You hard-hearted, dunderheaded, obstinate, rusty, crusty, musty, fusty, old savage!'" in "Three Sundays in a Week"; and Mrs. Fibalittle, Mrs. Squibalittle, and Mademoiselle Cribalittle in "Thingum Bob." (15)

What has Stauffer given us here but *morphological sets*?

Type: repetition: letters, syllables, and sounds

NOEMA: subtle, deliberately obscure speech; speech that intimates something rather than makes its meaning clear (another term is *intimitatio*). While Poe's critical prose can sometimes be difficult to follow – given his love of such things as foreignisms and periodicity combined with *hypotaxis* – I do not think he is ever purposely obscure. He has been known to praise plain language (see *aphelia*), and in the following excerpt he condemns obscurity, *noema*, in no uncertain terms:

> Either a man intends to be understood, or he does not. If he write a book which he intends *not* to be understood, we shall be very happy indeed not to understand it; but if he write a book which he means to be understood, and, in this book, be at all possible pains to prevent us from understanding it, we can only say that he is an ass – and this, to be brief, is our private opinion of Mr. Carlyle, which we now take the liberty of making public. (11: 177; see also 252)

We might consider Poe as wanting to apply this pronouncement more generally to the prose of all the Transcendentalists, whom he despised. Compare *noema* with *enigma* (a riddle) and *schematismus* (circuitious speech to conceal a meaning). Sonnino has quite a few examples (119–20).

Pronunciation: no E ma

Type: techniques of argument

NON SEQUITUR: really a term from logic but appropriate in our list of rhetorical terms insofar as rhetoric means the art of persuasion, the *non sequitur* (Latin: "it does not follow") occurs when a conclusion does not follow from the premise or premises intended to support it – that is, the premises are irrelevant to the conclusion:

> As it is well known that the "wise men" came "from the East," and as
> Mr. Touch-and-go Bullet-head came from the East, it follows that
> Mr. Bullet-head was a wise man. ("X-ing a Paragrab," 6: 229)

This is a simple syllogism – a logical equation consisting of two premises and a conclusion:

> Major premise: the wise men came from the East (general point);
> Minor premise: Mr. Bullet-head came from the East (specific point);
> Conclusion: Mr. Bullet-head was therefore a wise man.

This is a *non sequitur*, however, because the conclusion does not follow from the premises. The problem lies in the first premise: if it were to state that *all* wise men come from the East, the conclusion might be seen to follow, but it only claims that *certain* wise men came from the East, so it is not necessarily true that Mr. Bullet-head is wise. Poe is certainly aware of the faulty logic here, which he uses for satirical purposes.

Poe's knowledge of logic is also demonstrated now and then in his reviews. In "A Chapter of Suggestions," he uncovers a logical flaw known as the "undistributed middle term" (Poe provides the Latin, below), but it is also a type of *non sequitur*:

> *All* men of genius have their detractors; but it is merely a *non distributio medii* to
> argue, thence, that all men who have their detractors are men of genius. (14: 189)

There is no necessary link between the major term, "men of genius," and the minor term, "men who have their detractors." They do not overlap, so to argue that all men who have their detractors are men of genius would be a *non sequitur*. Poe again displays his knowledge of logic in his review of *Human Magnetism*: "Now the fallacy here is obvious, and lies in a mere variation of what the logicians style 'begging the question' [offering as proof of a conclusion not premises but simply the conclusion reasserted in another form] ... Now in the case of mesmerism our author is merely *begging the admission*" (12: 122).

Poe *does* seem to commit one particular fallacy now and then in his literary criticism: "poisoning the well" (see above). For more on logic and fallacies, see above under the various fallacies listed, as well as Lanham (77–8) and Corbett (43–80). Charles C. Walcutt attacks Poe's logic in "The Logic of Poe."

Pronunciation: non SE qui tur
Type: techniques of argument

NOTIONAL SET: a term from linguistics referring to a group of words linked on the basis of semantics – meaning. The words in a notional set do not necessarily *overlap* in meaning but are related in theme, idea ("notion"). Like Melville, Poe shows in several tales his understanding of the sea and ships via his use of nautical imagery or what we might call "nautical notional sets," as in this set from "King Pest":

> *seamen, crew, schooner, river, Tar, pennant, mast head, jib-boom, fins, sea-turtle, sea, lee-lurch, pump ship, clew up all sail, scud before the wind, Avast, shipmate, Davy Jones, stow away, hold, on board, ballast, seaports, full cargo, lubber, hull, top-heavy, raise a squall, stowage-room, marlin-spike, sea-boat, overstowed.*

We should find a similar set in *Pym,* "MS. Found in a Bottle," "A Descent into the Maelström," and, to a lesser extent, in a few other tales – for instance, "The Premature Burial." In "The Language and Style of the Prose," Stauffer notes Poe's use of "a specialized vocabulary" in some of his tales, often in the employment of verisimilitude (462). Thus, we can add certain notional sets as a characteristic of Poe's "versimilar" style.

When we pay attention to the classes of words and linguistic sets spoken or written by someone, we can often gain insights into that person's "soul," mind, personality, way of thinking about the world. Attention to notional sets in a given literary work can also help interpretation, too, and with Poe's protagonists – such as the homicidal narrators in "The Tell-Tale Heart" and "The Black Cat" – the notional sets they use can truly reveal their minds and give us a real sense of their concerns, values, even obsessions (monomania). As Ben Jonson wrote, *oratio imago animi* ("speech is the image of the mind"): "Language most shewes a man: speake that I may see thee" (*Timber or Discoveries*). The literary craftsman and psychologist Poe also believed this, and he gives us clues as to his narrators' monomanias through the notional sets they use. For instance, foregrounded in the confession of the narrator in "The Black Cat" is a notional set pertaining to ideas of the supernatural. As the notional set of time reveals the obsession of the paranoid schizophrenic in "The Tell-Tale Heart" (see under *chronographia* and chapters 1 and 2), so the notional set of the supernatural tells us about the obsessions, the view of the world, held by the protagonist in this tale of felines and uxoricide:

soul, Fiend, demon, fiendish, damnable, remorse, deadly sin, my immortal soul,
mercy of the Most Merciful and Most Terrible God, High God, demoniacal, guilt,
Arch-Fiend, hell, damned, damnation, witches, demons.

This narrator's view of life, clearly coloured by religion – belief in God, the Devil, Hell, damnation – contributes to his superstitious dread of divine portents and punishment. Had he been an agnostic or atheist, he would not have attached any supernatural significance to the events and images he witnessed, but his fervent belief in the world of the supernatural is his source of terror (see chapter 2).

Richard M. Fletcher writes extensively about Poe's diction in *The Stylistic Vocabulary of Edgar Allan Poe*, although he does not use the phrase *notional set* or engage in the kind of *rhetorical* examination that I do in this book. In his introduction Fletcher refers to Poe's style and literary techniques in terms of approbation: "as a craftsman and master manipulator of words he must be acknowledged as a genius of the very first rank" (5). In his chapter "The Poe Vocabulary," Fletcher looks closely at Poe's diction in a few of the short stories and provides – again, without using the term – several notional sets found there. Let me summarize briefly what Fletcher has concluded on this subject. First, he believes that it is the vocabulary of Poe's short stories "rather than other factors which distinguishes him from those other writers of the period who utilized Gothic materials" (63). After a look at the poetry – specifically, "The Bells" – Fletcher examines the diction of a few tales. In the context of "The Fall of the House of Usher," Fletcher remarks that "much of Poe's vocabulary is repetitious" and that he actually has a "limited repertoire" of words. He then provides some stock words and stereotypical phrases that, he insists, are "familiar favorites which appear and reappear throughout Poe's poetry and prose":

soundless, oppressive, singularly, dreary, melancholy, gloom, sentiment, depression
of soul, sensation, sickening of the heart, sublime, shadowy fancies, crowded upon
me, impression, lurid, lustre, ghastly, raven-haired, unearthly, ghoul, weir, tone-
less, sear, unalterable, ineffable, indescribable. (70–1)

Fletcher does not actually *prove* that these words appear over and over again in tale after tale, but most attentive readers of Poe's prose will probably be willing to accept that suggestion; and it is probably the frequency of such words and phrases that has prompted some critics (such as Spanier and Cox) to conclude that Poe's narrators are virtually one and the same, as well as identical with Poe. I attempt to show in chapter 1, however, that – despite the possible reappearance of some stock words and phrases – the notional sets in various tales are *different*, thus indicating that the narrators themselves differ from one another and from Poe.

Fletcher makes other notable observations about Poe's diction, discussing, for instance, his "ballad" and his "Gothic" vocabularies, and he does admit that, in Poe's detective fiction, "we find an altogether different vocabulary from that of 'Ligeia' or 'The Fall of the House of Usher'" (74). Fletcher's conclusion is that *three* distinctive vocabularies can be found in the Poe canon: "his mechanically stereotyped vocabulary ["limited repertoire"], his vocabulary of momentary inspiration [key words], and his vocabulary based on [literary and classical] allusion and analogy." When these three "are working in harmony with one another, we find Poe writing at his very best" (78).

Poe himself refers to his own "peculiarities of diction" in a letter to his friend Dr Snodgrass (4 June 1842). He does not elaborate on what he felt them to be, unfortunately. Still, that remark shows his sensitivity to matters of style (Ostrom, 202–3).

Type: repetition: clauses, phrases, and ideas
Type: "verisimilar"

OMINATIO: see *cataplexis*. Compare also with *paraenesis*.
Pronunciation: o mi NA ti o

ONEDISMUS: reproaching someone as ungrateful or impious. Here follows an indirect charge of ingratitude, although it might indeed be ironic:

> the Bostonians have no soul. They have always evinced towards us individually, the basest ingratitude for the services we rendered them in enlightening them about the originality of Mr. Longfellow [Poe frequently charged him with plagiarism]. ("Boston and the Bostonians," 13: 11)

Sonnino provides an alternate term, *exprobatio* (94).
Pronunciation: o ne DIS mus
Type: devices of vehemence
Type: techniques of argument

ONOMATOPOEIA: the use of words that sound like their meaning; or, more generally, the use of words that sound like some thing being signified. Poe had a good ear for the auditory qualities of the English language, as is shown both in his prose and poetry (see also under "auditory imagery"). "The Bells" is an extended exercise in *onomatopoeia*, and I quote the first stanza:

> Hear the sledges with the bells –
>   Silver bells!
> What a world of merriment their melody foretells!
>   How they tinkle, tinkle, tinkle,
>   In the icy air of night!
>   While the stars that oversprinkle
>   All the heavens, seem to twinkle
>   With a crystalline delight;
>   Keeping time, time, time,
>   In a sort of Runic rhyme,
>   To the tintinnabulation that so musically wells
>   From the bells, bells, bells, bells,
>   Bells, bells, bells –
> From the jingling and the tinkling of the bells. (7: 119)

Each stanza in this quaternion has its own story, mood, and tone, depending on the predominant sounds of the respective bells:

stanza 1: silver bells – courtship – *ink* sound
stanza 2: golden bells – wedding – *ing* sound
stanza 3: alarm bells – fire – *ang* sound
stanza 4: church bells – funeral – *oan* sound

I suspect that Poe is referring to *onomatopoeia* when he praises a poet thus: "In the 'pattering step,' &c., we have an admirable 'echo of sound to sense'" ("Henry B. Hirst," 13: 210).
Pronunciation: on o ma to po EI a
Type: description

OPTATIO: a fervent wish expressed to either God or humans:
> May God grant that we succeed! ("The Balloon-Hoax," 5: 236)

The device sometimes takes on a rather nasty air in Poe's literary criticism. In complaining about the refrain, "Yet I wail!", spoken too often by characters in *The Drama of Exile*, Poe says,
> God deliver us from any such wailing again! (12: 9)

To the poet William A. Lord, we get this:
> from any farther specimens of your stupidity, good Lord deliver us! (Review of *Poems*, 12: 161)

In his review of *Twice-Told Tales*, Poe is nicer to Hawthorne:

> May we live to hear them told a hundred times! (11: 103)

Pronunciation: op TA ti o
Type: devices of vehemence

ORACULUM: the quoting of God's words or commandments. We find this device in Poe's review of *Sacred Philosophy*:

> In the same way we have received an erroneous idea of the meaning of Ezek-
> iel XXXV., 7, where the same region is mentioned. The common version
> runs, – **"Thus will I make Mount Seir most desolate, and cut off from it**
> **him that passeth out and him that returneth."** (10: 84)

Elsewhere he provides the Hebrew version (Review of *Incidents of Travel in Central America*, 10: 180). Compare this device with *apomnemonysis*. Poe's knowledge of the Bible is well known to Poe specialists, and for a brief discussion of this topic, see under "leitmotif." His review of *Arabia Petræa* shows Poe to have been a fundamentalist at that period (1837), certainly where biblical prophecy is concerned.

Pronunciation: o RA cu lum
Type: example, allusion, and citation of authority
Type: techniques of argument

ORCOS: an oath expressed to confirm something being affirmed or denied, often by divine testimony (an "as-God-is-my-witness" type of statement). Here is an illustration from a letter to Sarah Helen Whitman, dated 18 October 1848:

> There is no oath which seems to me so sacred as that sworn by the all-divine
> love I bear you. – By this love, then, and by the God who reigns in Heaven, I
> swear to you that my soul is incapable of dishonor. (Ostrom, 393)

That is in response to a passage in Sarah's letter that runs thus: "How often I have heard men and even women say of you – 'He has great intellectual power, but *no* principle – *no* moral sense'" (392). Here is another to John Allan:

> I call God to witness that I have never loved dissipation. (41)

Pronunciation: OR cos
Type: devices of vehemence

OXYMORON: a "concatenation of modifier and modified that in most circumstances would contradict each other" (Cluett/Kampeas, 44);

a more straightforward definition is Lanham's: "a witty, paradoxical say-ing," a "condensed paradox" (106). We find the device in Poe's fiction as well as in his literary criticism:

> The author [Charles Dickens] possesses nearly every desirable quality in a writer of fiction, and has withal a thousand **negative virtues**. (Review of *The Posthumous Papers of the Pickwick Club*, 9: 205; see also 10: 92; 11: 280; 13: 134; 15: 255)

> His [Horace Greeley's] characters are scratchy and irregular, ending with an ***abrupt taper*** – if we may be allowed this contradiction in terms. (*Autography*, 15: 250)

> The impression left is one of a **pleasurable sadness**. ("The Poetic Principle," 14: 279)

> We thrill, for example, with the most intense of "**pleasurable pain**," over the accounts of the Passage of the Beresina. ("The Premature Burial," 5: 255)

By "pleasurable pain" Poe is referring to the theory of the sublime as found in Edmund Burke's *A Philosophical Enquiry into the Origin of Our Ideas of the Sublime and Beautiful*. The sublime is anything that frightens but thrills us simultaneously, such as a violent electrical storm; it fills us with what Burke, using another *oxymoron*, calls "delightful terror." Gothic writers have always employed the sublime in their works and Poe especially is a particularly adept student of the Burkean sublime.

Pronunciation: ox y MO ron

Type: balance, antithesis, paradox

PAEANISMUS: an exclamation of joy – a kind of *ecphonesis* (see above):

> Eureka! Pundit is in his glory. ("Mellonta Tauta," 6: 211)

Pronunciation: pae a NIS mus

Type: devices of vehemence

PALINDROME: words, phrases, verses, or sentences that read the same and make sense backwards as well as forwards (ABCCBA). The term means, after all, "running back again." Lanham compares the device to *chiasmos* (106; see also Dupriez's discussion [313–14]). In his chapter on Poe's use of the "biblical" style in prose, Forrest cites the following pas-sages to demonstrate how Poe approaches *palindrome*:

> "**It was night, and the rain fell; and, falling, it was rain, but, having fallen, it was blood**. And I stood in the morass among the tall lilies, and the rain fell upon my head ... And mine eyes fell upon a huge gray **rock which stood by**

the shore of the river, and was lighted by the light of the moon. And the rock
was gray, and ghastly, and tall, – and the rock was gray." ("Silence," 2: 221)
The *polysyndeton* (see below) and obsolete language ("mine eyes") in the
passage are, for me, anyway, a more convincing demonstration of Poe's
"biblical" language. At any rate, Poe's use of *palindrome* figures as well in
a single pair of names in "A Tale of the Ragged Mountains": the near-
perfect mirror-image version of the name "Bedlo[e]" – "Olbed" – reinforces the theme of metempsychosis, the transmigration of the soul,
from the British Olbed to the Virginian Bedlo[e].
Pronunciation: PAL in drome
Type: balance, antithesis, paradox
Type: repetition: words
Type: repetition: clauses, phrases, and ideas
Type: "biblical"

PARABLE: a kind of allegory or extended metaphor; an illustrative
story answering a question or pointing a moral or lesson. Consider "The
Masque of the Red Death" as a parable (see chapter 3).
Type: example, allusion, and citation of authority
Type: metaphorical substitutions and puns
Type: techniques of argument

PARADIASTOLE: making the best of a bad thing; the euphemistic
substitution of a negative word with something more positive. In his introduction to Machiavelli's *The Prince*, David Wootton calls chapters 16
to 18 of that work "a virtuoso exercise in *paradiastole*, the redescription of
behavior in order to transform its moral significance" (xxxiv). For example, what we call hypocrisy in a ruler, Machiavelli would call *craftiness* or
expediency; in other words, what most people consider a negative trait,
Machiavelli considers positive. We see, then, how the device, a technique
of argument, can involve essentially a Nietzschean revaluation of values.
We find an exemplification in "William Wilson":

> Who, indeed, among my most abandoned associates, would not rather have
> disputed the clearest evidence of his senses, than have suspected of such
> courses, the gay, the frank, the generous William Wilson – the noblest and
> most liberal commoner at Oxford – him whose follies (said his parasites) were
> but the follies of youth and unbridled fancy – **whose errors but inimitable
> whim – whose darkest vice but a careless and dashing extravagance?** (3: 316)

For even more striking examples, see chapter 2.

Pronunciation: pa ra di A sto le

Type: techniques of argument

PARADIEGESIS: an incidental narrative, a digressive story used to introduce one's argument (Lanham, 107). In his review of *Barnaby Rudge*, Poe wants to argue that, while having the freedom to praise literary works, the critic is justified in finding faults and in fact probably has an even greater obligation to do so. Just after commencing his remarks on Dickens' novel, Poe digresses with a classical anecdote to introduce his argument:

> Those who know us will not, from what is here premised, suppose it our intention, to enter into any wholesale *laudation* of "Barnaby Rudge." In truth, our design may appear, at a cursory glance, to be very different indeed. Boccalini, in his "Advertisements from Parnassus," tells us that **a critic once presented Apollo with a severe censure upon an excellent poem. The God asked him for the beauties of the work. He replied that he only troubled himself about the errors. Apollo presented him with a sack of unwinnowed wheat, and bade him pick out all the chaff for his pains.** Now we have not fully made up our minds that the God was in the right. (11: 41)

Taylor provides a slightly different definition: "Using an observation or fact as an occasion for further declaring one's meaning" (114). See also Lanham's definition of *digression* (54), and under that term, above. See also under "fable."

Pronunciation: pa ra di e GE sis

Type: amplification

Type: example, allusion, and citation of authority

Type: techniques of argument

PARADOX: an apparently contradictory or absurd statement that nevertheless contains a measure of truth or good sense. Unlike the *oxymoron* (see above), a paradox is an *extended* contradiction. Consider Poe's definition of what he calls the "imp of the perverse":

> In theory, **no reason can be more unreasonable** ... I am not more certain that I breathe, than that the assurance of the wrong or error of any action is often the one unconquerable *force* which impels us, and alone impels us to its prosecution. (6: 147)

Here is another exemplification:

> Others ... were restless in their movements, had flushed faces, and talked and gesticulated to themselves, as if **feeling in solitude on account of the very denseness of the company around.** ("The Man of the Crowd," 4: 135–6)

We even find an instance in Poe's literary criticism:

> Observe the silent refusal of Akinetos – the peculiar *passiveness* of his action – if we may be permitted the paradox. (11: 272)

He says elsewhere that Thomas Holley Chivers

> is at the same time one of the best and one of the worst poets in America.
>
> (*Autography*, 15: 241)

Paradox involves a deviation from conventional perceptions and opinions and "is a common element in epigrammatic writing," say Holman and Harmon (372). "The force of seeming self-contradiction makes the paradox a forceful rhetorical device," Espy maintains (118). Let us not forget Poe's famous definition of a long poem as a paradox. In this case, the paradox would *not* contain "a measure of truth or good sense," I should think. Perhaps Poe would have done better simply to call a long poem "a contradiction in terms."

Oddly enough, Poe actually condemns the use of paradoxes in the work of another writer:

> Sometimes we are startled by knotty paradoxes; and it is not acquitting their perpetrator of all blame on their account to admit that, in some instances, they are susceptible of solution. It is really difficult to discover anything for approbation, in enigmas such as
>
> > That bright impassive, passive angel-hood,
>
> or –
>
> > The silence of my heart is full of sound. (Review of *The Drama of Exile*, 12: 22; see also 23)

Type: balance, antithesis, paradox

PARAENESIS: exhortation; advice to beware of impending evil. Although it was one of Poe's critical rules not to tomahawk *female* writers – this rule based on his chivalric tenderness toward the "gentler sex" – we nevertheless find him feeling less gentlemanly toward certain women in his private letters. In an epistle of 24 November 1848, he admonishes Sarah Helen Whitman to beware the machinations of a Mrs Ellett:

On one point let me caution you, *dear* Helen. No sooner will Mrs E. hear of
my proposals to yourself, than she will set in operation every conceivable chi-
canery to frustrate me: – and, if you are not prepared for her arts, she will *in-
fallibly* succeed – for her whole study, throughout life, has been the
gratification of her malignity by such means as any other human being would
die rather than adopt. You will be sure to receive anonymous letters so skill-
fully contrived as to deceive the most sagacious. You will be called on, possibly, by persons whom you never heard of, but whom she has instigated to call
& villify me – without even *their* being aware of the influence she has exer-
cised. (Ostrom, 407)

This device compares with *cataplexis* (above), *ominatio*, and *admonitio*
("reminding, recalling to mind, suggestion" [Lanham, 2]). Compare also
with *adhortatio* and *dehortatio*.
Pronunciation: pa RAE ne sis
Type: devices of vehemence

PARALEIPSIS: pretending not to mention something while mentioning it (Cluett/Kampeas, 44):

I need not remind the reader that, from the long and weird catalogue of human miseries, I might have selected many individual instances more replete
with essential suffering than any of these vast generalities of disaster. ("The
Premature Burial," 5: 255)

If Poe's narrator "need not remind the reader," why does he go on to
mention that of which he need not remind us? We find *paraleipsis* several
times in Poe's prose (for instance, see also 10: 141). For more on this device (as it figures in Poe's critical book reviews), see chapter 5.
Pronunciation: pa ra LEP sis
Type: techniques of argument

PARALLELISM: the putting of like ideas in similar grammatical form,
often with *anaphora*. I have arranged a bit of prose from Poe's review of
Twice-Told Tales the better to illustrate the parallel grammatical form:

He [Nathaniel Hawthorne] has the purest style,
the finest taste,
the most available scholarship,
the most delicate humor,

the most touching pathos,

the most radiant imagination,

the most consummate ingenuity. (13: 155)

In a patient and intelligent discussion of style in "William Wilson" and "Ligeia," Stauffer maintains that "Parallelism may also be considered a form of rhythm, and Poe's parallelisms, although they appear infrequently in 'Ligeia,' are sometimes both logically and rhythmically parallel" ("Style and Meaning," 320). In this connection see also *isocolon* and *syncrisis*. Forrest considers "the Hebrew parallelism of members" an aspect of the "biblical" style and offers this passage from "The Premature Burial" as a sample:

they must sleep, or they will devour us – they must be suffered to slumber, or we perish. (5: 273)

Type: balance, antithesis, paradox

Type: repetition: letters, syllables, and sounds

Type: repetition: words

Type: repetition: clauses, phrases, and ideas

Type: "biblical"

PARANOMASIA: a scheme of repetition that involves the gathering up of an antithesis in two words of common root (Cluett/Kampeas, 45):

"The **riddle**, so far, was now **unriddled**." ("The Murders in the Rue Morgue," 4: 175)

But the England of Von Raumer will be sadly and wickedly **misconceived** if it be really **conceived** as militating against a Republicanism *here*. (Review of *England in 1835*, 9: 53)

Essentially, then, *paranomasia* is *polyptoton*, except that the words are antithetical; with *polyptoton* they are not. Cluett and Kampeas define the term differently from Corbett, Dupriez, and Lanham, however; these three consider the device to involve punning on the sounds and meanings of words that are not necessarily opposites in meaning. Certainly this definition compares with *polyptoton* (see below).

Pronunciation: pa ra no MA si a

Type: balance, antithesis, paradox

Type: repetition: letters, syllables, and sounds

Type: repetition: words

PARATAXIS (adjective: paratactic): a scheme involving phrases or independent clauses set one after the other without subordination and often without coordinating conjunctions (such as *and, but, or*) – the opposite of *hypotaxis* and similar to *asyndeton* (see above):

> She presented all the ordinary appearances of death. The face assumed the
> usual pinched and sunken outline. The lips were of the usual marble pallor.
> The eyes were lustreless. There was no warmth. Pulsation had ceased. ("The
> Premature Burial," 5: 257)

While the use of *hypotaxis* can slow the pace of a passage, the use of *parataxis* can speed it up. Note, too, that the paratactic sentences above are also right-branching and linear (they depend on the normal word order of subject-verb-object). Critics and students who despise Poe for his "style," either because of his hypotactic syntax or hyperbolic excesses, should consider the stylistic simplicity of the paratactic and emotionally low-keyed sentences above.

Pronunciation: pa ra TAX is

PARELCON: a kind of redundancy involving the use of unnecessary words – for instance, using two words, as if they were joined, where one should do. In examples from Sonnino (208–9) and Espy (194) the two words actually *are* joined – but it makes no sense to do this in English. In the following example from "Why the Little Frenchman Wears His Hand in a Sling," we have both a noun and a pronoun standing for the subject "widdy" (widow), but the pronoun is hardly necessary after the noun – it is superfluous:

> And wid that the **widdy, she** gits up from the sofy, and makes the swatest
> curtchy nor iver was seen. (4: 117)

We might also think of this example as a kind of tautology (see below). Clearly, *parelcon* is a kind of stylistic vice and as such should be (but is not) categorized by Lanham under his heading "Ungrammatical, illogical, or unusual uses of language" (195–6). Poe combines it here with *barbarismus* (see above) as part of the linguistic comedy of the tale (see also chapter 4).

In his review of the third edition of Griswold's *Poets and Poetry of America*, Poe takes Griswold to task for this grammatical vice, quoting a sentence from one of the latter's literary reviews: "'His chief characteristics pertaining to style, *they* will not long attract regard.' Here we have a gross grammatical error – *two* nominatives to *one* verb, 'characteristics' and 'they' to 'will'" (11: 237; see also 12: 12). Still, we find Poe doing the same thing in "William Wilson" – twice in the same sentence:

> My louder tones were, of course, unattempted, but then the **key, it** was identical; *and his singular **whisper, it** grew the very echo of my own.* (3: 309)

Presumably, Poe would defend his use of *parelcon* here, perhaps arguing that the repetition is for emphasis or that it mirrors the linguistic duplication of Wilson and his doppelgänger.

Pronunciation: pa REL con

Type: addition, subtraction, and substitution: words, phrases, and clauses

Type: repetition: clauses, phrases, and ideas

Type: ungrammatical, illogical, or unusual uses of language

Type: "comedic"

PARENTHESIS: a kind of *hyperbaton* that can also be related to *hypotaxis*, a parenthesis is a word, phrase, clause, or sentence – sometimes explanatory – parachuted into what is otherwise already a complete sentence; it can be separated from the larger sentence by commas, dashes, or square or round brackets. In his stylistic comparison of "Ligeia" and "William Wilson," Stauffer notes the different uses to which Poe puts parentheses in those two tales. He offers the following as the typically emotional parenthetical remarks in "Ligeia":

> Let me say only, that in Ligeia's more than womanly abandonment to a love, **alas!** all unmerited, all unworthily bestowed (2: 256)

> And (**strange, oh strangest mystery of all!**) I found, in the commonest objects of the universe, a circle of analogies to that expression. (252)

> I would call aloud upon her name ... as if ... I could restore her to the pathways she had abandoned – **ah, *could* it be forever?** – upon the earth. (261)

Poe, says Stauffer, "consistently uses parenthetical expressions in 'Ligeia' to emphasize or heighten the mood. Frequently they are in the form of interjections or exclamations" ("Style and Meaning," 321). Contrasting with the employment in that tale of parentheses for vehemence, in "William Wilson" they "are halting, hesitant, fussy, over-precise, reflecting the deliberations of a mind committed to discovering the truth. They contain additional, sometimes gratuitous, information that seems to satisfy the narrator's overwhelming need for facts and details. They also reflect the complexity of his mind" (327). I have isolated a few examples:

It was no doubt the anomalous state of affairs existing between us, which
turned all my attacks upon him, **(and there were many, either open or covert)** into the channel of banter or practical joke **(giving pain while assuming
the aspect of mere fun)** rather than into a more serious and determined hostility. (3: 307)

Parenthetical embedding is also strongly featured in the primary narrator's style in "The Thousand-and-second Tale of Scheherazade" (see under *hypotaxis* and chapter 4). In "The Language and Style of the Prose,"
Stauffer summarizes the various ways in which Poe employs parentheses
(464). For more on this stylistic feature, see Holman/Harmon (375) and,
for an extremely long consideration, Dupriez (325–7).

Type: addition, subtraction, and substitution: words, phrases, and clauses
Type: amplification

PAREURESIS : providing an excuse of such weight that it overcomes all
objections, accusations, complaints. Sonnino suggests that the excuse must
be premeditated (20). In his lengthy comments in "The Longfellow War,"
Poe answers the charge by an anonymous writer ("Outis") that his (Poe's)
critical book reviews have been generally scathing and filled with *ad hominem* arguments. I find the excuse wholly convincing and believe that here
Poe is at his rhetorical best:

no man can point to a single *critique*, among the very numerous ones which I
have written during the last ten years, which is either wholly fault-finding
[see *antanagoge*] or wholly in approbation; nor is there an instance to be discovered, among all that I have published, of my having set forth, either in
praise or censure, a single opinion upon any critical topic of moment, without attempting, at least, to give it authority by something that wore the semblance of a reason ... The fact is, that very many of the most eminent men in
America whom I am proud to number among the sincerest of my friends,
have been rendered so solely by their approbation of my comments upon
their own works – comments in great measure directed *against* themselves as
authors – belonging altogether to that very class of criticism which it is the
petty policy of the Outises to cry down, with their diminutive voices, as offensive on the score of wholesale vituperation and personal abuse. If, to be
brief, in what I have put forth there has been a preponderance of censure over
commendation, – is there not to be imagined for this preponderance a more
charitable motive than any which the Outises have been magnanimous

enough to assign me – is not this preponderance, in a word, the natural and inevitable tendency of all criticism worth the name in this age of so universal an authorship, that no man in his senses will pretend to deny the vast pre-dominance of good writers over bad? (12: 85–6)

Some rhetors also give us another definition of *pareuresis* – inventing a false pretext (see, for example, Dupriez, 355). Another term for *pareuresis* is *adinventio*. Cf *dicaeologia, praemunitio, proecthesis* (first definition), and *aetiologia,* all of which are exemplified elsewhere in this catalogue. While these other terms all involve excuse making, perhaps we can distinguish *pareuresis* by suggesting that the excuse offered in this case is irrefutable, while such may not be the case with the others.
Pronunciation: pa REU re sis
Type: techniques of argument

PARISON: see *isocolon.*
Pronunciation: PA ri son

PAROEMIA: see "proverb."
Pronunciation: pa ROE mi a

PAROMOLOGIA (sometimes spelled *paramologia*): conceding a point either because one believes it to be true or because one can strengthen one's own argument by the concession – giving away a weaker point to take a stronger one. Poe's literary reviews, which are often characterized by a very intense use of rhetoric, now and then display this intensely rhetorical device. In discussing the courageous frankness of the satirical poem *The Quacks of Helicon,* the Puritanical Poe complains about the poem's occasional vulgarity:

"Let what is to be said, be said plainly." True; but let nothing vulgar be *ever* said, or conceived. (10: 184)

Poe's fiction can be just as rhetorical as his criticism, especially his tales of murder:

True! – nervous – very, very dreadfully nervous I had been and am; but why *will* you say that I am mad? The disease had sharpened my senses – not destroyed – not dulled them. ("The Tell-Tale Heart," 5: 88)

To see how this device advances the forensic oratory of the narrator in that tale, see chapter 2. Dupriez has a long and thoughtful section on

this device, which he calls "concession": "Rhetorical concessions, or oratorical withdrawals, are acts of pseudo-generosity aimed only at convincing the jury [or, presumably, any other auditors] of the extent and force
of one's principal entitlement. The opposite is the *cession* or real relin-
quishment of a past claim" (110). We may wonder how to differentiate
between *paromologia* and *antistrephon* (see above). We also have *concessio*,
which Lanham defines as conceding a point "either to hurt the adversary
directly or to prepare for a more important argument" (38). I fail to see a
distinction between *paromologia* and *concessio*; perhaps the former involves some sort of confession while the latter does not; perhaps the latter involves more of a direct attack on the arguments of one's opponent.
Pronunciation: pa ro mo LO gi a
Type: techniques of argument

PARRHESIA: we find two definitions for this figure: (1) candid, frank
speech; and (2) "begging pardon in advance for necessary candor"
(Lanham, 110). A synonym is *licentia* – freedom, boldness, presumption.
This excerpt from a rather passionate letter to one of Poe's love interests
(Sarah Helen Whitman, 18 October 1848) illustrates the first definition:

> Let me speak freely to you *now*, Helen, for perhaps I may never thus be permit-
> ted to speak to you again – Let me speak openly – fearlessly – trusting to the
> generosity of your own spirit for a *true* interpretation of my own. I repeat, then,
> that I *dreaded* to find you in worldly circumstances superior to mine. So great
> was my *fear* that you were rich, or at least possessed some property which might
> cause you to *seem* rich in the eyes of one so poor. (Ostrom, 395)

Parrhesia figures as a deliberately chosen rhetorical device in *Eureka*. Poe
– or his *narrator*, as some scholars prefer to suggest – announces his plan
for the work (here is *digestion* – see above) and then provides some candid language in admitting the boldness of his vision:

> I design to speak of the *Physical, Metaphysical and Mathematical – of the Ma-
> terial and Spiritual Universe: – of its Essence, its Origin, its Creation, its Present
> Condition and its Destiny.* **I shall be so rash, moreover, as to challenge the
> conclusions, and thus, in effect, to question the sagacity, of many of the
> greatest and most justly reverenced of men.** (16: 185)

John P. Hussey considers *Eureka* as exhibiting the rules and structure of a
classical speech, and the narrator as adopting various appropriate personae throughout. Referring to the narrator's modest pose, above, Hussey
provides a good rationale for the use of *parrhesia*:

Given the fact that the narrator is about to take on the entire universe as well as the views of "many of the greatest and most justly reverenced of men" … he must, in the beginning, appear neither overweeningly arrogant nor incompetent. Indeed, as Blair [see chapter 2] suggests, he must be both modest and calm in order "to render the hearers docile, or open to persuasion" (Blair, II, 158). In his opening page, *Eureka's* narrator presents himself in just that way: as an earnestly humble seeker of a truth so "solemn" and "sublime" that he feels himself (or avers that he does) to be "rash" even to consider dealing with it. (40)

Pronunciation: par RHE si a

Type: techniques of argument

PERIERGIA: the unnecessary elaboration of a point:

> Your diddler is *nonchalant*. He is not at all nervous. He never *had* any nerves. He is never seduced into a flurry. He is never put out – unless put out of doors. He is cool – cool as a cucumber. He is calm – "calm as a smile from Lady Bury." He is easy – easy as an old glove, or the damsels of ancient Baiæ. ("Diddling Considered as One of the Exact Sciences," 5: 212)

"Diddling" is full of instances of *periergia*, as well as *exempla* and other types of amplification (see above under *amplificatio*). Cf *synonymia* and Lanham's second definition of *scesis onomaton*: "Using a string of synonymous expressions" (135).

Pronunciation: pe ri ER gi a

Type: amplification

Type: repetition: clauses, phrases, and ideas

PERIODIC SENTENCE: see under "left-branching sentence."

PERIPHRASIS: the designation of a noun by a more complex expression in several words (Dupriez, 336); the substitution of more words for less; circumlocution:

> A vivid fancy, an epigrammatic spirit … have made him very easily what he is, the most popular poet now living … and, perhaps, a slight modification at birth of that which phrenologists have agreed to term *temperament*, might have made him the truest and noblest **votary of the muse**. (Review of Thomas Moore's *Alciphron: A Poem*, 10: 71)

Pronunciation: pe RI phra sis

Type: amplification

Type: techniques of argument

PERISTASIS: amplifying by describing circumstances attending a person or thing. To enlarge the description of a person, we can mention parentage, nation, country, kind, age, gender, education, discipline, habit of body, fortune, condition, the nature of the mind, study, foredeeds, name (Espy, 198); of a thing, a subject, we can mention cause, occasion, instrument, time, mode (Sonnino, 210):

> Sir Huldbrand of Ringstetten, **a knight of high descent, young, rich, valorous, and handsome**, becomes slightly enamoured, at a tournament, of a lady Bertalda. (Review of *Undine: A Miniature Romance*, 10: 31)

The description of Sir Huldbrand is enlarged by Poe's mention of the knight's station in life, his age, his pecuniary status, a character trait, and his appearance. We may wonder how the device differs from *appositio* (see above), but while *appositio* involves amplification with the placement of an explanatory noun or noun phrase, without hypotactic linkage, beside a noun or pronoun, *peristasis* involves amplification that does, or can, involve hypotactic linkage. Examples provided by Sonnino and Espy are more complicated partly because they do not resemble apposition, which is fairly easy to identify.

Pronunciation: pe RI sta sis

Type: amplification

PERISTROPHE: "Converting an opponent's argument to one's use" (Lanham, 114). I do not find this device in other rhetorical catalogues; probably *antistrephon* (above) is provided as meaning the same thing. *Paromologia* (above) is similar. Poe uses the device in a rather nasty way in his magazine piece, "Achilles' Wrath." Responding to an abusive letter from a theatre manager, who describes himself as a "caterer for the public amusement" (12: 136), Poe ends this way:

> There is certainly not in New York, at the present moment, any other member of the theatrical profession, who either would have behaved with the gross discourtesy of this gentleman, or who, in inditing the preposterous letter published above, could have proved himself, personally, **so successful a "caterer for the public amusement."** (138–9)

Poe turns his adversary's own self-description against him, suggesting that, yes indeed, the public has certainly been amused by his silly letter!

Pronunciation: pe RI stro phe

Type: techniques of argument

PERSONIFICATION: see *prosopopoeia*, below. After quoting a passage of William Cullen Bryant's poetry, Poe says, "Happily to endow inanimate nature with sentience and a capability of action, is one of the severest tests of the poet" (13: 137).

PHILOPHRONESIS: an attempt to mitigate anger by gentle speech and humble submission; sometimes promises and flattery are involved. In Poe's play "Politian," Politian has sent word that he wishes to challenge Castiglione to a duel. Castiglione, puzzled by Politian's hostility, seeks him out and attempts to diffuse the situation:

My lord, some strange,
Some singular mistake – misunderstanding –
Hath without doubt arisen: thou hast been urged
Thereby, in heat of anger, to address
Some words most unaccountable, in writing,
To me, Castiglione; the bearer being
Baldazzar, Duke of Surrey. I am aware
Of nothing which might warrant thee in this thing,
Having given thee no offence. Ha! – am I right?
'T was a mistake? – undoubtedly – we all
Do err at times. (7: 77)

Another word for this device is *benevolentia*; Sonnino and Taylor also give us *exceptio benigna*.
Pronunciation: phi lo phro NE sis
Type: devices of vehemence
Type: techniques of argument

PHONOLOGICAL SET: a term from linguistics referring to a group of words linked on the basis of sound identity ("homophony" – having the same sound). In the following excerpt from a tale reflecting the literary battles of Poe's time and place, an editor responds to another editor's criticism that he (the first) uses too many *o*'s in his writing":

"So ho, John! how now? Told you so, you know. Don't crow, another time, before you're out of the woods! Does your mother *know* you're out? Oh, no, no – so go home at once, now, John, to your odious old woods of Concord [note the allusion to the Transcendentalists]! Go home to your woods, old owl, – go! You won't? Oh, poh, poh, John, don't do so! You've *got* to go, you

know! So go at once, and don't go slow; for nobody owns you here, you
know. Oh, John, John, if you *don't* go you're no *homo* – no! You're only a
fowl, an owl; a cow, a sow; a doll, a poll; a poor, old, good-for-nothing-to-
nobody, log, dog, hog, or frog, come out of a Concord bog. Cool, now –
cool! *Do* be cool, you fool! None of your crowing, old cock! Don't frown so –
don't! Don't hollo, nor howl, nor growl, nor bow-wow-wow! Good Lord,
John, how you *do* look! Told you so, you know – but stop rolling your goose
of an old poll about so, and go and drown your sorrows in a bowl!" ("X-ing a
Paragrab," 6: 232–3)

Long before the phrase "phonological set" was ever used, the classical
rhetors had already classified such sets with terms referring to devices of
sound – for example, *alliteration, homoioteleuton, homoioptoton*; consider
also rhyme, *assonance*, and *consonance*. For examples of most of these, see
under those headings.

Type: repetition: letters, syllables, and sounds

PLEONASM (*pleonasmus*): the repetition of an idea through words or
phrases (often parallel) that mean the same thing. For examples of pleonasm, see under "doublets" and *tautologia*. Poe sometimes uses the term
tautology when he is referring to pleonasms (see, for instance, 15: 177).

Despite his occasional use of pleonasm – sometimes accidental, some-
times deliberate – Poe was sure to catch it in the literature he reviewed.
In his comments on Robert Montgomery Bird's novel *The Hawks of
Hawk-Hollow,* for instance, Poe complains that

Occasionally we meet with a sentence ill-constructed – an inartificial adaptation of the end to the beginning of a paragraph – a circumlocutory mode of
saying what might have been better said, with brevity – now and then with a
pleonasm, as for example. "**And if he wore a mask in his commerce with
men, it was like that** *iron* **one of the Bastile** [sic], **which when put on, was
put on for life, and was at the same time of** *iron*." (8: 71; see also 13: 198;
Ostrom, 381)

"Pleonastic parallelism tends to be characteristic both of Ciceronianism and
of styles that employ the period," say Cluett and Kampeas. Although often
considered a vice, pleonastic expressions are sometimes used "for clarity, and
sometimes for expansion or filling out a figure of equality or stress" (49).
Pleonasm is "one of the most natural forms of emphasis," says Dupriez
(345), and sometimes can actually have a pleasing effect when used this way.

Sonnino quotes ancient rhetors who believe that a superfluity of words can give grace to one's speech "in the interest of either vehemence or exaggeration" (156). Cf *macrologia* (long-winded speech). Harmon and Holman insist that even the use of superfluous *syllables* constitutes pleonasm (393), although I have never heard pleonasm given this definition. We might call this *epenthesis* (see above), *paragoge*, or *prothesis* (see below) instead.
Pronunciation: ple o NASM
Type: amplification
Type: repetition: clauses, phrases, and ideas

PLEONASTIC DOUBLET: see under "doublets" and "pleonasm."

PLOCE: the repetition of a word with few words in between (cf *diacope*):

> I think it was his **eye**! yes, it was this! He had the **eye** of a vulture – a pale
> blue **eye**, with a film over it. ("The Tell-Tale Heart," 5: 88)

We see how the reappearance of a word can suggest a speaker's obsession, and certainly this narrator is a monomaniac where the old man's eye – an eye perhaps merely covered with cataracts – is concerned. Devices of repetition are foregrounded in "The Tell-Tale Heart," and there Poe combines frequently two such devices – *epizeuxis* and *diacope*. All figures that involve repetition can be used to indicate heightened emotions, and the *ploce, epizeuxis,* and *diacope* in this tale of paranoid schizophrenia undermine the frantic narrator's insistence that he can relate his story "calmly."
Pronunciation: PLO ce
Type: devices of vehemence
Type: repetition: words

POICILOGIA: overly ornate speech – too many figures. We might not expect to find this vice in Poe's writings if he really took to heart his criticism of Bulwer's prose. In his review of *Night and Morning*, Poe complains of Bulwer's "absolute mania of metaphor," and calls him "king-coxcomb of figures of speech" (10: 130). Lanham relates this term to two typologies: Asianism and Euphuism (116).
Pronunciation: poi ci LO gi a
Type: ungrammatical, illogical, or unusual uses of language

POLYPTOTON: repeated use of the same word or root as different parts of speech:

> The mountain trembled to its very base, and the **rock rocked**. ("A Descent into the Maelström," 2: 229; see also 223)

Poe employs the device in a rather nasty fashion in his scathing reviews of *Norman Leslie* and *Powhatan* (see chapters 4 and 5 respectively). His love of *polyptoton* for satirical purposes is even shown in a letter (25 December 1842) to James Lowell. He refers to Henry T. Tuckerman, who had rejected for publication "The Tell-Tale Heart":

> He writes, through his publishers, – "if Mr. Poe would condescend to furnish more **quiet** articles he would be a most desirable correspondent." All I have to say is that if Mr. T. persists in his *quietude*, he will put a **quietus** to the Magazine of which Mess. Bradbury & Soden have been so stupid as to give him control. (Ostrom, 220)

Although he uses *polyptoton* frequently, Poe objects to its use in a poem by Amelia Welby: "The repetition ('seemed,' 'seem,' 'seems,') in the sixth and seventh stanzas, is ungraceful" (11: 279). *Polyptoton* is labelled by Forrest (89) as *paranomasia*, which is a type of punning involving words that sound alike (see Dupriez, 328–30, and above).

Pronunciation: po LYP to ton

Type: repetition: words

POLYSYNDETON: the use of conjunctions (such as *and, or,* or *nor*) in a series of words, phrases, or clauses. *Polysyndeton* can be used to indicate not only a series of events passing, but also an abundance of things:

> "Is it Nergal of whom the idolater speaketh? – **or** Ashimah? – **or** Nibhaz? – **or** Tartak? – **or** Adramalech? – **or** Anamalech? – **or** Succoth-Benith? – **or** Dagon? – **or** Belial? – **or** Baal-Perith? – **or** Baal-Peor? – **or** Baal-Zebub?" ("A Tale of Jerusalem," 2: 217; see also 9: 83)

Stauffer believes that *polysyndeton* is a chief characteristic of what he calls Poe's "parabolic" style ("The Language and Style of the Prose," 459). It is well known that the device is frequent in the Bible, and some writers (for example, Poe and Melville) use *polysyndeton* to give passages a biblical "flavour" – to suggest that what they are writing has the weight of biblical pronouncement and truth. Here, for instance, is the ending of "The Masque of the Red Death":

And now was acknowledged the presence of the Red Death. He had come like a thief in the night. **And** one by one dropped the revellers in the blood-bedewed halls of their revel, **and** died each in the despairing posture of his fall. **And** the life of the ebony clock went out with that of the last of the gay. **And** the flames of the tripods expired. **And** Darkness **and** Decay **and** the Red Death held illimitable dominion over all. (4: 258)

Poe's one novel, *The Narrative of Arthur Gordon Pym of Nantucket*, similarly ends with foregrounded *polysyndeton*, complementing the biblical themes in that work. Forrest provides a lengthy and thoughtful discussion of this device in the Bible as it relates to Poe's own prose:

The most distinguishing characteristic of Scripture narrative is its extreme simplicity of structure. It moves forward by a succession of co-ordinate sentences and clauses usually connected by "and." They may be divided almost anywhere by periods, or they may be allowed to flow on undivided through paragraphs, chapters, and books. A scrutiny of chapter after chapter, and book after book, of the Hebrew Bible will show that they begin with "and." Even in the English translation the only pause for breath, so to speak, from the beginning of Genesis to the end of Numbers, is where Exodus opens with "now," instead of the "and" of the original. This is due in part to a love for polysyndeton, which shows itself in the repetition of other conjunctions also. But it is chiefly due to naïveté and unconscious simplicity. (84)

Forrest then offers a passage from "Silence" to illustrate *polysyndeton* – a good choice, since that device figures prominently in every single paragraph, almost every single clause. Forrest concludes, "Master stylist though he was, Poe was never able to surpass in his more independent productions the power and music of those pieces which were palpably modeled after the Bible" (100). Quinn suggests that "the indefiniteness of 'and' envelops biblical narratives … in mystery. Occasionally, in the Bible and elsewhere, repeated polysyndetons have an almost hypnotic power" (*Figures of Speech*, 12). He also notes that *polysyndeton* can slow the pace of a passage, "thereby adding dignity to what we say, much like the slow motion of a ceremony" (13).

Polysyndeton can sometimes have the opposite effect – that is, it can create a sense of the colloquial. The antithetical scheme is *asyndeton* (see above). We should note, finally, that *polysyndeton* also figures now and then in Poe's criticism and therefore not only, as Stauffer maintains, in his "parabolic" style:

> She is not so vigorous as Mrs. Stephens, **nor** so vivacious as Miss Chubbuck,
> **nor** so caustic as Miss Leslie, **nor** so dignified as Miss Sedgwick, **nor** so grace-
> ful, fanciful and *spirituelle* as Mrs. Osgood. (*The Literati of New York City*,
> Emma C. Embury, 15: 90)

Oddly enough, while loving the device and using it in so many ways, Poe objects to the use of *polysyndeton* in a poem by Amelia Welby: he mentions "the unpleasant repetition of '*and*,' at the commencement of the third and fifth lines" (11: 280). For more on *polysyndeton*, see Corbett (435–6) and chapter 5 (for Poe's satirical use of the figure).
Pronunciation: po ly SYN de ton
Type: repetition: words
Type: "biblical"

PRAECISIO: most rhetors equate this device with *aposiopesis* (see above): stopping before finishing a sentence. Arthur Quinn, however, differs from them in suggesting that *praecisio* involves *complete* silence – not the unwillingness to continue a sentence but an unwillingness to start it in the first place, an unwillingness to say *anything*. As he rightly admits, it is difficult to find examples of this. How do we quote someone saying nothing? If we accept Quinn's definition, certainly *praecisio* figures in "Hop-Frog":

> Trippetta, pale as a corpse, advanced to the monarch's seat, and, falling on her knees before him, implored him to spare her friend.
>
> The tyrant regarded her, for some moments, in evident wonder at her au-dacity. He seemed quite at a loss what to do or say – how most becomingly to express his indignation. At last, without uttering a syllable, he pushed her violently from him, and threw the contents of the brimming goblet in her face. (6: 221)

Pronunciation: prae CIS i o

PRAEMUNITIO: defending yourself in anticipation of an attack; strengthening your position beforehand. This device appears often in some of Poe's more famous tales, and he began the practice in "MS. Found in a Bottle," his first published tale:

> I have often been reproached with the aridity of my genius; a deficiency of imagination has been imputed to me as a crime; and the Pyrrhonism [ex-treme skepticism] of my opinions has at all times rendered me notorious ...

Upon the whole, no person could be less liable than myself to be led away
from the severe precincts of truth by the *ignes fatui* of superstition. I have
thought proper to premise this much, lest the incredible tale I have to tell
should be considered rather the raving of a crude imagination, than the positive experience of a mind to which the reveries of fancy have been a dead
letter and a nullity. (2: 1–2)

There is a distinctly *rhetorical* aspect not only to Poe's literary criticism,
where we would expect to find it, but even to some of his prose fiction.
He is so often attempting to *persuade* – that is, his narrators are. The
more wild and incredible a tale, the more ardently the storyteller will attempt what Poe called the "verisimilar style" – employ rhetorical devices
and other stylistic features designed to convince the reader that what
s/he is reading is a true account and not a hoax.

We also find *praemunitio* in Poe's tales of homicide, not so much for
the sake of verisimilitude but to anticipate and diffuse an attack on the
narrator's character – specifically, skepticism regarding his mental health:

If still you think me mad, you will think so no longer when I describe the
wise precautions I took for the concealment of the body. ("The Tell-Tale
Heart," 5: 92)

As with the use of *dicaeologia* on the part of some of Poe's narrators, this
narrator's use of *praemunitio* is pathetic, ironic, because clearly inadequate – outrageously unconvincing to anyone but himself.
Pronunciation: prae mu NI ti o
Type: techniques of argument

PRAEPARATIO: preparing an audience, reader(s), or interlocutor(s)
before telling them about something done. Dupriez (351) uses the term
praemunitio for this, refusing to make a distinction, and offers the following excerpt as an example. I prefer to see this excerpt as *praeparatio*
and to draw a distinction: *praemunitio* anticipates an attack; *praeparatio*
does not necessarily do so:

For the most wild, yet most homely narrative which I am about to pen, I neither
expect nor solicit belief. Mad indeed would I be to expect it, in a case where my
very senses reject their own evidence. Yet, mad am I not – and very surely do I
not dream. But to-morrow I die, and to-day I would unburthen my soul. My
immediate purpose is to place before the world, plainly, succinctly, and without
comment, a series of mere household events. ("The Black Cat," 5: 143)

Several of Poe's tales begin with short essays on various themes, concepts, that will be illustrated by the following narrative accounts; thus, the narrators prepare the audience to understand the specific cases to follow by illuminating the theories first – they engage in *praeparatio*. "The Murders in the Rue Morgue" commences with an essay on certain mental skills before we hear about their display by the amateur detective C. Auguste Dupin. "The Premature Burial" starts with several illustrations of untimely interment before we hear about how the narrator himself was apparently buried alive. "The Imp of the Perverse" begins with a short dissertation on that destructive and irresistible human impulse before the narrator provides three examples of it and finally his own case. I agree with Sandra Whipple Spanier (311), who quotes Eugene R. Kanjo with approval: "This essay-like introduction is not a failure of craft, as one critic contends, but a measure of Poe's craftiness" (41). This craftiness lies in Poe's use of the rhetorical tradition – here, in his employment of *praeparatio*. In such tales of homicide as "The Imp of the Perverse" and "The Tell-Tale Heart" – both of which essentially constitute forensic oratory (see chapter 2) – the narrator's use of *praeparatio* is essential to "soften up," *condition*, the hostile audience so that they may be more receptive to the murderer's point of view.

Sonnino (145) considers *praeparatio* synonymous with *aetiologia* (above).
Pronunciation: prae pa RA ti o
Type: techniques of argument

PRAGMATOGRAPHIA: the vivid description of an action or event (a kind of *enargia*). Pym describes the destruction of the ship *Jane Guy*:

> The savages … were upon the point of recommencing, when suddenly a mass of smoke puffed up from the decks, resembling a black and heavy thundercloud – then, as if from its bowels, arose a tall stream of vivid fire to the height, apparently, of a quarter of a mile – then there came a sudden circular expansion of the flame – then the whole atmosphere was magically crowded, in a single instant, with a wild chaos of wood, and metal, and human limbs – and, lastly, came the concussion in its fullest fury, which hurled us impetuously from our feet, while the hills echoed and re-echoed the tumult, and a dense shower of the minutest fragments of the ruins tumbled headlong in every direction around us. (*The Narrative of Arthur Gordon Pym of Nantucket*, 3: 216)

Anyone well acquainted with the prose fiction of Poe knows that *prag-matographia* abounds in his *oeuvre*.

Pronunciation: prag ma to GRA phi a

Type: description

PROECTHESIS: Lanham provides two definitions of this term: (1) "Defending what one has done or said, by giving reasons and circumstances" (cf *dicaeologia*); and (2) "pointing out what ought to have been done, and then what actually has been done" (119). We get an illustration of the second definition in Poe's review of *The Drama of Exile*:

> It would have been better for Miss Barrett if, throwing herself independently upon her own very extraordinary resources, and forgetting that a Greek had ever lived, she had involved her Eve in a series of adventures merely natural, or if not this, of adventures preternatural within the limits of at least a conceivable relation – a relation of matter to spirit and spirit to matter, that should have left room for something like palpable action and comprehensible emotion – that should not have utterly precluded the development of that womanly character which is admitted as the principal object of the poem. As the case actually stands, it is only in a few snatches of verbal intercommunication with Adam and Lucifer, that we behold her as a woman at all. (12: 4; see also 11: 117)

Essentially, *proecthesis* (second definition) is central to Poe's *modus operandi* as a critic. He himself suggests as much in "About Critics and Criticism": the critic must be concerned with "showing how the work might have been improved," as well as "pointing out and analyzing defects" (13: 194).

Pronunciation: pro EC the sis

Type: techniques of argument

PROGRESSIO: building a point around a series of comparisons – contrary sentences that answer one another (Sonnino, 111). In "The Longfellow War," Poe is attempting to refute the implied accusation, made by one "Outis," that he (Poe) plagiarized eighteen items from another poem for "The Raven." Poe examines each item one at a time, comparing his poem and the alleged source poem, gradually building his point – that the charges of plagiarism are groundless. Since Poe's use of *progressio* is extended over several pages, I shall quote only a small excerpt:

"*Third* – there is a bird," says Outis. So there is. Mine however is a raven, and
we may take it for granted that Outis' is either a nightingale or a cockatoo.
"*Fourth*, the bird is at the poet's window." As regards my poem, true; as regards
Outis', not: – the poet only *requests* the bird to come to the window. ["]*Fifth*,
the bird being at the poet's window, makes a noise." The fourth specification
failing, the fifth, which depends upon it, as a matter of course fails too. (12: 74)

Pronunciation: pro GRES si o
Type: balance, antithesis, and paradox
Type: techniques of argument

PROLEPSIS: anticipating objections and dealing with them:

An objection will be made: – that the greatest excess of mental power, however proportionate, does not seem to satisfy our idea of genius, unless we
have, in addition, sensibility, passion, energy. The reply is, that the "absolute
proportion["] spoken of, when applied to inordinate mental power, gives, as a
result, the appreciation of Beauty and a horror of Deformity which we call
sensibility, together with that intense vitality, which is implied when we speak
of "Energy" or "Passion." ("Fifty Suggestions," 14: 178)

We might not be surprised to find the device figuring in Poe's epistolary
quarrels with his stingy foster father, John Allan:

Under such circumstances, can it be said that I have no *right* to expect any
thing at your hands? **You may probably urge that you have given me a liberal education. I will leave the decision of that question to those who know
how far liberal educations can be obtained in 8 months at the University of
Va. Here you will say that it was my own fault that I did not return – You
would not let me return.** (Ostrom, 39)

Lanham supplies an extended discussion of this term with numerous
synonymous terms (120–1), and it is difficult to distinguish between it
and *praemunitio* (above). Sonnino, under the term *praesumptio*, provides
Lanham's and other definitions (146–7), one of which is that given by
Espy: dividing a general word afterwards into parts (200). Taylor concurs with this definition, which obviously brings to mind other terms of
amplification such as *diaeresis* (see above) and the second definition I
give (above) for *dinumeratio*.

Pronunciation: pro LEP sis
Type: techniques of argument
Type: amplification

PROSAPODOSIS: supporting each alternative, each division of a statement, with a reason:

> We complain ... secondly, of the blue-fire melo-dramatic aspect of the revolving sword; thirdly, **of the duplicate nature of the sword, which, if steel, and sufficiently enflamed to do service in burning, would, perhaps, have been in no temper to cut; and on the other hand, if sufficiently cool to have an edge, would have accomplished little in the way of scorching a personage so well accustomed to fire and brimstone and all that, as we have very good reason to believe Lucifer was.** (Review of *The Drama of Exile*, 12: 7)

This device is also called *redditio*. Clearly, it can be particularly devastating when used against an opponent because it can force him or her into a "damned if you do, damned if you don't" position – a dilemma (any "technique or argument which offers an opponent a choice, or a series of them, all of which are unacceptable" [Lanham, 54; see above]).

Pronunciation: pro sa PO do sis
Type: balance, antithesis, and paradox
Type: techniques of argument

PROSONOMASIA: calling by a name or nickname. The narrator of "How to Write a Blackwood Article" complains of her own nickname:

> My name is the Signora Psyche Zenobia. This I know to be a fact. Nobody but my enemies ever calls me **Suky Snobbs**. (2: 269)

Here is another example from Poe's criticism:

> What is he to **Jacques Bonhomme** or **Jacques Bonhomme** to him! (Review of *Charles O'Malley, the Irish Dragoon*, 11: 89)

Harrison's footnote informs us that *Jacques Bonhomme* is a nickname for the populace in the Middle Ages. Let us not forget Poe's nickname for the Bostonians; here he refers to the famous incident in which he contemptuously "hoaxed" a Boston audience by reading to them one of his juvenile poems:

> Never was a "bobbery" more delightful than that which we have just succeeded in "kicking up" all about Boston Common. We never saw the **Frog-Pondians** so lively in our lives. ("Boston and the Bostonians," 13: 5)

His nickname for the Brook Farmers is "Crazyites" (13: 27). His nickname for his mother-in-law, Mrs Clemm, was "Muddy." While a young student at Jefferson's University of Virginia, Poe himself was nicknamed "Gaffy" after a character in one of his early tales (now lost – Poe burned it in disgust when

his friends complained in fun that the name cropped up too frequently as he
recited the tale to them). As for the nickname, Poe was not amused.

Pronunciation: pro so no MA si a

Type: metaphorical substitutions and puns

Type: "comedic"

PROSOPOGRAPHIA: "A type of **Enargia** which vividly describes
the appearance of a person, imaginary or real, quick or dead" (Lanham,
123). See *effictio*. Taylor expands the definition thus: "Describing imaginary bodies, those which have no corporeal existence, such as harpies,
furies, devils" (123).

> They are neither man nor woman –
> They are neither brute nor human –
>> They are Ghouls: –
> And their king it is who tolls: –
> And he rolls, rolls, rolls,
>> Rolls
>>> A pæan from the bells!
> And his merry bosom swells
>> With the pæan of the bells!
> And he dances, and he yells. ("The Bells," 7: 121–2)

Prosopographia is foregrounded in "The Man of the Crowd," as the astute
narrator describes several types of people he sees in the busy London street,
in some cases exhibiting a Dupin-like (and Holmes-like) ability to deduce
their occupations simply by their appearances. It is also a central feature of
The Literati of New York City (see, for example, 15: 26). For more instances
of *prosopographia* in connection with phrenology, see under *enargia*.

Pronunciation: pro so po GRA phi a

Type: description

PROSOPOPOEIA: what we normally call "personification" (see
above) – giving abstract or inanimate objects human qualities or abilities. John Ruskin called this "pathetic fallacy":

> I looked upon the scene before me – upon the mere house, and the simple
> landscape features of the domain – upon the bleak walls – upon the **vacant
> eye-like windows**. ("The Fall of the House of Usher," 3: 273)

Ever since Poe's House of Usher, at least, it has been conventional to describe Gothic mansions in human terms: Hawthorne's House of the

Seven Gables, Shirley Jackson's Hill House (*The Haunting of Hill House*), and Stephen King's Overlook Hotel (*The Shining*) are all described in anthropomorphic terms. Roderick Usher believes that his house is *indeed* alive, sentient, and Poe supports this idea with the allegorical poem "The Haunted Palace," which appears in "Usher." Corbett suggests that *prosopopoeia* "is one of the figures that should be reserved for passages designed to stir the emotions" (451).

We find the device now and then in Poe's literary criticism, too:

The demands of Truth are severe. She has no sympathy with the myrtles. All *that* which is so indispensible in Song, is precisely all *that* with which *she* has nothing whatever to do. It is but making her a flaunting paradox, to wreath her in gems and flowers. ("The Poetic Principle," 14: 272; see also 9: 94)

Interestingly, about ten years earlier, Poe took Bulwer to task for doing exactly what Poe himself does in the above excerpt: "It is this coxcombry which leads him so often into allegory and objectless personification. Does he mention 'truth' in the most ordinary phrase? – she is with a great T, Truth, the divinity … That he has not yet discarded this senseless mannerism, must be considered the greater wonder, as the whole herd of his little imitators have already taken it up" ("Literary Small Talk," 14: 91–2). We can only conclude that when *Poe* engages in personification (*prosopopoeia*), it is *not* "objectless." In his review of Bulwer's *Night and Morning*, Poe makes a similar complaint – "His rage for personification is really ludicrous" (10: 130) – and demonstrates his familiarity with the rhetorical name for this device: "Nor does the commonplace character of anything which he wishes to personify exclude it from the prosopopœia" (131; see also 13: 19).

In reviewing Longfellow's *Voices of the Night*, Poe makes some highly intelligent criticisms of that poet's use of personification (10: 74–5). Poe complains that, while personifying night (Night), Longfellow's images at once further and interfere with the *prosopopoeia*. Night is pictured walking in her marble halls, which is fine, but then Longfellow uses the term *celestial* in conjunction with the corporate Night, thereby smashing the personified image of Night, bringing us back to *night*, as in *darkness*. In other words, as Poe observes, Longfellow's imagery is inconsistent: the images associated with personified Night should remain *concrete* (as in *marble halls*) rather than abstract (as in *celestial*).

Pronunciation: pro so po po EI a

Type: description

PROTHESIS (*prosthesis*): adding a letter or syllable at the front of a word without changing the word's meaning. In "Why the Little Frenchman Wears His Hand in a Sling" it is part of the Irishman's more general *barbarismus*:

> And is it ralelly more than the three fut and a bit that there is, inny how, of the little ould furrener Frinchman that lives just over the way, and that's **a oggling** and **a goggling** the houl day, (and bad luck to him,) at the purty widdy Misthress Tracle. (4: 115)

Pronunciation: PRO the sis
Type: addition, subtraction, and substitution: letters and syllables
Type: ungrammatical, illogical, or unusual uses of language
Type: "comedic"

PROVERB (adjective: proverbial): "A short, pithy statement of a general truth, one that condenses common experience into memorable form" (Lanham, 124). These, Lanham reminds us, include aphorisms (see above), adages, maxims, apothegms, gnomes, and *sententia*. He has a lengthy discussion (124–6), as do Dupriez (360–1) and Crowley (291–3). See also Cuddon (752–3), Harmon/Holman (415), and Baldick (180–1). Sonnino lists *sententia* with "gnome" (166–7). Espy lists "gnome" (177–8). Taylor provides and defines the term *paroemia* as "Quoting common proverbs" (117), while Lanham lists it as *synonymous* with "proverb" (109).

We might not expect to find too many of these in Poe, if we can believe he is in earnest when he writes of "the whole race of what are termed maxims and popular proverbs; nine-tenths of which are the quintessence of folly" (Review of Longfellow's *Ballads and Other Poems*, 11: 65). Then he quotes a specific example – which we can label *paroemia*, according to Taylor:

> One of the most deplorably false of them is the antique adage, *De gustibus non est disputandum* – there should be no disputing about taste.

Elsewhere he provides another, this time in English:

> "Necessity," says the proverb, "is the mother of Invention." (13: 175)

Type: example, allusion, and citation of authority

PROZEUGMA: when a verb is expressed in the first clause but omitted (yet understood) in subsequent clauses – a scheme of omission (minus additioning). In the following quote I insert a caret to mark the missing verb *became*:

Those eyes! those large, those shining, those divine orbs! they **became** to me
twin stars of Leda, and I /\ to them devoutest of astrologers. ("Ligeia," 2: 252)
Prozeugma means "to join in front," and we see how the initial verb joins
(governs) words in subsequent clauses. This device is one of several that
can speed up the pace of a passage and make for expressive concision. It
is one of Poe's most frequently used figures of brevity.
Pronunciation: pro ZEUG ma
Type: addition, subtraction, and substitution: words, phrases, and clauses
Type: brevity

PUN: a play on words involving either one word with more than one
meaning or two words that sound the same but have different meanings.
When the word is repeated with the two different senses, we call the device *antanaclasis* (see above). Michael J.S. Williams draws our attention
to the puns in "The Gold-Bug": "The puns are most obvious in the
transcriptions of Jupiter's speech – where visual as well as aural puns are
at work – but they also pervade the narrative" (176). He then refers to
the scene in which the narrator, Legrand, and Jupiter are digging in a
grave-like pit for treasure:

> We dug very steadily for two hours. Little was said; and our chief embarrass-
> ment lay in the yelpings of the dog, who took exceeding interest in our
> proceedings … The noise was, at length, very effectually silenced by Jupiter,
> who, getting out of the hole with a **dogged** air of deliberation, tied the brute's
> mouth up with one of his suspenders, and then returned, with a **grave**
> chuckle, to his task. (5: 115–16)

In his Marginalia Poe expresses impatience with writers who employ
puns too extensively, however – specifically with British poet, editor, and
humorist Thomas Hood. Hood became well known for his clever and
skillful punning but, says Poe,

> during the larger portion of his life, he seemed to breathe only for the pur-
> pose of perpetrating puns – things of so despicable a platitude that the man
> who is capable of habitually committing them, is seldom found capable of
> anything else. Whatever merit *may* be discovered in a pun, arises altogether
> from *unexpectedness*. This is the pun's element and is two-fold. First, we de-
> mand that the *combination* of the pun be unexpected; and, secondly, we
> require the most entire unexpectedness in the pun *per se*. A rare pun, rarely
> appearing, is, to a certain extent, a pleasurable effect; but to no mind,
> however debased in taste, is a continuous effort at punning otherwise than

unendurable. The man who maintains that he derives gratification from any such chapters of punnage as Hood was in the daily practice of committing to paper, should not be credited upon oath. (16: 177; see also 12: 213–15)

Still, Peithman insists, quite rightly, that "Poe, like Thoreau, was fond of wordplay, and 'death-watch' [a phrase used in 'The Tell-Tale Heart' to describe an insect] is also a vigil held over a dying person" (136, n10) – a reference to the narrator's watch over the old man whom he is about to murder. In "Lionizing" we also find Poe punning on "nosology": it really means the science of diseases, but the narrator defines it as "the Science of Noses" (2: 36). Punning is a device found often enough in Poe's comedic tales and it joins *soraismus, barbarismus, bomphiologia, epenthesis,* and *prosonomasia* as evidence of Poe's linguistic sportiveness – although Symons is less impressed with Poe's wordplay, insisting that "he uses an abundance of appalling puns" (208). Here are some further samples:

In Spain they are [use] *all* curtains – a nation of **hangmen**. ("The Philosophy of Furniture," 14:101)

Some of our foreign lions [celebrities] resemble the human brain in one very striking particular. They are without any **sense** themselves, and yet are the centres of **sensation**. ("Fifty Suggestions," 14: 171)

This second example also illustrates quite well *assonance* (the short *e* sound) and *polyptoton* (for both, see above). Poe even uses a pun to deride an author who he feels is a "wholesale" quack guilty of hoaxing the public with a particularly bad book:

He acts upon the principle that if a thing is worth doing at all it is worth doing well: – and the thing that he "**does**" especially well is the public. (Review of *The Sacred Mountains,* 13: 209)

Even in one of his letters (8 August 1839), Poe can be found punning:

I intend to **put up** with nothing that I can *put down* (excuse the pun) and I am not aware that there is any one in Baltimore whom I have particular reason to fear in a regular set-to. (Ostrom, 114)

If we can stand it, here is one more (from a letter of 14 June 1848):

How happens it that you have flown away to **Providence**? or is this a **Providential** escape? (Ostrom, 370)

Discussions of various kinds of puns can sometimes be a little bewildering. See, for instance, Lanham (12; 126–8), Abrams (151–2), Corbett (447–8), and Dupriez (43–5; 364–5). For more on the use of puns as part of Poe's linguistic humour, see chapter 4. As well, see Stauffer's *The Merry Mood* (9–10; 14). Type: "comedic"

PYSMA: asking many questions requiring diverse answers (Lanham, 128):

> yonder scampers a ragged little urchin. **Where is he going? What is he bawling about? What does he say?** ("Four Beasts in One; The Homo-Cameleopard," 2: 208)

Sonnino, referring to the use of *pysma* in orations, notes that this device can be used "to underline emotions such as admiration, determination and indignation" (153), and Espy (202) quotes the sixteenth-century rhetor Henry Peacham, who says that this device makes an oration "sharp and vehement": "Now thus many questions together, are as it were like unto a courageous fighter, that doth lay strokes upon his enemy so thick and so hard that he is not able to defend or bear half of them." Indeed, *pysma* can be used as a wonderfully intimidating device. It can also be considered a type of rhetorical question if the many questions asked do not require answers but are asked simply to bully someone or to express emotion. In his more vehement literary reviews, Poe sometimes uses rhetorical questions to express indignation (*subjectio, epiplexis, hypophora*), and we find *many* instances of *pysma* in his review of Griswold's third edition of *The Poets and Poetry of America* (see chapter 5).

Pronunciation: PYS ma

Type: devices of vehemence

Type: techniques of argument

RANGE DOUBLET: a word-pair wherein the members refer to the range of a group:

> Seven of the crew (among whom was the cook, a negro) were rummaging the staterooms on the larboard for arms, where they soon equipped themselves with **muskets and ammunition**. (*The Narrative of Arthur Gordon Pym of Nantucket*, 3: 49)

Type: balance, antithesis, paradox

RATIOCINATIO: reasoning by asking ourselves questions:

> Besides, granting that we were still in the neighbourhood of the island, why should not Augustus have visited me and informed me of the circumstances? (*The Narrative of Arthur Gordon Pym of Nantucket*, 3: 27)

Pronunciation: ra ti o ci NA ti o

Type: techniques of argument

REDITUS AD PROPOSITUM: "returning to the subject after a digression" (Lanham, 194). In the silly comedic tale "Loss of Breath," the narrator looks for his missing breath:

> Long and earnestly did I continue the investigation: but the contemptible reward of my industry and perseverance proved to be only a set of false teeth, two pairs of hips, an eye, and a bundle of *billets-doux* from Mr. Windenough to my wife. I might as well here observe that this confirmation of my lady's partiality for Mr. W. occasioned me little uneasiness. That Mrs. Lacko'breath should admire anything so dissimilar to myself was a natural and necessary evil. I am, it is well known, of a robust and corpulent appearance, and at the same time somewhat diminutive in stature. What wonder then that the lath-like tenuity of my acquaintance, and his altitude, which has grown into a proverb, should have met with all due estimation in the eyes of Mrs. Lacko'breath. **But to return.**
>
> **My exertions, as I have before said, proved fruitless.** (2: 154)

For *digressio*, see above.

Pronunciation: RE di tus ad pro PO si tum

Type: techniques of argument

REDUCTIO AD ABSURDUM: not a rhetorical figure but a term describing a rhetorical strategy: to "disprove a proposition, one validly deduces from it a conclusion self-contradictory or contradictory to acknowledged facts" (Lanham, 130). I think we see this strategy at work in Poe's review of *George Balcombe*:

> For the occasional *philosophy* of Balcombe himself, we must not, of course, hold the author responsible. It might now and then be more exact. For example. "I am not sure that we do not purchase all our good qualities by the exercise of their opposites. How else does experience of danger make men brave? If they were not scared at first, then they were brave at first. If they were scared, then the effect of fear upon the mind has been to engender courage." As much, perhaps, as the effect of truth is to engender error, or of black paint to render a canvass [sic] white. *All* our good qualities purchased by the exercise of their opposites! Generalize this dogma, and we have, at once, virtue derivable from vice. (9: 263)

Deductive reasoning moves from the general to the specific, so Poe takes Balcombe's "philosophy" as a general rule – all our good qualities are purchased by the exercise of their opposites – and deduces a self-contradictory conclusion, namely, that virtue (Poe's specific) comes from vice. Poe's

powers of logic are evident here. We find another instance in his review of
Barnaby Rudge – embedded in an instance of *paraleipsis* (see above):

> But we have no idea, just now, of persecuting the Tittlebats [*tapinosis*] by too
> close a scrutiny into their little opinions. It is not our purpose, for example,
> to press them with so grave a weapon as the *argumentum ad absurdum*, or to
> ask them why, if the popularity of a book be in fact the measure of its worth,
> we should not be at once in condition to admit the inferiority of "Newton's
> Principia" to "Hoyle's Games;" of "Earnest Maltravers" to "Jack-the-Giant-
> Killer," or "Jack Sheppard," or "Jack Brag;" and of "Dick's Christian Philoso-
> pher" to "Charlotte Temple," or the "Memoirs of de Grammont," or to one
> or two dozen other works which must be nameless. (11: 40)

Pronunciation: re DUC ti o ad ab SUR dum
Type: techniques of argument

RESTRICTIO: excepting part of a statement already made:

> "True! – nervous – very, very dreadfully nervous I had been and am; but why
> *will* you say that I am mad?" ("The Tell-Tale Heart," 5: 88)

See chapter 2 for a discussion of the narrator's strategic use of *restrictio*
(along with *paromologia*) in the context of his forensic oratory. This is a
highly rhetorical device, and that it can be found in Poe's literary criticism should not surprise us:

> "Vocal music," says L'Abbate Gravina, "ought to imitate the natural language
> of the human feelings and passions, rather than the warbling of Canary birds,
> which our singers, now-a-days, affect so vastly to mimic with their quaver-
> ings and boasted cadences." **This is true only so far as the "rather" is con-
> cerned.** (Review of *George P. Morris*, 10: 42)

Pronunciation: re STRIC ti o
Type: techniques of argument

RETICENTIA: telling or requesting someone to shut up; a warning
to speak no more. This device hardly needs an example, but I give one
anyway:

> *Castiglione.* 'T was a mistake? – undoubtedly – we all
> Do err at times.
> *Politian.* Draw, villain, and **prate no more!** ("Politian," 7: 77)

Several rhetors consider this device similar to *aposiopesis* (above).
Pronunciation: re ti CEN ti a
Type: devices of vehemence

RHETORICAL QUESTION: a question asked without requiring an answer. We can distinguish between four kinds, all of which are defined above:

- *epiplexis*
- *erotema* (sometimes called *erotesis*)
- *hypophora*
- *ratiocinatio*

A rhetorical question is asked not to elicit information but to express emotion, as with *erotema* and *epiplexis*. One of Poe's most vehement reviews – on Griswold's *The Poets and Poetry of America* – is absolutely loaded with rhetorical questions (11: 220–43); they are largely responsible for its emotional *bite*. Corbett says the rhetorical question also "can be an effective persuasive device, subtly influencing the kind of response one wants to get from an audience"; thus, it can be more effective than a direct assertion (454). In fact, Dupriez says a rhetorical question is a "disguised assertion" (370). At the same time, the rhetorical question challenges the members of an audience and makes them more alert, as Corbett rightly points out (292). To the four above, we might add

- *pysma*
- *subjectio*

For the first, see above; for the second, see below.

RIGHT-BRANCHING SENTENCE: a sentence that begins with a main (independent) clause followed by at least one dependent clause. The R-B sentence is also called a "loose" or "unsuspended" sentence and is complete grammatically well before the end; the material that follows in the dependent clause(s) seems incidental:

> I knew what the old man felt, and pitied him, although I chuckled at heart.
>
> ("The Tell-Tale Heart," 5: 90)

See also "left-branching sentence," above. As a *left*-branching sentence the above excerpt would begin with the dependent rather than the independent clauses, and would read, "Although I chuckled at heart, and pitied him, I knew what the old man felt." Poe's use of both left- and right-branching sentences shows his stylistic versatility (see chapter 1).

In his review of *Spain Revisited*, Poe loses patience with a right-branching sentence that is too long, too loose. He quotes from the book and then comments (*epicrisis*):

"Carts, and wagons, caravans of mules, and files of humbler asses came pouring, by various roads, into the great vomitory by which we were entering, laden with the various commodities, the luxuries as well as the necessaries of life, brought from foreign countries or from remote provinces, to sustain the unnatural existence of a capital which is so remote from all its resources, and which produces scarce anything that it consumes."

This sentence, although it would not be too long, if properly managed, is too long as it stands. The ear repeatedly seeks, and expects the conclusion, and is repeatedly disappointed. It expects the close at the word *"entering"* – and at the word *"life"* – at the word *"provinces"* – and at the word *"resources."* Each additional portion of the sentence after each of the words just designated by inverted commas, has the air of an after-thought engrafted upon the original idea. (9: 9–10)

That last observation is a good description of the right-branching sentence structure. Perhaps we can conclude from this passage that Poe generally disapproved of sentences that were too "loose," too "unsuspended."

SARCASMUS: (*sarcasmos*) mockery, sneering, scoffing – a "bitter jibe or taunt" (Lanham, 135). This device does not necessarily have to involve irony (Sonnino, 124), as our word *sarcasm* suggests, but when it does Espy notes (130) that the irony is bitter. We find an instance of sarcasm in Poe's review of *Lafitte: The Pirate of the Gulf*:

Count D' Oyley ... makes his escape from the rendezvous with his mistress and Juana. In so doing he has *only* [my italics] to dress his mistress as a man, and himself as a woman, to descend a precipice, to make a sentinel at the mouth of the cave drunk, and so walk over him – make another drunk in Lafitte's schooner, and so walk over him – walk over some forty or fifty of the crew on deck – and finally to walk off with the longboat. These things are trifles with a man of genius – and an author should never let slip an opportunity of displaying his invention. (9: 109–10)

See also the discussion of *sarcasmus* in chapter 5.
Pronunciation: sar CAS mus
Type: devices of vehemence

SCESIS ONOMATON: (1) a group of words (mostly nouns and adjectives) that might be a full sentence were it not for the complete lack of verbs – in other words, what we call a sentence fragment:

> Then the ardent, the eager, the simple-minded, the generous and the devoted
> Mary Musgrove! (Review of *Horse-Shoe Robinson*, 8: 8)

Now and then we do find the occasional fragment in Poe's criticism. This,
I am sure, is not a matter of oversight on his part but a stylistic licence he
allows himself. With *scesis onomaton*, often each single noun has a single
adjective joined to it, which would make for syntactical parallelism. Both
Espy and Sonnino treat this term as a single word: *scesisonomaton*.

(2) Another definition provided by Lanham is: "Using a string of synonymous expressions" (135):

> It has the air of a **happy chance**, of a **God-send**, of an **ultra-accident**, in-
> vented by the playwright by way of compromise for his lack of invention.
> ("The American Drama," 13: 68)

We may wonder how that definition differs from *synonymia* – amplification by synonym (Lanham, 149) – *periergia* (see above), *iteratio* (above),
and *commoratio* (above).

Pronunciation: SCE sis o NO ma ton

Type: ungrammatical, illogical, or unusual uses of language

SCHEMATISMUS: circuitous speech to conceal a meaning. The desire to be indirect may arise for several reasons: fear or politeness; a wish
to please the auditor(s) with figurative rather than direct language; a
sense of fun; or, if we believe Poe's definition of the "imp of the perverse," a longing to act against one's own best interests (perhaps in a
perverse and daring kind of fun):

> There lives no man who at some period has not been tormented ... by an
> earnest desire to tantalize a listener by circumlocution. The speaker is aware
> that he displeases; he has every intention to please; he is usually curt, precise,
> and clear; the most laconic and luminous language is struggling for utterance
> upon his tongue ... he dreads and deprecates the anger of him whom he ad-
> dresses; yet, the thought strikes him, that by certain involutions and paren-
> theses, this anger may be engendered. ("The Imp of the Perverse," 6: 148)

In the following letter to "Annie" (January 1849), Poe uses *schematismus*
almost certainly for the sake of politeness, delicacy – he is alluding to his
suicide attempt (see Ostrom, 402):

> The reports, if any such there be – may have arisen, however, from **what I
> did in Providence on that terrible day – you know what I mean**: – Oh – I
> shudder even to think of it. (Ostrom, 418)

Cf *periphrasis, noema,* and *enigma.*
Pronunciation: sche ma TIS mus

SERIATION : a scheme of repetition involving setting together grammatically parallel units – words, phrases, clauses, sentences – in groups of two,
three, or more (Cluett/Kampeas, 52). Nominal seriation is foregrounded in
"The Man of the Crowd," but I offer the following example from *Pym* exemplifying the seriation of single words – it is a list, a catalogue:

> He had on board, as usual in such voyages, **beads, looking-glasses, tinder-
> works, axes, hatchets, saws, adzes, planes, chisels, gouges, gimlets, files,
> spokeshaves, rasps, hammers, nails, knives, scissors, razors, needles, thread,
> crockery-ware, calico, trinkets, and other similar articles.** *(The Narrative of
> Arthur Gordon Pym of Nantucket,* 3: 149)

Like *epicrisis* (see above), catalogues of nouns (nominal seriation) are
found now and then in *Pym* functioning as part of Poe's strategy of verisimilitude (what he termed the "plausible or verisimilar style"); that is,
when he lists nautical items and species of flora and fauna, for example,
he is attempting to give his readers the impression that the antarctic voyage Pym describes is a factual account and not fiction. *Pym* is, of course,
a hoax, but surely Poe's attention to detail, his catalogues, give the appearance of truth that must have fooled some of his readers into believing Pym's fantastic account a matter of truth rather than imagination.
Poe's strategy is the same in another nautical hoax, "MS. Found in a
Bottle": there Poe provides details of the stowage of the narrator's vessel
with nominal seriation:

> She was freighted with **cotton-wool and oil**, from the Lachadive islands. We
> had also on board **coir, jaggeree, ghee, cocoa-nuts, and a few cases of opium.**
> (2: 2)

According to Claude Richard (as translated by Mark L. Mitchell), "all of
the provisions stocked on board really come from the Lacquedive Islands
– the list is found, moreover, in the *Encyclopedia Brittanica*" (192).

In addition to lists of nouns, as above, we can also find verbal, adjectival, and adverbial seriation, for instance. Here is some adjectival seriation (which also constitutes *bdelygma* – see above) from the same novel:

> In truth, from everything I could see of these wretches, they appeared to be
> the most **wicked, hypocritical, vindictive, bloodthirsty, and altogether
> fiendish** race of men upon the face of the globe. (234)

Espy's term for a piling up of adjectives is *synathroesmus* (137). Here is some adverbial seriation from *The Literati of New York City*:

> The "Anastasis" is **lucidly, succinctly, vigorously** and **logically** written.
> ("George Bush," 15: 6)

Seriation can mean more than simply lists of nouns, verbs, adjectives, and adverbs, however; it can involve a complex catalogue of several types of couplings (doublets, triplets), repetition, and grammatical parallelism – for instance, *anaphora, antistrophe, epanaphora, epistrophe, isocolon, parison*. The catalogue as a whole can be fairly regular or more "chaotic," irregular, asymmetrical. It can also involve several types of minus additioning, including *ellipsis, syllepsis,* and the various types of *zeugma*. Its clauses might end with either neutral or satirical continuators. It might also display much end-linkage. All of these features (and more) have been identified – brilliantly, I think – by Louis T. Milic in the catalogues of Jonathan Swift. Here is a long catalogue from "The Man of the Crowd" embodying many of the aforementioned features that characterize Swift's own inventories:

> Descending in the scale of what is termed gentility, I found darker and deeper themes for speculation. I saw Jew pedlars, with hawk eyes flashing from countenances whose every other feature wore only an expression of abject humility; sturdy professional street beggars scowling upon mendicants of a better stamp, whom despair alone had driven forth into the night for charity; feeble and ghastly invalids, upon whom death had placed a sure hand, and who sidled and tottered through the mob, looking every one beseechingly in the face, as if in search of some chance consolation, some lost hope; modest young girls returning from long and late labor to a cheerless home, and shrinking more tearfully than indignantly from the glances of ruffians, whose direct contact, even, could not be avoided; women of the town of all kinds and of all ages – the unequivocal beauty in the prime of her womanhood, putting one in mind of the statue in Lucian, with the surface of Parian marble, and the interior filled with filth – the loathsome and utterly lost leper in rags – the wrinkled, bejewelled and paint-begrimed beldame, making a lost effort at youth – the mere child of immature form, yet, from long association, an adept in the dreadful coquetries of her trade, and burning with a rabid ambition to be ranked the equal of her elders in vice; drunkards innumerable and indescribable – some in shreds and patches, reeling, inarticulate, with bruised visage and lack-lustre eyes – some in whole although filthy garments, with a slightly unsteady swagger, thick sen-

sual lips, and hearty-looking rubicund faces – others clothed in materials which had once been good, and which even now were scrupulously well brushed – men who walked with a more than naturally firm and springy step, but whose countenances were fearfully pale, whose eyes hideously wild and red, and who clutched with quivering fingers, as they strode through the crowd, at every object which came within their reach; beside these, pie-men, porters, coal-heavers, sweeps; organ-grinders, monkey-exhibiters and ballad mongers, those who vended with those who sang; ragged artizans and ex-hausted laborers of every description, and all full of a noisy and inordinate vi-vacity which jarred discordantly upon the ear, and gave an aching sensation to the eye. (4: 138–9)

Below, I have schematized the passage the better to show the types of seria-tion – the doublets (which are underlined) and triplets (doubly under-lined) – and schemes of repetition, parallelism, and minus additioning.

Descending in the scale of what is termed gentility, I found <u>darker and deeper</u> themes for speculation.

I saw Jew pedlars, with hawk eyes flashing from countenances whose ev-ery other feature wore only an expression of abject humility;

[I saw] sturdy professional street beggars scowling upon <u>mendicants of a better stamp, whom</u> despair alone had driven forth into the night for charity;

[I saw] <u>feeble and ghastly</u> <u>invalids, upon whom</u> death had placed a sure hand, and who <u>sidled and tottered</u> through the mob, looking every one beseechingly in the face, as if in search of some chance consola-tion, some lost hope;

[I saw] modest young girls returning from <u>long and late</u> labor to a cheerless home, and shrinking more tearfulLY than indignantLY from the glances of <u>ruffians, whose</u> direct contact, even, could not be avoided;

HOMOIOPTOTON

[I saw] women of the town of all kinds and of all ages

(1) – the unequivocal beauty in the prime of her womanhood, put-ting one in mind of the statue in Lucian, with the surface of Parian marble, and the interior filled with filth

(2) – **the** loathsome and utterly lost leper in rags

DIAERESIS

ANAPHORA

(3) – **the** <u>wrinkled, bejewelled and paint-begrimed</u> beldame, making a lost effort at youth

(4) – the mere child of immature form, yet, from long association, an adept in the dreadful coquetries of her trade, and burning with a rabid ambition to be ranked the equal of her elders in vice;

[I saw] drunkards <u>innumerABLE and indescribABLE</u>

$\boxed{\text{HOMOIOPTOTON}}$

(1) – some in <u>shreds and patches</u>, reeling, inarticulate, with bruised visage   and

                                               lack-lustre eyes

DIAERESIS

(2) – some in whole although filthy garments, with a <u>slightLY un-steady swagger, thick sensual lips, and hearty-looking rubicund faces</u>

(3) – others clothed in materials which had once been good, and which even now were scrupulousLY well brushed

(4) – men $\boxed{\text{HOMOIOPTOTON}}$

ANAPHORA

who walked with a more than naturalLY <u>firm and springy</u> step,   but

whose countenances were fearfulLY pale,

whose eyes [were] hideousLY <u>wild and red</u>, and

$\boxed{\text{PROZEUGMA}}$

who clutched with quivering fingers, as they strode through the crowd, at every object which came within their reach;

[I saw] beside these,

pie-men,

portERS, $\boxed{\text{HOMOIOTELEUTON}}$

coal-heavERS,

sweeps;

[I saw] organ-grindERS,

monkey-exhibitERS   and $\boxed{\text{HOMOIOTELEUTON}}$

ballad mongERS,

$\boxed{\text{PLOCE}}$ those who vended   with

                  those who sang;

[I saw] ragged   artizans   and

exhausted laborers

    of every description, and all full of a <u>noisy and inordinate</u> vivac-ity which

        jarred discordantly   upon   the ear,   and

        gave an aching sensation   to   the eye.

NOMINAL SERIATION

In this catalogue, which is one of the most stylistically interesting passages in Poe's prose, we have schemes of verbal and phonetic repetition, syntactical parallelism, and smaller inventories within the larger inventory. The whole is controlled by a scheme of omission, *prozeugma* (the missing but understood phrase "I saw" after each semicolon) but schemes of amplification especially abound. The whole is an amplification of the opening phrase "themes for speculation," and within the particularization of that phrase are yet other particularizations (*diaeresis*), the first of which follows "women of the town" (of which the narrator provides four types). Some syntactical parallelism is maintained with the repetition at the beginning of each clause of the determiner-article *the*. The second instance of *diaeresis* follows the phrase "drunkards innumerable and indescribable," and again we are given four types. Then we are given some nominal seriation following the phrase "beside these." Thus, within the category of humanity we have further sub-categories.

While the narrator is breaking down the population into sub-types, he is simultaneously giving a sense of the *oneness* of the whole through his use of punctuation. Poe's use of the dash here is a bit unorthodox: he uses it to separate sub-types between semicolons. He could have used periods in place of the semicolons and semicolons in place of the dashes – but the use of periods especially would have intensified the sense of *separateness* to the individuals in the catalogue. The virtue of omitting periods and linking the various human types in the inventory (a sentence a page and a half long!) is to provide a sense of the *unbroken flow of humanity* moving past the narrator's coffee-house window – a *sea* of flesh and colour (and note this extended metaphor at work). Also connecting the individuals in this unbroken flow of humanity, in addition to the punctuation, is the occasional use of end-linkage ("mendicants of a better stamp, whom"; "invalids, upon whom"; "ruffians, whose") – see the dotted underlining. Thus, while Poe's use of amplification takes this mass of humanity and breaks it down into *particulars* (*diaeresis*, nominal seriation), his use of punctuation and end-linkage simultaneously provides or restores a sense of the *whole*, of *connectedness*.

Large catalogues like this often depend on schemes of repetition and syntactical balance, parallelism; seriation, after all, by definition, involves these. The missing but understood phrase "I saw" after each semicolon provides an implied *anaphora* (initial repetition), and we do get some explicitly anaphoric repetition/parallelism with "whose countenances were fearfully pale, whose eyes hideously." A sense of balance is also present in the many doublets, while phonetic repetition and parallelism appear in the instances of *homoioptoton* and *homoioteleuton*. Other instances of phonological repetition are found in the several alliterations, most of which involve the letter *l* ("long and late"; "loathsome and utterly lost leper"). Finally, syntactical parallelism is assured through such couplings as "bruised visage and lack-lustre eyes," "those who vended with those who sang," "ragged artizans and exhausted laborers," "jarred discordantly upon the ear, and gave an aching sensation to the eye."

All in all, like Swift's catalogues (as Milic has shown), this one contains frequent doublets, end-linkage, seriation, some syntactical regularity through verbal and phonetic repetition and schemes of balance, some minus additioning, and *asyndeton*. The inventory as a whole is irregular, syntactically asymmetrical, but within this chaotic heap of words we find small instances of syntactical symmetry – balance, parallelism. One wonders whether Poe had been inspired, stylistically, by the prose of Swift for "The Man of the Crowd."

Pronunciation: ser i A tion

Type: amplification

Type: balance, antithesis, paradox

Type: description

Type: "verisimilar"

SERMOCINATIO: answering the remarks or questions of a pretended interlocutor:

> But if it be asked – "What is the design – the end – the aim of English
> Grammar?" our obvious answer is, "The art of speaking and writing the
> English language correctly:". ("The Rationale of Verse," 14: 212–13)

This device as Poe uses it, above, compares with *praemunitio* (defending yourself from an anticipated attack), but I would say that *sermocinatio* does not necessarily involve a defence; *praemunitio* always does (cf *prolepsis*). We can also see that *sermocinatio* compares with *hypophora* (providing answers to your own rhetorical questions – see above); *dialogismus* (speaking in another person's character – see above); and the second definition, given above, of *ethopoeia*. Dupriez relates *sermocinatio* to the interior dialogue (131–2). Espy quotes ancient rhetors to whom the device meant feigning the

remarks or questions of actual persons: "Cicero … gave meet speech to the person whom he feigned to speak, whether he were his adversary or his friend. He brought in Milo speaking valiantly; Anthony arrogantly; Nevius wickedly; Erutius impudently – ever framing their speech according to their nature" (203). The example from Poe, on the other hand, does not feign a question from any particular person known to Poe, but I assume it exemplifies *sermocinatio* nevertheless. Sonnino quotes Erasmus as saying that this "figure is found in histories, but is more common in the poets" (168). Certainly it is found often in *Eureka*, which John P. Hussey considers a kind of classical oration; and as such, it necessarily contains a section characterized by *refutatio*, the refutation of imagined or real objections – the fifth of the six parts of a classical speech. *Sermocinatio* is part of that section.
Pronunciation: ser mo ci NA ti o
Type: techniques of argument

S I M I L E : explicit comparison of two unlike things using either *like* or *as*:
 I bounded **like** a madman through the crowded thoroughfares. ("The Imp of the Perverse," 6: 152)

Poe appears to have believed that this most well known of tropes could function in more than merely an ornamental way: in "The Purloined Letter" he has his detective, Dupin, note that "some color of truth has been given to the rhetorical dogma, that metaphor, or simile, may be made to strengthen an argument, as well as to embellish a description" (6: 47); however, Poe asserts that this "dogma" is *false* in an 1841 review of Dickens (10: 143). Still, Poe does not like similes much; in his Marginalia he writes, "Direct similes are of too palpably artificial a character to be artistical. An artist will always contrive to weave his illustrations into the metaphorical form" (16: 27). He elaborates in his review of *Alciphron: A Poem*:

 Similes (so much insisted upon by the critics of the reign of Queen Anne) are never, in our opinion, strictly in good taste, whatever may be said to the contrary, and certainly can never be made to accord with other high qualities, except when naturally arising from the subject in the way of illustration – and, when thus arising, they have seldom the merit of novelty. To be novel, they must fail in essential particulars. The higher minds will avoid their frequent use. They form no portion of the ideal, and appertain to the fancy alone. (10: 68)

We now know why we do not find a lot of similes in Poe's works, given his "higher" mind. Nevertheless, we do find the occasional simile even in Poe's literary criticism:

> How truthful an air of deep lamentation hangs here upon every gentle sylla-ble! It pervades all. It comes over the sweet melody of the words, over the gentleness and grace which we fancy in the little maiden herself, even over the half-playful, half-petulant air with which she lingers on the beauties and good qualities of her favorite – like the cool shadow of a summer cloud over a bed of lilies and violets. (Review of *The Book of Gems*, 9: 102)

Here is a nasty one from Poe's review of *Guy Fawkes*:

> We say, however, that from all that appears in the novel in question, he may be as really ignorant as a bear. (10: 216)

One place where Poe provides a great many similes, many more than we might expect from him, is in the mawkish and highly puffed review of *The Dream, and Other Poems*, by a female poet (10: 103–4). Poe was ob-viously willing to ignore his usual credo about similes for the sake of a poetess. Still, he insisted that, when used, they must be wholly appropri-ate and not bathetic; after quoting from *Poems*, by William A. Lord, he says, "The disfiguration to which we allude, lies in the making a blazing altar burn merely like a blazing cresset – a simile about as forcible as would be the likening an apple to a pear, or the sea-foam to the froth on a pitcher of Burton's ale" (12: 149).

Pronunciation: SI mi le

Type: description

Type: metaphorical substitutions and puns

SOLECISMUS (adjective: solecistic): a type of *enallage* (see above) – speaking incorrectly because of the ignorant misuse of cases, genders, and tenses (Lanham, 142). Lanham notes that the term referred originally to words used improperly in combination while *barbarismus* (see above) re-ferred to an error in a single word (cf malapropism). In Poe's "The Specta-cles," we get a sample of the bad English of a French lady, Eugénie Lalande:

> Monsieur Simpson vill pardonne me for not compose de butefulle tong of his contrée so vell as might. It is only de late dat I am arrive, and not yet ave de opportunité for to – l'étudier.
>
> Vid dis apologie for de manière, I vill now say dat, hélas! – Monsieur Simpson ave guess but de too true. Need I say de more? Hélas! am I not ready speak de too moshe? (5: 191)

In his review of Mrs Norton's *The Dream, and Other Poems,* Poe displays his familiarity with the term *solecism,* and its meaning, in comparing Mrs Norton with another British poetess, Mrs Hemans:

> Mrs. Norton will now and then be betrayed into a carelessness of diction; Mrs. Hemans was rarely, if ever, guilty of such solecisms. Such expressions, for instance, as the "harbouring" land, the "guiding" hand, the "pausing" heart, the "haunting" shade, and others of like character, taken at random from the volume before us, though not strictly improper, yet, as they are plainly expletive, and weaken, instead of strengthening a sentence, are never to be found in the poems of Mrs. Hemans, or of any one "learned in the craft." (10: 100–1; see also 12: 133)

For brief but interesting discussions of the term, see Dupriez (424–5) and Holman/Harmon (487). For another example, see under *barbarismus.*
Pronunciation: so le CIS mus
Type: ungrammatical, illogical, or unusual uses of language

SORAISMUS (sometimes spelled *soroesmus*): mingling languages either through ignorance or a desire to show off – or, I would add, for the sake of *linguistic playfulness.* Poe's prose is sprinkled liberally with instances of *soraismus* – this is one reason why some commentators despise his writing as pretentious. The first detective in literature, Poe's brilliant but arrogant and pretentious C. Auguste Dupin, is guilty of this kind of accumulation now and then, and if we do not want to accuse Dupin of showing off, we might at least accuse Poe:

> "'*Il y a à parier,*'" replied Dupin, quoting from Chamfort, "'*que toute idée publique, toute convention reçue, est une sottise, car elle a convenu au plus grand nombre.*' The mathematicians, I grant you, have done their best to promulgate the popular error to which you allude, and which is none the less an error for its promulgation as truth. With an art worthy a better cause, for example, they have insinuated the term 'analysis' into application to algebra. The French are the originators of this particular deception; but if a term is of any importance – if words derive any value from applicability – then 'analysis' conveys 'algebra' about as much as, in Latin, '*ambitus*' implies 'ambition,' '*religio*' 'religion,' or '*homines honesti,*' a set of *honorable* men." ("The Purloined Letter," 6: 43–4)

This *soraismus* involves a mingling of English, French, and Latin. Poe began learning both Latin and French (as well as Greek) when a schoolboy in England between his seventh and twelfth year (1815–20); back in Richmond, Virginia, his foreign-language studies continued at the English and Classical School. As a seventeen-year-old (1826), he entered the University of Virginia, enrolling in the schools of ancient and modern languages. Poe "was a member of the classes in Latin and Greek, French, Spanish, and Italian, and attended them regularly" (Woodberry, 26). By the end of the academic term, in December, "Poe came home with the highest honors in Latin and French" (Woodberry, 29; see also the Harrison biography in *The Collected Works* and *The Poe Log*, by Thomas and Jackson). For more thorough investigations of Poe's multilingual talents, see Emma Katherine Norman, "Poe's Knowledge of Latin," and Edith Philips, "The French of Edgar Allan Poe." Poe may also have known German, although scholars disagree about this point. Yet, in an article on "Secret Writing," Poe challenged readers of *Graham's Magazine* to send in ciphers, "and the key-phrase may be either in French, Italian, Spanish, German, Latin, or Greek, (or in any of the dialects of these languages,) and we pledge ourselves for the solution of the riddle" (14: 124).

In a letter to his friend Frederick Thomas, we find Poe discussing language acquisition and recommending what we call today *French immersion*. At the same time, the comments suggest something about how Poe himself may have studied and picked up foreign languages:

Touching your study of the French language. You will, I fear, find it difficult – as, (if I rightly understood you,) you have not received what is called a "classical" education. To the Latin & Greek proficient, the study of all additional languages is mere play – but to the non-proficient it is anything else. The best advice I can give you, under the circumstances, is to busy yourself with the theory or grammar of the language as little as possible & to read *side-by-side* translations continually, of which there are many to be found. I mean French books in which the literal English version is annexed page per page. Board, also, at a French boarding-house, and force yourself to speak French – bad or good – whether you can or whether you *cannot*. (Ostrom, 190; see also 192)

Dupriez never mentions the term *soraismus* but does give us *peregrinism* – "The use of linguistic elements borrowed from a foreign language. Elements include: the sound system, graphy, and sentence-melodies as well as grammatical, lexical, or syntactic forms, and even meanings and connotations" (332). A synonym is "foreignism" and, as the passage above shows, many foreignisms are found in Poe's works. Certainly he employs many Gallicisms (French introduced into English), Latinisms, and some Germanisms.

Although he does not use the term, Richard Fletcher considers Poe's use of *soraismus* as part of his "third vocabulary," which depends on allusions and analogies:

> Critics frequently comment, usually in disparaging terms, on his insistence at using French or German expressions in his writing, as well as his inclination to pepper his pages with Latin and Greek epigrams. Certainly the tradition in English literature had been a strong one up to Poe's time, the familar essay of the early nineteenth century being a medium that was peculiarly dependent for effect on the ability of its author to quote at fluent length from the most diverse sources in English, French and Classical prosody, while establishing recondite metaphorical allusions and analogies from the most diverse sources and fields. To the extent that Poe regarded himself as an equivalent American familiar essayist he would of course be justified in imitating the tendencies and techniques of the English Romanticists. (76)

For instance, we have this from his review of *Our Amateur Poets*, No. III:

> We may convey some general idea of them [William Ellery Channing's mistakes] by two foreign terms not in common use – the Italian *pavoneggiarsi*, "to strut like a peacock," and the German word for "sky-rocketing," *schwärmerei*. (11: 174–5)

In "How to Write a Blackwood Article," however, Poe shows his willingness to make fun of *soraismus* – of writers who show off by writing in or quoting from foreign languages. He has Mr Blackwood give the following advice to Miss Psyche Zenobia, a budding writer:

> "There's nothing goes down so well, especially with the help of a little Latin … ' *The venerable Chinese novel Ju-Kiao-Li*.' Good! By introducing these few words with dexterity you will evince your intimate acquaintance with the language and literature of the Chinese. With the aid of this you may possibly get along without either Arabic, or Sanscrit, or Chickasaw. There is no passing muster, however, without Spanish, Italian, German, Latin, and Greek." (2: 278)

For an extended study of how Poe ridicules some of the very tricks he himself employs in prose, in relation to "How to Write a Blackwood Article" and the companion piece "A Predicament: the Scythe of Time," see McElrath's "Poe's Conscious Prose Technique."

While Poe in all seriousness employs foreignisms in his own prose but ridicules the use of *soraismus* in the abstract, in a literary review he also condemns another author for that device – or *vice*. Referring to Bulwer's *Night and Morning*, he says this:

Among the *niaiseries* of his style we mention the coxcombical use of little French sentences, without a shadow of an excuse for their employment … And again, when, at page 49, Fanny exclaims, *"Méchant,* every one dies to Fanny!"* why could not this heroine as well confined herself to one language? At page 38 the climax of absurdity, in this respect, is fairly capped; and it is difficult to keep one's countenance, when we read of a Parisian cobbler breathing his last in a garret, and screaming out, *"Je m' étouffe* – air!"* (10: 129) He also ridicules a poet for his use of Latinisms: "Now, no one is presupposed to be cognizant of any language beyond his own; to be ignorant of Latin is no crime; to pretend a knowledge is beneath contempt" (Review of *The Poetry of Rufus Dawes,* 11: 137).
Pronunciation: so ra IS mus
Type: example, allusion, and citation of authority
Type: ungrammatical, illogical, or unusual uses of language

SUBJECTIO: the questioner suggests the answer to his or her own question (Lanham, 145). In his cruel magazine review of Griswold's third edition of *The Poets and Poetry of America,* Poe attacks Griswold using *subjectio*:

Why was Frederick W. Thomas insulted with a place as the author of *one* song, among the miscellaneous writers, after his having been written to, and "his biography and best articles" solicited? **Was it not because he did not obey your dictatorial and impertinent request to write *for you* the biography of Mrs. Welby?** (11: 240)

We may indeed wonder how *subjectio* differs from another type of rhetorical question, *hypophora* (asking questions then answering them). Sonnino considers the terms synonymous (173–4). Judging solely by Lanham's definition, I might suggest that we differentiate between them by considering *subjectio* a question answered with another question (which shows the answer to be diffidently proposed – as in Poe's use of it, above), while considering *hypophora* a question answered with a statement (which shows the answer to be confidently proposed).
Pronunciation: sub JEC ti o
Type: techniques of argument

SYLLEPSIS: a kind of minus additioning in which a verb agrees grammatically with only one of the subject-nouns or subject-pronouns it governs. Because this device involves a breakdown in grammatical congruence, it is a stylistic vice, an error. In the following example I place a caret where the missing verb *was* should be. Read it with the omitted verb to see the grammatical incongruence:

> His forehead **was** lofty and very fair; his nose [was] a snub; his eyes /\ large, heavy, glassy and meaningless. ("Mystification," 4: 103)

Clearly, the verb *was* agrees with the first singular subjects, *forehead* and *nose*, but not with the second subject, the plural noun *eyes*. Poe makes the same error in "The Poetic Principle":

> And just as the lily **is** repeated in the lake, or the eyes of Amaryllis [is repeated] in the lake. (14: 273)

Some confusion exists on the part of rhetors regarding the definitions of and distinction between *syllepsis* and *zeugma*. While I agree with the definitions of Lanham (145) and Cluett/Kampeas (54), Corbett offers several examples of *zeugma* that he labels *syllepsis* (448), and Dupriez correctly points out the error (440). Cf *ellipsis, prozeugma,* and *zeugma.*

Even though his own grammar could slip now and then (see also 10: 89), Poe ridicules an instance of *syllepsis* in Theodore S. Fay's novel *Norman Leslie.* Poe, after calling Fay's style "unworthy of a school-boy" (8: 60), provides this passage from the novel: "'You are both right and both wrong – you, Miss Romani, [are both right and both wrong] to judge so harshly of all men who are not versed in the easy elegance of the drawing room, and your father [are both right and both wrong] in too great *lenity* towards men of sense, &c'." Poe continues: "This is really something new [no, it is *not*], but we are sorry to say, something incomprehensible. Suppose we translate it." Then Poe rewrites the passage, quite correctly doing away with the *syllepsis*: "'You are both right and both wrong – you, Miss Romani, *are both right and wrong* [Poe's italics] to judge so harshly of all not versed in the elegance of the drawing-room, &c; and your father *is both right and wrong* [Poe's italics] in too great lenity towards men of sense'" (61).

Pronunciation: syl LEP sis
Type: subtraction: words, phrases, and clauses
Type: brevity
Type: ungrammatical, illogical, or unusual uses of language

SYMPLOCE: a scheme of repetition involving the use of *anaphora* and *epistrophe* together – that is, a succession of clauses having the same beginning and ending:

In the deepest slumber – **no**! **In** delirium – **no**! **In** a swoon – **no**! **In** death –
no! even in the grave all is not lost. ("The Pit and the Pendulum," 5: 68–9)
Symploce can involve exact or nearly exact parallel grammatical structure,
as in the above excerpt. All schemes of repetition can be used to suggest
vehemence, heightened emotions.
Pronunciation: SYM plo see
Type: balance, antithesis, paradox
Type: devices of vehemence
Type: repetition: words

SYNAERESIS: see under *synalepha*.

SYNALEPHA: a kind of elision – omitting letters so that two words
are joined:
Doth o'er us pass, when, as **th'expanding** eye [etc.]. ("Stanzas," 7: 18)
Quinn says that essentially any contraction is a *synalepha* – *don't*, *it's*,
can't, and so on (*Figures of Speech*, 22). See under *syncope* and *elision* for
Poe's attitude toward any kind of omissions in poetry. That he does not
approve, despite his own use of the device, is demonstrated by some remarks he makes in his review of the poem *Orion*. After quoting several
lines, in one of which "*th' excrescence*" figures, Poe refers to this as "a very
blameable concision" (11: 262).
Lanham (147) reminds us that Quintilian considered *synalepha* synonymous with *synaeresis*, which means "drawing together, contraction" –
"Pronouncing as a diphthong two adjacent vowels that belong to different
syllables within a single word: Phaethon" (146). Interestingly, Poe shows
his awareness of the idea of *synaeresis* in *Eureka* when he mentions Alexander Von Humboldt's *Cosmos*: "His design is simply synœretical" (16:
187). In "The Rationale of Verse," he defines the term: "*Blending* is the
plain English for *synæresis* – but there should be *no* blending" (14: 231).
Pronunciation: syn a LE pha
Type: addition, subtraction, and substitution: letters and syllables
Type: ungrammatical, illogical, or unusual uses of language

SYNATHROESMUS (*synathrismos*): a heaping up of words – see *congeries*, *accumulatio*, seriation. Some rhetors note that the term involves
giving details then gathering them up to recapitulate (for example,

Joseph, 117). Sonnino discusses it under different headings with subtle distinctions (56–7); see also Taylor (128). Dupriez considers the device as *accumulatio* (9–12). Espy, however, insists on defining *synathroesmus* as a piling up of adjectives (137; and see *epitheton*). Here is an exemplification from one of the more rhetorically rich passages in Poe's literary criticism:

> For what are the **inane** and **purchased** adulations which fall to the lot of the conqueror – what, even, are the **extensive** honours of the **popular** author – his **far-reaching** fame, his **high** influence, or the **most devout public** appreciation of his works – to that **rapturous** approbation, that **spontaneous, instant, present,** and **palpable** applause – those **irrepressible** acclamations, those **eloquent** sighs and tears, which the **idolized** Malibran at once heard, and saw, and deeply felt that she deserved? (Review of *Memoirs and Letters of Madame Malibran*, 10: 91)

Pronunciation: syn a THROES mus
Type: amplification
Type: description

SYNCHISIS (*synchysis; confusio*): see under *anoiconometon*.
Pronunciation: SYN chi sis

SYNCHORESIS: "The speaker gives his questioner leave to judge him" (Lanham, 147):

> I have then to refute only the accusation of mangling by wholesale – and I refute it by the simplest reference to *fact*. **What I have written remains; and is readily accessible in any of our public libraries.** ("The Longfellow War," 12: 85)

This is an implicit rather than explicit invitation to the questioner, "Outis," to judge Poe – whether he has mangled "by wholesale" the works he reviewed – by visiting the libraries and reading for himself what Poe indeed wrote.
Pronunciation: syn cho RE sis
Type: techniques of argument

SYNCOPE: removing a letter(s) or a syllable(s) from the middle of a word to contract it – obviously a type of *elision* (see Harmon/Holman for an interesting discussion of the device [510]). The figure appears now and then in Poe's poetry:

Helen, thy beauty is to me
  Like those Nicéan barks of yore,
That gently, **o'er** a perfumed sea. ("To Helen," 7: 46)

Here is another example:

Above the closed and fringéd lid
'Neath which thy **slumb'ring** soul lies hid. ("The Sleeper," 7: 51)

Although *syncope* appears in Poe's poetry, consider the following comments he makes in his discussion of the device in "The Rationale of Verse":

Others ... would insist upon a Procrustean adjustment thus (del'cate) – an adjustment recommended to all such words as *silvery, murmuring,* etc., which, it is said, should be not only pronounced, but written, *silv'ry, murm'ring,* and so on, whenever they find themselves in trochaic predicament. I have only to say that ... all words, at all events, should be written and pronounced *in full,* and as nearly as possible as nature intended them. (14: 232–3)

Clearly, then, even though he was forced to use it occasionally in his own poetry, Poe did not like the artificiality of *syncope* – a type of *metaplasm* (the transformation of a word) – any more than he approved of the artificiality of *hyperbaton* in poetry (see above). Neither did he like *synaeresis* – "Pronouncing as a diphthong two adjacent vowels that belong to different syllables within a single word: Pha͜eton" (Lanham, 146). As he says in "The Rationale of Verse," *"Blending* is the plain English for *synæresis* – but there should be *no* blending" (231). For more on *elision,* see under that term.

Interestingly, Poe employs the term *syncope* but with its medical rather than grammatical definition: "An occasional swoon is a thing of no consequence, but 'even Stamboul must have an end,' and Mr. Bulwer should make an end of his syncopes" (Review of *Night and Morning,* 10: 129).

Pronunciation: SYN co pe
Pronunciation: syn AE re sis
Type: addition, subtraction, and substitution: letters and syllables
Type: ungrammatical, illogical, or unusual uses of language

SYNCRISIS: comparison and contrast in two parallel clauses:
Yet differently we grew – I ill of health, and buried in gloom – she agile, graceful, and overflowing with energy; hers the ramble on the hill-side – mine the studies of the cloister – I living within my own heart, and addicted body and soul to the most intense and painful meditation – she

roaming carelessly through life with no thought of the shadows in her path, or the silent flight of the raven-winged hours. ("Berenice," 2: 18)

The device figures now and then in Poe's literary criticism as well. Considering Donne and Cowley, then Wordsworth and Coleridge, Poe writes,

> With the two former ethics were the end – with the two latter the means. The poet of the *Creation* wished, by highly artificial verse, to inculcate what he considered moral truth – he of the *Ancient Mariner* to infuse the *Poetic Sentiment* through channels suggested by mental analysis. (9: 95)

See also "parallelism" and *isocolon*.

Pronunciation: SYN cri sis

Type: balance, antithesis, paradox

SYNECDOCHE: a trope, a kind of metaphor: understanding one thing with another, substituting a part for the whole or the whole for a part. In his review of *The Drama of Exile*, Poe quotes four lines from Elizabeth Barrett's work –

> Hear the **steep generations**, how they fall
> Adown the visionary **stairs** of Time,
> Like the supernatural thunders – far, yet near,
> Sowing their fiery echoes through the hills! –

then complains about "the misapplication of 'steep,' to the 'generations,' instead of to the 'stairs' – a perversion in no degree to be justified by the fact that so preposterous a figure as *synecdoche* exists in the school books" (12: 23; see also 13: 201). That would seem to tell us what Poe's attitude toward *synecdoche* is, even though we find a similar device, *metonymy* (see above), and other metaphorical substitutions in his works (see "The Terms by Type"). For extended discussions of *synecdoche*, see Dupriez (445–7), Corbett (445–6), and Quinn (*Figures of Speech*, 56–8), and cf *antonomasia*.

Pronunciation: syn EC do che

Type: metaphorical substitutions and puns

SYNGNOME: forgiveness of injuries. In "Some Words with a Mummy," the narrator and his scientific friends attempt to revive a mummy through the use of a Voltaic pile:

> we made, upon the spot, a profound incision into the tip of the subject's nose, while the Doctor himself, laying violent hands upon it, pulled it into vehement contact with the wire.

Morally and physically – figuratively and literally – was the effect electric. In the first place, the corpse opened its eyes … turning to Messieurs Gliddon and Buckingham, it addressed them, in very capital Egyptian, thus:

"I must say, gentlemen, that I am as much surprised as I am mortified, at your behaviour. Of Doctor Ponnonner nothing better was to be expected. He is a poor little fat fool who knows no better. **I pity and forgive him.**" (6: 122–3)

We find a somewhat comedic instance in *The Literati of New York City*:

Mr. [Lewis Gaylord] Clark once did me the honor to review my poems, and – **I forgive him.** (15: 115)

Pronunciation: SYN gno me

Type: devices of vehemence

SYNONYMIA: amplification by synonym – using different words to express the same thought:

"Now, Bon-Bon, do you behold the thoughts – the **thoughts**, I say – the **ideas** – the **reflections** – which are being engendered in her pericranium?" ("Bon-Bon," 2: 138)

Synonymia compares with the second definition of *scesis onomaton*, as provided by Lanham (135), *iteratio* (above), one definition of *palilogia* (Lanham, 106), and *commoratio* (above). See also *amplificatio*. We can consider these terms synonymous, and they figure often in *Eureka*, where it seems that Poe, aware of the difficult ideas he is trying to convey, feels compelled to repeat them in different ways in an attempt to make his meaning clear.

Pronunciation: syn o NY mi a

Type: amplification

Type: repetition: clauses, phrases, and ideas

SYSTROPHE: heaping up definitions of a thing without getting to its *essence*, its *substance* (Sonnino, 58; Joseph, 109–11, 313); heaping up descriptions of a thing without defining it (Lanham, 149). In Poe's play "Politian," Lalage heaps up descriptions of America without using its name or defining it ("the northernmost continent of the Western Hemisphere, extending from Central America to the Arctic Ocean"):

Knowest thou the land

With which all tongues are busy – a land new found –

Miraculously found by one of Genoa –

A thousand leagues within the golden west?
A fairy land of flowers, and fruit, and sunshine,
And crystal lakes, and over-arching forests,
And mountains, around whose towering summits the winds
Of Heaven untrammelled flow – which air to breathe
Is Happiness now, and will be Freedom hereafter
In days that are to come? (7: 73–4)

This device is also called *conglobatio* and compares with seriation (congeries).
Pronunciation: SYS tro phe
Type: amplification
Type: description

TAPINOSIS: undignified language that debases, belittles, a person or thing. Lanham suggests that the use of this device is "generally considered a vice, not a self-conscious technique" (149), but it is easy to imagine the *deliberate* use of belittling language – as in this example:

"I have been guilty of certain **doggerel** myself." ("The Purloined Letter," 6: 34)

Sometimes the figure may belittle by exaggeration (Cuddon, 957). *Tapinosis* obviously compares with *meiosis* (see above) – Peacham calls it an excess of *meiosis*. And see Dupriez under "extenuation" and Sonnino under *humiliatio*.

Tapinosis is central to "The Literary Life of Thingum Bob, Esq.," as the editors of various magazines belittle Thingum's poetry by referring to it with such terms as *verses* and *lines*; they refer to the poet himself with such degrading terms as *poetaster* and *scribbler*. The irony, of course, is that he has plagiarized and sent excerpts from such poets as Dante, Homer, and Milton. Poe clearly seems to be suggesting his contempt for the editors of his day.

We should not be surprised to find *tapinosis* figuring now and then in Poe's occasionally scathing literary reviews:

There are many mere **versifiers** included in the selection who should have been excluded. (Review of Griswold's *The Poets and Poetry of America*, 11: 125)

Perhaps no work ever appeared whose announcement created a greater sensation among the **poetasters** of the land. (Review of Griswold's *The Poets and Poetry of America*, 11: 221)

Elsewhere he accumulates his instances of *tapinosis*:

the small geniuses – the literary Titmice – the animalculae. (Review of *Barnaby Rudge*, 11: 39)

In another place we have this:

> We are at a loss to know by what right, human or divine, **twaddle** of this character is intruded into a collection of what professes to be *Poetry.* (Review of *Our Amateur Poets,* No. I – Flaccus, 11: 163; see also 15: 260)

Somewhere else Poe refers to the "customary verbiage" of the British critics (Review of *Orion,* 11: 251).

Pronunciation: ta pi NO sis
Type: devices of vehemence
Type: metaphorical substitutions and puns

TAUTOLOGIA (tautology): the needless repetition of the same idea in different words:

> To him a *pas de papillon* has been an **abstract conception**. ("Loss of Breath," 2: 162; see also 12: 23 and 13: 201 for "abstract idea")

Here are three other examples:

> He then took a gracious leave of Mr. Butt, and **returned back** to the counting-house. (Review of *Peter Snook*, 14: 79)

> In our last number, we took occasion to say that a **didactic moral** might be happily made the *under-current* of a political theme. (Review of Longfellow's *Ballads and Other Poems*, 11: 79)

> we should have been pleased to see the vivacious defence of the dissolute Coelius, and (that last oration of the noble Roman), the fourteenth of his **indignant Philippics** against Anthony. (Review of *Select Orations of Cicero*, 9: 267)

In *Eureka* Poe provides the phrase *limited sphere*, then admits that a "sphere is *necessarily* limited" – but he defends his redundancy: "I prefer tautology to a chance of misconception" (16: 242n).

While providing the occasional tautology, Poe could detect one easily enough in the works he reviewed. He quotes a passage from Bulwer's novel *Night and Morning* – "And at last silenced, if not convinced, his eyes closed, and the **tears yet wet** upon their lashes, fell asleep" – and rewrites it to omit the dangling participles. Then Poe says this: "It will be seen that, besides other modifications, we have ,... omitted 'wet' as superfluous when applied to tear; who ever heard of a dry one?" (10: 127). In his review of *The Drama of Exile*, Poe complains about "from whence" (12: 27). See also 11: 32–3; Ostrom, 151.

The term *nugatio* is mentioned by Sonnino (134) as an alternative, and some rhetors also define *tautologia* as the needless and wearisome repetition of the same word. To complicate matters, see Dupriez (451–2).

Pronunciation: taw to LO gi a
Type: amplification
Type: repetition: words
Type: repetition: clauses, phrases, and ideas

TESTAMENTUM: "will; something acknowledged before witnesses" (Lanham, 150); "a piece of literature that 'bears witness to' or 'makes a covenant with' in the biblical sense" (Harmon/Holman, 516); "an affirmation" (Cuddon, 962):

> His Majesty selected a narrow slip of parchment, and from it read aloud the following words:
>
> "In consideration of certain mental endowments which it is unnecessary to specify, and in farther consideration of one thousand louis d'or, I being aged one year and one month, do hereby make over to the bearer of this agreement all my right, title, and appurtenance in the shadow called my soul. (Signed) A ... " ("Bon-Bon," 2: 144–5)

This example of a testament is, in fact, a pact with the Devil. This definition of the device, however, differs from Sonnino's (176), which is synonymous with *diatyposis* (see above).
Pronunciation: tes ta MEN tum

THAUMASMUS: an exclamation of wonder:

> It was the work of the rushing gust – but then without those doors there DID stand the lofty and enshrouded figure of the lady Madeline of Usher. ("The Fall of the House of Usher," 3: 296)

Taylor gives this definition: "Marvelling at some state of affairs, such as why a thing was done or not done, some strange event, or secret cause" (131).
Pronunciation: thau MAS mus
Type: devices of vehemence

THRENOS: a lamentation, an expression of sorrow, often for the dead:

> For, alas! alas! with me
>   The light of Life is o'er!
> "No more – no more – no more –"
> (Such language holds the solemn sea
>   To the sands upon the shore)
> Shall bloom the thunder-blasted tree,
>   Or the stricken eagle soar!

And all my days are trances,
    And all my nightly dreams
Are where thy grey eye glances,
    And where thy footstep gleams –
In what ethereal dances,
    By what eternal streams. ("To One in Paradise," 7: 86)

With all the dead ladies in Poe's poetry and prose, we would expect to find many instances of *threnos*. "Annabel Lee" is an extended example. After all, Poe confesses in "The Philosophy of Composition" that death is the most melancholy topic of all and that the death "of a beautiful woman is, unquestionably, the most poetical topic in the world" (14: 201). *Threnos*, for Poe, is actually something that can cause us a certain amount of pleasure – he uses the oxymoron "pleasurable sadness" ("The Poetic Principle," 14: 279).

Pronunciation: THRAE nos
Type: devices of vehemence

TOPOGRAPHIA: (a type of *enargia*), the vivid description of a place. This scheme differs from *topothesia*, below, in that *topographia* is the clear description of a real rather than an imaginary place. The details given of Landor's cottage may be an instance of *topographia* insofar as that cottage is said to be modelled on Poe's own at Fordham, outside of New York. Passages in "The Elk" are extended exemplifications of *topographia* insofar as they portray certain places in the eastern United States. The narrator describes the brook Wissahiccon, which is

narrow. Its banks are generally, indeed almost universally, precipitous, and consist of high hills, clothed with noble shrubbery near the water, and crowned at a greater elevation, with some of the most magnificent forest trees of America, among which stands conspicuous the *liriodendron tulipiferum*. The immediate shores, however, are of granite, sharply-defined or moss-covered, against which the pellucid water lolls in its gentle flow, as the blue waves of the Mediterranean upon the steps of her palaces of marble. Occa-sionally in front of the cliffs, extends a small definite *plateau* of richly herb-aged land, affording the most picturesque position for a cottage and garden which the richest imagination could conceive. The windings of the stream are many and abrupt, as is usually the case where banks are precipitous, and thus the impression conveyed to the voyager's eye, as he proceeds, is that of an endless succession of infinitely varied small lakes, or, more properly speaking, tarns ... the height of the hills on either hand, and the density of the foliage, conspire to produce a gloominess, if not an absolute dreariness of effect. (5: 160)

In considering such luxuriantly descriptive landscape pieces as "The Domain of Arnheim," "Landor's Cottage," "The Island of the Fay," and "The Elk," Woodberry reminds us, quite rightly, how they "bring out strongly the extent to which his [Poe's] work is dependent for its effect directly on the senses" (329). Numerous instances of *topographia* figure in "The Thousand-and-second Tale of Scheherazade."

Pronunciation: top o GRA phi a

Type: description

TOPOTHESIA: a description (*enargia*) of an imaginary place:

> By a route obscure and lonely,
> Haunted by ill angels only,
> Where an Eidolon, named Night,
> On a black throne reigns upright,
> I have reached these lands but newly
> From an ultimate dim Thule –
> From a wild weird clime that lieth, sublime,
> Out of Space – out of Time.
> Bottomless vales and boundless floods,
> And chasms, and caves and titan woods,
> With forms that no man can discover
> For the tears that drip all over;
> Mountains toppling evermore
> Into seas without a shore;
> Seas that restlessly aspire,
> Surging, unto skies of fire;
> Lakes that endlessly outspread
> Their lone waters – lone and dead, –
> Their still waters – still and chilly
> With the snows of the lolling lily. ("Dream-Land," 7: 89)

Sonnino (212) quotes the sixteenth-century rhetor Henry Peacham, who says that "This figure is proper to poets and is seldom used of orators." The poet Poe, of course, specializes in this device not only in his poetry but also

in his fiction. "The Domain of Arnheim," for instance, is an exploration of
the theories of the beautiful and picturesque applied to landscape garden-
ing, and the tale's entire second half is a description of Arnheim, an artificial paradise on Earth – "the phantom handiwork, conjointly, of the
Sylphs, of the Fairies, of the Genii, and of the Gnomes" (6: 196).

   We also have "Landor's Cottage: A Pendant to 'The Domain of Arnheim'." That piece really has no plot; it is extended *topothesia* – an exercise in picturesque description of a place, almost as if Poe were engaging
in one of the *progymnasmata,* the set of elementary exercises used by
rhetoric teachers from classical to Renaissance times; one such exercise
(*ekphrasis* or *ecphrasis*) involved the description of such things as people,
plants, animals, actions, times, places, and seasons (see Crowley, 321–4).
"The treatment," says Donald Lemen Clark, "should involve the use of
many descriptive figures, both schemes and tropes, in presenting a vivid
imitation of the subject" (Covino/Jolliffe, 629; see also under *enargia*).
In "Landor's Cottage," Poe employs a great deal of imagery, largely chromatic, in addition to *characterismus, hydrographia,* and a good deal of
dendrographia (see above for each). It is almost as if Poe were describing
the details of a painting, or a series of paintings, that he had in front of
him when he composed the piece – which is certainly a vivid *word picture.* In its extravagant, sensuous descriptions, "Landor's Cottage" compares with the vivid imagery of Irving's landscape descriptions in "The
Legend of Sleepy Hollow" (another New York piece, allegedly).

   Sometimes Poe gets carried away with his descriptions, however, as
when his measurements become *too* precise:

> The little vale … could not have been more than four hundred yards long;
> while in breadth it varied from fifty to one hundred and fifty, or perhaps two
> hundred … The widest portion was within eighty yards of the southern
> extreme … Here a precipitous ledge of granite arose to a height of some
> ninety feet; and, as I have mentioned, the valley at this point was not more
> than fifty feet wide. ("Landor's Cottage," 6: 258–9)

No one not armed with surveying equipment and knowledge of trigo-
nometry could give us some of those overly precise, fastidious, measurements. Ketterer complains of all the "compass-point" identifications in
"Landor's Cottage," suggesting that they are actually counterproductive
as aids to *enargia*: "Paradoxically, these fixes are so frequent and so

specific that they have a dizzying effect on the reader and make it impossible for him to visualize the scene" (210).
Pronunciation: top o THE si a
Type: description

TRAIECTIO IN ALIUM: pushing responsibility onto another. Once Poe became notorious for his "tomahawk" style of literary criticism, apparently people started to attribute anonymous scathing reviews to *him*. Now and then he found himself pleading innocent:

> Some five years ago there appeared in the "Messenger," under the editorial head, an article on the subject of the "Pickwick Papers" and some other productions of Mr. Dickens. This article, which abounded in well-written but extravagant denunciation of everything composed by the author of "The Curiosity Shop," and which prophesied his immediate downfall, we have reason to believe was from the pen of Judge Beverly Tucker. We take this opportunity of mentioning the subject, because the odium of the paper in question fell altogether upon our shoulders, and it is a burthen we are not disposed and never intended to bear. (15: 195; see also 75; Ostrom, 202, 294, and 332)

See also chapter 5.
Pronunciation: tra IEC ti o in A li um
Type: techniques of argument

TRICOLON: "the three-unit pattern common in many prose styles" (Lanham, 154). In the following passage, Poe provides *two* instances of the tricolonic arrangement:

> [1a] He must *walk*, [1b] he must leap ravines, [1c] he must risk his neck among precipices, or he must leave unseen [2a] the truest, [2b] the richest, and [2c] most unspeakable glories of the land. ("The Elk," 5: 158)

These exemplifications also illustrate expansion (see above): in the first example of *tricolon*, the second clause has more syllables than the first and the third more than the second; in the next example, the first two clauses are equal in syllabic length but the third has more. Lanham calls it a subtype, tricolon *crescens*. Poe was quite fond of the tricolonic arrangement. Cf triplet.
Pronunciation: TRI co lon

TRIPLET: a series of three items; like doublets, a kind of seriation. Triplets tend to consist of an initial item followed by a doublet. Here is an example of a triplet involving adjectives in a passage on style from "The Imp of the Perverse":

> The speaker is aware that he displeases; he has every intention to please; he is usually **curt, precise, and clear**. (6: 148)

The following is a triplet involving nouns – a nominal triplet – from "The Black Cat":

> Having procured **mortar, sand, and hair**, with every possible precaution, I prepared a plaster which could not be distinguished from the old, and with this I very carefully went over the new brick-work. (5: 153)

Here is a verbal triplet from "Thou Art the Man":

> Having thus arranged the box, I **marked, numbered and addressed** it as already told. (5: 309)

After providing several examples of triplets from "William Wilson," Stauffer concludes that "Such formal groupings of three elements are often found in Poe's periodic sentences ... Less formal groupings of threes occur not only in the formal rational style, but also in Poe's emotional style, as in the first paragraph of 'William Wilson,' suggesting, therefore, that such groupings are a characteristic trait which at the same time links these two tales" ("Style and Meaning," 327). Triplets, as I show above, link many, perhaps all, of Poe's tales. He clearly liked them.

Type: amplification

Type: balance, antithesis, paradox

Type: description

ZEUGMA: a scheme of omission in which one verb – or another kind of word – is used for two or more objects to each of which it stands in a different relation:

> "But, under the real circumstances of the case, if we are to suppose gold the motive of this outrage, we must also imagine the perpetrator so vacillating an idiot as **to have abandoned his gold and his motive together**." ("The Murders in the Rue Morgue," 4: 179)

This example confirms Dupriez's remark that, "In English, zeugma frequently unites an abstract with a concrete term" (475). Here are other instances, suggesting that Poe appreciated *zeugma*:

she grows melancholy and ... **throws aside her bread-and-butter for desper-ation and a guitar.** (Review of *The Swiss Heiress*, 9: 187)

In this, our second "Chapter on Autography," **we conclude the article and the year together.** (15: 209)

Like Dupriez, Lanham (159–61) and Cluett/Kampeas (58) have lengthy and lively commentaries on this device and its similarities with others. We must not confuse *zeugma* with *syllepsis* (see above). Cf *hypozeugma,* *mesozeugma,* and *prozeugma.* For a discussion of the comedic uses of *zeugma,* and further instances, see chapter 4.

Pronunciation: ZEUG ma

Type: addition, subtraction, and substitution: words, phrases, and clauses

Type: brevity

The Terms by Type

ADDITION,
SUBTRACTION,
AND SUBSTITU-
TION: LETTERS
AND SYLLABLES

antistoecon
aphaeresis
apocope
diastole
elision
epenthesis
expansion
metathesis
prothesis
synalepha
synoeresis

ADDITION,
SUBTRACTION,
AND SUBSTITU-
TION: WORDS,
PHRASES,
AND CLAUSES

alleotheta
appositio
asyndeton
brachylogia
continuators
diazeugma
ellipsis
enallage
epexegesis
hypozeugma
mesozeugma

parelcon
parenthesis
prozeugma
syllepsis
zeugma

AMPLIFICATION

accumulatio
appositio
auxesis
bomphiologia
climax
cohortatio
commoratio
continuators
diaeresis
diallage
digestion
dinumeratio
distinctio
epexegesis
epicrisis
epimone (leitmotif)
epitheton
exergasia
expansion
iteratio
macrologia
metanoia
paradiegesis
parenthesis
periergia
periphrasis
peristasis
pleonastic doublet

prolepsis
seriation
synathroesmus
synonymia
systrophe
tautologia
triplet

BALANCE,
ANTITHESIS,
PARADOX

antanagoge
anticategoria
antimetabole
antiphrasis
antisagoge
antistrophe
antithesis
antithetic doublet
chiasmos
climax
contrarium
dialysis
dilemma
disjunctio
horismus
hypophora
hypozeuxis
inclusio
isocolon
oxymoron
palindrome
paradox
parallelism
paranomasia

pleonastic doublet
progressio
range doublet
seriation
symploce
syncrisis
triplet

BREVITY

asyndeton
brachylogia
brevitas
diazeugma
ellipsis
epitrochasmus
hypozeugma
mesozeugma
oxymoron
prozeugma
syllepsis
zeugma

DESCRIPTION

anemographia
astrothesia
characterismus
chronographia
dendrographia
dialogismus
effictio
enargia
encomium
epic simile
epitheton
ethopoeia
geographia

hydrographia
imagery
onomatopoeia
pragmatographia
prosopographia
prosopopoeia
adjectival/adverbial
seriation
simile
synathroesmus
systrophe
topographia
topothesia
adjectival/adverbial
triplet

DEVICES OF
VEHEMENCE

accumulatio
adhortatio
adynata
amphidiorthosis
anacoluthon
anamnesis
anaphora
anticategoria
antiphrasis
antirrhesis
apocarteresis
apodioxis
aporia
aposiopesis
apostrophe
ara
asphalia
bathos
bdelygma

cataplexis
categoria
cohortatio
commiseratio
commoratio
communicatio
comprobatio
consolatio
deesis
dehortatio
diatyposis
dicaeologia
ecphonesis
enargia
encomium
epanalepsis
epanaphora
epiphonema
epiplexis
epistrophe
epitrope
erotesis
euche
euphemism
eustathia
exuscitatio
hyperbaton
hyperbole
hypophora
indignatio
iteratio
mempsis
metastasis
onedismus
optatio
orcos
paeanismus
philophronesis

ploce
pysma
reticentia
sarcasmus
symploce
syngnome
thaumasmus
threnos

EXAMPLE,
ALLUSION, AND
CITATION OF
AUTHORITY

anamnesis
apodixis
apomnemonysis
chreia
diatyposis
epicrisis
exemplum
fable
martyria
oraculum
parable
paradiegesis
paroemia
proverb
soraismus

METAPHORICAL
SUBSTITUTIONS
AND PUNS

adianoeta
allegoria
analogy
antanaclasis

antistasis
antonomasia
asteismus
catachresis
epic simile
euphemism
fable
meiosis
metaphysical conceit
metonymy
parable
prosonomasia
prosopopoeia
schematismus
simile

REPETITION:
LETTERS,
SYLLABLES,
AND SOUNDS

alliteration
assonance
cacophonia
consonance
homoioptoton
homoioteleuton
morphological set
parallelism
paranomasia
phonological set

REPETITION:
WORDS

anadiplosis
anaphora
antanaclasis

antimetabole
antistasis
antistrophe
climax
diacope
epanalepsis
epanaphora
epimone (leitmotif)
epistrophe
epizeuxis
inclusio
palindrome
parallelism
paranomasia
ploce
polyptoton
polysyndeton
symploce
tautologia

REPETITION:
CLAUSES,
PHRASES,
AND IDEAS

commoratio
disjunctio
end-linkage
epanalepsis
epimone (leitmotif)
epistrophe
exergasia
homiologia
inclusio
isocolon
iteratio
notional set
palindrome

parallelism

parelcon

periergia

pleonastic doublet

synonymia

tautologia

TECHNIQUES

OF ARGUMENT

adhortatio

adynata

amphidiorthosis .

analogy

antanagoge

antirrhesis

antisagoge

apodioxis

apodixis

apomnemonysis

apophasis

aporia

aposiopesis

cacosistaton

charientismus

chreia

cohortatio

communicatio

comprobatio

contrarium

dehortatio

deliberatio

diaeresis

diallage

dialogismus

dialysis

diatyposis

dicaeologia

digestion

digressio

dilemma

dinumeratio

distinctio

eidolopoeia

enthymeme

epanorthosis

epicrisis

epitrope

erotesis

ethopoeia

euphemism

exemplum

expeditio

exuscitatio

fable

fallacy of the appeal to

ignorance

fallacy of assertion

fallacy of false cause

fallacy of hasty gener-

alization

fallacy of irrelevant

thesis

fallacy of poisoning

the well

fallacy of special

pleading

fictio

hypophora

indignatio

martyria

medela

meiosis

metanoia

metastasis

noema

onedismus

oraculum

parable

paradiastole

paradiegesis

paraleipsis

pareuresis

paromologia

parrhesia

periphrasis

philophronesis

praemunitio

praeparatio

proecthesis

progressio

prolepsis

pysma

ratiocinatio

reditus ad propositum

reductio ad absurdum

restrictio

sermocinatio

simile

subjectio

synchoresis

traiectio in alium

UNGRAMMATICAL,

ILLOGICAL,

OR UNUSUAL USES

OF LANGUAGE

acyrologia

alleotheta

amphibologia

anacoluthon

anoiconometon

antistoecon

aphaeresis
aschematiston
barbarismus
cacemphaton
cacophonia
cacozelia
catachresis
elision
enallage
graecismus
hendiadys
hyperbaton
metaphysical conceit
metathesis
non sequitur
parelcon
poicilogia
prothesis
solecismus
soraismus
syllepsis
synalepha
synchisis

"BIBLICAL"

adhortatio
asyndeton
dehortatio
diatyposis
epimone (leitmotif)
epizeuxis
inclusio
palindrome
parallelism
polysyndeton

"COMEDIC"

antistoecon
barbarismus
bathos
bomphiologia
epenthesis
metathesis

parelcon
prosonomasia
puns (asteismus)

"VERISIMILAR"

apodixis
apomnemonysis
barbarismus
epicrisis
exemplum
martyria
metathesis
nominal seriation
notional set

Conclusion

I believe that the preceding catalogue of terms from classical rhetoric, linguistics, and informal logic reinforces what the previous five chapters are intended to demonstrate: Poe was a clever rhetorician and a meticulous, conscientious, and sometimes innovative literary craftsman – a brilliant stylist. We have seen several aspects of Poe's literary credo, one of which is that style should reflect character. Another is that a writer should be stylistically versatile. Both those rules are illustrated easily by an examination of Poe's narrators, who are stylistically distinct from one another and from Poe himself (who is therefore *not* a literary twin of each of his storytellers). We have discovered, as well, that he was clearly aware of the traditional stylistic typologies, knew some of the classical names for rhetorical figures, and picked up his knowledge of these aspects of prose both informally or formally. While it is difficult to *prove* the sources of his linguistic and argumentative versatility – this is not a source study, after all (although I would be inclined to favour Blair and Quintilian; we also know he read Cicero) – he had numerous textbooks at his disposal, contemporary and ancient, which could have instilled in him not only the ability to demolish opponents rhetorically but also a keen and profound sensitivity to the possibilities of language – to amplify thoughts, to delight with humour, to express oneself concisely, to startle with paradoxes and puns, to express the wide range of human emotions, to hoax the gullible through verisimilitude, to create vivid word pictures through precise descriptions, to deride the grammatical weaknesses of poets and novelists, to add dignity to prose through stylistic mimicry of the Bible – and the list goes on.

The extent to which the numerous stylistic devices found in Poe's prose fall into all fourteen of Lanham's rhetorical categories – not to mention the three I have added ("comedic," "biblical," and "verisimilar") – suggests the impossibility of forcing Poe into any of the traditional typologies. Does he write in the "plain" style (*aphelia*)? Sometimes – but not always. Does his prose display aspects of Ciceronianism? Sometimes – but not always. Are his tales characterized by turgidity and bombast? Sometimes – but not always. Are we safer going with Stauffer's categories (see appendix 1)? Maybe, but the same pitfalls exist there as with traditional typologies. Perhaps it is safest simply to list some of the patterns we have found without committing ourselves to stylistic paradigms. The key word here is *patterns*. It might be argued that a stylistical/rhetorical examination such as I have done in this book would similarly turn up hundreds of figures of speech and thought in the writings of *any* highly productive creative writer – Melville, for instance. That *may* be true – and it may not. If it is, we then must ask whether those tropes and schemes are incidental, ornamental, or otherwise strategically employed. *Patterns* would certainly differ from writer to writer. Would we find the same number of descriptive figures in Hemingway as in Poe? the same devices of vehemence in James as in Melville? as many schemes of omission in Hawthorne as in Hammett? the same types and number of tropes in Stowe as in Cain? Stylistic signatures are as various as written signatures, or fingerprints.

We have seen the conclusions drawn about *Poe's* prose in chapters 1–5. What additional conclusions does the catalogue enable us to make? Here are some:

· That Poe rarely falls back on clichés but, when he does, he – like Thoreau – often gives them a twist.

· That he enjoys various types of seriation (nominal, verbal, adjectival, adverbial, clausal) and that his catalogues can be quite complicated and both symmetrical (balanced) *and* asymmetrical ("chaotic") simultaneously. His use of lexical catalogues may be inspired by other seriators, notably Swift and Rabelais, both of whom Poe read. Among its functions, *nominal* seriation contributes to the "verisimilar" style of Poe's hoaxes.

- That these lists in Poe often conclude with continuators (satirical, neutral, or eulogistic).
- That he uses devices of brevity *as well as* devices of amplification – this is one facet of the many-sided argument made throughout this text that we cannot pigeonhole Poe's "style."
- That he is skilled in his role as literary reviewer in uncovering the grammatical flaws of other writers but that he is occasionally guilty of a blunder himself (*syllepsis, enallage, hendiadys, tautologia*).
- That he employs all types of imagery as well as all or nearly all of the devices of description listed by Lanham. Every careful reader of Poe *knows* that he is a highly descriptive writer, but our task has been to substantiate that claim and, with precise labels and analysis, explore its subtleties and intricacies – and thus avoid the impressionism that can characterize the most irresponsible statements about style.
- That some of his descriptive passages (*enargia*) have been criticized as being *too precise* (Irving and Ketterer).
- That his belief in the claims of phrenology and physiognomy is often behind his detailed descriptions of characters (*enargia, effictio, characterismus, prosopographia*).
- That, like Shakespeare, Poe is an eminently *emotional* writer, figures of vehemence being featured in every type of literature he wrote: poetry, personal letters, reviews, critical theory, fiction long and short. He expresses a gigantic range of human emotions through dozens of devices, often even using figures of repetition for their potential to express ardency. This is perhaps no surprise coming from the passionate and histrionic Poe.
- That those devices of repetition – involving elements at every level of the prose: letters, syllables, sounds, words, phrases, clauses, ideas – are among the most foregrounded in his prose and function in a variety of ways in addition to the expression of vehemence.
- That, while Poe is famous for devices of sound that lead to auditory agreeableness in his poetry, these same (such as *alliteratio, assonance, consonance*) are often found in his prose as well, not just the tales but even the criticism. He is very much a writer whose *prose* appeals to the ear. Not surprisingly, he is sensitive to *cacophonia* and condemns writers, especially poets, in whose works it is found.
- That when he decides to combine periodicity and *hypotaxis*, his sentences often become so long and complicated as to necessitate devices

of summary such as *epanalepsis* or devices of repetition such as what
Dupriez calls *restart*. These are frequent in his prose.

- That he is a consistently *rhetorical* writer, techniques of argument being featured in every type of prose he wrote. In his letters, reviews, and
critical theory he speaks, of course, in his own voice, but he often cre-
ates remarkable although typically deluded rhetoricians in his tales of
homicide.

- That, while he is a skilled and intimidating rhetorician and logician,
his own exercises in argumentation sometimes display weaknesses
through the use of analogical reasoning ("analogic is not logic"), various fallacies (appeal to ignorance, assertion, irrelevant thesis, special
pleading, the intentional fallacy), or underhandedness (*apophasis*, well
poisoning, *paraleipsis*).

- That he loves syntactical balance, parallelism (including doublets) –
often antithetical; but he also loves syntactical expansion, often
through tricolonic arrangements.

- That among his favourite stylistical devices, in addition to puns and
allegoria (his love of which is well known), are *chiasmos, antimetabole,
zeugma,* climax, *litotes, chronographia, epanorthosis,* parenthesis, *metanoia, oxymoron, polysyndeton, praeparatio,* seriation, *soraismus,* and the
various kinds of rhetorical questions – these last used particularly in
his more impassioned critical reviews.

- That among components of his literary credo we find the following:
  – one should never compare the picturesque or the natural sublime
  with artificial objects, for the bathetic is always the result;
  – in poetry one should always avoid devices of contraction (elisions) as
  well as *hyperbaton*, both of which are artificial;
  – one should avoid similes but, if they must be used, they should be
  used appropriately (certainly not bathetically);
  – one should eschew similes in favour of metaphors, but one should
  be careful not to employ metaphors indiscriminately – more generally, one should not pile on figures of speech (avoid *poicilogia*);
  – one should avoid *noema* (unless for artistic purposes) in order to be
  clear;
  – one's use of imagery associated with personification (*prosopopoeia*)
  should be consistent and not interfere with or contradict the personification;

- right-branching sentences should not be overly long – should not be too "loose."
- That he is quick to condemn other poets and prose writers for stylistic features that he himself employs on occasion (allegory, types of elision, *hyperbaton*, *cacozelia*, paradoxes, puns, *ellipsis, bomphiologia, enargia, hypotaxis, inclusio, macrologia*, paradox, *parelcon, pleonasm, polyptoton, polysyndeton, prosopopoeia*, similes, *soraismus*). Sometimes, however, Poe uses these devices deliberately for various artistic reasons and therefore presumably could justify *his own* use of them.
- That when he is at his best, style is related to theme and characterization – the linguistic related to the extralinguistic (for instance, see *homiologia, hypotaxis*, imagery, *inclusio, meiosis, paradiastole*).

I do not pretend that *all* of these insights are original with me and have not been considered by other scholars who have studied Poe's styles. Still, I suspect that most of the above *is* new and should prove useful and stimulating to those readers who are interested in the technicalities of Poe's prose and who wish to carry this stylistical/rhetorical approach to Poe further. As well, it is my wish that Poe scholars who hitherto have had negative preconceptions about his prose, or who have analysed it to some extent and found it wanting, will see that prose in a more sympathetic, a more positive, light as a result of this study – or, to put it more bluntly, that they will learn to give credit where credit is due.

While the excerpts in the rhetorical catalogue cover Harrison's entire Virginia edition of Poe's works, in the chapters I have only analysed in detail a few of Poe's major tales. And despite the excellent and patient studies of Stauffer, Gargano, McElrath, Forrest, Fletcher, Cox, Gooder, Spanier, Williams, and others, I am sure that much work remains to be done – for, as Tennyson's Ulysses insists, "all experience is an arch where-thro'/ Gleams that untravell'd world whose margin fades/ For ever and for ever when I move."

Stauffer on Poe's "Five Styles"

My intention throughout chapter 1 was to demonstrate that not only is it impossible to talk about Poe's "style" but also that Poe cannot easily be placed onto the Procrustean bed of any conventional stylistic typology. Recognizing these truths, Donald B. Stauffer has nevertheless – and rather *courageously* – attempted to define other stylistic typologies based on the Poe *oeuvre* ("The Language and Style of the Prose"). Poe, he believes, did not write in a single style: *he has five distinct styles* that divide into two broad categories. I have taken the liberty of charting the two categories, the five typologies, and their characteristics (see Table 2).

Like Stauffer, I have seized on Poe's own discussion of the "plausible or verisimilar" style (see "The Terms by Type"). Stauffer, however, is unable to provide many features of this alleged style; he confesses that the "plausible style itself is more easily illustrated than described" (458). In the catalogue of rhetorical devices (and other terms) that forms the backbone of this study, I have listed several figures that might be said to constitute or at least contribute to this style. For Stauffer's "circumstantial detail," I would list certain notional sets and seriation (catalogues often are themselves notional sets). We can also add *apodixis, apomnemonysis, barbarismus* and *metathesis* (for dialectal verisimilitude), *epicrisis, exempla,* and *martyria.* As exemplifying the plausible style, Stauffer recommends all of Poe's hoaxes and "Items purported to have appeared in newspapers, such as those in 'the Murders in the Rue Morgue'" (458).

I would add those stylistic features that might mimic the terse style of journalism, certainly *brachylogia* and *brevitas* (which indeed are exemplified by the newspaper reports in "Rue Morgue" – see the catalogue under those terms).

The "analytical" style, of course, is shown in all of Poe's critical essays and reviews and "comes closest to being Poe's 'own' style," Stauffer maintains (458); certainly one might concur on the basis of the stylistic features of Poe's business letters – but *not* his disgustingly overcharged *love* letters. Stauffer quotes Gorham Munson (*Style and Form in American Prose*), who says that Poe's syntax in the literary criticism "embodies the technique of mathematical proof – the *quod erat demonstrandum* followed by examples supporting the principle set forth in the generalization." Indeed, Poe often makes a point of avoiding what logicians call the "fallacy of assertion" (see the catalogue), not remaining content simply to express an opinion but insisting on supplying *proof* for it – at least, evidence. Completing his discussion of the analytical style, Stauffer says, "In its logical movement, it follows the eighteenth-century *ordonnance* [Stauffer borrows this word from Tate] characteristic of Franklin, Burke, Marshall, and the lawyers and statesmen whose works Poe studied closely in the 1830s" (459). As for rhetorical devices, it should go without saying that *epicrisis* (quoting a passage and commenting on it) is foregrounded in Poe's reviews. The ever-pretentious Poe allows *soraismus* to figure heavily, too (but this is true of his prose generally; see the catalogue).

According to Stauffer, Poe's alleged "hyperbolic" style is found in his satires and other comedic tales – "strained efforts at humor" (459). The terms listed in the chart under "HYPERBOLIC" are not all features of *style* insofar as I understand the term and have defined it near the beginning of chapter 1, but my catalogue of rhetorical devices and other literary terms makes clear that I too have identified certain stylistic features that are typically found in Poe's comedies and that we might add to this category (see chapter 4). These are not comedic in themselves but Poe puts them to comedic use; other than *bathos* (certainly in "The Premature Burial"), they are mostly there for the sake of *linguistic* (largely dialectal) humour: for example, *antistoecon, barbarismus, bomphiologia, epenthesis, metathesis,* and *prosonomasia.* Stauffer suggests that Poe's "fondness for verbal horseplay marks the hyperbolic style as separate and distinct from other ratiocinative styles" (459).

Table 2
Poe's "Five Styles" According to Donald B. Stauffer

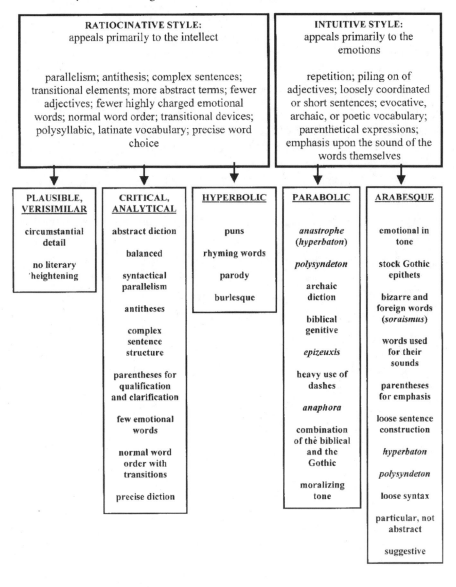

RATIOCINATIVE STYLE: appeals primarily to the intellect parallelism; antithesis; complex sentences; transitional elements; more abstract terms; fewer adjectives; fewer highly charged emotional words; normal word order; transitional devices; polysyllabic, latinate vocabulary; precise word choice			INTUITIVE STYLE: appeals primarily to the emotions repetition; piling on of adjectives; loosely coordinated or short sentences; evocative, archaic, or poetic vocabulary; parenthetical expressions; emphasis upon the sound of the words themselves	
PLAUSIBLE, VERISIMILAR	**CRITICAL, ANALYTICAL**	**HYPERBOLIC**	**PARABOLIC**	**ARABESQUE**
circumstantial detail	abstract diction	puns	*anastrophe (hyperbaton)*	emotional in tone
no literary 'heightening	balanced	rhyming words	*polysyndeton*	stock Gothic epithets
	syntactical parallelism	parody	archaic diction	bizarre and foreign words (*soraismus*)
	antitheses	burlesque	biblical genitive	words used for their sounds
	complex sentence structure		*epizeuxis*	parentheses for emphasis
	parentheses for qualification and clarification		heavy use of dashes	loose sentence construction
	few emotional words		*anaphora*	*hyperbaton*
	normal word order with transitions		combination of the biblical and the Gothic	*polysyndeton*
	precise diction		moralizing tone	loose syntax
				particular, not abstract
				suggestive

The "parabolic" style figures mainly in Poe's parables and fables, says Stauffer. Clearly, in such works as "Silence" and the angelic dialogues, Poe is cultivating, displaying, an old-fashioned, even biblical, style suitable to the "moralizing tone" of those pieces. This is not to say that Poe is being *didactic* in any conventional religious sense (we all know of his distaste for the didactic in literature), but such stylistic features as *polysyndeton*, archaic diction, *hyperbaton*, the biblical genitive, and various devices of repetition (not just *anaphora*, as given by Stauffer, but *epimone*, *epizeuxis*, *inclusio*, and *palindrome*, for instance) give these works a biblical "flavour" suitable for the truths or at least philosophical-metaphysical concepts that Poe offers to his readers (see my comments on "The Masque of the Red Death" in chapter 3). Stauffer completes his discussion of the parabolic style thus: "Poe's debt not only to the Bible but to such Bulwer-Lytton tales as 'Monos and Daimonos' is clear. Whether he is satirizing Bulwer, as in 'Silence,' or using Bulwer's technique to create a desired effect, the parabolic style combines the biblical and the Gothic; however, it is relatively rare in Poe" (459).

The "arabesque" style is essentially that of Poe's most famous – his Gothic – tales. The arabesque and parabolic together "embody the characteristics most often associated with Poe's fictional prose," says Stauffer (459) – and surely, for the most part, it is the stylistic features of those typologies that have aroused the critical disgust of the scholars and writers with whom we began chapter 1. While the parabolic is a special form of the arabesque, Stauffer insists that the latter is more emotional and contains a broader range of stylistic qualities (see Table 2). Indeed, and I would add to his list many devices of verbal repetition – such as *epizeuxis*, *diacope*, *anaphora*, *epistrophe*, *anadiplosis*, *epanalepsis*, *ploce* – none of which is a device of emotion *per se* but all of which can be used to indicate vehemence (see my analysis of the stylistic features of "The Tell-Tale Heart"). Additionally, we can add virtually *all* of the figures listed in "The Terms by Type" under the heading "Devices of vehemence." Figures such as *ecphonesis*, apostrophe, *adynata*, *antirrhesis*, *bdelygma*, *dehortatio*, *adhortatio*, *optatio*, *thaumasmus*, *threnos*, and all rhetorical questions come to mind immediately. The intuitive aspects of the arabesque "make it suitable for rendering abnormal mental states or bizarre or unusual situations and settings. It lies at the opposite end of the spectrum from the analytical style" (460).

Stauffer should be congratulated for his attempt to dispel the old misconception that Poe wrote in a single style (and an obnoxious one at that). Furthermore, Stauffer does not make the mistake of suggesting that other writers wrote in "verisimilar" or "hyperbolic" styles. He would seem to be of the "individualist" school. That is the safer position: he is confining his pronouncements about style to an individual author. Unfortunately, Stauffer's own typologies are subject to some of the same criticisms that the conventional ones are (such as the Ciceronian, the Senecan, the Elizabethan). For one thing, no "Ciceronian" writer (let us say, Milton) wrote purely Ciceronian prose all the time; other alleged stylistic features surely must have intruded now and then. Is Poe's "ratiocinative" style *always* and *entirely* free of the characteristics of the "intuitive" style? Is the reverse true as well? Figures of verbal repetition are supposedly absent from the ratiocinative style, but I can easily find numerous instances of verbal repetition in the many reviews Poe wrote. Stauffer very likely would concede that some stylistic overlapping certainly occurs and would probably insist that the five typologies he has suggested represent stylistic *tendencies* in the various kinds of prose that Poe wrote. But that overlapping occurs at all represents one of the dangers in attempting to establish typologies in the first place. Perhaps the safest approach is simply to do what I am attempting in this book – to identify rhetorical and other stylistic patterns and to suggest the ways these relate to the extralinguistic, if possible – but to stop short at establishing typologies. I feel safer staying with Lanham's *types*.

Another problem in Stauffer's essay is the weakness of his case, certainly in the section on Poe's five styles. That is, he does not really provide sufficient supporting evidence from the prose to demonstrate that this or that stylistic feature typifies this or that typology. He offers only one quotation to demonstrate aspects of the ratiocinative style, one to demonstrate the intuitive style, and virtually none to show the other five more particular typologies. Granted, he does explore the issue more fully in the following sections on diction and rhetorical devices, but it seems to me that to make a truly convincing argument he would have to devote far more than just over nine pages to the question. Perhaps his editor imposed severe restrictions regarding length; in this case, we can only hope that Stauffer is putting his keen critical energies into a monograph or book on Poe's "five styles."

Paranoid Schizophrenia in "The Tell-Tale Heart"

In our time, creative writers are expected to do their "homework," and consequently to find "modern" scientific accuracy in a literary text comes as no surprise. To discover similar scientific accuracy in a text from an early period is a different matter, one that involves questions not only about the sophistication of the artist in question but also about the sophistication of the science of his/her time. A case in point is "The Tell-Tale Heart." Poe's confessional tale features a psychologically ill protagonist who recalls his grisly murder of an old man, his living companion, and who tries to explain the reasons for both this abominable act and his ultimate confession. My purpose in the following essay is to demonstrate the extent to which Poe's characterization of this narrator corresponds with current psychoanalytic profiles of the "paranoid schizophrenic" personality. Subsequently, my purpose is to consider the "science" of Poe's time to show how it "anticipates" current thinking and so provides the context for Poe's own acute insights into the nature, cause, and consequences of this kind of mental illness.

According to current psychological theory, the "active" phase of paranoid schizophrenia is preceded by a "prodromal" phase during which premonitory symptoms occur, one of which is "superstitiousness" (*DSM-III-R*, 195; referred to more vaguely as "unusual or odd beliefs" or "magical thinking" in the *DSM-IV*, 278).[1] In Poe's tale, what precipitated the narrator's insanity and the subsequent murder was his irrational obsession with

the old man's so-called "Evil Eye." The narrator freely admits to his auditors that this was his *primum mobile*: "yes, it was this! He had the eye of a
vulture – a pale blue eye, with a film over it. Whenever it fell upon me,
my blood ran cold; and so by degrees – very gradually – I made up my
mind to take the life of the old man, and thus rid myself of the eye forever" (5: 88). Although it might be argued that the madman's comments
about the "Evil Eye" constitute his rationalization about his decision to
murder, the way he describes the object suggests that the "Eye" was indeed what drove him to commit his atrocities. Although mad, he is not
entirely an unreliable narrator, for what we should consider here is the
way his *idée fixe*, his superstition concerning the "Evil Eye," generated a
kind of anxiety or "overwhelming stress" which, according to current theories, can lead to a full schizophrenic breakdown (Sue, 441–2).

A major symptom of the active phase of schizophrenia involves hallucinations, and it is here that Poe critics have come closest to identifying
the specific nature of the narrator's mental condition. For example, before she abandons herself to a Freudian interpretation, Marie Bonaparte
refers to "auditory hallucinations of paranoia" (498). Similarly, in their
anthology of short fiction, *The Abnormal Personality Through Literature*,
Alan Stone and Sue Smart Stone include "The Tell-Tale Heart" in a
chapter on psychotic symptoms – specifically, hallucinations. Closest to
a more precise identification of the narrator's condition is John E. Reilly,
who describes the protagonist as a paranoid schizophrenic (5–6).[2] To
Reilly, the key index to the narrator's condition is his "hyperacusis," but
it is at this point that his analysis falls short and the directions from current research become important.

According to modern researchers, paranoid schizophrenics often experience sensory perceptions that are not directly attributable to environ-
mental stimuli. They also note that 74 per cent of schizophrenics suffer
from auditory hallucinations: they hear sounds that are not real to others
(Sue, 428). Usually these sensorial illusions involve voices that the victim
perceives as originating outside his/her head, but occasionally "the auditory hallucinations are of sounds rather than voices" (*DSM-III-R*, 189).

Poe's narrator insists that his "disease had sharpened [his] senses – not
destroyed – not dulled them," and that "Above all was the sense of hearing acute." Yet when he goes on to add, "I heard all things in the heaven
and in the earth. I heard many things in hell" (88), his absurdly grandiose

claim encourages us to suspect related claims he makes regarding his auditory capacity. He explains, for example, that "there came to my ears a
low, dull, quick sound, such as a watch makes when enveloped in cot-
ton" (91). He interprets this sound as the beating of the old man's heart,
but it would have been impossible for him to hear such a noise unless his
ear were against the old man's chest. Some scholars argue, in turn, that
the narrator was in fact hearing his own heart (Shelden, 77; Hoffman,
232; Howarth, 11). While such an interpretation is possible, the narrator's
claim to hear things in heaven, hell, and the earth makes it more logical
to conclude that the sound he heard was not the beating of his own
heart, but rather was an auditory hallucination.

To Reilly, the cause of the sound was actually an insect called the
"lesser death-watch," but he also admits that there are certain discrepan-
cies in his theory: "Whereas the narrator heard the sound on two occasions during the night of the murder, the ticking of the lesser death-
watch is said to continue for hours. Moreover, the narrator reports that
the sound he heard increased in tempo just before the murder and grew
in volume on both occasions, whereas the ticking of the lesser death-
watch is uniformly faint" (5). Reilly then tries to account for the discrep-
ancies by saying that the narrator's "subjective sense of time accelerated
the regular ticking of the lesser death-watch" and its volume (7). Such an
explanation is, however, entirely unnecessary if we view the protagonist
as a paranoid schizophrenic. If we see him as suffering from auditory
hallucinations, then we do not need to suggest any material source,
whether insect or heart, for the sounds he claims to have heard; they
originated inside his head (see also Peithman, 136n10).

The narrator, of course, insists that "the noise was not within my ears"
(94), but such a disclaimer simply highlights another, the most common,
symptom of schizophrenia – a lack of insight: "during the active phase
of their disorder, schizophrenics are unable to recognize that their thinking is disturbed" (Sue, 426; also *DSM-IV,* 279). Although Poe's narrator
admits to having some kind of sensorial disease, he is obviously unaware
that it is a mental aberration: "why *will* you say that I am mad?"; "You
fancy me mad. Madmen know nothing. But you should have seen *me*";
"have I not told you that what you mistake for madness is but over
acuteness of the senses?"; "If still you think me mad, you will think so
no longer when I describe the wise precautions I took for the conceal-

ment of the body" (88, 91, 92). One of the greatest sources of irony – and perhaps *pathos* – in the tale is the narrator's vehement insistence that he is sane rather than insane.

The protagonist's inflated opinion of himself is also in keeping with the current view that a "common delusion among paranoid schizophrenics involves exaggerated grandiosity and self-importance" (Sue, 439; also *DSM-IV*, 275). Poe's narrator brags and boasts specifically of his brilliant circumspection in preparing to murder the old man: "You should have seen how wisely I proceeded – with what caution – with what foresight – with what dissimulation I went to work! ... Never before that night, had I felt the extent of my own powers – of my sagacity. I could scarcely contain my feelings of triumph" (88–9). The narrator believes that he has engaged in what Thomas de Quincey thinks of as "the fine art of murder." He would agree with the facetious de Quincey that a murder can be a very meritorious performance – when committed by a man of superior powers.

Not only was the murder performed with circumspection and with finesse but so was the disposal of the corpse; Poe's narrator believes that in hiding the evidence of his crime he had considered every possible contingency:

If still you think me mad, you will think so no longer when I describe the wise precautions I took for the concealment of the body ... I then took up three planks from the flooring of the chamber, and deposited all between the scantlings. I then replaced the boards so cleverly, so cunningly, that no human eye – not even *his* – could have detected any thing wrong. There was nothing to wash out – no stain of any kind – no blood-spot whatever. I had been too wary for that. A tub had caught all – ha! ha! (92–3)

Then this *narrator gloriosus* boasts of the "enthusiasm of my confidence," and of "my perfect triumph."

Other symptoms of paranoid schizophrenia include shifts of mood (Sue, 433–4) – referred to in the *DSM-IV* as "unpredictable and untriggered agitation" (276) – and Poe's madman exhibits these in a number of ways. When he begins his recall, he boasts of "how calmly I can tell you the whole story" (88), and indeed his recollection starts calmly enough. As soon as he begins to recall the alleged beating of the old man's heart, however, he becomes frenetic and he loses his composure: "The old man's terror *must* have been extreme! It grew louder, I say, louder every moment! ... Yet, for some minutes longer I refrained and stood still. But the beating grew louder, louder! I thought the heart must burst. And now a new anxiety seized me – the sound would be heard by a neighbour! The old man's hour had come!" (92). Poe dramatizes the madman's shift from calmness to hysteria by the increased use of such rhetorical devices as repetition (*diacope, epizeuxis, ploce*), exclamations, emphatic utterances (italics), and the dash (see chapter 1 for a more in-depth examination of the style of this tale, and chapter 2 for the rhetoric). After he confesses how he murdered the old man, Poe's narrator calms down again – until he relates how the police entered his house and the sound of the "heartbeat" recommenced, at which point he becomes one of the most hysterical, most frenzied narrators in all of Poe's fiction.

Associated with the narrator's mood alterations are other symptoms of schizophrenia, including the display of emotions that are at variance with the normal reaction to a given situation: "Schizophrenic patients may exhibit wild laughter or uncontrollable weeping that bears little relationship to current circumstances ... Schizophrenics may express the wrong emotions or may express them inappropriately" (Sue, 433–4; also *DSM-IV*, 279). Evidencing this trait, Poe's protagonist recalls with delight the artful way he performed the most hideous of crimes. He assumes, as well, that his audience shares similar emotions; relating his stealth and patience while putting his head into the old man's chamber, he explains, "Oh, you would have laughed to see how cunningly I thrust it in! ... To think that there I was, opening the door, little by little, and he not even to dream of my secret deeds or thoughts. I fairly chuckled at the idea" (89–90). Although he pitied his intended victim, he nevertheless "chuckled at heart." In addition, the care he displayed in avoiding bloodstains is for him a great source of complacency and humour: "A tub had caught all – ha! ha!" (93).

Complications of schizophrenia include "violent acts" (*DSM-III-R*, 191), and, of course, the murder of the old man is clearly the ultimate manifestation of such a tendency. Indeed, he exemplifies this statement from the *DSM-IV*: "the combination of persecutory and grandiose delusions with anger may predispose the individual to violence" (287). Not all paranoid schizophrenics are homicidal maniacs, however; often if they are violent at all the violence is turned against themselves rather than others, and "10 per cent of individuals with Schizophrenia commit suicide" (*DSM-IV,* 280). Clearly, though, Poe's schizophrenic is the most dangerous kind: his violence is turned outward, and he originally had no intention of coming to harm himself.

Features of paranoid schizophrenia associated with violence include anxiety, anger, and argumentativeness (*DSM-IV,* 287). The anxiety of Poe's narrator is something he admits to and, indeed, stresses at the outset: "True! – nervous – very, very dreadfully nervous I had been and am" (88). Anger and argumentativeness are also evidenced in his response to the police: "I arose and argued about trifles, in a high key and with violent gesticulations ... I foamed – I raved – I swore!" (94). Such symptoms constitute what is currently labelled "dysphoric mood" (*DSM-IV,* 279); a more general term is "grossly disorganized behavior," which can involve "shouting or swearing" (*DSM-IV,* 276). Poe's frenetic narrator also illustrates the "extreme intensity in interpersonal interactions" that often characterizes the schizophrenic (*DSM-IV,* 287).

Unfortunately for Poe's agitated and vehement narrator, what finally proved his undoing is yet another symptom of his disease: delusions of persecution. Psychologists note that "deluded individuals believe that others are plotting against them, are talking about them, or are out to harm them in some way. They are constantly suspicious, and their interpretations of the behavior and motives of others are distorted" (Sue, 438–9; also *DSM-IV,* 275). When Poe's narrator invited the three officers in, he was at first certain that they suspected nothing; then his auditory hallucination began again and eventually he became convinced that they could not fail to hear the sound that was tormenting him:

It grew louder – louder – *louder!* And still the men chatted pleasantly, and smiled. Was it possible they heard not? Almighty God! – no, no! They heard! – they suspected! – they *knew!* – they were making a mockery of my horror! – this I thought, and this I think. But anything was better than this agony! Anything was more tolerable than this derision! I could bear those hypocritical smiles no longer! I felt that I must scream or die! and now – again! – hark! louder! louder! louder! *louder!* (94)

Just as current researchers note the way paranoid schizophrenics might see a "friendly, smiling bus driver ... as someone who is laughing at them derisively" (Sue, 439), so the smiles of the police served only to convince Poe's narrator that they were conspiring against him – with the end result being his confession: "'Villains!' I shrieked, 'dissemble no more! I admit the deed!'"

What especially recommends a view of the narrator as a paranoid schizophrenic is that it uncovers the most plausible reason why he confessed. Contrary to the explanations usually given, I would argue that Poe's madman revealed his crime not because of a guilty conscience, not because some "imp of the perverse" goaded him into confessing, not because he hates himself and really wanted to be caught – not because he has self-destructive tendencies, in other words – but because he suffers from delusions of persecution. He believed that the officers had discovered his crime and he could not bear the thought that they were mocking him. As Reilly notes, "the narrator purged his rage by exposing what be believed was the hypocrisy of the police," and thus "self-incrimination" was merely the by-product (7).

The time span of "The Tell-Tale Heart" – from the time Poe's narrator began looking in on the old man every night at midnight, until the consummation of the murder, and even while he is confessing and insisting upon his sanity – corresponds nicely with the active phase of paranoid schizophrenia. According to the *DSM-III-R*, the active phase is of at least a week's duration and is characterized by the manifestation of psychotic symptoms (194). Apparently Poe's narrator had been suffering such symptoms for this same time period, at least: he speaks of "the whole week before I killed him" (89), and when he mentions the "low, dull, quick sound" that he attributes to the old man's heart, he says that he "knew that sound well" (91). In other words, he had been experiencing his auditory hallucinations during the week before the murder, not just on the night of the crime. The *DSM-IV* has changed the week-long active-phase period to one month (274), but it is no trouble at all to consider the week-long period of psychosis for Poe's schizophrenic as being bracketed by a slightly longer time frame.

It is one thing to apply twentieth-century psychology to Poe's tales but it is quite another to account for the fact that Poe has given us a paranoid schizophrenic in the *absence* of twentieth-century psychology. In Poe's day the field of scientific psychology was relatively young and schizophrenia did not even have a specific name; it was not until 1898 that Emil Kraepelin labelled the disease "Dementia Praecox," and it was given its modern name by Eugen Bleuler only in 1911. Thus, Poe portrayed a paranoid schizophrenic decades before nosologists labelled and separated that disease from other mental abnormalities.

Several explanations for this situation are possible. One is that Poe himself had experienced symptoms of paranoid schizophrenia and used these as the basis for his narrator in "The Tell-Tale Heart." Another hypothesis is that Poe's portrait is purely a product of his imagination (and it is therefore a matter of coincidence that he portrayed what twentieth-century psychology calls a paranoid schizophrenic). The explanation I would like to advance and support, however, is that Poe acquired his knowledge of the symptoms by familiarizing himself with the scientific theories of his time.

The allusion to the phrenologist Spurzheim in "The Imp of the Perverse"; the references to the "moral treatment" of the insane in "Dr. Tarr and Prof. Fether"; the review of Mrs L. Miles' *Phrenology* in the *Southern Literary Messenger* – these and other references to coeval theories of psychology in his works show that Poe was very much a student of mental diseases. He may have learned a great deal from his discussions with medical men, such as his friend Joseph Evans Snodgrass, a Baltimore physician, or his own doctor, John Kearsley Mitchell, or Pliny Earle (a physician and psychiatrist who dealt extensively with the insane at asylums in both Pennsylvania and Bloomingdale – see Ostrom, 147, 451), but probably he gleaned information from literary sources as well.

I.M. Walker is only one of several scholars – including Phillips ("Mere Household Events"), Smith ("Psychological Context," *Analysis*), and Jacobs (*Poe: Journalist & Critic*) – who insist that Poe was familiar with the works of the psychologists of his day: "With his passion for scientific fact and his interest in abnormal mental states, Poe would have been likely to turn to systems of contemporary psychology in the same way that modern writers have turned to Freud and Jung. Moreover, in Poe's day ... information regarding both mental and physical diseases was readily available to the intelligent layman, not only in the original works of the scientists, but also in popular journals and encyclopaedias" (588). A specialized publication, the *American Journal of Insanity*, began appearing in 1844 (a few months before the final publication of "The Tell-Tale Heart" in the

Broadway Journal on 23 August 1845). As for books, Paige Matthey Bynum notes that "Between 1825 and 1838, the Philadelphia publishing house of Carey and Lea published almost twice as many medical books as those in any other category except fiction, and mental health was a staple concern in these works" (150). In the bibliography to *The Analysis of Motives*, Smith lists many works on psychology that were extant in Poe's America – books in English describing the various symptoms that characterize the abnormal mental state of his narrator in "The Tell-Tale Heart."

Such descriptions are scattered, however. Because the science of psychology was in its infancy, there was much confusion and disagreement between medical men on how to classify and relate the symptoms of insanity. While twentieth-century students can find entire chapters devoted solely to schizophrenia in various manuals and textbooks, it is more difficult to find specific chapters that group only the features of this disease in the books by Poe's contemporaries. Their categories were very broad and often vague.

Occasionally, however, we can find three or more of the symptoms listed together. One of the earlier texts available to Poe was John Haslam's *Observations on Madness and Melancholy* (1809). In a general chapter on insanity – "Symptoms of the Disease" – Haslam refers to suspiciousness (42) and later to auditory hallucinations and violence (69). In the next chapter he provides particular case studies. One of these, "Case XVI," concerns a man whose "temper was naturally violent, and he was easily provoked ... He would often appear to be holding conversations: but these conferences always terminated in a violent quarrel between the imaginary being and himself. He constantly supposed unfriendly people were placed in different parts of the house to torment and annoy him" (118–19). Here we have not only violence and argumentativeness but also the two essential psychotic features of paranoid schizophrenia that modern psychologists have identified (*DSM-IV*, 285): delusions (of persecution) and the most common kind of auditory hallucination – that involving voices.

Haslam's "Case XX" involves a woman who, like the male patient, evinced violent tendencies and delusions of persecution in addition to mood shifts and optical and olfactory hallucinations: "At the first attack she was violent, but she soon became more calm. She conceived that the overseers of the parish, to which she belonged, meditated her destruction ...

She fancied that a young man, for whom she had formerly entertained a partiality, but who had been dead some years, appeared frequently at her bed-side, in a state of putrefaction, which left an abominable stench in her room" (126–7). Haslam also notes that the woman began to suffer her mental affliction "shortly after the death of her husband." The likelihood that the demise of her spouse created the extreme stress that triggered her breakdown corresponds with the current view that a "psychosocial stressor" may trigger the active phase of schizophrenia (*DSM-III-R*, 190).

In his introduction to a recent edition of Haslam's work, Roy Porter observes that "Historians of psychiatry have credited Haslam with giving the first precise clinical accounts of … schizophrenia" (xxvii). Prior to the publication of "The Tell-Tale Heart," however, there were also other works that described the illness. In his *Treatise on Insanity and Other Disorders Affecting the Mind* (1837), for example, the American physician James Cowles Prichard records the case of a young man who suffered from what he calls "moral insanity":

He frequently changed his residence, but soon began to fancy himself the object of dislike to every person in the house of which he became the inmate … On being questioned narrowly as to the ground of the persuasion expressed by him, that he was disliked by the family with which he then resided, he replied that he heard whispers uttered in distant apartments of the house indicative of malevolence and abhorrence. An observation was made to him that it was impossible for sounds so uttered to be heard by him. He then asked if the sense of hearing could not, by some physical change in the organ, be occasionally so increased in intensity as to become capable of affording distinct perception at an unusual distance … This was the only instance of what might be termed hallucination discovered in the case after a minute scrutiny [by physicians]. (38)

Apparent in this case are delusions of persecution and voice hallucinations. The young man's query about the possibility of hearing sounds at great distances, furthermore, certainly recalls Poe's insane narrator. Finally, the patient's hypothesis that his disorder is physiological rather than mental also indicates that he too lacks insight into his true psychical condition – another symptom of paranoid schizophrenia.

Other works on abnormal mental states that were written during Poe's day and describe symptoms of schizophrenia include Isaac Ray's *A Trea-*

tise on the Medical Jurisprudence of Insanity (1838), in which he cites
Joseph Mason Cox's *Practical Observations on Insanity* (1804). In a chapter on "General Moral Mania," Ray quotes Cox's report of a certain variety of "maniacs" who

take violent antipathies, harbor unjust suspicions ... are proud, conceited and
ostentatious; easily excited ... obstinately riveted to the most absurd opinions;
prone to controversy ... always the hero of their own tale, using ... unnatural
gesticulation, inordinate action ... On some occasions they suspect sinister intentions on the most trivial grounds; on others are a prey to fear and dread from
the most ridiculous and imaginary sources ... If subjected to moral restraint, or
a medical regimen, they yield with reluctance to the means proposed, and generally refuse and resist, on the ground that such means are unnecessary where no
disease exists. (172–3)

The symptoms Cox describes correspond very closely to those current
psychologists associate with paranoid schizophrenia, just as they also
closely match those evinced by the narrator of "The Tell-Tale Heart": violence, delusions of persecution and of grandeur, mood shifts, nervous-
ness, and a lack of insight into his own psychopathy.

Clearly, then, Poe and his contemporaries were describing paranoid
schizophrenia, even if its symptoms were classified under the broad
heading "Moral Insanity," which, as Norman Dain observes, "served as a
catchall for many forms of mental illness" in the early nineteenth century (73) – and which, as Bynum confirms, would indeed have been the
way Poe's contemporaries would have diagnosed the condition of his
narrator. Accordingly, although romanticists may like to see Poe as a tormented artist who wrote "The Tell-Tale Heart" to explore or to purge
himself of his own psychotic or self-destructive tendencies, it seems better to regard him as a sophisticated writer who consulted scientific books
and journals in an attempt to achieve accuracy and verisimilitude in his
own works – the same Poe who familiarized himself with, for instance,
the writings of Sir John Herschel, Thomas Dick, and John P. Nichol for
the astronomy in *Eureka*, and whose reviews of Washington Irving's *Astoria* and J.N. Reynolds's "South Sea Expedition" informed *Pym*. For
Poe to consult psychology texts for the sake of scientific precision in
"The Tell-Tale Heart" would have been typical of his standard practice.[3]

In many ways, therefore, Poe is a precursor of modern artists who find in science not a threat but an ally, and the sophistication of his insights might encourage us to be more humble about our own sophistication. His insights might make us wonder whether the major contribution of twentieth-century psychology has taken the form of new knowledge or whether it consists instead in naming and classification, for it appears that Poe and his contemporaries knew a good deal about paranoid schizophrenia – even if they did not use this terminology.

Notes

INTRODUCTION

1 In a letter to Poe (30 October 1845), Thomas Chivers refers to the aforementioned Ainsworth. More importantly, he uses a term from classical rhetoric with the apparent understanding that Poe was familiar with it: "Ainsworth places a *diæresis* over the first vowel of the diphthong" (17: 218–19; my italics). This would correspond to the second definition of that term (see my catalogue).

CHAPTER ONE

1 This aesthetic credo – that style must be adapted to subject, to theme – should figure even in poetry, Poe believed. In his review of Longfellow's *Ballads and Other Poems,* he says of Longfellow's verses, "The metre is simple, sonorous, well-balanced and *fully adapted to the subject*" (my italics; 11: 78).
2 Perhaps the best and most patient of early defences of Poe as a stylist is Stauffer's "Style and Meaning in 'Ligeia' and 'William Wilson'." In this excellent essay Stauffer makes a most sensible assertion in maintaining that
> No judgment of the quality of a style can legitimately be made separately from a critical consideration of the work in which it is found. It is often disturbing to find remarks about the style of an author which seem to be based on the reader's own personal tastes, rather than upon his awareness

that the style is inseparable from the work itself and must therefore, like its symbols, its metaphors, and its paradoxes, be organically related to it. Such an assumption must be insisted upon in the instance of Poe, who was not a careless, haphazard writer, but a conscious and skilled craftsman – technician even – who carefully calculated the means by which to bring about his celebrated "unity of effect." (316)

Another early, sensitive, and sensible study of Poe and his stylistic techniques is Joseph R. McElrath's "Poe's Conscious Prose Technique": "Poe reveals how keenly conscious he was of the characteristic traits of his own crafts-manship" (38).

Stauffer and McElrath engage in close and patient examinations of Poe's prose to determine his talents as a writer and his artistic codes guiding style. A complementary approach is to read through his literary criticism (six volumes in the Harrison edition), as well as *The Literati of New York City* and *Autography* (both in Harrison's volume 15). In these seven volumes, Poe makes *hundreds* of observations regarding style; some concern the writing of the particular authors being reviewed, others are more general statements about style (formulae). We learn, for instance, that, to Poe, style pertains to more than just grammar, syntax, and diction. In his remarks on W.E. Channing, he criticizes another reviewer for his inappropriately narrow ideas about style:

To detect occasional, or even frequent inadvertences in the way of bad grammar, faulty construction, or mis-usage of language, is not to prove impurity of *style* – a word which happily has a bolder signification than any dreamed of by the Zoilus of the Review in question. Style regards, more than anything else, the *tone* of a composition. All the rest is not un-important, to be sure, but appertains to the minor morals of literature, and can be learned by rote by the meanest simpletons in letters – can be carried to its highest excellence by dolts, who, upon the whole, are despi-cable as stylists. (*Autography*, 15: 227)

Now *those* are significant observations, and they give us useful clues in help-ing us to judge Poe as a literary critic and writer of prose fiction. Had more Poe scholars taken the time, and shown the patience, necessary to work through Poe's criticism, they might have been prevented from making many wrongheaded assumptions and statements about his writing.

3 In his introduction to *Edgar Allan Poe: Selected Prose and Poetry*, W.H. Auden also acknowledges the rightness of Poe's prose insofar as it reveals the characters of his protagonists:

Poe is sometimes attacked for the operatic quality of the prose and *décor* in his tales, but they are essential to preserve the illusion. His heroes cannot exist except operatically. Take, for example, the following sentence from *William Wilson*:

> Let it suffice, that among spendthrifts I out-heroded Herod, and that, giving name to a multitude of novel follies, I added no brief appendix to the long catalogue of vices then usual in the most dissolute university of Europe.

In isolation, as a prose sentence, it is terrible, vague, verbose, the sense at the mercy of a conventional rhetorical rhythm. But dramatically, how right; how well it reveals the William Wilson who narrates the story in his real colors, as the fantastic self who hates and refuses contact with reality. (*Recognition*, 221–2)

4 In a review of the work of Amelia Welby, Poe expresses his distaste for *hyperbaton* (and other stylistic liberties) in poetry: "All contractions are awkward. It is no paradox, that the more prosaic the construction of verse, the better. Inversions [*hyperbaton*] should be dismissed. The most forcible lines are the most direct. Mrs. Welby owes three-fourths of her power (so far as style is concerned), to her freedom from these vulgar and particularly English errors – elision and inversion" (16: 58). The closer the syntax of poetic lines is to that of normal English, the better – the more natural it is, Poe believed (quite rightly). As the lines from his prose piece "The Tell-Tale Heart" show, however, he recognized the usefulness of *hyperbaton* to express emotional frenzy in a mad narrator.

5 In "The Angelic Imagination" Tate makes an intriguing observation: "Poe is the transitional figure in modern literature because he discovered our great subject, the disintegration of personality, but kept it in a language that had developed in a tradition of unity and order" (*Recognition*, 241–2). If I understand Tate correctly, he is suggesting that the language, the stylistic features, of any given Poe tale are unable to convey adequately the full disintegration of personality, by which I take him to mean madness: "without the superimposed order of rhetoric the disorder hidden beneath would explode to the surface, where he would not be able to manage it." I conclude, however, that in his best tales Poe does take the language of disintegration as far as he can. Consider the linguistic frenzy of the schizophrenic in "The Tell-Tale Heart." Poe employs language superbly to convey the terrible anxieties, the rage, the argumentativeness (*antirrhesis*), the overwhelming stress, and the mood

shifts of his tortured protagonist. There is *one* symptom schizophrenics can
display that Poe does not duplicate, for if he had made the attempt the narrator's account would have been incomprehensible:

> A disturbance in the form of thought is often present. This has been re-
> ferred to as "formal thought disorder," and is different from a disorder in
> the content of thought. The most common example of this is loosening
> of associations [sometimes called "derailing," "word salad," or "cognitive
> slippage"], in which ideas shift from one subject to another, completely
> unrelated or only obliquely related subject, without the speaker's display-
> ing any awareness that the topics are unconnected. Statements that lack a
> meaningful relationship may be juxtaposed, or the person may shift idio-
> syncratically from one frame of reference to another. When loosening of
> associations is severe, the person may become incoherent, that is, his or
> her speech may become incomprehensible. (*Diagnostic and Statistical
> Manual of Mental Disorders-III-R*, 188; see also *DSM-IV*, 276)

Occasionally we can find psychology textbooks that provide examples of this
cognitive slippage. Davidson and Neale quote the following words from a
schizophrenic: "lettuce is a transformation of a dead cougar that suffered a
relapse on the lion's toe. And he swallowed the lion and something happened. The … see, the … Gloria and Tommy, they're two heads and they're
not whales. But they escaped with herds of vomit, and things like that"
(265). Note how this person jumps from bizarre topic to topic, the thematic
connection between them tenuous or nonexistent (much like in some undergraduate essays). Consider the same feature in the conversation of another patient, quoted by Bootzin, Acocella, and Alloy: "I use Cover Girl
creamy natural makeup. Oral Roberts has been here to visit me … This
place is where *Mad* magazine is published. The Nixons make Noxon metal
polish. When I was a little girl, I used to sit and tell stories to myself [and it
goes on like this for some time]" (367). They also offer the following statement as another instance of "word salad":

> It's all over for a squab true tray and there ain't no music, there ain't no
> nothing besides my mother and my father who stand alone upon the
> Island of Capri where there is no ice, there is no nothing but changers,
> changers, changers. That comes like in first and last names, so that thing
> does. Well, it's my suitcase, sir. I've got to travel all the time to keep my
> energy alive. (373)

Here are three cases in which "the disorder hidden beneath" explodes to the surface in linguistic utterances absolutely alien to normal comprehension. Had Poe attempted to duplicate this loosening of associations in his tales, they would have been unreadable, not to mention unpublishable – and *he* might have been committed to an asylum. As things stand, he took the language of mental disturbance as far as he could.

CHAPTER TWO

1 Indeed! In a brief history of American oratory from 1788 to 1860, Aly and Tanquary say this:

> Any classification of speeches by occasions is likely to leave the false impression that the Americans spoke only on occasion. The fact is, however, that speechmaking went on in the daily exercise of life in situations and under conditions that defy classification. And if no situation requiring speechmaking was at hand, then one was invented. The literary society, the "bee," the debating society, and the lyceum were largely given over to speechmaking in one form or another. (89)

2 That is worth repeating: Poe took a course in elocution. Ota Thomas informs us that courses devoted to the delivery of speeches were developed at American colleges in the early 1800s. The teaching of speech came to be recognized "as a separate and distinct subject field":

> In 1806 John Quincy Adams was appointed to the Boylston Chair of Rhetoric and Oratory at Harvard. It was the first such appointment in the United States. Previously the subject had been taught by some tutor who also instructed in numerous other fields and was frequently not specifically prepared for teaching speech. But after Adams began his duties, other colleges established similar professorships. (196–7)

In his notes on Bishop Doane's signature, Poe refers to that man's "professorship of Rhetoric and Belles Lettres in Washington College, Hartford" (*Autography,* 15: 257). In his 1836 review of *An Address Delivered Before the Students of William and Mary College,* Poe says this: "For a degree in the *classical* department it is necessary that the candidate should not only be proficient in the studies just mentioned, but that he should obtain a certificate of qualification on the junior mathematical, *rhetorical* and historical courses" (9: 193–4; my italics). Clearly, Poe valued the teaching of rhetoric, particularly for classicists such as himself.

3 In "Poe's Knowledge of Latin," Norman tells us that "Poe quotes from no less than twenty-three Latin writers. He refers to four others. He reviewed at one time or another texts of the works of Sallust and Ovid, and several of his criticisms show his acquaintance with Latin grammars" (73). Of the Roman rhetoricians, Poe quotes Cicero six times and alludes to him seven times; Quintilian he quotes twice. The great Latin poets put rhetorical study "to its most effective and lasting use during later antiquity" (Crowley, 27), and of these, Poe quotes Virgil twenty-three times, Horace seventeen times, and Ovid ten (Norman, 73). (Norman's count differs from that of Campbell; see "Poe's Reading," 191.) While he does make a few errors in quoting from the Latin writers, most of Poe's quotations are accurate; Norman concludes: "We may infer, I think, that Poe, although he had obtained no such thorough acquaintance with Latin as we should expect of a scholar, nevertheless acquired in his several years' study of the subject a good working knowledge for his purpose as critic and reviewer" (77).

4 Generally, Ota Thomas notes that, in the nineteenth century, "The classical rhetorical principles expounded in the American colleges found practical application in frequent disputes, as well as in the older, accepted types of collegiate speaking exercises. Furthermore, specialized and intensive training in elocution supplemented the persuasive techniques acquired in the rhetoric classes" (195).

5 Mechanistic delivery concentrates on "the use of pitch, intensity, rate, and quality of the voice, as well as movements of hands, head, eyes, and other parts of the body" (Ota Thomas, 203). Vocal and physical communication was extremely important, and Walker's *Elements of Elocution* was one of the principal books devoted to the orator's bodily movements; Walker based his teaching "on observations of dance, musical, and theatrical performance" (Covino/Jolliffe, 43). William Russell (see below) and Porter were both Walker adherents, but the most monumental book devoted to mechanistic oratory was Gilbert Austin's *Chironomia; or a Treatise on Rhetorical Delivery: Comprehending Many Precepts, Both Ancient and Modern, for the Proper Regulation of the Voice, the Countenance, and Gesture* (1806). Covino and Jolliffe say that Austin "grounded his teaching in a self-proclaimed scientific study of effective delivery" (see also Ota Thomas, 206). This book contains dozens of figures of gestures involving the hands, feet, and entire bodies (poses that would strike us as hilarious today and would get a modern speechifier laughed off the stage). Books published in nineteenth-century America that

show Austin's influences include Increase Cooke's *The American Orator* (1819), Russell's *American Elocutionist* (1844), Rufus Claggett's *Elocution Made Easy* (1845), Merritt Caldwell's *A Practical Manual of Elocution* (1845), and C.P. Bronson's *Elocution; or Mental and Vocal Philosophy* (1845), in its fifth edition by 1845 (see Robb and Thonssen, xviii). In the same oratorical tradition is Dr James Rush's *Philosophy of the Human Voice*, "the greatest single influence upon the development of elocution in America … The book was immediately popular, and … remained the supreme authority on voice through most of the nineteenth century" (Ota Thomas, 207).

6 It has been customary to see this tale as a *confession*, but it becomes clear that the narrator has *already* confessed to the murder of the old man, his former living companion. The tale, then, is not so much a confession as a *defence*; as I am about to show, "The Tell-Tale Heart" is actually a specimen of courtroom rhetoric – judicial, or forensic, oratory. This is not to say that the narrator is necessarily arguing in a court of law; he may be speaking to his auditor(s) in a prison cell – but that he *is* telling his side of the story to someone (rather than writing to himself in a journal) is clear by his use of the word "you"; and that he is speaking rather than writing is clear by his exhortation to "hearken" (listen) to what he has to say. The important point is that his spoken account is forensic insofar as that means a legal argument in self-defence.

7 We might also consider the narrative an extended example of *progressio*, building a point around a series of comparisons (Lanham, 119) – in this case, between the narrator and a true lunatic.

8 For a more in-depth consideration of the theory of perversity in "The Black Cat" and other Poe tales, see Vitanza's "'The Question of Poe's Narrators': Perverseness Considered Once Again."

9 Amper argues that the body seen behind the bedroom wall of the narrator's burnt house is not that of a cat but actually of his previously murdered wife; McElroy insists that the body is indeed that of Pluto but that it got there because the narrator deliberately plastered it over after cutting the poor feline down from the tree; Matheson sees alchoholism and the narrator's innate evil and sadistic tendencies as responsible for everything that happens; Crisman reads "The Black Cat" as a simple domestic tale of marital jealousy.

10 Badenhausen adopts an existential point of view in interpreting "The Black Cat" – an interpretation that ignores the formal qualities of the text considerably (for instance, the "supernatural notional set" and imagery). This is

not to say that existential readings of Poe are inappropriate, and I am certainly inclined to see the usefulness of this approach when applied especially
to "The Pit and the Pendulum" and "The Masque of the Red Death" (see
chapter 3). Without doing a stylistic analysis, Badenhausen also makes some
comments about the rhetoric in "The Black Cat": "Poe's narrator turns away
from the truth and as a result condemns himself to the rhetorical prison of
his tale ... he chooses to manipulate the reader throughout his narrative
with multiple evasions and explanations. While this tactic proves the narrator's worth as a skillful storyteller and allows him to succeed as a rhetorician,
it also induces him to fail as a human being" (496). The extent to which I
agree with Badenhausen's comments will become evident, but I should say
now that the rhetoric of this frantic protagonist does not succeed, either
with us or with him.

11 Amper resists vigorously a supernatural explanation of the events recorded in
"The Black Cat," arguing that such an "interpretation, while offering logical
consistency, is far from satisfying. It seems entirely out of keeping with the
psychological tenor of the tale and with the body of Poe's work" (481). We
must remember, however, that Poe's Gothic tales typically offer both natural
and supernatural interpretations, sometimes several of each within a single
work. It is true, though, as Amper insists, that Poe's Gothic tales are also psychological explorations – I have shown as much in my discussions of "The
Tell-Tale Heart"; however, I see no reason why we cannot consider "The
Black Cat" simultaneously as a supernatural tale and a study in psychology –
specifically, of how the human mind attempts to deal with manifestations of
the supernatural (the "Gothic psychomachy") – as in Shirley Jackson's *The
Haunting of Hill House.*

   I find my reading of this tale far more satisfying than Amper's naturalistic
interpretation:

   the narrator murdered his wife, not impulsively on the cellar stairs as he asserts, but willfully and with malice aforethought at the very time he claims
   to have killed his cat; the supposed cat-killing is a fiction he invents in order
   to assuage his guilt and, more immediately, to explain away the mysterious
   "apparition" on the bedroom wall that threatens to expose his crime; the alleged appearance of a second cat is also a fiction, cooked up to explain the
   continued existence of the supposedly dead cat; it is actually Pluto that is
   discovered in the basement wall with the wife's body. (476)

Amper admits that these conclusions "seem at first astonishing," and they remain so, to my way of thinking. Her attempt to justify these conclusions leads to what I consider a misreading of the tale, as well as to assumptions (479n) and speculations (480n) – violations of Occam's Razor – to interpretations for which we can easily supply alternatives, and to guesses about the narrator's "subconscious" (if we cannot even prove it to exist within real humans, why fall back on it with fictitious humans?). In short, Amper's attempt to avoid a supernatural interpretation gets her into trouble, as it would any reader. This is not to say that natural explanations for the events of the tale are not available (see below on alcoholism), but they can sometimes be Procrustean exercises. Still, Amper's article is ingenious in its own way and deserves to be read.

12 Alcohol plays a key role in bringing about the change in the narrator from a gentle husband and animal lover to a murderer. In the nineteenth century, alcohol was readily available and drunkenness was a serious social problem; America was known as the "alcoholic republic." Long before the era of Prohibition in the United States, the Temperance Movement was only one of many reform movements that characterized the social life of America. Perhaps not surprisingly, it was led by Christian women, and the narrator's wife in Melville's "The Apple-Tree Table" seems to be a supporter of temperance. Alcohol is what really triggers the change in the narrator of "The Black Cat." We might even consider this tale a kind of temperance tract about the evils of drink (although Matheson says that, while Poe borrows some of the language and motifs of temperance literature, "The Black Cat" is in fact a critique of that genre). With some apparent remorse, the narrator confesses, "my general temperament and character – through the instrumentality of the Fiend Intemperance – had (I blush to confess it) experienced a radical alteration for the worse. I grew, day by day, more moody, more irritable, more regardless of the feelings of others. I suffered myself to use intemperate language to my wife. At length, I even offered her personal violence" (5: 144–5). Feminists might even seize on this story as a fictional record of wife abuse; certainly it culminates in uxoricide.

The theme of alcoholism can also be seen to contribute a naturalistic interpretation of some events in the tale. Alcoholism is the most common malady that will incite delirium tremens. Symptoms of the D.T.s are great confusion, the shakes, and terrifying visual hallucinations – all of which can last for several hours or days (Galloway maintains that the "raucous fantasies of 'The Angel of the Odd'" are brought on by the narrator's delirium tremens [20]). If we can postulate that the alcoholic narrator may be suffering from hallucinations, it may be that there really is no gallows-shaped splotch of fur on the second cat's chest and that the shape on the wall after the house burned down is not that of a hanged cat (the neighbours apparently see something but no one ever confirms what the narrator claims to see – see also Matheson [78]). Perhaps his intense shame and guilt are why he hallucinated (projected?) these images – interpreted them to have personal significance. Still, what really matters is not the possible naturalistic explanation of events but how the frantic narrator interprets those events. Unfortunately for his emotional and psychological well-being, it never occurs to him that his visions could be alcohol-related hallucinations, despite his desperate longing to find some rational explanation.

13 The image of the "nightmare" appears as well in Poe's *Autography*: "His [Colonel Stone's] MS. is heavy and sprawling, resembling his mental character in a species of utter unmeaningness, which lies like the nightmare, upon his autograph" (15: 214). We find the image again in Poe's prospectus for *The Penn Magazine*. He lists a number of faults with current magazines, saying that they hang "like nightmares" upon American literature (17: 60).

14 Harry Levin writes that Poe "prefers to dwell upon the psychology of crime rather than upon the ethics of guilt" (*The Power of Blackness*, 146). I am inclined to agree; the "ethics of guilt" is Hawthorne's territory. He often depicts the guilty soul; Poe is more interested in criminal psychology – getting into the mind of the culprit. In his other tales of murder, Poe gives us studies in psychology and crime, then. He is doing this in "The Black Cat" too, but in this tale the folklore, religious language, and the religious terror of supernatural punishment that the narrator displays, make this the most Hawthornesque of Poe's tales.

The tale was written around the same time that Poe reviewed Hawthorne's collection of stories, *Twice-Told Tales*, so Poe may indeed have been influenced by Hawthorne when he wrote "The Black Cat." It is well known that Poe admired Hawthorne, as did the latter's one-time neighbour, Melville. In his review, Poe says that in his work Hawthorne "evinces extraordinary genius, having no rival either in America or elsewhere" (13: 141). Then follow some characteristic Poesque superlatives – *hyperbole* – along with a nice use of *anaphora* and *parison*: "He has the purest style, the finest taste, the most available scholarship, the most delicate humor, the most touching pathos, the most radiant imagination, the most consummate ingenuity" (13: 155).

15 Gargano insists that the theory of perverseness – the uncontrollable desire that sometimes comes upon us to act against our own best interests by harming ourselves or breaking the law – is nothing more than an attempt on the narrator's part to avoid responsibility for his sin, a slippery rationalization ("Poe's Narrators," 171; also "Perverseness Reconsidered"). I would suggest, rather, that it is an alternative theory in the form of a psychological explanation provided by the narrator as a smokescreen to hide his real motive for hanging Pluto. Although I have said that the narrator's rhetoric is normally inner-directed, here is one place in the tale where it is aimed more towards his readers than himself:

> And then came, as if to my final and irrevocable overthrow, the spirit of PERVERSENESS. Of this spirit philosophy takes no account. Yet I am not more sure that my soul lives, than I am that perverseness is one of the primitive impulses of the human heart – one of the indivisible primary faculties, or sentiments, which give direction to the character of Man. Who has not, a hundred times, found himself committing a vile or a silly action, for no other reason than because he knows he should not? … It was this unfathomable longing of the soul to vex itself – to offer violence to its own nature – to do wrong for the wrong's sake only – that urged me to continue and finally to consummate the injury I had inflicted upon the unoffending brute. One morning, in cool blood, I slipped a noose about its neck and hung it to the limb of a tree. (5: 146)

One persuasive device he employs is *erotesis* (*erotema*), a rhetorical question implying strong affirmation or denial: "Who has not, a hundred times, found himself committing a vile or a silly action, for no other reason than because he knows he should not? Have we not a perpetual inclination, in the teeth of our best judgment, to violate that which is Law, merely because we understand it to be such?" The narrator's use of *erotema* is a desperate rhetorical attempt to encourage acceptance in his readers of the theory of perversity. Through *erotema* he is asking them to think deductively (to move from the general to the specific) by saying something like this: "Look, everyone has succumbed to perverse impulses now and then, right? So you'll believe me when I tell you that perversity overcame me, too, on the occasion when I hanged my poor cat." Poe must have known what Corbett confirms, that this type of rhetorical question "can be an effective persuasive device, subtly influencing the kind of response one wants to get from an audience … By inducing the audience to make the appropriate response, the rhetorical question can often be more effective as a persuasive device than a direct assertion would be" (454).

CHAPTER THREE

1 The great clock in "The Devil in the Belfry" also has seven built into it: seven faces, one for each side of the steeple.

2 A similar thing happens in "The Devil in the Belfry": Weber suggests that the impish figure who causes temporal chaos in the Dutch borough of Vondervotteimittiss symbolizes the minute hand and that the belfry symbolizes the hour hand. I disagree with the latter assertion: rather, the belfry and its steeple simply constitute a clock within a clock (the larger clock of the borough itself – just as the large ebony clock in "Masque" is a clock within the larger clock of the abbey); it is the belfry-man, the bell-ringer, who represents the hour hand. After all, he is described as being fat (253), as the hour hand is the fatter of the two hands on a clock's face, and, when the devil figure overcomes him, he sits "upon the belfry-man, who was lying upon his back" (257) – just as a minute hand lies upon the hour hand when they come together to strike twelve o'clock, which is exactly what is happening (even though a thirteenth hour is about to strike, as well). Thus, the devil figure and the belfry-man parallel Prince Prospero and the Phantom, minute and hour hands respectively.

3 Here is another interesting point: in "Hawthorne's 'Plagiary': Poe's Duplicity" Regan, looking for possible sources in Hawthorne for "The Masque of the Red Death," cites one of his Twice-Told Tales: "The action of 'Howe's Masquerade' opens with a reminder that 'eleven strokes, full half an hour ago, had pealed from the clock of the Old South' and it ends with the music of a dead march" at midnight (290). Regan does not make the connection, but the events of "Howe's Masquerade" begin at 11:30 p.m. and end at 12:00 – the same allegorical time span that covers the climactic finale of "Red Death." If Poe was indeed inspired by Hawthorne, then, he may have taken the idea of the fatal thirty-minute time span from "Howe's Masquerade" (but see n4).

4 Charles N. Watson, Jr, suggests even more: that Poe got some of his ideas for "The Masque of the Red Death" from reading two specific Twice-Told Tales

of Hawthorne's, "The May-Pole of Merry Mount" and "The Haunted Mind."
As well as "Howe's Masquerade," Regan considers "Lady Eleanore's Mantle"
and other "legends of the Province House" additional Hawthorne tales that
inspired Poe ("Hawthorne's 'Plagiary'"). The danger with all influence criticism, of course, is that critics risk committing the fallacy in logic known as *post
hoc, ergo propter hoc* – "after this, therefore because of this" (also called the fallacy of "False Cause" or "Questionable Cause"). While Poe might have borrowed from Hawthorne, scholars should not forget the possibility that both
authors borrowed from a common source, if they borrowed at all.

5 In "The Hoax of the Red Death: Poe as Allegorist," Ruddick gives us an extended and thoughtful consideration of whether the tale falls into the category of allegory or not. He concludes that we cannot read the tale as such;
however, in trying to demonstrate this thesis, he does a better job of per-
suading me that the tale *is* allegorical. He quotes from Fletcher's book *Allegory: The Theory of a Symbolic Mode* in noting that an allegory must have
"periodic repetitions" (then shows us several in the tale) and a "kakodaemon" (then shows that Prospero "seems perfectly to fit Fletcher's description
of the typical kakodaemon" [270]). Next, Ruddick notes that "The 'Masque'
of the tale's title further suggests an allegorical dimension," that the "text ...
seems to indicate that the tale is an allegory" too (271), and finally that it
"borrows the major encoding device of contagion from Christian allegory"
(273). So far so good, but then he brings us back to the essay's central
premise: "should we discern even one major allegorical equation ... then we
must surely account in a similar manner for all the other main elements in
the tale: the Prince, the courtiers, the abbey, the suite of rooms, the ebony
clock, and the Red Death itself" (268). He seems to imply that if even one
element does not work allegorically then the tale as a whole cannot be so
read, and the one element that cannot be seen to function this way is the colour imagery, Ruddick believes (while black and red have fairly clear meanings, the other colours do not). To his argument I would make two
objections: first, some scholars do believe they have solved the riddle of the
colour imagery – see, for example, Pitcher (73), Vanderbilt (142 and 149n),
Pope-Hennessy (141), Peithman (116–17), and Cheney (37); second, I believe
Ruddick's central premise is faulty; even if we cannot come up with an explanation of the allegorical significance of the colours, that does not mean
we should throw out any and all allegorical interpretations of the other elements in the tale.

CHAPTER FOUR

1 Jesse Bier also claims to have found humour in Poe's poetry. He speaks,
   for instance, of the "overt humor" in "Al Aaraaf," suggesting that Poe "is
   spoofing the overwhelming Miltonic mode" (370). Later, Bier considers
   "The Raven":

   > Here Poe's serious, obsessive effort at lamentation is undercut by several
   > comic devices, both intentional and unintentional. There are inane
   > rhymes: "surely, that is" with "window lattice" and "what thereat is" …
   > which are triumphs in their way. There is metric absurdity and bathetic
   > overwriting: "What this grim, ungainly, ghastly, gaunt and ominous bird
   > of yore/ Meant in croaking 'Nevermore!'" There is witless alliteration and
   > assonance rather than true punning: "Whether *Temp*ter sent, or whether
   > *temp*est tossed." And, finally, there is anticlimax that utterly deflates and
   > destroys the best half-line in all his poetry: "Take thy beak from out my
   > heart," he concludes the penultimate stanza but adds, "and take thy form
   > from off my door!" (373)

   Stauffer, on the other hand, insists that humour, according to Poe, was "'directly antagonistical' to the soul of the Muse" (*Merry Mood*, 7); he admits a
   few lines later, however, that Poe did occasionally insert some of the comedic
   into his verse, and then spends several pages looking at some of the humorous poetry (7–9).
2 Stauffer discusses briefly "a national tempest in a teapot" that arose over the
   issue of Poe's humour or lack thereof in 1911. While the editors of the *Empo-
   ria Gazette* and *Chicago Tribune* objected strenuously to the claim that Poe
   was funny, the editor of the *Denver Republican* countered that "there are half
   a dozen of Poe's sketches of humor which give Poe a real claim as an American humorist" (quoted in *Merry Mood*, 4).
3 Some of Poe's contemporaries were clearly delighted with his comedy. In a
   letter of 21 February 1847, Thomas Chivers wrote to Poe, "I read your tale of
   the 'Spectacles' to some ladies here the other day, and they shouted – particularly at that place where you speak of the old lady's '*Bustle!* When they
   heard of the '*Universe of Bustle*' maybe they did n't [sic] laugh – '*up to the
   hearing of the Gods*'" (17: 279). James Paulding, in a letter (3 March 1836) to
   the editor White, mentions Poe's "fine humor" (17: 378). Thus, Stauffer
   should qualify his observation that "In his own lifetime Poe's readers did not
   think of him as a humorist" (*Merry Mood*, 1).

4 Stauffer begins his small book on Poe's humour by noting that, "In 1940 the
  French surrealist poet André Breton assembled an anthology of black humor. In it he included Jonathan Swift, Alfred Jarry, and Edgar Allan Poe"
  (*Merry Mood*, 1). It seems odd that Poe himself should have written black
  humour, considering his attitude toward a passage in *Life of Petrarch*:

  > We observe, also, far more serious defects – defects of *tone*. These sen-
  > tences, for instance, are in shockingly bad taste, – "The most skilful phy-
  > sicians stood aghast at this disease (the plague). The charlatan rejoiced at
  > it, *unless it attacked himself*, because it put quackery on a par with skill;
  > and compassionate women assisted *both physicians and quacks in doing no
  > good to their patients … This was a dance of the king of terrors over the earth,
  > and a very rapid one.*" Attempts at humour on such subjects are always ex-
  > ceedingly *low*. (Review of *Life of Petrarch*, 10: 205–6)

  But consider "King Pest"! And as for exceedingly tasteless humour, consider
  this passage from "Loss of Breath" describing the narrator's hanging. True,
  this tale is a parody of those published in *Blackwood's*, but that does not excuse Poe:

  > As for the jerk given to my neck upon the falling of the drop, it merely
  > proved a corrective to the twist afforded me by the fat gentleman in the
  > coach.
  >
  > For good reasons, however, I did my best to give the crowd the worth
  > of their trouble. My convulsions were said to be extraordinary. My spasms
  > it would have been difficult to beat. The populace *encored*. Several gentle-
  > men swooned; and a multitude of ladies were carried home in hysterics.
  > (2: 160–1)

  I make the point later that Poe sometimes employed literary techniques as a
  fictionist that he condemned as a critic.

5 In this connection, see also Harry M. Bayne, "Poe's 'Never Bet the Devil
  Your Head' and Southwest Humor," as well as Stauffer's brief discussion of
  "Thou Art the Man" as frontier humour (*Merry Mood*, 19–20).

6 But I *shall* mention a few of the scholarly studies that deal with comedy, sat-
  ire, and hoaxing in Poe's works – for instance, J. Gerald Kennedy's "The
  Preface as a Key to the Satire in *Pym*"; Richard P. Benton's "Poe's 'Lionizing':
  A Quiz on Willis and Lady Blessington" and "Is Poe's 'The Assignation' a
  Hoax?"; G.R. Thompson's "Is Poe's 'A Tale of the Ragged Mountains' a
  Hoax?"; Alexander Hammond's "A Reconstruction of Poe's 1833 'Tales of the
  Folio Club': Preliminary Notes," "Poe's 'Lionizing' and the Design of 'Tales

of the Folio Club'," and "Edgar Allan Poe's 'Tales of the Folio Club': The
Evolution of a Lost Book"; Thomas O. Mabbott's "On Poe's Tales of the Folio Club"; Benjamin Franklin Fisher IV's *The Very Spirit of Cordiality: The
Literary Uses of Alcohol and Alcoholism in the Tales of Edgar Allan Poe*, "Blackwood Articles á la Poe: How to Make a False Start Pay," and "Poe's 'Tarr and
Fether': Hoaxing in the Blackwood Mode"; Gargano's "The Distorted Perception of Poe's Comic Narrators"; William Whipple's "Poe's Political
Satire"; Claude Richard's "The Tales of the Folio Club and the Vocation
of Edgar Allan Poe as Humorist." See the bibliography for complete publication information.

7 This is *bathos* on the dramatic level. We find it on the sentence level in "Loss
of Breath." As the narrator describes how two cats started nibbling on his
nose, Poe begins with the grandeur of an epic simile (a two-pronged one, actually) – but consider how it ends: "as the loss of his ears proved the means of
elevating, to the throne of Cyrus, the Magian, or Mige-Gush, of Persia, and
as the cutting off his nose gave Zopyrus possession of Babylon, so the loss of a
few ounces of my countenance proved the salvation of my body" (2: 159).

8 Stauffer discusses the comedic sarcasm on the part of Dupin and the narrator directed at the uncomprehending Prefect of Police in "The Purloined
Letter" (*Merry Mood*, 19).

9 Weeks has more to say about Jupiter's role as laughing stock, and again the
humour is linguistic:

> Once out on the treasure hunt, Legrand's negro servant, Jupiter, has to
> climb a tree and seek out a skull on one of the limbs. He has then to drop
> the gold bug, attached to a string, through the skull's left eye. Up in the
> tree, when told to look for the skull's left eye, he exclaims: 'Hum! hoo!
> Dat's good! why dare ain't no eye left at all.' In his day, this humour was
> spontaneously written – and read – and imitated throughout the years
> which followed. In its total climax, it can be found in the zany dialogue of
> the Marx Brothers. (87)

The pun on *left* is *antanaclasis* (see the catalogue and chapter 5).

10 I could easily have cited more instances of humour in Poe's literary reviews,
and the "humor of scorn" is a theme that overlaps this chapter and chapter 5.
This point – about the connection in Poe's prose between humour and his
linguistic weaponry (in other words, *satire*) as a critic – is emphasized by a
passage from Weeks:

Curiously enough, one of Poe's pieces of criticism, 'William Ellery Channing', was selected by E.B. and Katharine S. White for their *Subtreasury of
American Humor,* 1941 … In this piece, Poe's phlegmatic satire disposes of
Channing's *Poems*: 'His book contains about sixty-three things, which he
calls poems, and which he no doubt seriously supposes so to be. They are full
of all kinds of mistakes, of which the most important is that of their having
been printed at all. They are not precisely English – nor will we insult a great
nation by calling them Kickapoo; perhaps they are Channingese.' (76)
Stauffer also has several paragraphs on the humour of Poe's critical reviews
(*Merry Mood,* 9–13). Indeed, that Poe was conscious of his deliberate use of
humour in his role as literary critic is demonstrated by a remark he makes to
Griswold in a letter (24 February 1845): "I believe that in 'funny' criticism (if
you wish any such) Flaccus will convey a tolerable idea of my style, and of
my serious manner Barnaby Rudge is a good specimen" (Ostrom, 279–80).

11 Stauffer also discusses certain devices of comedic repetition, though without
using any terms from stylistics (*Merry Mood,* 15). He lists the rhyming sur-
names in "The Spectacles" (Croissart, Froissart, Voissart, Moissart), "King
Pest" (Pest-Ilential, Pest-Iferous, Ten-Pest), and "Thingum Bob" (Fibalittle,
Squibalittle, Cribalittle). He might have compared these with *homoioteleuton*
and *homoioptoton* (see the catalogue of rhetorical terms) or considered these
similar-sounding names part of a morphological set (see the catalogue). At
any rate, they also comprise Poe's linguistic comedy.

12 It is almost as if Poe's frame narrator is manifesting one symptom of the
"imp of the perverse":

There lives no man who at some period, has not been tormented … by an
earnest desire to tantalize a listener by circumlocution. The speaker is
aware that he displeases; he has every intention to please; he is usually
curt, precise, and clear; the most laconic and luminous language is struggling for utterance upon his tongue; it is only with difficulty that he re-
strains himself from giving it flow; he dreads and deprecates the anger of
him whom he addresses; yet, the thought strikes him, that by certain involutions and parentheses, this anger may be engendered. (6: 148)

It would seem clear, however, that Poe wants to amuse rather than anger his
readers through the "involutions and parentheses" of the narrator of "The
Thousand-and-second Tale of Scheherazade." If we *are* annoyed, it is the
same kind of amused annoyance that we feel listening to Grampa Simpson.

13 I cannot help one more time quoting Stauffer, whose critical footsteps I have
    encountered repeatedly on the path before me while preparing this study.
    Here Stauffer quotes William Carlos Williams, who "long ago noticed Poe's
    affinity with Twain when he remarked in *In the American Grain* that there is
    in his work 'a primitive awkwardness of diction, lack of polish, colloquialism
    that is, unexpectedly, especially in the dialogues, much in the vein of Mark
    Twain'" (*Merry Mood*, 22).

CHAPTER FIVE

1 The risks were great and the results ultimately devastating in their total effect. As for the risks, Lowell (17: 121) wrote to Poe to beware of wounding
   the feelings of the poet Rufus Dawes, whom Poe had tomahawked in the
   October number of *Graham's* (see 11: 131–47). In those days of duelling to
   avenge one's honour, Poe would have been wise to listen to such advice. This
   warning appears in a letter of 19 November 1842; the next month, Lowell
   wrote Poe telling him of Henry Tuckerman's refusal to publish "The Tell-
   Tale Heart" in his *Boston Miscellany*, speculating that Poe's remarks on Tuckerman in the *Autography* may be to blame (Poe had called him "an insufferably tedious and dull" writer [15: 217]). In a letter written precisely two years
   later, Lowell again seemed to take pleasure in suggesting that Poe's critical reviews were still hurting his chances to succeed with publishers: "I also took
   the liberty of praising you to a Mr. Colton, who has written 'Tecumseh' …
   & whom I suspect, from some wry faces he made on first hearing your
   name, you have cut up" (17: 195). That Poe made powerful enemies among
   the literary cliques of his time and place – the Griswold case is only the most
   notorious – is well known to Poe specialists. Harrison's volume of Poe correspondence shows that Poe's literary enemies and their supporters were
   slandering his reputation years, even decades, after his death. In his final
   years, they were apparently sabotaging his attempts to establish the *Stylus*
   and to remarry.
       Much of this fallout was the direct result of Poe's tomahawking critical
   reviews. He did attempt to engage in damage control, however: he now and
   then found himself apologizing to those whom he had slashed, including
   Griswold (17: 170; Ostrom, 275), Chivers (Ostrom, 207), and Cornelius
   Mathews (Ostrom, 245). Sometimes the apologies would be offered to those

from whom Poe needed a loan or some other favour. Griswold was often the target.

2 Poe was often praised highly for his critical courage. His friend F.W. Thomas wrote to tell Poe that Robert Tyler valued his opinion "more than any other critic's in the country – to which I subscribed" (17: 105); Thomas goes on to suggest that he uses Poe as a touchstone against which to measure the critical opinions of others (106). The rather sycophantic Chivers called Poe "the best critic in this Country" (116) and Lowell praised him as "almost the only *fearless* American critic" (120), one who is able "to keep our criticism in a little better trim" (139). One thing that Lowell admired most about Poe was the latter's scrupulous attempts to avoid the fallacy of assertion in his reviews – his insistence on buttressing his arguments with exemplifications from the text: "You occasionally state a critical proposition from which I *dissent*, but I am always satisfied. I care not a straw *what* a man says, if I see that *he* has *his* grounds for it, & knows thoroughly what he is talking about. You might cut me up as much as you pleased & I should read what you said with respect, & with a great deal more of satisfaction, than most of the praise I get, affords me" (159). Anna Cora Mowatt sent Poe a comedy to peruse, telling him that "your criticisms will be prized" (208). By 1849 Poe finally had made contact with a man able to give the *Stylus* project a great boost, financially – and who stipulated that, if they became partners in the project, Poe would have complete editorial control. E.H.N. Patterson's letter of 7 May summarized much of what was wrong with American literary criticism – and these failings were those against which Poe himself had railed and for which he had attempted to provide an antidote:

> Our Literature is, just now, sadly deficient in the department of criticism. The Boston Reviewers are, generally, too much affected by local prejudices to give impartial criticisms; the Philadelphia Magazines have become mere monthly bulletins for booksellers; Willis does not, with his paper, succeed, *even tolerably,* as a critic; in fact, I seldom find any critique so nearly according with my own idea of the *true aim* and *manner* of criticism as were yours, while you had charge of that department in *Graham's* and *Burton's.* (352–3)

One of the great tragedies and ironies of American literary history is that, with his beloved *Stylus* project finally on the verge of becoming a reality, Poe would be dead five months later.

APPENDIX TWO

1 The abbreviation refers to the standard reference work in the field of psychology, *Diagnostic and Statistical Manual of Mental Disorders*. When it appeared in *Mosaic* (1992), this essay referred to the revised third edition of the *DSM*; since then a fourth edition has come out. In their respective chapters on schizophrenia there are no substantial changes, but I shall employ both editions here – *DSM-III-R* because it sometimes provides more useful quotations, *DSM-IV* for slightly revised data.

2 Eleven years before the publication of this essay in *Mosaic*, Stephen Peithman labelled the protagonist in "The Tell-Tale Heart" correctly: "He seems also to be a paranoid schizophrenic, with delusions of persecution accompanied by hostility and aggressiveness" (135). I wonder why Peithman hedges ("seems") and why he did not explore the insight fully (the diagnosis is confined to a mere annotation). Fortunately, from my point of view, Peithman did not elaborate; at any rate, I owe him an apology for not discovering his insight in time to give him credit in the *Mosaic* essay.

3 This theory that Poe engaged in research while writing his prose fiction certainly seems substantiated by a remark he makes in a letter (2 July 1844) to James Russell Lowell: "I scribble all day, and *read all night*" (Ostrom, 256; my italics). Even better is a statement he makes in a letter (26 June 1849) to George Eveleth:

> The essay you enclose, on the igneous liquidity of the Earth, embodies some truth, and evinces much sagacity – but no doubt ere this you have perceived that you have been groping in the dark as regards the general subject. Before theorizing ourselves on such topics, it is always wisest to make ourselves acquainted with the actually ascertained facts & established doctrines. (Ostrom, 449)

This point is clearly made in the context of scientific studies, and although Poe's remark insofar as his own work is concerned is made in the context of *Eureka*, there is no reason to suppose the methodology to which he refers is not equally applicable to tales as clinically precise as "The Tell-Tale Heart."

Bibliography

Abel, Darrel. "A Key to the House of Usher." *The University of Toronto Quarterly* 18 (Jan. 1949): 176–85.

Abrams, M.H. *A Glossary of Literary Terms.* 5th ed. Toronto: Holt 1988.

Ainsworth, William Harrison. "Maniacal Style and Furibund Story." 1853. *Moby-Dick.* Eds Harrison Hayford and Hershel Parker. Norton Critical Editions. New York: Norton 1967. 619–21.

Allen, Hervey. *Israfel: The Life and Times of Edgar Allan Poe.* New York: Doran 1927.

Aly, Bower, and Grafton P. Tanquary. "The Early National Period, 1788–1860." In *A History and Criticism of American Public Address.* Ed. William Norwood Brigance. Vol. 1. 1943. New York: Russell 1960. 55–110.

American Psychiatric Association. "Schizophrenia." In *Diagnostic and Statistical Manual of Mental Disorders.* 3rd ed., rev. Washington, D.C.: American Psychiatric Association 1987. 187–98.

– "Schizophrenia and Other Psychotic Disorders." In *Diagnostic and Statistical Manual of Mental Disorders.* 4th ed. Washington, D.C.: American Psychiatric Association 1994. 273–90.

Amper, Susan. "Untold Story: The Lying Narrator in 'The Black Cat'." *Studies in Short Fiction* 29 (1992): 475–85.

Anderson, Gayle Denington. "Demonology in 'The Black Cat'." *Poe Studies* 10 (Dec. 1977): 43–4.

Arnold, John. "Poe's 'Lionizing': The Wound and the Bawdry." *Literature and Psychology* 17 (1967): 52–4.

Auden, W.H. Introduction. *Edgar Allan Poe: Selected Prose and Poetry.* In *The Recognition of Edgar Allan Poe: Selected Criticism Since 1829.* Ed. Eric W. Carlson. Ann Arbor, MI: University of Michigan Press 1966. 220–30.

Badenhausen, Richard. "Fear and Trembling in Literature of the Fantastic: Edgar Allan Poe's 'The Black Cat'." *Studies in Short Fiction* 29 (1992): 487–98.

Baldick, Chris. *Oxford Concise Dictionary of Literary Terms.* Oxford and New York: Oxford University Press 1990.

Bayne, Harry M. "Poe's 'Never Bet the Devil Your Head' and Southwest Humor." *ARLR* 3 (1989): 278–9.

Beaver, Harold, ed. *The Science Fiction of Edgar Allan Poe.* New York: Penguin 1976.

Benton, Richard P. "Is Poe's 'The Assignation' a Hoax?" *Nineteenth-Century Fiction* 18 (1963): 193–7.

– "Poe's 'Lionizing': A Quiz on Willis and Lady Blessington." *Studies in Short Fiction* 5 (spring 1968): 239–44.

Bier, Jesse. *The Rise and Fall of American Humor.* New York: Holt 1968.

Bittner, William. *Poe: A Biography.* London: Elek 1962.

Blair, Walter. "Poe's Conception of Incident and Tone in the Tale." *Modern Philology* 41 (May 1944): 228–40.

Bloom, Harold. Introduction. *Modern Critical Interpretations: The Tales of Poe.* New York: Chelsea 1987. 1–15.

Bonaparte, Marie. "The Tell-Tale Heart." *The Life and Works of Edgar Allan Poe: A Psycho-Analytic Interpretation.* Trans. John Rodker. 1949. New York: Humanities 1971. 491–504.

Bootzin, Richard R., Joan Ross Acocella, and Lauren B. Alloy. "Schizophrenia and Paranoia." In *Abnormal Psychology: Current Perspectives.* 1972. 6th ed. Toronto: McGraw 1993. 363–89.

Buranelli, Vincent. *Edgar Allan Poe.* New York: Twayne 1961.

Burke, Edmund. *A Philosophical Enquiry into the Origin of our Ideas of the Sublime and Beautiful.* 1757. Ed. Adam Phillips. Oxford and New York: Oxford University Press 1990.

Bynum, Paige Matthey. "'Observe How Healthily – How Calmly I Can Tell You the Whole Story': Moral Insanity and Edgar Allan Poe's 'The Tell-Tale Heart'." In *Literature and Science as Modes of Expression.* Ed. Frederick Amrine. Boston Studies in the Philosophy of Science 115. Boston: Kluwer 1989. 141–52.

Campbell, Killis. "Poe's Knowledge of the Bible." *Studies in Philology* 27 (1930): 546–51.

– "Poe's Reading." *University of Texas Studies in English* 5 (1925): 166–96.

– "Poe's Treatment of the Negro and of the Negro Dialect." *University of Texas Studies in English* 16 (1936): 106–14.

Cassale, Ottavio. "The Dematerialization of William Wilson: Poe's Use of Cumulative Allegory." *South Carolina Review* 11 (1978): 70–9.

Caputi, Anthony. "The Refrain in Poe's Poetry." *American Literature* (1953). Rpt. in *On Poe: The Best from American Literature*. Ed. Louis J. Budd and Edwin H. Cady. Durham and London: Duke University Press 1993. 92–101.

Cheney, Patrick. "Poe's Use of *The Tempest* and the Bible in 'The Masque of the Red Death'." *English Language Notes* 20 (March-June 1983): 31–9.

Clark, Donald Lemen. "The Progymnasmata." In *Rhetoric: Concepts, Definitions, Boundaries*. Eds. William A. Covino and David A. Jolliffe. Toronto: Allyn 1995. 620–31.

Cleman, John. "Irresistible Impulses: Edgar Allan Poe and the Insanity Defense." *American Literature* 63 (Dec. 1991): 623–40.

Clemens, Samuel (Mark Twain). *The Adventures of Huckleberry Finn*. 1884. Eds Walter Blair and Victor Fisher. Berkeley: University of California Press 1985.

– "To William Dean Howells." 18 Jan. 1909. In *Mark Twain's Letters*. Ed. Albert Bigelow Paine. Vol. 2. New York: Harper 1917. 830.

Clendenning, John. "Anything Goes: Comic Aspects in 'The Cask of Amontillado'." In *American Humor: Essays Presented to John C. Gerber*. Ed. O.M. Brack, Jr. Arizona: Arete 1977. 13–26.

Clough, Wilson O. "The Use of Color Words by Edgar Allen [sic] Poe." *PMLA* 45 (June 1930): 598–613.

Cluett, Robert, and Rina Kampeas. *Grossly Speaking*. Toronto: Discourse 1979.

Cmiel, Kenneth. "Rhetoric." In *A Companion to American Thought*. Eds Richard Wightman Fox and James T. Kloppenberg. Cambridge: Blackwell 1995. 592–3.

Cohen, Carl, and Irving M. Copi. *Introduction to Logic*. 9th ed. New York: Macmillan 1994.

Cohen, Hennig. "A Comic Mode of the Romantic Imagination: Poe, Hawthorne, Melville." In *The Comic Imagination in American Literature*. Ed. Louis D. Rubin, Jr. New Jersey: Rutgers 1973. 85–99.

Connor, Frederick W. "Poe and John Nichol: Notes on a Source of *Eureka*." In *... All These to Teach*. Eds Robert A. Bryan et al. Gainesville, FL: University of Florida Press 1965. 190–208.

Corbett, Edward P.J. *Classical Rhetoric for the Modern Student.* 1965. 3rd ed. New York: Oxford University Press 1990.

Covino, William A., and David A. Jolliffe. *Rhetoric: Concepts, Definitions, Boundaries.* Toronto: Allyn 1995.

Cox, James M. "Edgar Poe: Style as Pose." *Virginia Quarterly Review* 44 (winter 1968): 67–89.

Crisman, William. "'Mere Household Events' in Poe's 'The Black Cat'." *Studies in American Fiction* 12 (1984): 87–90.

Crowley, Sharon. *Ancient Rhetorics for Contemporary Students.* Toronto: Allyn 1994.

Cuddon, J.A. *Penguin Dictionary of Literary Terms and Literary Theory.* 3rd ed. New York: Penguin 1992.

Dain, Norman. *Concepts of Insanity in the United States, 1789–1865.* New Brunswick, NJ: Rutgers University Press 1964.

Dameron, J. Lasley. "Poe, 'Simplicity,' and *Blackwood's Magazine.*" *Mississippi Quarterly* 51 (spring 1998): 233–42.

Davidson, Edward H. Introduction. *Selected Writings of Edgar Allan Poe.* Boston: Houghton 1956. vii-xxviii.

– *Poe: A Critical Study.* Cambridge: Belknap 1957.

Davidson, Gerald C., and John M. Neale. "Schizophrenia." In *Abnormal Psychology.* 1974. 7th ed. Toronto: Wiley 1998.

de Navarre, Marguerite. *The Heptameron.* Trans. P.A. Chilton. New York: Penguin 1984.

DeShell, Jeffrey. *The Peculiarity of Literature: An Allegorical Approach to Poe's Fiction.* Madison: Fairleigh Dickinson University Press 1997.

Dupriez, Bernard. *A Dictionary of Literary Devices: Gradus, A-Z.* Trans. Albert W. Halsall. Toronto: University of Toronto Press 1991.

Eddings, Dennis W. *Poe's Tell-Tale Clocks.* Baltimore: Enoch Pratt Free Library and the Edgar Allan Poe Society of Baltimore 1994.

– ed. *The Naiad Voice: Essays on Poe's Satiric Hoaxing.* Port Washington, NY: Associated Faculty Press 1983.

Eliot, Thomas Sternes. "From Poe to Valéry." In *The Recognition of Edgar Allan Poe: Selected Criticism Since 1829.* Ed. Eric W. Carlson. Ann Arbor, MI: University of Michigan Press 1966. 205–19.

Engel, S. Morris. *With Good Reason: An Introduction to Informal Fallacies.* 4th ed. New York: St. Martin's 1990.

Espy, Willard R. *The Garden of Eloquence: A Rhetorical Bestiary.* 1983. New York: Dutton 1985.

Fiedler, Leslie. *Love and Death in the American Novel.* Rev. ed. New York: Stein and Day 1966.

Fisher, Benjamin Franklin. "Blackwood Articles à la Poe: How to Make a False Start Pay." *RLV* 39 (1973): 418–32.

– "Playful 'Germanism' in 'The Fall of the House of Usher': The Storyteller's Art." In *Ruined Eden of the Present: Hawthorne, Melville, and Poe.* Eds G.R. Thompson and Virgil L. Lokke. West Lafayette, Indiana: Purdue University Press 1981. 355–74.

– "Poe's 'Tarr and Fether': Hoaxing in the Blackwood Mode." *Topic* 31 (1977): 29–40.

– *The Very Spirit of Cordiality: The Literary Uses of Alcohol and Alcoholism in the Tales of Edgar Allan Poe.* Baltimore: Edgar Allan Poe Society 1978.

Fletcher, Richard M. *The Stylistic Development of Edgar Allan Poe.* The Hague, Paris: Mouton 1973.

Forrest, William Mentzel. *Biblical Allusions in Poe.* New York: Macmillan 1928.

Frushell, Richard C. "'An Incarnate Night-Mare': Moral Grotesquerie in 'The Black Cat'." *Poe Studies* 5 (1972): 43–4.

Fuller, Margaret. "Poe's Tales." In *The Recognition of Edgar Allan Poe: Selected Criticism Since 1829.* Ed. Eric W. Carlson. Ann Arbor, MI: University of Michigan Press 1966. 17–18.

Galloway, David. Introduction. *The Other Poe: Comedies and Satires.* Ed. David Galloway. New York: Penguin 1983. 7–22.

Gargano, James W. "'The Black Cat': Perverseness Reconsidered." *Texas Studies in Literature and Language* 2 (summer 1960): 172–8.

– "The Distorted Perception of Poe's Comic Narrators." *Topic* 16 (1976): 23–43.

– "The Theme of Time in 'The Tell-Tale Heart'." *Studies in Short Fiction* 5 (summer 1968): 378–82.

– "The Question of Poe's Narrators." In *Poe: A Collection of Critical Essays.* Ed. Robert Regan. Twentieth Century Views. Englewood Cliffs, NJ: Prentice 1967. 164–71.

Gooder, R.D. "Edgar Allan Poe: The Meaning of Style." *The Cambridge Quarterly* 16 (1987): 110–23.

Gray, Martin. *A Dictionary of Literary Terms.* 2nd ed. Essex: Longman 1992.

Hammond, Alexander. "Edgar Allan Poe's 'Tales of the Folio Club': The Evolution of a Lost Book." *Poe at Work: Seven Textual Studies.* Ed. Benjamin Franklin Fisher IV. Baltimore: The Edgar Allan Poe Society 1978. 13–43.

– "Poe's 'Lionizing' and the Design of 'Tales of the Folio Club'." *Emerson Society Quarterly* 18 (1972): 154–65.

- "A Reconstruction of Poe's 1833 'Tales of the Folio Club': Preliminary Notes."
  Poe Studies 5 (1972): 25–32.

Harmon, William, and C. Hugh Holman. *A Handbook to Literature.* 7th ed.
  New Jersey: Prentice 1996.

Harrison, James A. *Biography. The Complete Works of Edgar Allan Poe.* Vol. 1. Ed.
  James A. Harrison. 1902. New York: AMS 1965.

Haslam, John. *Observations on Madness and Melancholy.* 2nd ed. London:
  J. Callow 1809.

Hoffman, Daniel. "Grotesques and Arabesques." *Poe Poe Poe Poe Poe Poe Poe.*
  Garden City: Doubleday 1972. 226–32.

Hough, Robert L. Introduction. *Literary Criticism of Edgar Allan Poe.* Regents
  Critics Series. Lincoln, NE: University of Nebraska Press 1965. ix–xxviii.

Howarth, William L. Introduction. In *Twentieth-Century Interpretations of
  Poe's Tales: A Collection of Critical Essays.* Englewood Cliffs, NJ: Prentice 1971.
  1–22.

Hubbell, Jay B. "Edgar Allan Poe." In *Eight American Authors: A Review of Research and Criticism.* Rev. ed. New York: Norton 1971. 3–36.

Hungerford, Edward. "Poe and Phrenology." *American Literature* 2 (1930): 209–
  31. Rpt. in *On Poe: The Best from American Literature.* Eds Louis J. Budd and
  Edwin H. Cady. Durham and London: Duke University Press 1993. 1–23.

Hussey, John P. "Narrative Voice and Classical Rhetoric in *Eureka.*" *American
  Transcendental Quarterly* 26 (spring 1975): 37–42.

Jacobs, Robert D. *Poe: Journalist & Critic.* Baton Rouge: Louisiana State University Press 1969.

- "Rhetoric in Southern Writing: Poe." *Georgia Review* 12 (1958): 76–9.

James, Henry. "Comments." In *The Recognition of Edgar Allan Poe: Selected
  Criticism Since 1829.* Ed. Eric W. Carlson. Ann Arbor, MI: University of
  Michigan Press 1966. 65–7.

Joseph, Sister Miriam. *Shakespeare's Use of the Arts of Language.* New York:
  Hafner 1966.

Kanjo, Eugene R. "'The Imp of the Perverse': Poe's Dark Comedy of Art and
  Death." *Poe Newsletter* 2 (Oct. 1969): 41–4.

Kaplan, Sidney. "An Introduction to *Pym.*" In *Poe: A Collection of Critical Essays.* Ed. Robert Regan. Englewood Cliffs, NJ: Prentice 1969. 145–63.

Kaufhold, Jack. "The Humor of Edgar Allan Poe." *Virginia Cavalcade* 29
  (1980): 136–43.

Kennedy, J. Gerald. "The Preface as a Key to the Satire in *Pym.*" *Studies in the
  Novel* 5 (summer 1973): 191–6.

Ketterer, David. *The Rationale of Deception in Poe.* Baton Rouge: Louisiana State University Press 1979.

Kierly, Robert. "The Comic Masks of Edgar Allan Poe." *Umanesimo* 1 (1967): 31–41.

Kopely, Richard. "Hawthorne's Transplanting and Transforming 'The Tell-Tale Heart'." *Studies in American Fiction* 23 (autumn 1995): 231–41.

Kremenliev, Elva Baer. "The Literary Uses of Astronomy in the Writings of Edgar Allan Poe." PhD diss. University of California 1963.

Lanham, Richard A. *A Handlist of Rhetorical Terms.* 2nd ed. Berkeley and Los Angeles: University of California Press 1991.

Levin, Harry. "Notes from Underground." In *The Power of Blackness: Hawthorne, Poe, Melville.* Chicago: Ohio University Press 1958. 132–64.

Lewis, Paul. "Poe's Humor: A Psychological Analysis." *Studies in Short Fiction* 26 (fall 1989): 531–46.

Lowell, James Russell. "Edgar Allan Poe." In *The Recognition of Edgar Allan Poe: Selected Criticism Since 1829.* Ed. Eric W. Carlson. Ann Arbor, MI: University of Michigan Press 1966. 5–16.

Mabbott, Thomas Ollive, ed. *The Collected Works of Edgar Allan Poe.* Cambridge, MA: Harvard University Press 1978.

– "On Poe's Tales of the Folio Club." *Sewanee Review* 36 (1928): 171–6.

Machiavelli, Niccolò. *The Prince.* Trans. David Wootton. Indianapolis: Hackett 1995.

Madden, Fred. "Poe's 'The Black Cat' and Freud's 'The Uncanny'." *Literature & Psychology* 39 (1993): 52–62.

Matheson, T.J. "Poe's 'The Black Cat' as a Critique of Temperance Literature." *Mosaic* 19 (summer 1986): 69–81.

Matthiessen, F.O. *American Renaissance: Art and Expression in the Age of Emerson and Whitman.* 1941. New York: Oxford University Press 1968.

May, Charles E. *Edgar Allan Poe: A Study of the Short Fiction.* Boston: Twayne 1991.

McElrath, Joseph R. "Poe's Conscious Prose Technique." *NEMLA Newsletter* 2 (1970): 34–43.

McElroy, John Harmon. "The Kindred Artist; or, The Case of the Black Cat." *Studies in American Humor* 3 (1976): 103–17.

McLuhan, Herbert Marshall. "Edgar Poe's Tradition." *Sewanee Review* 52 (winter 1944): 24–33.

Melville, Herman. *Billy Budd, Sailor.* Eds Harrison Hayford and Merton M. Sealts, Jr. Chicago: University of Chicago Press 1962.

Meyers, Jeffrey. *Edgar Allan Poe: His Life and Legacy.* New York: Scribner's 1992.

Milic, Louis T. "Metaphysical Criticism of Style." In *New Rhetorics*. Ed. Martin Steinmann, Jr. New York: Scribner's 1967. 161–75.

Montaigne, Michele de. *Essays*. Trans. J.M. Cohen. New York: Penguin 1978.

Mooney, Stephen L. "The Comic in Poe's Fiction." *American Literature* 33 (1962): 433–41.

– "Comic Intent in Poe's Tales: Five Criteria." *Modern Language Notes* 76 (1961): 432–4.

Munson, Gorham B. *Style and Form in American Prose*. Washington, New York: Kennikat 1969.

Murray, Angus Wolfe, ed. *Comic Tales of Edgar Allan Poe*. Edinburgh: Canongate 1973.

Nänny, Max. "Chiastic Structures in Literature: Some Forms and Functions." In *The Structure of Texts*. Ed. Udo Fries. Tübingen: Gunter Narr 1987. 83, 91–6.

Norman, Emma Katherine. "Poe's Knowledge of Latin." *American Literature* 6 (1934): 72–7.

Ostrom, John Ward. *The Letters of Edgar Allan Poe*. 2 vols. Cambridge, MS: Harvard University Press 1948.

Parks, Edd Winfield. *Edgar Allan Poe as Literary Critic*. Georgia: University of Georgia Press 1964.

Peithman, Stephen, ed. *The Annotated Tales of Edgar Allan Poe*. New York: Doubleday 1981.

Philips, Edith. "The French of Edgar Allan Poe." *American Speech* 2 (1927): 270–4.

Phillips, Elizabeth C. "'His Right of Attendance': The Image of the Black Man in the Works of Poe and Two of His Contemporaries." *No Fairer Land: Studies in Southern Literature Before 1900*. Eds J. Lasley Dameron and James W. Matthews. Troy, NY: Whitson 1986. 172–84.

– "Mere Household Events: The Metaphysics of Mania." *Edgar Allan Poe: An American Imagination*. Port Washington: Kennikat 1979. 97–137.

Pitcher, Edward William. "Horological and Chronological Time in 'Masque of the Red Death'." *American Transcendental Quarterly* 29 (winter 1976): 71–5.

Poe, Edgar Allan. *The Complete Works of Edgar Allan Poe*. Ed. James A. Harrison. 17 vols. 1902. Rpt. New York: AMS 1965.

Pollin, Burton R. "The Role of Byron and Mary Shelley in 'The Masque'." In *Discoveries in Poe*. Notre Dame, IN: University of Notre Dame Press 1970. 75–90.

– ed. *Word Index to Poe's Fiction.* New York: Gordian 1982.

Pope-Hennessy, Una. *Edgar Allan Poe: A Critical Biography.* 1934. New York: Haskell 1971.

Porter, Roy. Introduction. In John Haslam, *Illustrations of Madness.* New York: Routledge 1988. xi–lxiv.

Powell, Nicolas. *Fuseli: The Nightmare.* New York: Viking 1973.

Prichard, James Cowles. *A Treatise on Insanity and Other Disorders Affecting the Mind.* Philadelphia: Haswell, Barrington, and Haswell 1837.

Quinn, Arthur. *Figures of Speech: 60 Ways to Turn a Phrase.* Salt Lake City: Smith 1982.

Quinn, Arthur Hobson. *Edgar Allan Poe: A Critical Biography.* New York: Appleton 1941.

Quirk, Tom. "What if Poe's Humorous Tales Were Funny?: Poe's 'X-ing a Para-grab' and Twain's 'Journalism in Tennessee'." *Studies in American Humor* 3 (1995): 36–48.

Ray, Isaac. *A Treatise on the Medical Jurisprudence of Insanity.* Boston: C.C. Little and J. Brown 1838.

Regan, Robert. Introduction. *Poe: A Collection of Critical Essays.* Ed. Robert Regan. Englewood Cliffs, NJ: Prentice 1967. 1–13.

– "Hawthorne's 'Plagiary': Poe's Duplicity." *Nineteenth-Century Fiction* 25 (1970–71): 281–98.

Reilly, John E. "The Lesser Death-Watch and 'The Tell-Tale Heart'." *American Transcendental Quarterly* 2 (1969): 3–9.

Richard, Claude. "The Tales of the Folio Club and the Vocation of Edgar Allan Poe as Humorist." Trans. Mark L. Mitchell. *University of Mississippi Studies in English* 8 (1990): 185–99.

Robb, Mary Margaret, and Lester Thonssen, eds. *Chironomia or A Treatise on Rhetorical Delivery,* Gilbert Austin. 1806. Landmarks in Rhetoric and Public Address. Carbondale and Edwardsville: Southern Illinois University Press 1966.

Roppolo, Joseph Patrick. "Meaning and 'The Masque of the Red Death'." In *Poe: A Collection of Critical Essays.* Ed. Robert Regan. Englewood Cliffs, NJ: Prentice 1967. 134–44.

Roth, Martin. "Inside 'The Masque of the Red Death'." *SubStance* 13 (1984): 50–3.

Rourke, Constance. "I Hear America Singing." *American Humor: A Study of the National Character.* New York: Doubleday 1931. 133–62.

Ruddick, Nicholas. "The Hoax of the Red Death: Poe as Allegorist." *Sphinx* 4 (1985): 268–76.

Shaw, George Bernard. "Edgar Allan Poe." In *The Recognition of Edgar Allan Poe: Selected Criticism Since 1829*. Ed. Eric W. Carlson. Ann Arbor, MI: University of Michigan Press 1966. 95–100.

Shelden, Pamela J. "'True Originality': Poe's Manipulation of the Gothic Tradition." *American Transcendental Quarterly* 29 (1976): 75–80.

Short, Bryan C. *Cast by Means of Figures: Herman Melville's Rhetorical Development*. Amherst: University of Massachusetts Press 1992.

Silverman, Kenneth. *Edgar A. Poe: Mournful and Never-Ending Remembrance*. New York: HarperCollins 1991.

Smith, Allan Gardner. "Chapter Two: Edgar Allan Poe." *The Analysis of Motives: Early American Psychology and Fiction*. Amsterdam: Rodopi 1980. 38–75.

– "The Psychological Context of Three Tales by Poe." *Journal of American Studies* 7 (1973): 279–92.

Sonnino, Lee A. *A Handbook to Sixteenth-Century Rhetoric*. London: Routledge 1968.

Spanier, Sandra Whipple. "'Nests of Boxes': Form, Sense, and Style in Poe's 'The Imp of the Perverse'." *Studies in Short Fiction* 17 (summer 1980): 307–16.

Stauffer, Donald Barlow. "The Language and Style of the Prose." In *A Companion to Poe Studies*. Ed. Eric W. Carlson. Westport, CT: Greenwood 1996. 448–67.

– *The Merry Mood: Poe's Uses of Humor*. Baltimore: Enoch Pratt, Edgar Allan Poe Society and the University of Baltimore 1982.

– "Style and Meaning in 'Ligeia' and 'William Wilson'." *Studies in Short Fiction* 2 (1965): 316–30.

Stepp, Walter. "The Ironic Double in Poe's 'The Cask of Amontillado'." In *Modern Critical Interpretations: The Tales of Poe*. Ed. Harold Bloom. New York: Chelsea 1987. 55–61.

Stone, Alan A., and Sue Smart Stone. "Psychotic Symptoms." *The Abnormal Personality Through Literature*. Englewood Cliffs, NJ: Prentice 1966. 126–31.

Sue, David, Derald Sue, and Stanley Sue. *Understanding Abnormal Behavior*. 2nd ed. Boston: Houghton 1986. 425–45.

Symons, Julian. *The Tell-Tale Heart: The Life and Works of Edgar Allan Poe*. 1978. New York: Penguin 1981.

Tate, Allen. "The Angelic Imagination." In *The Recognition of Edgar Allan Poe: Selected Criticism Since 1829*. Ed. Eric W. Carlson. Ann Arbor, MI: University of Michigan Press 1966. 236–54.

– "Our Cousin, Mr. Poe." In *Poe: A Collection of Critical Essays*. Ed. Robert Regan. Twentieth Century Views. Englewood Cliffs, NJ: Prentice 1967. 38–50.

Taylor, Warren. *Tudor Figures of Rhetoric*. Whitewater, WI: Language 1972.

Thomas, Dwight, and David K. Jackson. *The Poe Log: A Documentary Life of Edgar Allan Poe 1809–1849*. Boston: Hall 1987.

Thomas, Ota. "The Teaching of Rhetoric in the United States During the Classical Period of Education." In *A History and Criticism of American Public Address*. Ed. William Norwood Brigance. Vol. 1. 1943. New York: Russell 1960. 193–210.

Thompson, G.R. "Is Poe's 'A Tale of the Ragged Mountains' a Hoax?" *Studies in Short Fiction* 6 (summer 1969): 454–60.

– "On the Nose – Further Speculation on the Sources and Meaning of Poe's 'Lionizing'." *Studies in Short Fiction* 6 (fall 1968): 94–6.

Tomlinson, David. "The Humor of Edgar Allan Poe: Poe's Humor in Summary." 1997. 3 March 2000 <http://odur.let.rug.nl~usa/E/Poe_humor/ poe6.htm>

Toner, Jennifer Dilalla. "The 'Remarkable Effect' of 'Silly Words': Dialect and Signature in 'The Gold-Bug'." *Arizona Quarterly: A Journal of American Literature, Culture and Theory* 49 (spring 1993): 1–20.

Trieber, J. Marshall. "The Scornful Grin: A Study of Poesque Humor." *Poe Studies* 4 (1971): 32–4.

Vanderbilt, Kermit. "Art and Nature in 'The Masque of the Red Death'." *Nineteenth-Century Fiction* 22 (March 1968): 379–89. Rpt. in *Edgar Allan Poe: A Study of the Short Fiction*. Charles E. May. Boston: Twayne 1991. 140–50.

Vitanza, Victor J. "'The Question of Poe's Narrators': Perverseness Considered Once Again." *American Transcendental Quarterly* 38 (spring 1978): 137–49.

Walcutt, Charles C. "The Logic of Poe." *College English* 2 (1941): 438–44.

Walker, I.M. "The 'Legitimate Sources' of Terror in 'The Fall of the House of Usher'." *Modern Language Review* 61 (1966): 585–92.

Watson, Charles N., Jr. "'The Masque of the Red Death' and Poe's Reading of Hawthorne." *The Library Chronicle* 45 (1981): 143–9.

Weaver, Aubrey Maurice. "And Then My Heart with Pleasure Fills … " *Journal of Evolutionary Psychology* 9 (Aug. 1989): 317–20.

Weber, Jean-Paul. "Edgar Poe or the Theme of the Clock." In *Poe: A Collection of Critical Essays*. Ed. Robert Regan. Englewood Cliffs, NJ: Prentice 1967. 79–97.

Weeks, Donald. "The Humour of Edgar Allan Poe." *Maatstaf* 26 (1978): 75–89.

Weissberg, Liliane. "In Search of Truth and Beauty: Allegory in 'Berenice' and 'The Domain of Arnheim'." In *Poe and His Times: The Artist and His Milieu*.

Ed. Benjamin Franklin Fisher IV. Baltimore: The Edgar Allan Poe Society 1990. 66–75.

Wheat, Patricia H. "The Mask of Indifference in 'The Masque of the Red Death'." *Studies in Short Fiction* 19 (winter 1982): 51–6.

Whipple, William. "Poe's Political Satire." *UTSE* 25 (1956): 81–95.

Wilbur, Richard. "The House of Poe." In *Poe: A Collection of Critical Essays.* Ed. Robert Regan. Englewood Cliffs, NJ: Prentice 1967. 98–120.

Williams, Michael J.S. *A World of Words: Language and Displacement in the Fiction of Edgar Allan Poe.* Durham and London: Duke University Press 1988.

Winters, Yvor. "Edgar Allan Poe: A Crisis in the History of American Obscurantism." In *The Recognition of Edgar Allan Poe: Selected Criticism Since 1829.* Ed. Eric W. Carlson. Ann Arbor, MI: University of Michigan Press 1966. 176–202.

Woodberry, George E. *Edgar Allan Poe.* 1885. New York, London: Chelsea 1980.

Wootton, David. Introduction. *The Prince.* By Nicolò Machiavelli. Indianapolis and Cambridge: Hackett 1995. xi-xliv.

Zapf, Hubert. "Entropic Imagination in Poe's 'The Masque of the Red Death'." *College Literature* 16 (fall 1989): 211–18.

Zimmerman, Brett. "A Catalogue of Rhetorical and Other Literary Terms from American Literature and Oratory." *Style* 31 (winter 1997): 730–59.

– "A Catalogue of Selected Rhetorical Devices Used in the Works of Edgar Allan Poe." *Style* 33 (winter 1999): 637–57.

– "*Allegoria* and Clock Architecture in Poe's 'The Masque of the Red Death'." *Essays in Arts and Sciences* 29 (Oct. 2000): 1–16.

– "Frantic Forensic Oratory: Poe's 'The Tell-Tale Heart'." *Style* 35 (spring 2001): 34–49.

– "'I could read his prose on salary, but not Jane's': Poe's Stylistic Versatility." *Language and Discourse* 5 (winter 1997): 97–117.

– "'Moral Insanity' or Paranoid Schizophrenia: Poe's 'The Tell-Tale Heart'." *Mosaic* 25 (spring 1992): 39–48.

Index

logue, 270; *hypotaxis*, 234; *hypozeuxis*, 236

parelcon, 72, 76, 83–4, 270–1, 335

parenthesis, xxi; in catalogue, 271–2; circumlocution, 201, 235, 371n12; *epexegesis*, 204; *hyperbaton*, 232; Poe's fondness for, 334; *schematismus*, 298

pareuresis, 185, 272–3

parison, 236, 242; describing Hawthorne, 364n14; Gorgias, 33; seriation, 300. *See also isocolon*

Parks, Edd Winfield, 87, 104

paroemia. See proverb

paromologia: *antistrephon*, 135; in catalogue, 273–4; *epitrope*, 210; *peristrophe*, 97, 276; *restrictio*, 295; in "Tell-Tale Heart," 36, 40

parrhesia, 274–5

Partisan, The (Simms), 129

pathetic fallacy, 288

pathopoeia, 240

pathos, appeal to, 37, 40, 42, 173, 249

Paulding, James Kirke, 101, 368n3

Peacham, Henry, 94, 186, 293, 317, 321

Peithman, Stephen: on "Black Cat," 44; on "Masque," 52, 55, 367n5; puns in Poe, 292; on "Tell-Tale Heart," 344, 374n2

Penn, The, 102–3, 364n13

peregrinism, 308

periergia, 120, 275, 298

periphrasis, 275

peristasis, 276. *See also appositio*

peristrophe, 88, 97–8, 130, 135, 276

permissio. See epitrope

peroratio, 187, 206

persiflage, 163. *See also charientismus*

personification, 277. *See also prosopopoeia*

Philips, Edith, 308

Phillips, Elizabeth C., 77, 349

philophonesis, 247, 277

Philosophical Enquiry into the Origin of our Ideas of the Sublime and Beautiful, A (Burke), 237, 264

"Philosophy of Composition, The" (Poe): *aetiologia*, 115; *assonance*, 148; *inclusio*, 239; *metaphora*, 251; refrain, 244; *threnos*, 320

"Philosophy of Furniture, The" (Poe), 71, 166, 292

phonological set, 228, 277–8

phrenology, 3, 246; *chronographia*, 169; *efficio*, 190; *enargia*, 195–6; phrenologists, 275; *prosopographia*, 288, 333; Spurzheim, 349

physiognomy, 3, 190, 195, 333

Pilgrim's Progress, The (Bunyan), 60

"Pit and the Pendulum, The" (Poe): *allegoria*, 62; alliteration, 117; clocks in, 51; *epistrophe*, 207; existential reading of, 362n10; humour in, 65; imagery, 237; sensation tale, 111; *symploce*, 312

Pitcher, Edward William, 51, 55, 367n5

pleonasm, xvii, 8, 189, 278–9, 335. *See also* doublets

ploce, xxii, 240; *antanaclasis*, 98; in Appendix One, 340; in catalogue, 279; in "Man of the Crowd," 302; in "Tell-Tale Heart," 21, 346

Poe, Neilson, 217

"Poetic Principle, The" (Poe): *brevitas*, 158; *commoratio*, 173; *digressio*, 186; *dinumeratio*, 188; *epanaphora*, 202; *epilogos*, 206; fallacy of poisoning the well, 223; *isocolon*, 242; oxymoron, 264; *prosopopoeia*, 289; *syllepsis*, 311; *threnos*, 320

poicilogia, xvi, 279, 334

"Politian" (Poe), 145, 175, 277, 295, 316

Pollin, Burton R., 30, 56

polyptoton: in catalogue, 280; comedic, 72, 84; in critical reviews,

"Rime of the Ancient Mariner, The" (Coleridge), 315
Rollin, Charles, 30
Roppolo, Joseph Patrick, 55
Roth, Martin, 56
Rourke, Constance, 65–6, 72
Ruddick, Nicholas, 52, 55, 58, 367n5
Ruskin, John, 288

sarcasmus (sarcasm), xx, 88–90, 132, 149, 297
scesis onomaton, 275, 297–8, 316
Schadenfreude, 75, 80, 90
schematismus, 257, 298–9
Scott, Walter, 104
"Scythe of Time, The" (Poe), 51
"Secret Writing" (Poe), 308
Senecan prose, 5–6, 13, 27, 341
seriation, xxi; *accumulatio*, 110; adjectival, 299; adverbial, 300; *amplificatio*, 120; in Appendix One, 337; in catalogue, 299–304; *congeries*, 174–5; *isocolon*, 242; in "Man of the Crowd," 304; nominal, 176, 205, 247, 299, 302–3; Poe's fondness for, 334; Poe's use of, 322; *synathroesmus*, 312; *systrophe*, 317; triplets, 324; verisimilitude, 322
sermocinatio, 304–5

"Shadow – A Parable" (Poe), 51
Shakespeare, William: *anthimeria*, 194; *As You Like It*, 55; *aschematiston*, 147; evil rhetoricians in, 34, 50; figures of vehemence, 333; "linguistic bumpkins," 83; style and character, 15
Shakespeare's Use of the Arts of Language (Joseph): *anthimeria*, 194; *aschematiston*, 147; *chria*, 167; *eciasis*, 183; *meiosis*, 248; *synathroesmus*, 313; *systrophe*, 316
Shaw, George Bernard, xiii, 6
Shelden, Pamela J., 43, 44, 344
Sheridan, Thomas, 30
Short, Bryan C., 29, 30
sicca. See *aschematiston*
Sigourney, Lydia Huntley, 102
"Silence – A Fable" (Poe): in Appendix One, 340; clocks in, 51; *epizeuxis*, 210; palindrome, 265; *polysyndeton*, 281; refrain, 244
Silverman, Kenneth, 32
simile, xxii; in catalogue, 305–6; Dupin on, 32; *metaphora*, 251; used appropriately, 334; warnings about, 335. *See also* epic simile
Simms, William Gilmore, 89

"Sleeper, The" (Poe), 183, 314
Smith, Allan Gardner, 349–50
Snodgrass, Joseph Evans, xvii, 196, 215, 261, 349
solecisme. See *solecismus*
solecismos. See *solecismus*
solecismus, xviii, 194, 306–7
"Some Words with a Mummy" (Poe), 32, 67, 125, 315–16
"Sonnet – To Science" (Poe), 145
Sonnino, Lee, 73, 107, 147
soraismus, xxi, 111; in Appendix One, 338; *cacozelia*, 160; in catalogue, 307–10; linguistic sportiveness, 292; Poe's fondness for, 334; warnings about, 335
soroesmus. See *soraismus*
Southern Literary Messenger: article on Headley and Channing, 85; article on phrenology, 195, 349; Poe's severity in, 103; review of Cicero's orations, 33; Tucker in, 323
Spanier, Sandra Whipple: Poe and his narrators, 14, 27, 260; on *praeparatio*, 37, 284; studies of Poe, 335
"Spectacles, The" (Poe): *apodixis*, 142; *barbarismus*, 78; Chivers, 368n3; comedic repetition in, 371n11; *euche*,